Eddie Young Publishers
P.O. Box 60, Nylstroom, 0510
Tel. (01531) 2954

© Eddie Young Publishers
P.O. Box 60, Nylstroom 0510, South Africa.
Tel. (01531) 2954.

First edition: October 1992
ISBN 0-620-17149-9

Printed and bound by Promedia Printers and published and distributed by Eddie Young Publishers.

Every care has been taken to ensure that the information contained in this book is as accurate as it could be made at the time of going to press, but no responsibility can be accepted for errors or omissions.

GAME FARMING
AND
WILDLIFE MANAGEMENT

— Eddie Young

Translated from the Afrikaans by Sharon Slavik.

Revised and edited by Nicki Young.

Eddie and Targa

PREFACE

It gives me great pleasure, but with a measure of sadness, to write the preface to this updated, English version of the very successful book, "Wildboerdery en Natuurreservaatbestuur" written by Dr Eddie Young.

This book was the first of its kind ever published and contained a wealth of practical information for prospective as well as established game farmers, nature conservation students and farm managers.

However, much has changed since the publication of this book in 1984. Thanks to the initiation by Eddie, and his tireless efforts in this regard, game farmers have finally been granted property rights over the animals on their farms. Various other laws and/or policies pertaining to wildlife management and game farming have since been amended or adapted due to suggestions and motivations by him and have been included in this book.

There has long been a need for an English edition of "Wildboerdery en Natuurreservaatbestuur" and the translation thereof was one of the many projects which Eddie was planning for 1991. However, Eddie's life was tragically ended in an aircraft accident near our farm on 8 August 1990 when he was assisting the South African Police in a poaching investigation.

Encouraged by warmly persistent friends, I have taken it upon myself to finish this task for him, assisted by his meticulous and characteristically detailed notes. I would like to dedicate this book to the memory of Dr Eddie Young, pioneer game farmer, wildlife vet, researcher, conservationist, author, husband and father: his spirit was as large as the Africa he so loved. Eddie believed it was his life task to protect and conserve God's wonderful creation and he fulfilled it magnificently. It was truly an honour to know him.

Nicki Young

CONTENTS

1. CONSERVATION OR COMMERCIAL ENTERPRISE?

South Africa hosts a wealth of indigenous plant and animal species. Stop and think for a moment of the colourful profusion of our Cape Fynbos, Namaqualand's dancing floral carpet of wild-flowers, and the dense bushveld of the Transvaal and Natal; of the demure beauty of the Kalahari — or the overall splendour of our whole country — and we find that this natural treasure chest holds more than 20 000 different species of trees, shrubs and plants. This exceeds even the large number of species found in the United States of America — a diversity made all the more remarkable by the fact that it is condensed into an area approximately one seventh the size of the USA.

Add to this colourful landscape the exquisite calls of almost 800 different birds — approximately 10 per cent of all the earth's species — and the image conjured up is that of a true paradise. It sounds almost too good to be true, yet these are actual facts about the beautiful country that we are privileged to live in.

But how many of us still attach any particular value to this unique natural heritage? Many seem to have become hardened by the demands of enterprise and materialistic progress. Perhaps we no longer have the capacity or the desire to appreciate the miracles of creation around us! An even more disturbing phenomenon, worse than this indifference to nature, is the destructive frenzy that drives some people — ostensibly in the interest of progress — to watch with satisfaction as primeval forests topple before bull-dozers; to fail to see the unassuming little red flowers, hidden in the grass, vanish under the sharp blades of the plough. A compromise between progress and preservation can certainly be found, provided that our outlook on life begins to incorporate a true appreciation of our earth and all its beauty.

There are several references in the Bible to man's responsibility towards creation: for example "The Lord God placed the man in the Garden of Eden to work it, and take care of it" (Genesis 2:15).

South Africans have, as a nation, gained a reputation over the years for living close to nature, and we can feel especially proud and grateful for the wonderful diversity of wild mammals still found in our country. No fewer than 400 different species and subspecies abound here! Once again, South Africa surpasses America, since this number of species does not even occur in North and South America combined.

It has been claimed that, since Jan van Riebeeck set foot on the Cape shore, approximately one out of every hundred of the world's larger animal species has died out. Thanks to our fore-fathers' conservation-mindedness, South Africa has lost only three larger mammal species. The fact that the blue antelope, the Cape lion and the true quagga have become extinct is nevertheless still ascribed by certain international conservation groups to the selfishness and neglect of South African hunters and farmers!

The last blue antelope (bloubok) disappeared from its South African habitat and thus also into extinction during the last century. The last Cape lion was shot in 1836, in the vicinity of what was to become the Hendrik Verwoerd Dam. Until recently, it was thought that the history of another remarkable species drew to a tragic close on 12 August 1883 when the last quagga died in a zoo. We in South Africa are regarded as leaders in the field of nature conservation, but the above events will unfortunately always stand as black milestones along the road of South Africa's development!

In sharp contrast to these unhappy events, considerable praise is due to those farmers who contributed to South Africa's fine conservation successes through their far-sighted and determined measures to preserve rare game species.

In 1885, when skin traders and mange had decimated black wildebeest populations and the last remaining herds were facing extinction, the Terblanches, the du Plessis's and other conservation-minded farmers undertook to protect these vulnerable wildebeest herds. As time passed, they supplied breeding animals to the provincial nature reserves in the Transvaal and the Orange Free State, and today, thanks to the efforts of these farmers, the black wildebeest once again occurs in large numbers.

The bontebok, another rare species found only in the Republic, also owes its continued existence to the fine conservation measures of certain farmers. When it became clear that the numbers of the last herds of this antelope were decreasing rapidly, Alexander van der Byl in 1837 captured approximately 30 to 40 bontebok and placed these for protection in a special enclosure on his farm in the Bredasdorp district. This positive example was followed by the Albertyns and the van Bredas of Bredasdorp. These animals' numbers continued to drop, however, and by 1930 hardly 20 remained. The ensuing energetic efforts of the National Parks Board succeeded in increasing the numbers of this beautiful animal to such an extent that, today, more than 220 bontebok are found in the Bontebok National Park and elsewhere in the Republic. Thus the van der Byls, the Albertyns and the van Bredas earned themselves, and also the Republic, honourable mention in history books as well as publications of conservation groups throughout the world.

Equally commendable was Hans Lombaard's donation to the National Parks Board of eleven Cape mountain zebra which he had been protecting on his farm. At one stage, when indiscriminate hunting had destroyed all but a few mountain zebra, Mr Lombaard and his fellow farmers protected this animal to such an extent that subsequent conservation efforts by the National Parks Board and the Cape Department of Nature Conservation resulted in our country's now being the proud host of more than 560 Cape mountain zebra. About 75 per cent of these unique animals are at present under the special protection of the National Mountain Zebra Park near Cradock in the Cape Province.

The above examples illustrate some successful rescue efforts by farmers — beacons in the history of nature conservation, even on an international level!

South African farmers are continuing to make history, on what is possibly an even larger scale. As owners of a major portion of the land, farmers are ideally placed to preserve our country's natural resources. Some base their conservation activities on a sincere interest in and love for nature. Others regard conservation as a personal mission.

Over many years, this close involvement of farmers with nature has led to the commercial exploitation of game, culminating in recent years in the development of a new and profitable form of land use. Game farming has, in fact, only recently been recognised by the Department of Agriculture as a new form of farming.

While many agriculturalists tend to regard game farming merely as a supplementary source of meat, a number of incidental uses also ensue from it. On several farms meat production, although substantial, has already begun to assume a secondary role. Regardless of whether the primary aim of game farming is nature conservation or agricultural exploitation, this industry is here to stay, and game farms offer just as agreeable and welcome a refuge to hunters, adventurers and jaded city-dwellers as they do to the herds of game thriving on them.

As is probably the case with any relatively new industry which must compete for its viability, opinions often diverge as to the position that game farming should occupy within the general agricultural framework. Detractors are inclined to place undue emphasis on the role of game in transmitting disease, while ignorance regarding the feeding requirements and grazing habits of game also frequently leads to unjustified antagonism. The view that game farming should be undertaken solely on idle land, or in regions unsuited to stock farming, is certainly not beneficial to the game industry, and is based on ignorance and prejudice.

As a supplementary source of animal production, the advantages of combining stock and game farming should be self-evident. A typical example of complementary food utilisation is found on a bushveld farm, where cattle feed mainly on grass, kudu and other browsers on the lower shrubs and herbaceous plants, and giraffe on leaves in the treetops at a height of approximately 6 m. Livestock and predominantly graminivorous game (grazers) can also profitably be kept together, provided that their numbers are controlled.

Game farming on its own has already shown that it can succeed, but it can also hold disadvantages in certain circumstances. When, for example, insufficient numbers of grazers such as zebra, wildebeest, hartebeest or buffalo occur on a farm, grassland may become very dense. Optimum veld use is not possible in these conditions. Tall grassveld and particularly underutilised sour grassveld are furthermore avoided by species of game such as wildebeest and blesbok. Veldfires in dense grassland usually inflict greater damage to trees and undergrowth and also pose a greater threat to the survival of game during uncontrollable blazes.

Although one can profitably keep livestock and game together on the same farm, or game on its own, the best option, to my mind, is to keep game and livestock separately on the same farm, where circumstances allow this. Competition for available water and grazing is sometimes used as an argument against the presence of game on farms utilised predominantly for stock farming. The daily water requirements of game, which will be discussed in more detail later, are very modest, particularly in the case of browsers. In fact, the resistance of game to drought holds numerous advantages in regions where water is scarce. However, the fact that certain species of game can survive in arid or semi-arid conditions does not imply that these are the conditions under which game should generally be kept or used for farming. There are definite indications that nutritionally deficient grazing can, although to a lesser extent than in livestock, also sometimes lead to lower productivity in game. Our indigenous game species should therefore be afforded a reasonable opportunity of proving their worth under optimum conditions.

Competition for the same food sources should not pose problems, either, provided that the feeding requirements and grazing habits of all the types of game and livestock concerned are taken into account, and that the necessary control over numbers is exercised in order to prevent overgrazing.

Bush encroachment is assuming alarming proportions in certain areas of the bushveld. This phenomenon is already causing severe problems on certain cattle farms. Although further research in this field is recommended, it seems logical that certain types of game could only improve the situation by counteracting encroachment in several ways. Here, once again, browsers could prove extremely beneficial on a cattle farm.

It is generally known that some species of game can safely eat a variety of poisonous plants which are toxic to livestock. In areas where major poisonous plants are prevalent, certain species of game could therefore possibly be kept more safely and beneficially than livestock. A word of caution is needed here, however. In conditions where game is kept in small fenced areas or exposed to extreme drought, animals could eat certain plants which, in normal circumstances, they would avoid. The seeming ability of game to thrive in areas containing poisonous plants is therefore due not only to a natural immunity of certain species to the toxic elements in poisonous plants, but also to their avoidance of these plants.

The significance of game farming, in my opinion, lies not only in the adaptability of different species of game to diverse and often

Farmers are of the best conservationists in the country. The black wildebeest (left), the Cape mountain zebra (right) and the bontebok would in all probability have been extinct if conservation-minded farmers had not stepped in to take protective action.

unfavourable conditions, but also to the numerous ways in which game and game farms can be utilised. Whereas cattle farming is, from an economic viewpoint, primarily aimed at food production and the supply of breeding stock, game offers the game farmer additional advantages.

Next to oil production, tourism represents the largest single industry in the world. In South Africa, the income derived each year from tourism amounts to several hundred million rands. Game farms are increasingly being used for tourism and hunting purposes. In addition to ensuring a steady income from biltong hunters, a kudu bull, for example, could earn the game farmer more than a thousand rand on the trophy market. In the case of certain other types of game the income from hunting is much higher. It is not unusual nowadays for game farmers to receive a hunting fee of more than R400 per hunter per day — provided that the hunting facilities and opportunities on a game farm are of an acceptable standard. The price of the trophy and the value of the meat are excluded from this fee. Into the bargain, the meat generally remains the property of the farmer, since the foreign hunter is only interested in the trophy.

Bushveld holidays and tourism in private conservation areas are also becoming fashionable. Hiking trails in game areas, for which the landowner receives remuneration, are becoming increasingly popular, while luxury accommodation for the more sophisticated guests on certain game farms is already earning the host more than R400 per night per person.The overwhelming population growth — numbers are expected to double during the last thirty years of this century — could cause the demand for outdoor recreation on private property to increase sharply, and a considerable rise in the price of venison, as a delicacy and health food, is likely.

The value and full potential of the game farming industry and game trading can hardly be determined accurately, owing to a lack of relevant statistics. It is estimated, however, that hunters spent approximately R7 million rand on their sport in Namibia in one year. Foreign hunters are also beginning to find South Africa very attractive.

Furthermore, in 1981 the amount of foreign exchange earned from venison exports amounted to more than twice the income derived from the combined export of fresh-frozen mutton, lamb and domestic goatmeat. This is no small feat for so young an industry.

The above-mentioned exports represent only approximately 1 100 tons of venison, however. This is about 40 per cent of the estimated 2 760 tons of venison processed by registered businesses in South Africa and Namibia during 1981. In the same year, West Germany's population of 61 million consumed approximately 72 times more venison. According to an informative report by Dr J D G Steenkamp of Vleissentraal, West Germany imported the equivalent of 73 589 tons of venison and 78 000 tons of pigeon and rabbit meat between January and November 1981. A huge potential market exists overseas for South African venison. In addition to the above, game, venison and by-products such as hides, skins and ivory to the value of millions of rands are marketed annually within the country. At present, Vleissentraal's marketing strategy for venison is also largely aimed at the local consumer. As the population figures and the per capita income of the country's people increase, the demand for meat may be expected to rise accordingly.

Game farming is much like a diamond with many different facets. While hunting opportunities for our South African hunters, bushveld holidays for the city-dweller and biltong during the winter may be the most important by-products for the local consumer, visits by overseas trophy hunters, the export of venison and the development of holiday opportunities for foreign tourists represent far greater possibilities for the country's economic prosperity.

With the necessary support from all the government bodies concerned, the game industry can play an increasingly important role in earning foreign exchange, as well as supplying meat and recreational opportunities for our country's own people.

Farmers spend millions of rands annually to develop private conservation areas and to establish game in regions where it was driven to extinction in the past.

Commercial utilisation of game is recognised by the Departement of Agriculture as a new form of farming.

2. FINANCIAL IMPLICATIONS OF A GAME FARMING ENTERPRISE

Game farming can be very lucrative, but it also entails enormous costs. Land and game are expensive, and development costs high. As with any other form of farming, thorough financial planning is consequently of the utmost importance.

Without venturing into a detailed discussion, I should like to give prospective game farmers some indication of the categories of expenditure for which provision should be made. This information is based on personal experience of game farming acquired over the past 26 years.

In this chapter it is assumed that a relatively undeveloped farm has been purchased and needs to be given a solid foundation for further development. Specific costs are not mentioned, since these can vary from time to time and from farm to farm, and can consequently be misleading. Using the following guidelines as a basis, however, quotations can be obtained, and expected costs calculated by prospective farmers.

CAPITAL EXPENDITURE AND DEVELOPMENT COSTS

Purchase of farm
Acquisition of vehicles, tractor, trailer and other farm machinery and tools
Development of roads and firebreaks
Boreholes, motors, pumps, pipes, dams and other irrigation
Erection of game-proof fences and holding pens
Purchase and establishment of breeding game
Construction of living quarters, storerooms and other buildings
Tourist and guest facilities
Field abattoir

RUNNING COSTS

Maintenance of roads and firebreaks
Maintenance of game-proof fences
Maintenance of buildings and guest facilities
Maintenance of vehicles and machinery
Fuel, oil and lubricants
Helicopter and transport services
Game capture drugs and equipment
Professional game capture services
Supplementary feeding and mineral licks
Worm remedies, other parasiticides, and veterinary medicines
Salaries, wages and rations
Insurance, medical aid schemes and contributions to unemployment insurance fund
Professional consultation services
Veterinary inspection services and other government services
Licences and permits
Advertising, brochures and pamphlets
Telephone, postage and stationery
Interest and bank charges
Diverse farm expenses

Naturally the primary management objective will vary from farm to farm, and all game farmers will not erect tourist facilities or spend equal amounts on items such as insurance, consultation

The drilling of boreholes and the erection and maintenance of pumps, dams and other irrigation can require a huge capital outlay on a farm.

services, supplementary feeding and game capture drugs. Items of a more general nature will now be discussed.

The purchase price of land varies considerably, often even within the same district or region. Land prices are also rising steadily. In areas of the North-Western Transvaal abounding in game, R400,00 per hectare was considered too expensive by some only a few years ago. At present game farms in this area are being sold at up to R1 000,00 per hectare. No one knows what will happen in future. The fact remains, however, that many game and stock farmers have over the years gained more from the appreciation of their farms than from the sale of game or stock bred on these farms.

As a word of caution to prospective buyers, I must emphasize that an area of land surrounded by a game-proof fence does not necessarily constitute a good game farm. The unfortunate misconception that poor land which is unsuitable for stock farming can and should be used for game farming continues to persist and can lead to unnecessary losses.

Choosing a suitable game farm will be discussed more fully in a later chapter. Meanwhile buyers are strongly advised to ob-

Four wheel drive vehicles and dart guns are synonomous with game farming and necessitate considerable additional expenditure.

tain expert advice regarding the suitability of farms for game farming before making large financial investments.

One's choice of suitable vehicle(s), tractor and equipment can also considerably influence the initial scale of expenditure. Expensive four-wheel-drive trucks and hunting vehicles are obviously recommended in mountainous, sandy, clayey and other impassable terrain, but quite often these are unnecessary luxuries. A tractor, a trailer and a good road-grader are, in my opinion, essential, particularly if firebreaks have to be made and maintained. A flat-bed trailer with movable sides is very useful, not only for routine farm use, but also for transporting game crates and other equipment.

For at least two good reasons, a carefully planned network of roads and firebreaks is indispensable on a game farm. First, veld fires can easily be controlled and there is a far smaller risk of the whole farm burning down at once. Seen from the point of view of tourism or game viewing, as well as for game census and game cropping purposes, more roads obviously offer greater accessibility to larger areas of a game farm. Particularly in dense bush and mountainous areas, the construction and maintenance of roads is an expensive undertaking and generous allowance should be made for this in the budget.

Although game generally requires little drinking water, it is nevertheless essential that sufficient drinking water should be available and that adequate watering points are introduced at strategic spots. Veld utilisation is largely influenced by the location and distribution of watering points and a water supply programme should therefore be drawn up to provide this essential amenity.

The erection of game-proof fences represents another particularly large expenditure. Where jumping game such as impala and kudu have to be kept in, a suitable fence of approximately 2,4 m with 21 strands can barely be erected at present for less than R5 000 to R6 000 per kilometre. Depending on the type of fence and whether or not use is made of the services of contractors, the cost can even be much higher.

The movements of springbok and certain other types of game can fortunately be restricted by lower and much cheaper fences. Besides perimeter fences, provision should also be made for the subdivision of the farm into more than one camp, as well as for the erection of smaller capturing and holding pens.

Conservation-minded farmers generally endeavour to establish as wide a variety of game as possible on their game farms. The keeping of game on small farms is usually officially discouraged, whereas the establishment of large herds of breeding game on very large farms can be a very costly exercise. It is nevertheless wise not to begin farming with very small groups of breeding game of any species, since larger breeding herds have a greater chance of survival and can ensure a croppable population of game sooner. At current prices of more than R200 per impala, R900 per kudu, R2 000 for a waterbuck, R6 000 to R7 000 for a giraffe and more than R20 000 each for the rarer species, a prospective buyer must necessarily set aside considerable sums of money in his planning and calculations for the acquisition of game. Care should also be taken with the choice of game species, since not only the habitat requirements of the game itself but also the primary goals of the farmer (for example meat production, trophy hunting or tourism) will determine which types of game are suitable.

The shared use of expensive equipment by farmers on neighbouring farms can contribute to making game farming more profitable.

In addition to a suitable home for the farmer or his manager, provision must be made for living quarters for farm workers, adequate storage space for vehicles, tractors, tools, game capture equipment, animal feeds, and so forth. Suitable confinement facilities for quarantine purposes, for instance, or for the isolation and treatment of sick or injured animals, or for hand-rearing young antelope, may also be needed in certain cases. Cheaper, temporary cages or smaller pens, consisting of plastic-covered fences, are often a more practical alternative, however. Considerable savings can, once again, be achieved through careful advance planning, with the advice and assistance of an expert.

When consideration is given to the possible construction of hunting camps and tourist facilities, it should be borne in mind that the most expensive and luxurious facilities are not always necessarily the most suitable and most popular. Many hunters may, for example, prefer a tented camp in the bush to rondavel accommodation of five-star quality, while modern youngsters are satisfied with the barest minimum on walking trails. Game farms are also not all equally well suited to tourism, and therefore expenditure on any tourist facilities should be weighed up thoroughly in advance.

If a farmer wishes to equip his farm for trophy hunting and he would like to have overseas hunters using his farm, he must take into account the minimum requirements laid down by the authorities for hunting camps and facilities. In addition to suitable accommodation, all hunting vehicles, rifles, facilities for processing trophies and personnel services must also comply with the requirements laid down.

The construction of even a small abattoir which complies with veterinary requirements for export purposes is seldom justified on even large meat production farms. Mobile abattoirs which are supplied under certain conditions by meat exporters frequently offer a cheaper solution and better service. In most cases a clean and insect-free slaughtering place and/or biltong room is advisable, however, and funds should be set aside accordingly.

On an efficiently managed game farm, running costs can be considerably lower than on most stock farms. Except for the hunting, culling and game capture activities during autumn and winter, little more than maintenance work is required on most game farms for more than half of the year. Considerable savings in terms of salaries, wages, housing and rations can be expected, since game farming is not a labour-intensive industry.

As can be deduced from the preceding paragraphs, farmers stand to save considerable amounts by involving experts with sufficient practical experience in the purchase and planning of their farms and the management of their farming activities.

Helicopter and other aviation services for game census and/or culling purposes is another large but necessary expenditure for which farmers have to provide periodically. A regular aerial census every few years is strongly recommended, especially in areas where it is difficult to count game using any other method.

Any game capturing method is an expensive procedure. If a game farmer purchases his own capturing equipment such as dart guns, game capture drugs, material for capture corrals, etc., a game farmer can prepare himself to lay out another ten to twenty thousand rand. In most instances it will be justified to make use of the services of professional game capture teams instead.

In my opinion insufficient and/or indiscriminate use is made of mineral licks and supplementary feeding. The conception that game should look after itself and that man should not interfere with the natural course of events is outdated and can only lead to unnecessary production losses. Any game farmer who cares for his animals will have to be willing to budget for costs in respect of animal feeds. Although these costs are usually not large, the purchase of lucerne and feeding bales and pellets during unexpected droughts can, just as on a stock farm, require substantial expenditures.

It is hoped that the above information will not deter any prospective game farmer from his purpose, but that it will, instead, enable him, in his own interest and that of the industry, to plan ahead and be better prepared for the new venture. It goes without saying that any form of farming is a costly undertaking these days, and game farming is certainly no exception.

Fortunately a well managed game farm is able not only to provide the owner with much pleasure and satisfaction, but a steady income can also in most cases be earned through the sale of breeding game and venison, skins, trophies and other by-products, as well as from tourism and hunting. Whether the expected income from the above-mentioned and other forms of utilisation can make game farming on a specific farm sufficiently profitable is for the game farmer himself to decide. Without thorough advance planning and the associated calculation of expected income and expenditure, any form of farming remains a gamble. It is my opinion, nonetheless, that game farming remains a wonderful experience with enormous challenges and endless possibilities.

3. CO-OPERATIVE NATURE CONSERVATION AND GAME FARMING

Some years ago the Natal Parks Board took the lead in initiating the concept of "conservancies". Mr Nick Steele, originator of this remarkable conservation idea, realised the importance of more active participation by landowners in conservation activities, and put the system to the test with the co-operation of the farming community in Natal. Under the leadership of Mr Tom Kerr, the first conservancy was founded in the Balgowan District in August 1978. Groups of farmers from other districts were also organised into nature conservation committees.

PRINCIPLE OF OPERATION

Each group of farmers appointed one black game guard or more, and specific tasks were allocated to these guards. Their most important tasks were to patrol the joint properties of the group of farmers concerned on a regular and intensive basis and to deter poachers. The system was, and remains, a huge success!

During 1981 I, together with representatives of Organised Agriculture and the Transvaal Division of Nature Conservation, had the privilege of visiting various conservancies in Natal as guests of the Natal Parks Board. During this visit evidence was revealed of hundreds of wire snares removed from the veld in one conservancy, and 318 grain-bags of protected plants confiscated in another conservancy thanks to the excellent co-operation of the conservation committee concerned and the South African Police. These plants had been removed from the veld for use by witchdoctors for their ostensible curative properties. The extent of this illegal form of veld robbery was staggering — in one conservancy alone, 6 tons of illegally gathered veld plants were confiscated. We became profoundly aware that the effective protection of our unique natural heritage, especially on private farms, could only succeed with efficient organisation and with the necessary co-operation of landowners.

SUCCESSFUL APPLICATION IN NATAL

The Natal farmers are completely convinced of the fruitfulness of their co-operative ventures and are amazed at the success experienced almost immediately after the inception of new conservancy committees. Additional conservancy committees are still being formed, and the following statistics, which were obtained with the kind co-operation of Gary Davies of the Natal Parks Board, indicate the success that has been achieved:

Number of private conservancies in Natal 140
Number of farmers participating 1 628
Total area of private conservancies .... 1,1 million ha
Number of black game guards 424
Game guards salary .... R250 — R500 p.m.

According to the committee members, stray dogs and snare-setting poachers pose the biggest problem. These problems have, in most conservancies, been eliminated or, at the very least, brought under control.

ADVANTAGES OF COMMON CONSERVATION PRACTICES

If the statistics given have convinced you that the conservancy system could also be of value in your area, you might consider establishing a conservancy committee as soon as possible, either through your local farmers' association (preferably so) or through direct contact with the farmers in the vicinity and in consultation with your Nature Conservation department. Advantages of this concept, which you could mention to your fellow farmers, include the following:

1. More regular contact between farmers which is, in these times, of obvious importance.
2. The establishment of a cost-effective patrol service which can deter poachers in the most effective way possible.
3. The systematic and regular removal of snares which pose a threat to game as well as livestock.
4. Efficient control of stray dogs which catch and kill game and domestic stock and encourage the spreading of rabies.
5. Discouraging theft of livestock and firewood, farm equipment and farm produce. Since this patrol service was introduced, all forms of farm theft in conservancies in Natal have declined sharply. Without exception, the farmers who employed game guards felt that the saving achieved through the prevention of theft was sufficient to compensate for the cost of these patrol services.
6. Regular reports concerning strange tracks and movements of suspect persons have also repeatedly contributed to a more satisfying security situation. Naturally good co-operation must exist between the conservancy committees and the police.
7. In the space of less than a year, several committees reported that not only had the numbers of game and birds increased, but game had become much tamer and could therefore be spotted more easily on farms, probably thanks to the improved control of stray dogs.
8. The removal and in some cases total eradication of rare and precious veld plants could hardly be prevented in a more efficient manner.
9. Regular inspections of game fences, in particular, can prevent game from escaping from fenced areas.
10. Veld fires can be reported sooner and fought more efficiently on a co-operative basis.

These and numerous other examples of conservation successes can largely be ascribed to the excellent services of competent game guards. Candidates for this important task must be selected with care, and receive better remuneration than labourers in the same area. It should be seen as a prestige job and the game guards should not associate unnecessarily with the local population. Some feel that it may even be advisable to recruit candidates for these sought-after posts from other regions. The game guards are on duty at all times, and especially over weekends, except for a leave period of approximately three weeks each year. Because they work over weekends, they should receive approximately four days' occasional leave per month, which can be accumulated. Remuneration agreements and salary scales will naturally differ from region to region, and can be determined individually by each conservancy committee.

Arming the game guards is considered essential, and permission for this is required from the South African Police. In Natal, semi-automatic shotguns have proved satisfactory.

SHARED USE OF SERVICES AND RESOURCES

Farmers in other provinces may feel that the system used in Natal would not function equally well in their areas. The system does, however, lend itself to adaptation to various regional needs and I should like to encourage farmers to take the initiative and, in consultation with the South African Police and Nature Conservation, to decide how co-operative nature conservation could best be applied in their specific areas.

In remote regions where game is still abundant, such as the Northern and Eastern Transvaal, I would also suggest the possible sharing of hunting and game culling facilities and personnel.

Hunting contractors and/or professional hunters who wish to arrange and conduct hunting trips for overseas hunters must meet certain minimum requirements in respect of hunting vehicles, camping facilities, personnel and hunting equipment. Only qualified hunting contractors may advertise overseas and act as hosts, while only qualified professional hunters may accompany the overseas hunters on their hunting expeditions. In order to obtain these qualifications, special theoretical and practical examinations have to be passed and hunting contractors must spend considerable capital in order to establish the necessary facilities and services, if he does not already have them.

To me it does not seem practical for all game farmers, and other farmers who have game on their farms, to take the required examinations and acquire the necessary facilities and personnel in order to be allowed to enjoy the benefits of an income from overseas hunters. However, the co-operative concept, based on the conservancy system used in Natal, offers a very acceptable alternative! If farmers with hunting farms form a group and make use of the services of a qualified hunting contractor/ professional hunter, farm game could be utilised better, and thus also contribute to the earning of foreign currency. Similarly the hunting contractor would be able to offer a greater variety of game species in larger hunting areas within the same region,

which can only be to the benefit of the hunting industry. Thus the landowner can obtain the best prices for his trophy animals, while the hunting contractors/professional hunters are simultaneously able to offer a better and more extensive service in the national interest.

The co-ordinated cropping of game for export purposes, for example, can also be promoted by the co-operative system. The Division of Veterinary Services sets certain requirements in respect of game cropping teams and game vehicles, which would certainly make the shared use of such services and facilities much more economical. Export firms are moreover willing to place mobile slaughtering and refrigeration facilities at the disposal of farmers, provided that a minimum number of carcasses per day or per week can be guaranteed. In cases where it is difficult or even impossible for individual farmers to offer such a guarantee, the shared use of such facilities and services by a group of farmers on adjacent farms would, once again, contribute to the better utilisation of farm game for export purposes.

Certain universities and colleges endeavour to train nature conservation students who can eventually provide a useful information service to game farmers. However, nature conservation officers employed by official organisations are spread rather thinly and agricultural information officers are not always appropriately trained, and therefore the appointment of farm managers with a good basic training in agricultural and nature conservation principles can only be to the benefit of the game farming industry. While it may not be feasible for individual farmers to appoint such an expert, it could in some cases be done by a group of farmers together. The question arises whether other experts, such as veterinarians and other agriculturalists, could not also thus be accommodated and utilised better in our rural areas.

Game capture equipment and transport services are expensive. Few farmers have the necessary knowledge or can afford the equipment and vehicles to capture and sell their own live game profitably. Once again the old adage "unity is strength" holds true, and farmers can only benefit from combining forces and sharing facilities and services.

These few examples simply illustrate how the system of co-operative nature conservation, which has already been very successful in Natal, can be adapted and even expanded to meet different needs both locally and elsewhere in the Republic.

4. SELECTING A SUITABLE GAME FARM

A game farm must possess the necessary infrastructure to function efficiently. If an undeveloped farm of average size is bought, further expenditure on improvements and the establishment of game can easily cost the new owner an additional amount running into six figures. The nature and location of the farm furthermore determine the type of game that can be kept on it and for which forms of utilisation the farm is suitable. Factors such as disease control areas are also of the utmost importance if, for example, the export of venison is envisaged.

Buyers of game farms sometimes tend to throw all other considerations overboard when, overwhelmed by the beautiful natural surroundings, signs of abundant game and brand-new game fences, they reach for their wallets without further ado. Although game farms are becoming exceedingly rare in certain regions and a wide choice is not always possible, a considerable amount of money can be saved on the cost of development and the resettlement of game if the farm is evaluated critically beforehand. However, a great part of the pleasure and satisfaction of game farming undeniably lies in developing the farm and releasing game in your own small earthly paradise.

To assist prospective buyers I have summarized some of the most important information that should be obtained in respect of a game farm:

IMPORTANT INFORMATION FOR EVALUATING A GAME FARM

Name of the farm and geographic location

— Name(s) of the farm and number(s)
— Province
— District
— Geographic location

Size and price

— Deed of transfer for correct size
— Price and remuneration agreement
— Financing

Particulars regarding environment

— Transvaal Highveld, Lowveld, Cape fynbos, Karoo, etc.
— Dense or mixed bushveld, savanna, grassveld, etc.
— Mountainous or broken terrain or plains
— Perennial rivers, dry sand beds, streams
— Vlei areas or wetlands with or without water
— Soil type(s), rainfall and climate
— Nature and condition of grazing

Game (and livestock) on farm

— Types and numbers
— Census data or certificate of nature conservation officer
— Permanent or migrant game

Improvements

— Game fences
  — outer fences
  — pens and capture corrals
  — types of fence
  — condition of fences
— Water supply
  — equipped boreholes and production capability (borehole tests)
  — natural sources and permanence (full particulars)
  — reservoirs, pipelines and watering troughs
  — adequate or insufficient
— Roads and firebreaks
— Houses and outbuildings (condition and value)
— Tourist and hunting facilities
— Slaughtering and cooling facilities

Vehicles and farm machinery

— Vehicles
— Tractor, trailer, tools
— Motors, pumps, generators
— Other farm machinery and equipment

Infrastructure and nearby facilities

— Road and rail links
— Public roads and railway lines through or alongside farm
— Air services and nearest landing strip and international airport
— Nearest city or town
— Nearest hospital, first-aid services
— Nearest school
— Nearest game abattoir or depot
— Telephone, radio communications and electricity supply

Existing staff and support services

— Staff: permanent and temporary
— Service contracts amd remuneration
— Professional services and/or supervision
— Game capture and culling teams in vicinity

Important information and exemptions

— Enzootic stock disease area, e.g. foot-and-mouth disease, anthrax, etc.
— Veterinary control measures and restrictions in area
— Control over movements of game and game products
— Exemption of enclosed farm by Nature Conservation Ordinance

Statements and records

— Deed of transfer for farm
— Mortgages, leases, servitudes
— Other obligations pertaining to farm
— Specified income statement
  — meat exports
  — local meat and biltong sales
  — hides and skins
  — sale of breeding game
  — income from hunting
  — earnings from tourism
  — other income
— Statement of assets and liabilities, as well as recent tax statements

POSSIBLE LOCAL RESTRICTIONS ON FARMING ACTIVITIES

The above information is useful not only for budgeting purposes, but also for determining the practical feasibility of the industry, as illustrated by the following brief examples:

Game farmers in the Orange Free State are subject to the control measures of their own province's Nature Conservation Division, which differ from those of the Natal Parks Board, for example. Veterinary control measures also differ from region to region and from one area to another, especially in enzootic foot-and-mouth areas. Especially as regards veterinary control in respect of the transport and export of game and game products, the geographic location of the farm is of the utmost importance in certain circumstances. Whereas game movements in disease-free areas, although subject to permit control, is allowed almost freely, antelope, other susceptible game species and their meat and other unprocessed by-products may often not be removed from a farm in an enzootic foot-and-mouth disease area.

Notwithstanding these restrictions on venison production and sales, farms in foot-and-mouth areas can, owing to the big game found there, often be highly sought after by tourists and trophy hunters. Regardless of where a game farm is situated, I strongly advise potential buyers to consult the state veterinarian or live-stock inspector in advance to ascertain what disease control measures may from time to time govern domestic stock and game in the area.

NATURE OF THE HABITAT

The nature of the habitat is also of the utmost importance, since the habitat preferences of the different game species vary considerably. For example springbok, which thrive naturally in the Free State, Namibia, parts of the Cape and in the Southern Transvaal, may hardly survive a year when released in the bushveld regions of the Northern or Eastern Transvaal. Conversely, the latter regions offer a favourable habitat to most of the other important farm game species.

Just as hard as I find it to picture klipspringers on the open grass plains of the South-Western Transvaal, so incongruous a waterbuck must feel in the Kalahari. More will follow in a later chapter about the adaptability of game to regions other than their natural habitats and the desirability of resettling game beyond their historic distribution areas. Meanwhile I shall merely say that often the most important consideration when selecting a game farm is the ability of the environment to support the greatest possible variety of species. The diverse soil types and plant life found in a varied landscape comprising mountainous or broken terrain and river beds, vlei areas or wetlands often offer the widest possible range of habitats which, once other possible limitations have been taken into account, support the greatest number of species.

If trophy hunting or tourism is not so important a consideration, and you prefer larger numbers of a smaller variety of game species for biltong hunting or meat production, for example, you might require quite a different sort of a farm. The open grassland and scrubveld that comprises a large portion of our country has an allure of its own and, amongst other things, makes a noteworthy contribution to the country's venison export industry. While proponents of game farming often use the advantages of mixed game and stock farming in bush-dense regions as a motivation for the better utilisation of farm game, intensive farming with, for instance, blesbok, and particularly springbok, can in certain circumstances offer a better alternative for the export industry.

SUITABLE FARM SIZE

Although suitable sizes for game farms will be discussed in more detail later, it should preliminarily be pointed out that certain provincial nature conservation authorities lay down minimum requirements in respect of the size of game farms that may be game-fenced. It is therefore advisable to obtain the necessary details from your local nature conservation officer.

In practice it has been demonstrated time and again that larger game farms offer game better chances for survival, while very small game farms can easily become overgrazed and lead to other management problems. Depending on the nature and availability of grazing and the types and numbers of game that must be supported, it is generally accepted that farms smaller than 50 hectares are, in most cases, too small for game-fencing. There are, however, exceptions!

The larger the area, naturally, the more game can be kept on it. In the bushveld regions of the Transvaal, game farms of approximately 500 hectares can support considerable numbers of game, while farms of 1 000 hectares and more are generally quite common. In the drier parts of the country and in regions where grazing is more vulnerable, larger farms are recommended.

River banks, vlei areas and pans usually offer suitable habitats for bushbuck, reedbuck, waterbuck and various other species. Rivers flowing through farms can, however, create problems in the rainy season, when game fences may be swept away. Game fences near rivers and streams should therefore be inspected with particular care.

Although vlei areas can contribute to heavy infestations of certain internal parasites, this is not always inevitably so. When one takes into account the diverse advantages offered by vlei areas, especially with regard to water-loving game species and the protection and possible utilisation of waterbirds, the risks inherent in vlei areas should be evaluated in a broader perspective.

CONDITION OF GRAZING

The nature and condition of the grazing is obviously very important. Depending on the species of game that are to be kept on

The establishment of breeding nuclei of different species is an expensive process. Prospective game farmers must budget generously for this, unless the farm already hosts sufficient game.

the farm, not only the condition of the grass, but also that of the trees, shrubs and vegetation, should also be evaluated, preferably with the assistance of an expert. The availability of suitable browse within reach of the game species concerned is just as important as a good ground cover of suitable types of grass. Overutilisation by browsers is usually characterised by the relative absence of leaves and twigs for a metre or two above ground level, especially during the time of the year when deciduous trees and shrubs have not yet shed their leaves.

Excessive bare patches, erosion and the general presence of stick-grass species and pioneer grasses usually, depending on the region concerned, indicate overutilisation and damage to the grass stratum. The grazing habits of game differ considerably from those of cattle, however, and, as mentioned, game often prefers short grassveld, for example in brackish areas, above dense sour grassveld with an excess of thatch and turpentine-grass and other unpalatable types of grass. Once again the guidance and advice of an expert, and specifically someone with a thorough practical knowledge of game, is highly recommended when evaluating a farm for game farming purposes.

NUMBERS OF GAME

Claims regarding the numbers of game occurring on a farm are unfortunately often misleading. The value of game already present on an established game farm can, in some cases, exceed R300 000, and therefore it is mostly justified to spend one to two thousand rand on an aerial game census. Although no census method is absolutely accurate, a good aerial census should at least provide a satisfactory indication of the species and numbers of game on the farm. It should also be established beyond any doubt that this game is enclosed on the farm permanently and will not roam across to the neighbour's farm the very next day.

IMPROVEMENTS

Without going into too much detail about the presence or absence, as well as quality, of fences, waterholes, roads and firebreaks, homes and outbuildings, facilities for tourists, hunting, slaughtering and cooling, vehicles and farm machinery and tools,

prospective buyers should naturally take into account the value of all improvements and equipment when estimating the value of a farm. In some cases it may be cheaper and more realistic to buy a relatively undeveloped farm at a lower price and to develop and settle game on it in accordance with one's own planning.

TRANSPORTATION AND COMMUNICATION NETWORKS

Links to transportation and communication networks are an important consideration . Professional game capture teams with large trucks sometimes find it impossible to reach certain farms, while other farms are so remote from civilization that it is impractical for the owner, tourists or hunters to visit the farm over weekends.

While road and rail links in the vicinity are very useful, railway lines or roads crossing or running alongside a farm often give rise to veld fires and poaching.

In view of veterinary restrictions governing the maximum permissible duration for the transport of game carcasses from a game farm to the nearest game abattoir or depot, particularly for export purposes, such facilities in the immediate vicinity of a game farm are a definite advantage. The lack of such facilities in the vicinity can sometimes be overcome by making use of mobile abattoir services, such as those offered by certain major export companies in certain circumstances.

RECORDS AND INCOME STATEMENTS

The value of consulting available records and statements when estimating a farm's productivity cannot be overemphasized. In the case of established farms, specified income statements and particularly tax sheets of the preceding few years can certainly provide an accurate indication of the expected income and expenditures of the farm in question. This information, together with the opinions of private experts and/or the local information officers of the Departments of Agriculture and of Conservation, as well as a thorough inspection of the farm, should enable any prospective buyer to draw a reasonable comparison between different prospects and to make the correct choice regarding his own game farm.

5. FARM GAME SPECIES

In South Africa the more than 30 antelope species and other ungulates offer great opportunities for meat production, hunting and other forms of game utilisation. The production and survival capacity of the different species in our varying climatic conditions, as well as the popularity of specific species for, say, trophy hunting and tourism, are but a few of the factors to be considered when selecting suitable species of farm game.

SUITABLE CARCASS SIZE

South African venison appears to be extremely popular overseas. Some years ago, almost R10 million's worth of fresh frozen venison was exported. Since small reindeer carcasses are traditionally dressed and utilised in European countries, small carcasses of approximately 18 to 23 kilograms are preferred. Springbok carcasses are particularly popular, while young impala and blesbok are also very sought after. The prices paid by venison exporters to game farmers for game carcasses over the past few years have therefore also been better for the smaller categories of carcass. For local use and also for the possible utilisation and export of deboned venison, the size of the carcass is less critical. Information concerning the average carcass mass of the most important game farm species is given in Chapter 19.

EFFICIENT FODDER UTILISATION AND PRODUCTIVITY

Whereas the traditional selection and breeding of farm stock has largely concentrated on production capability, the advantage of our indigenous game species lies especially in their adaptability and their ability to survive. Cattle can admittedly, as is claimed, grow twelve times as rapidly as elephant on a given energy intake. Experiments under artificial conditions, where the fodder conversion and growth rate of eland, for example, are compared with those of cattle, have also yielded interesting results. It is probably to be expected that domestic animals which have for many years been bred under intensive-farming conditions specifically for production properties will fare better in such experiments. However, when these animals are returned to their natural environment, a different picture emerges. For example, illuminating research by Dr Ian Hofmeyr has revealed that eland utilise approximately 130 different plant species. Like the kudu and other species of game, the eland also feeds off a variety of plants that are classified poisonous to livestock. Even during the winter the browsing species, in particular, such as kudu, bushbuck, nyala and giraffe, feed off leaves, which have a much higher nutritional value than grass.

Herds of thriving springbok and gemsbok on some of the

In the past it was believed that only tame game could be successfully used for farming. Eland become very tame, can be milked like cows and are the ideal species of farm game in regions where ticks and diseases that are transmitted by ticks are not a problem.

The impala is particularly immune to disease, can withstand long periods
without water, especially in summer, and during severe droughts can thrive
in areas where cattle and sheep would not survive.

poorest grazing, sleek impala on damaged veld on which live-stock could survive with difficulty, if at all, and game in their thousands in all parts of our country which have mostly stood the test of time without man's assistance and particularly without supplementary feeding, surely offers adequate proof of the hardiness of our indigenous game species and of their capacity for survival under unfavourable conditions.

Based on these characteristics, selective game breeding aimed specifically at increased productivity should pose unique challenges to today's breeders.

RESISTANCE TO DROUGHT

It is common knowledge that certain game species are better equipped than livestock or other game species to survive under arid or semi-arid conditions and/or to withstand protracted droughts. Gemsbok, springbok, eland, steenbok and duiker are a few examples of game which can survive with little or no water.

IMMUNITY TO DISEASE

More than one third of Africa is still plagued by tsetse and naga-na. In these areas, where stock farming can hardly be under-taken successfully without enormous expenditure, together with the frequently associated pollution of rivers and streams and the poisoning of wild animals with insecticides, large herds of almost every species of game thrive. Foot-and-mouth disease, swine fever and bovine malignant catarrh provide further exam-ples of diseases to which our domestic farm animals are sus-ceptible and as a result of which huge losses can be incurred. In

the past, especially, wild game was generally held responsible for the incidence of these diseases, with or without justification.

In the interest of the stock farming industry and the country's economy no risks should be taken when moving game which could contribute to the spread of foot-and-mouth disease or swine fever, for example. However, it is surely also a valid viewpoint that anyone who walks around barefoot amongst thorns is almost certain to get hurt! Why farm with livestock in areas where foot-and-mouth disease pose a constant threat? Game, and particularly big game such as buffalo, has remarkable value for hunting and tourism, and surely has the right to exist in certain areas. Indeed, the question involuntarily arises whether the immunity of game to these significant livestock diseases should not in certain instances be regarded as a great advantage in favour of game farming in enzootic disease regions.

Although game in general, and particularly under natural con-ditions, is more immune to diseases and parasite infestations, it should be kept in mind that eland, for example, often fare poorly owing to severe tick infestations and that springbok from areas that are free of heartwater should not summarily be released in heartwater areas, owing to their susceptibility to this disease (see Chapter 18).

PREDATION AND SURVIVAL

All types of game do not fare equally well in areas where pred-ators commonly occur. Blesbok and springbok often suffer heavily where jackals and other predators are found, while game species which hide their young for the first few weeks or months after birth also sometimes lose many calves or lambs to predators. Despite the high reproduction rate of roan antelope — a roan antelope cow can produce six calves in five years — research by Dr Salomon Joubert in the Kruger Park has shown, for example, that a cow has an 80 per cent chance of losing her calf during the first six weeks after birth. While the calves are initially hidden they easily fall prey to predators and also die from numerous other causes. Survival statistics of young animals serve as one of the most important criteria determining the survival success of a specific type of game in a specific area.

OTHER IMPORTANT FACTORS

It is only logical that a species's habitat and feeding preferences and its grazing habits should also be taken into account when the suitability of a species is evaluated for a specific region.

The territorial behaviour patterns, aggression or mutual tolerance and other behaviour patterns and herd habits of game differ from species to species, and contribute to the fact that all species do not fare equally well under restricted conditions.

In addition, the monetary value of rare species and the popularity of certain species amongst trophy hunters also play an important role in the choice of game species for specific purposes. There is furthermore the contentious point of view that game should be restricted to their historical distribution areas only.

SABLE ANTELOPE
Hippotragus niger

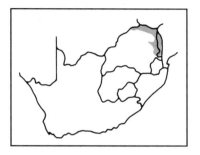

Photograph: Transvaal Nat. Cons. Division

GENERAL INFORMATION

Natural distribution: Northern and north-eastern Botswana, Zimbabwe (they have largely disappeared from the central plateau), Mozambique, south of the Zambezi river with the exception of the extreme southern parts and some areas in the south-east. In South Africa natural populations are found in the northern and eastern Transvaal (Smithers, 1983).

Conservation status: Rare.

Limiting factors: High calf mortality. Predation, veld degradation, due to competitive overgrazing by other ungulates, unsuitable habitat with nutritionally inferior grazing in late winter, disease and parasites.

Habitat: Vleis and grassveld with medium length to long grasses, bordered by savanna veld, are generally preferred.

Preferred food types: Grass. Exceptionally browse.

Sexual maturity: Females at 2 years and males about 3 years.

Gestation period: 261 — 281 days.

First calf born: When cow is about 3 years old.

Calving interval: On average, every year.

Mating season: Autumn and winter.

Calving season: Peak in summer.

Number of young: One at a time. Twins not recorded.

Longevity: 18 years.

Body weight (adults): 180 — 230 kg (396 — 506 lb.).

Shoulder height (adults): 135 cm (54 in.).

Horns: Both sexes. Longer and more heavily ridged in bulls.

Of the three subspecies of sable, *H. niger niger* is the one found in South Africa, and elsewhere south of the Zambezi river. *H. niger kirkii* occurs north of the Zambezi.

Only three South African antelope species have backward-sweeping horns, viz. the sable antelope (swartwitpens), roan (bastergemsbok) and the extinct blue antelope (bloubok). The sable antelope is slightly smaller than the roan but has considerably longer horns.

The giant sable
The giant, or royal sable, *H. niger variani*, restricted in its distri-

bution to Angola, is probably the most impressive of all antelope. Its very long horns and facial markings distinguish this subspecies from our own. Unlike our indigenous sable, the white markings, extending downwards from near the base of the horns, do not go right down to the muzzle, giving the giant sable's face a darker, almost black appearance.

Before the Angolan war, an estimated 500 to 3 000 giant sable were strictly protected in that country. How many of them, if any, still survive there today is not known.

Typical sable country

Dr J.H. Grobler, who studied sable intensively in Zimbabwe, describes a typical sable home range very appropriately as 'areas of grassland and woodland with a varied amount of granite hills with associated koppie vegetation, and with at least one permanent water point in the area.'

Being gregarious, sable are found in small herds, exceptionally in large congregations of up to a few hundred animals, particularly toward the end of the dry season and in areas where they still occur in large numbers.

The adult females in a herd establish a definite hierarchical order. The most dominant cow usually acts as herd leader and will take the initiative when the herd moves to another area, in keeping watch and when fleeing from danger.

The breeding or nursery herd, which basically consists of cows, heifers, young bulls and calves, and at times a patriarchal bull, live in and move across a home range area some 200 to 400 hectares in size.

The home range of the breeding herd may overlap with that of one or more territorial bulls. Once a territorial bull has taken over a herd, he will defend it possessively against any other adult bulls. Should a female dare to try to escape or to run in the direction of another territorial bull, the herd bull will run past her and drive her back with sweeping horns and disgusted snorts.

Young bulls are driven out of the breeding herds by the patriarchal bull when they show the first signs of sexual maturity at about three years of age. They then either join bachelor herds, which may consist of up to 10 bulls, usually about three to six years old, or remain solitary and live in a territory some 25 to 40 hectares in size. Some of these territories may overlap with one or more home ranges of breeding herds. Stripped bark and trees and shrubs with broken branches may indicate that a territorial sable bull could be present in the area.

Vicious fighting

When scaring off intruding males, the territorial bull adopts a typical stiff-necked posture with the chin tucked in, the neck muscles bulging and the long mane erect. The stiffly held tail is nervously twitched as the two bulls approach each other sideways. At this stage one of the bulls may surrender and run away with his tail clamped between the hindlegs. Alternatively the combatants may drop to their knees, delivering deadly blows with sweeping horns. For an hour or more the fight may continue, with clashing horns and penetrating screams audible over a considerable distance. These combats often end in the death of one or both of the contestants.

The sable has a varied vocabulary. It ranges from the better-known warning snort of the adult animals to the softer, high-pitched screams of the calves when danger is sensed. Dr Grobler describes the call of a calf, in search of its mother, as bird-like, while a cow, in search of its calf, will emit a series of short grunts. When fighting, the bulls repeatedly emit a very high-pitched bleating squeal.

Sable are normally of a shy nature, avoiding contact with humans. However, when they have been chased and are tired or wounded, this beast, with its dangerous horns, is among the few antelope I know of that will fiercely retaliate. It will at times even defy a pride of lion.

Feeding habits

When not disturbed, sable may graze for days in a very small area a few hectares in size before moving to another part of their home range. Most of the feeding takes place during the early morning and late afternoon when it is cool. During the hot hours of the day they lie up or simply stand, resting, while chewing the cud.

Unlike species such as blesbok and wildebeest, which prefer short grass, sable normally graze on grass of medium height. They are very selective in their feeding habits.

Like all other grazers they show a definite preference for new growth and are attracted by recently burnt veld. Predominantly grazers, they occasionally browse on trees and shrubs, particularly towards the end of winter when the nutritional value of grass is low. Fruits and pods of the raisin bush (*Grewia spp.*), buffalo-thorn (*Ziziphus mucronata*) and of the sickle bush (*Dichrostachys*) and Acacia species are sometimes eaten.

The nutritional value of the veld, particularly towards late winter, largely determines the well-being of sable in a particular area. They tend to avoid heavily overgrazed areas, while heavy mortalities may occur during severe droughts.

Undernourished individuals may be further weakened by internal parasites, to the extent that weakened individuals may even be caught by hand.

Bone chewing has also been recorded. This may reveal a phosphorous deficiency in a particular area and could have the added disadvantage of animals contracting and dying from botulism. This, however, has not yet been confirmed. Balanced mineral licks could meet the nutritional needs of sable in deficient areas, at the same time reducing the urge to pick up bones.

Research by Dr Dave Wilson has revealed that some sable are infected with Babesia and Cytauxzoon blood parasites. The Babesia parasites are related to protozoa causing red water disease in cattle and biliary fever in horses and dogs. Animals harbouring these parasites do not necessarily develop clinical symptoms. When their resistance is broken down, by malnourishment or stress, for instance, the affected animal could theoretically die from an overwhelming infection.

A fungal disease, dermatophilosis, can occasionally affect sable (and roan) calves under continually wet conditions. Hair loss and dermatitis in young sable may be due to this disease.

Sable are usually found near open water, seldom moving more than three kilometres from it. They drink regularly, about once a day and normally during the hot hours. They are fastidious animals and often walk knee-deep into the water to avoid the muddiness along the edges of a pool.

Good breeders

Females become sexually mature at two years of age, have their first calves when three years old, and thereafter calve almost every year. Cows older than 10 years old are still capable of breeding.

Calves may be born at any time of the year. In general, however, sable are seasonal breeders, dropping their calves mostly from January to March, with a peak around February.

Shortly before giving birth the pregnant cow leaves the herd. When born, the golden-brownish baby weighs about 13 to 18 kilograms. It is not very mobile during the first two weeks, which possibly explains the high mortality rate in sable calves, due to predation.

During the first two weeks the cow hides her young baby nearby in dense grass and only visits it every now and then to let it suckle. After being licked clean by its mother, the calf may move to some alternative hiding place, thereby lessening the chances of being found by a predator. During these first few weeks it is not a strong runner and depends largely on camouflage and hiding. A small calf in hiding can be approached on foot and stroked, without it even attempting to flee. Sometimes several young calves are hidden in close proximity.

When young calves are flushed from their hiding places and chased, they usually run for some distance and when tired, they drop down and hide in the long grass.

Calf mortality is very high and it is calculated that despite a high calving rate the real recruitment rate per breeding herd from the young of the year is about 26 to 29 per cent. If all females of three years and older do in fact have calves every year, it is estimated that about half the calves die within the first year of life.

Weaning of the calves seems to take place when they are about 6 to 8 months old. They sometimes form nursery groups, frequently with an adult cow or some yearlings in attendance.

Natural enemies
Lion, leopard, spotted hyena, crocodile and man count among the sable antelope's enemies. In certain areas leopard are important enemies, as they may prey heavily on young calves.

The sable's inquisitive but aggressive nature and its sometimes bold attitude towards lions frequently make it easy prey for the big cats. When the herd decides to flee, as a last-moment decision, it is the younger members of the herd which sometimes do not get away quickly enough from the attacking predators.

When one considers that the sable is a rare species, it comes as a shock to read that no fewer than 31 000 sable were shot in Zimbabwe until 1952, as part of the tsetse fly control programme.

Farming sable antelope
There are about 1 453 sable in the Kruger Park, 130 in provincial nature reserves in the Transvaal and more than 1 300 on private farms in the same province.

In areas with suitable habitat and grazing, it should be possible to keep sable on relatively small farms. As already mentioned, a breeding herd requires a home range of about 200 to 400 hectares. Should adequate feeding conditions prevail throughout the year and the number of competitive grazers and predators be low, sable should theoretically do well on many farms in South Africa. Sable can usually be confined on a game farm by low game fencing. A strong, 1,8 metre high fence will normally suffice.

Establishing as many breeding herds of sable over as wide a range of suitable farms and reserves as possible is obviously the surest way of ensuring the survival of this beauty of all beauties in its homeland, southern Africa.

ROAN ANTELOPE
Hippotragus equinus

Photograph: Koos Delport

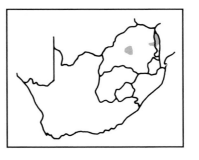

GENERAL INFORMATION

Natural distribution (S.A.): Northern and Eastern Transvaal.
Conservation status: Rare and threatened.
Limiting factors: Disease, carnivores, habitat, social behaviour.
Habitat: Savanna with long grassveld.
Preferred food types: Grass.
Sexual maturity: Bulls 31 months, cows 20 — 22 months.
First calf born: Cow ± 32 months.
Mating season: Throughout the year.
Gestation period: ± 280 days.
Calving season: Throughout the year.
Number of young: One. Twins unknown.
Period between calves: ± 317 days.
Body weight (adults): 227 — 272 kg (504 — 604 lb.).
Shoulder height (adults): 125 — 150 cm (50 — 60 in.).
Horns: Both sexes.

After the eland, the roan antelope (together with the kudu) is the second largest African antelope species. The roan is closely related to the sable antelope and belongs to the same genus. The extinct blue antelope (bloubok) also belonged to this genus.

The newborn calves are a light to rich reddish-brown colour, which changes to the greyish brown colour of the adult animals when they are between two to four months old.

Bulls and cows both carry horns. In animals older than two years, the bull's horns are noticeably thicker than those of the cows. The roan and sable antelope are of the few African antelope species which have backward sweeping horns.

It is possible to estimate the age of roan by the size and shape of the animal's horns. From the age of two to twelve months, the roan calf's straight, spiked horns develop more or less in relation to its age. When the animal is between 10 and 12 months old, the first ridge is formed at the horn base. For the next two years, until the age of three years, eight ridges per year are formed. After this age, it becomes difficult to determine the age of an animal by this method. In very old animals, the ridges on the horns begin to wear down from the horn base upwards and the tips of the horns also become blunt and shorter.

Roan are almost always found in small herds. Herd size usually varies from between three to twelve animals. Their senses are well developed and it is difficult to approach these wary animals. Roan are aggressive antelope and a wounded animal can be dangerous. The cows seem intolerant of weaker animals within the herd and constantly maintain a seniority hierarchy.

Why are they so rare ?
Roan breed faster and produce more young than most other large antelope species. The cow usually mates within two to four weeks after the birth of her calf, and in this manner can produce six calves every five years. During her lifetime, a roan cow can give birth to between ten and eleven calves. The puzzling question which arises is: if roan are capable of prolific breeding, why are they so rare ?

The following limiting factors may, to a greater or lesser degree, be responsible for the rarity of this impressive antelope:

Agricultural and other developments have been largely responsible for the disappearance of roan from their original distribution areas. Roan are particularly sensitive to disturbance and they will usually move away to a quieter, more peaceful area. Excessive hunting in the past has surely also played a part in the decline in roan numbers.

Disease, particularly anthrax, can have a very negative effect on the roan population. For example, in 1960 and 1970, 41 and 38 roan, respectively, died of anthrax in the Kruger National Park.

Dr Salomon Joubert, warden of the Kruger National Park, who can surely be regarded as the expert on roan, found that the inherent behavioural patterns of this antelope are one of its biggest limiting factors. The bulls fight viciously and evict each other from the herd. Only one breeding bull is allowed in every herd. This bull's own male calves are driven from the herd when they are between two and three years old. These animals are forced to seek refuge elsewhere, possibly in a less suitable area. This renders them more prone to attack by predators. Injuries and mortalities among the fighting bulls, amongst other things, may result in almost twice as many cows as bulls surviving, after being born in an equal ratio. The outcast bulls live alone, or form bull herds. When these bulls are about five or six years old, they may succeed in driving off the older bulls, and claim their own harems.

Areas suited to the habitat requirements of roan are

diminishing in size. Established herds which live in an area of about 60 to 100 square kilometres do not defend a staked out territory from other roan or drive off other herds. However, the limited number of animals in a particular herd, as well as the general intolerance toward other herds in the same area, results in a relatively small number of roan being found in a fairly large area, the unwelcome herd once again having to find a less suitable refuge elsewhere.

Roan are selective grazers. The tops of long grass stalks, leaves and the growing points of grass species are favoured. Roan do not mix freely with other herds of wild animals, such as wildebeest or zebra, and avoid areas which have been over-grazed. Once again, the roan's finicky nature makes it difficult for the species to adapt to changing conditions.

Furthermore, it is important that roan avoid short grassveld and rear their young in long grassveld. The calves are hidden in the long grass for the first six weeks of life and are left alone for most of the day. In the first two weeks after birth, these calves are not able to escape from danger. In short grassveld, which provides little shelter, the young calves are obviously more at risk.

The concentration of other game species in an area where roan occur, can cause further problems for the latter. Under these conditions, disease is rampant and parasites flourish, both being more easily transmitted from one animal to another. In dry areas, they may even have to compete for available water. Predators abound near such concentrations of game and this may pose a further threat to the roan. This is particularly true where roan may have to drink from an isolated waterhole, where lions lie in wait for thirsty animals for days on end.

Amongst predators, lions count as the roan's chief enemy. Research done over many years in the Kruger National Park by Dr U. de V. Pienaar, has shown that as many as 86 per cent of roan kills were attributable to lions. Other enemies are leopard, cheetah, wild dog, spotted hyena and even black-backed jackal, which may prey on young animals.

In the Kruger National Park, Dr Salomon Joubert studied a herd of roan in a fenced-in area of 2,6 square kilometres. The nett increase in the population was 100 per cent. Studies done outside of this protected area, however, showed a 70 per cent mortality rate among calves in the first six weeks of life and an 80 per cent mortaliy rate during the first three months. Adequate shelter, plentiful food and water and protection from lions and other predators in the fenced-off camp, as well as the absence of other limiting factors which are a problem where roan have to compete with large herds of other game, are apparently re-sponsible for the higher survival rate of roan within the protected camp.

Research has also revealed that roan numbers begin to decline where more than one roan to about nine or ten hectares (26 — 28 animals per square mile) is kept. It is a well-known ecological fact that high population density also limits the numbers of certain other species. The good news gleaned from this research is that the optimum carrying capacity for large game in a suitable habitat can be as high as 30 to 33 animals on a relatively small game farm of 300 hectares.

Veld fires are also a limiting factor, as calves may be trapped and burn to death. Rain, accompanied by cold winds, may also be responsible for losses amongst roan herds.

In the Kruger National Park, as many roan as possible are inoculated annually against anthrax. This is done by firing dart syringes into the animals from a helicopter. Single outbreaks of anthrax, particularly in small nature reserves, can decimate entire populations and the good example set by the Parks Board should be followed by others to afford the necessary protection to these rare animals.

The policy of the Transvaal Division of Nature Conservation to establish breeding herds in different areas can also contribute greatly to the preservation of the species. However, like Dr Joubert, I would like to see the implementation of a conservation strategy which allows selected farmers with suitable game farms and good conservation records, the opportunity to protect breeding herds on their farms. Many farmers would be prepared to allow breeding of rare and endangered species on their farms at no cost.

GEMSBOK
Oryx gazella gazella

Photograph: Koos Delport

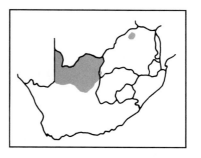
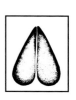

Body weight (adults): 180 — 240 kg (396 — 528 lb.)
Shoulder height (adults): About 120 cm (48 in.)
Longevity: 20 years.
Horns: Both sexes. Usually longer in females.

Different species

Three species of oryx are known; two of which live in Africa. The gemsbok, *Oryx g. gazella*, is the one we know in South Africa. The scimitar horned oryx *O. dammah*, is an inhabitant of desert regions in North Africa, from Nigeria to Libya and the Sudan. The Arabian oryx, *O. leucoryx*, is a smaller species, almost pure white in colour. Captive herds of the latter, which is an endangered species, have been established in the United States and Africa in an attempt to prevent extinction of the species.

Oryx gazella, to which our indigenous gemsbok belong, has 5 different subspecies. These include the Beisa oryx, *O.g. beisa*, of Ethiopia and Somalia, the fringe-eared oryx, *O.g.callotis*, of Kenya and Tanzania, *O.g. gallurum* of the Sudan and Ethiopia and *O.g.annectans* from Kenya and Somalia. The latter two subspecies could, in fact, be the same animal but might have been wrongly classified as two separate subspecies.

To me the gemsbok is certainly one of the most handsome of all antelope. Standing about 120 cm (48 in.) at the shoulder, the gemsbok, the only oryx species which occurs naturally in southern Africa, is the largest of the oryxes, and also carries the longest horns. The gemsbok's body build, the way it gallops and its long, hairy tail, gives it a somewhat horsey appearance.

These extremely wary animals of the open plains rely strongly on their keen eyesight to detect predators and flee at great speed at the first signs of approaching danger.

It is commonly believed that gemsbok calves are born with horns. The truth is that only short horn buds are present at birth.

Both male and female gemsbok carry horns. In the female the horns are generally longer and lighter in build.

The gemsbok is a formidable fighter. It uses its long, needle-sharp horns with unbelievable accuracy. When approached too closely, it will unhesitatingly turn on its pursuer. When approached by game captors in a catching vehicle, gemsbok are said to have punctured a tyre of the vehicle with a quick jab of the horns. The gemsbok can flick off a stone thrown at it, and I

GENERAL INFORMATION

Natural distribution (Southern Africa): Namibia (but largely absent in the south and south west), Botswana (mainly in semi-desert areas), western Zimbabwe, northern Cape and extreme south-western Transvaal.
Conservation status: Fairly abundant.
Limiting factors: Predation. Inability to adapt when released in areas with unsuitable habitat.
Habitat: Semi-desert. Shrub and grassveld.
Preferred food type: Grass. Exceptionally browse. Also Tsamma melons, bulbs and tubers.
Sexual maturity: Females about 2 years. Males presumably a little later.
Gestation period: 261 to 275 days.
Mating season: Mainly autumn.
Calving season: Peak in summer.
Calves born: One. Twins not recorded.
Calving interval: About one year.

have been told that it is even fast enough to deflect a dart syringe fired at it, by using its horns.

In their attempts to avoid the gemsbok's long horns, Kalahari lions are reported to have discovered a weak point in the anatomy of the gemsbok. Prof. Fritz Eloff, well-known zoologist and expert on the behaviour of the animals of the Kalahari, noticed that lions have adapted their hunting techniques to deal with gemsbok. Instead of going for the animal's forequarters, the lion flings its full weight on the back part of the fleeing gemsbok's body, snapping the spine just in front of the hips. Once paralysed, the gemsbok is then again approached and killed.

The gemsbok's forehooves are typical of animals with heavy forequarters, larger than the hind hooves. The spoor is characteristically heart-shaped with sharp tips.

Gemsbok will drink when water is readily available. In desert conditions, however, they obtain some of the required moisture from succulent roots and tubers, which they dig out from the sand with their hooves, and from Tsamma melons, a wild cucumber-like fruit which grows in desert areas.

Gemsbok avoid excessive moisture loss through sweating and panting by being passive during the hot hours of the day. They are more active during the early mornings, late afternoons and at night. Research has revealed that some desert plants absorb considerable amounts of atmospheric moisture at night. By eating these plants at night, the gemsbok also obtains some of its much needed water from these 'hygroscopic' plants.

Other animals, not adapted to desert conditions, lose enormous amounts of moisture through their skins (sweating) and lungs (breathing and panting). These natural evaporative cooling processes are brought about and stimulated by even a small rise in body temperature. The gemsbok, unique in this way, can have its body temperature rise past all average physiological norms, without these dehydrating mechanisms being activated.

Its temperature rises to levels which could cause thermal brain damage in other species. But nature has made provision for this. Blood carried from the gemsbok's heart to its brain first flows past the animal's nasal passages where the warm blood, flowing through a network of thin-walled membranes in the animal's nose, is cooled down by the relatively cooler air that the animal breathes. Consequently, cooler blood is pumped to the gemsbok's brain, enabling it to survive under extremely hot and dry conditions. Once it gets cooler, later in the day, the gemsbok also cools down and resumes its activities, searching for succulent food to replenish its water supply.

Even under extreme desert conditions the gemsbok's rumen (stomach) contents have a high percentage of moisture. Bushman hunters squeeze out a hunted gemsbok's stomach contents to obtain water which they strain through a sieve of grass, before drinking the foul-smelling liquid.

Gemsbok do not occur naturally in Malawi and Zambia. They are found in South-West Angola, in parts of Botswana and Namibia, the northern parts of the Cape Province and in the far northern and south-western Transvaal. Lately, game farmers have also established gemsbok elsewhere in South Africa.

When gemsbok are released on game farms they often do exceedingly well. But sometimes they don't adapt at all. They sometimes flourish for several years on certain game farms but then their numbers gradually decline for no apparent reason.

Preliminary observations indicate that, when gemsbok are released in an area with well-drained, sandy soil, with short annual grasses, they usually do very well. On game farms with heavier, clay soils and dense stands of grass, the success rate is variable.

Badly adapted, malnourished and sick gemsbok lose weight and may become heavily infested with ticks. In severe cases, concomitant screw-worm infestation sometimes causes severe feet lesions which may result in death, as the animal is unable to walk and feed, and so dies of starvation.

Of all the South African antelope, the gemsbok seems to be one of the species most susceptible to extremely cold conditions.

Gemsbok are mostly found in small herds, which may join up to form large congregations during droughts, or when they concentrate in areas with green grass after the first spring rains fall in a localized area.

Old bulls often live a solitary life. The bulls are territorial but are generally more tolerant of other bulls than the males of most other territorial antelope species. Each territorial male occupies a territory about four to ten square kilometres in size. When about five to seven years old, these territorial bulls play a major role in breeding. They actively herd animals of mixed or nursery herds into their territories, where mating takes place.

A game-proof fence, only 1,8 metres high (compared with a 2,4 metre fence for kudu, eland, waterbuck and impala) should normally suffice for gemsbok. Sixteen strands of wire, evenly spaced over the height of 1,8 metres, is recommended.

Calculated at an estimated dressed carcass weight of about 55 per cent of its live weight, an eviscerated gemsbok carcass (adult animal) should weigh about 100 — 140 kilograms (220 — 308 lb.) Its meat is said to be comparable in palatability to that of the eland.   I foresee an increase in the price of gemsbok at auctions and other sales and game farmers who have successfully established gemsbok on their farms can consider themselves very fortunate. Very popular with game viewers and hunters alike, the gemsbok is a more than worthwhile acquisition to any game farm.

ELAND
Taurotragus oryx

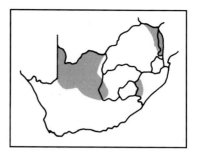

Photograph: Transvaal Nat. Cons. Division

GENERAL INFORMATION

Natural distribution (S.A.): Northern and eastern Transvaal, western Natal, northern Cape.
Conservation status: Relatively abundant.
Limiting factors: Excessive hunting (earlier), shrinking habitat, tick infestations.
Habitat: Savanna, grassland, semi-desert areas.
Preferred food types: Predominantly browsers.
Sexual maturity: Bulls 18 months, cows 15 months.
Mating season: Throughout the year, especially October to January.
Gestation period: 271 days.
First calf born: Cow 26 — 31 months.
Calving interval: 334 — 374 days.
Number of calves: One, occasionally twins.
Longevity: 23½ years.
Body weight (adults): 460 — 910 kg (1022 — 2022 lb.).
Shoulder height (adults): 150 — 170 cm (60 — 68 in.).

Eland are more prolific breeders than, for example, Afrikaner cattle, make better use of the leaves of trees and shrubs than do cattle, are generally better able to adapt to extremely hot, dry regions and even flourish under these conditions, produce very tasty meat and are easily tamed. Eland have been a favourite game species for farming purposes for the past 130 years because of these outstanding qualities.

There are three subspecies of eland. They occur from the Cape in the south to the fringes of the Sahara desert in the north.

Prof. J.D. Skinner calculated that, in 1973, some 6 800 eland occurred in South Africa and Namibia. This figure included approximately 1 000 to 1 500 animals in the Kalahari Gemsbok National Park, where these animals seasonally migrate between South Africa and Botswana. Approximately two thirds of all the eland in South Africa were found on private game farms at that time.

Not only is the eland the largest antelope species in Africa, it is also one of the biggest antelope in the world. In fact, a large eland can weigh more than a big, adult buffalo and this huge antelope is taller than either the buffalo or the domestic cow.

In spite of their size, eland can jump very high and a 2.4 m high fence is required to confine them. If specific eland are reared in a camp with a 1,7 m high fence, this fence will be adequate to keep them in.

Eland utilise some 130 tree and shrub species for food. Plant and weed species which are almost never eaten by domestic stock sometimes comprise the most important food types of the eland. Eland even do well in areas where 'gifblaar' (*Dichapetalum cymosum*), which causes stock losses, is found.

Eland will utilise green grass during summer, but they eat considerably less grass during winter. In winter, leaves and pods constitute their main diet. Eland use their horns to pull leafy branches within reach and these may even be broken off. Thin twigs are eaten as well as the leaves.

The leaves off which the eland lives not only provide more than twice as much protein as the grass which is eaten by cattle, but also provide more moisture during the dry months. This contributes to the fact that eland are able to go without water for longer periods.

When water is freely available, eland will drink regularly. In semi-desert areas, they dig up moisture-rich tubers and eat tsammas, which makes it possible for them to go without water for long periods.

Although research has shown that cattle can be fattened more successfully than eland under intensive conditions, the latter grow fast and can put on 840 g of weight per day.

The bulls weigh much more than the cows when they are fully grown, but the female animals grow proportionately faster in relation to their adult mass. The bulls reach about 25 per cent of their adult weight when they are one year old, compared to 40 per cent for the cow. At three years of age, this figure is 62 per cent for the bull and 75 per cent for the cow. Eland cows are mature when they are between five and six years old, and bulls when they are between six and seven years of age.

Both sexes carry horns. The horn buds are present at birth. The bull's horns are heavier and have a prominent ridge, which is clearly visible on the horns when the animal is 15 months old. The horns of the eland cow are smoother and lighter. The horns may already be 75 cm long when the animal is 18 months old.

The patch of brown-coloured hair on the forehead of eland bulls has a strong smell because of glandular secretions. Scent communication plays an important part in the life of the eland.

The carcass yield of eland is between 48 and 54 per cent and some 82 per cent of the dressed carcass, or 48 per cent of the total body mass, is meat. Eland venison is of the tastiest venisons and, because of its low fat content, is an ideal source of red meat for the health conscious.

Eland are nomadic and migrate over long distances. New plant growth after veld fires and the general availability of their preferred food types usually determine the nature and extent of their wanderings. The home range of eland cows and the younger animals is usually considerably larger than that of the bulls, and can extend over an area of approximately 200 square kilometres.

Eland spoor is very similar to that of domestic cattle. The eland's front hooves are bigger than its hind hooves. Walking eland can be heard from a distance. A distinctly audible clicking noise, apparently originating from the knee joints, can be heard over a distance of 100 metres and further on a quiet night. This clicking betrays their presence and may make it easier for carnivores and humans to hunt these animals.

Many attempts at cross-breeding eland with cattle have been made, without success. Even attempts at artificial insemination have failed.

Formerly, eland were widely distributed over southern Africa. However, man and his cattle have significantly disturbed the eland's natural habitat. Their nomadic behaviour has been curbed by the erection of cattle fences and their natural grazing areas have been taken over by cattle. More significant problems are tick infestations, and, to a lesser degree, cattle diseases such as heartwater, which are synonymous with cattle farming. This has made it almost impossible to relocate eland successfully in areas where they used to occur naturally.

The eland's skin over the neck, behind the shoulders, under the abdomen, between the hindlegs, and under the tail appears to be very soft and pliable and is easily attacked by ticks. However,

the skin of an eland makes very good and strong leather thongs. It is claimed that a single thong of about 150 metres in length can be cut from the skin of one, large eland.

In areas where heavy tick infestations are common, the genital organs of eland bulls are often so damaged that they are unable to breed. The cow's udders are also damaged by ticks and resulting ulcers to such an extent that they are unable to suckle their calves. In such instances it is wise to capture the young calves and hand-rear them. These calves soon become tame, are very easy to rear and can usually be weaned at between five and nine months of age.

Tame eland have successfully been driven into a crush and dipped to control tick numbers. Products such as Amitras (Triatix, Coopers), which require treatment of only a portion of the body in order to kill off all the ticks, makes tick control much easier.

Where cattle and eland are kept together on a farm, it is prudent to dip the cattle regularly in order to control tick numbers and so give the eland the opportunity to build up a measure of natural resistance against ticks.

Eland are gregarious animals and up to 1 000 animals have been counted in a single herd (Smithers, Botswana). Adult bulls are often seen alone or in small bull herds.

Bulls are sexually mature at 18 months of age, but generally breed when they are quite a bit older, as they are kept away from the cows by the older, stronger bulls. In theory, eland cows can produce a calf every year, from the age of two years. In reality, the period between calves is about 334 to 374 days. Some cows will skip a year and, as a result, researchers calculate the average annual increase in the population at 83 per cent of the adult cows.

The young calves are hidden by their mothers for the first two weeks after birth. Thereafter, the cows and their calves may form a separate little herd, apart from the large herd. If such a herd of cows and calves is persistently pursued, the cows may, on passing through a dense patch of bush, unobtrusively hide their calves and continue running, unperturbed, to distract the pursuers.

On average, an eland will live for 14 to 16 years. There is a case of an eland cow reaching the age of 23½ years, and having her last calf when she was 19 years old.

When the older animals lose some of their body hair, the darker coloured skin shows through, hence the term, "blue bulls" given to very big, old eland bulls.

KUDU
Tragelaphus strepsiceros

GENERAL INFORMATION

Natural distribution (S.A.): Northern, eastern and western Transvaal, north-eastern Natal, north-eastern and south-eastern Cape.
Conservation status: Relatively abundant.
Limiting factors: Drought, carnivores, disease and excessive hunting.
Habitat: Savanna and mountainous areas.
Preferred food types: Leaves, twigs, pods and fruit.
Sexual maturity: Bulls 14 months (mate later), cows 17 months.
Mating season: Mostly from July to September.
Calving Season: January — May. Peak in February. Occasionally throughout the year.
Gestation period: ± 210 — 240 days.

First calf born: Cow 24 months.
Calving interval: 1 year (occasionally 2 years).
Number of calves: One. Twins unknown.
Longevity: 11 + years.
Body weight (adults): 170 — 260 kg (377 — 577 lb.).
Shoulder height (adults): 125 — 140 cm (50 — 56 in.).

The kudu is generally considered to be the most impressive of all the antelope species. Usually only the bulls carry horns. Sometimes, as a freak of nature, cows also have horns, which are thin and unnaturally curved.

A kudu's age can be determined by counting the transverse ridges on the bull's horns and taking note of the shape of the horns. Research by Dr Dave Wilson showed that the straight

28

Photograph: Lorna Stanton, S.A. National Parks Board

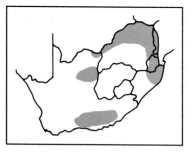

horns of a heifer calf form the first curve at between 14 and 17 months of age and that the first spiral in the horns is complete by the age of 2 years. The other 2½ spirals which are seen on big trophy bulls can take another 4½ years to form.

Kudu occur primarily in the bushveld regions of the country. Deserts, open grassveld and very dense forests are mostly avoided. In semi-desert areas, kudu are generally found in localised herds, where there is sufficient food and shelter for the animals. As with impala and other game species, the kudu is particularly fond of broken terrain with sufficient bush. They are normally not found too far from water.

The kudu is predominantly a browser. Trees, shrubs and herbs of some 150 species are utilised by them. Some of these are considered to be very poisonous to cattle, but most of them have no adverse effect on the kudu.

Sickle bush (*dichrostachys cinerea*) and rough leaved raisin (*grewia flavescens*) represent, amongst others, important feed trees in the rainy season, while the very young leaves of the peeling-bark ochna (lekkerbreek) (*Ochna pulchra*) and red syringa (*Burkea africana*) are utilised, possibly beyond expectation, in the early spring. The tough leaves of the latter are only exceptionally eaten by cattle or game at other times.

In winter when food is scarce, kudu may feed on the poisonous Candelabra trees (*Euphorbia* species). The poisonous milky sap of the plant may fall into the feeding animal's eyes, causing acute blindness.

Grass is exceptionally eaten, and then only small quantities of the new growth of the more juicy species such as buffalo grass

(*Panicum maximum*). During the dry season kudu do not compete significantly with cattle for available grass. Taking this into account, it is not appropriate to compare the utilisation of veld by kudu and cattle in terms of large animal units.

Kudu mortalities sometimes occur during late winter and early spring. Various theories have been offered for this phenomenon, most of which I feel are of more theoretical interest than of practical value. The fact is that these deaths occur mostly when the available food has been eaten by game, cattle and insects and, because of late rains and the low moisture content in the soil, there is not sufficient new growth to sustain the animals.

On farms with mountains or river frontage, kudu mortalities are lower, because in these areas there is usually enough food to ensure survival, even during the mentioned critical time of the year.

Although kudu may die on small, confined game farms under the above circumstances, large-scale mortalities may also occur in large, open areas such as the Kruger National Park and neighbouring nature reserves. This happens because the kudu are no longer able to move freely to areas such as mountains, rivers, streams or even cultivated lands in search of food.

Kudu are usually found in small herds. These herds are normally largest during the breeding season in June and July and in the calving season, during November to January.

The big, old trophy bulls are seldom seen, but seem to appear from nowhere during the mating season. Because June and July are also favourite hunting months, there is a distinct danger that these superb animals may be over-exploited by hunters. The habit of certain so-called hunters to lie in wait for these animals at waterholes poses a further threat to the big bulls.

At the beginning of the hunting season, many kudu cows may still be suckling their calves. As the kudu cows hide their calves when they are very young, it is sometimes difficult for a hunter to ascertain whether a cow has a calf or not. Consequently, these cows are often shot, leaving the orphaned babies to starve to death. Although it may be too late to hunt in September and November, and particularly to make biltong, this is the best time to cull excess kudu because most of the calves will have been weaned. Unfortunately, many animals are in poor condition at this time of the year, and some cows may be heavily pregnant.

Kudu are quite resistant to most of the important stock diseases, but anthrax and rabies can wipe out large numbers of these animals.

The carcass yield of a kudu is about 60 per cent and, according to a study made by the Rudman brothers from Glen Conor in the Cape, the average carcass weight of bulls and cows (head, feet and innards removed) is about 120 kilograms. The average for kudu bulls, according to research by Dr Huntley, is 134 kilograms.

Kudu which are hand-reared normally remain tame for life and even adult wild animals which are caught and kept in captivity soon become quite tame. These, and many other advantageous character traits, make this beautiful animal one of the best candidates for game farming in areas with suitable habitat.

BUSHBUCK
Tragelaphus scriptus

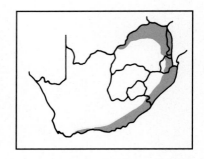

GENERAL INFORMATION

Natural distribution (S.A.): Widely distributed in the Transvaal, excluding the grassland areas, eastern Natal, western Cape, north-eastern Namibia, Okavango Delta, along the Chobe river and eastern Botswana.
Conservation status: Abundant.
Limiting factors: Shrinking habitat, predation.
Habitat: Dense bush with permanent water supplies.
Preferred food types: Leaves.
Sexual maturity: Rams ± 10 months, ewes 14 months.
Mating season: Throughout the year.
Lambing season: Throughout the year, peak in summer.
Gestation period: 180 days.
Number of lambs: One.
Longevity: ± 11 years.
Body weight (adults): 24 — 54 kg (53 — 119 lb.).
Shoulder height (adults): 70 — 80 cm (28 — 32 in.).
Horns: Only the males carry horns.

Bushbuck are very shy, secretive and almost solitary animals. Adult rams and ewes are usually seen singly. However, small groups consisting of adult females, or an adult female with her lamb or subadult offspring are sometimes observed. It is unusual to encounter two or more bushbuck rams together. Small congregations of bushbuck can be found in favourite feeding places, such as thick riverine bush.

As their name implies, bushbuck are found in dense bush, where they lie up for most of the day, unless the weather is cool and overcast, when they will move about to feed. They move about actively and feed during late evenings, at night and early mornings.

When it is hot and dry they will remain in thick riverine bush in the same small area close to water, and their home ranges are only about 0,4 hectares in size. During the wet season, when water is freely available, they will move further and then they have home ranges of about 6,0 hectares.

Bushbuck have very well developed senses of hearing, sight and smell. This is probably one of the factors that has enabled them to exist in close proximity to human development. In spite of being hunted with dogs and snares, particularly, they continue to survive close to large centres such as Port Elizabeth. They are very wily animals and a hunter must be very skilful if he wishes to obtain a bushbuck trophy.

Adult bushbuck are preyed upon by the larger carnivores, such as leopards, spotted hyenas and wild dogs, while the lambs are caught by pythons and caracals. Both the ram and ewe emit a loud, baboon-like warning bark when they become aware of danger. The voice of the ram is louder and harsher than that of the female. During dark nights in wilderness areas, the sound of the bushbuck's repeated bark may mean that a leopard is on the prowl.

Cornered or wounded bushbuck rams are very aggressive, as many a hunter has found out to his cost. They will attack fiercely and fearlessly under these circumstances and may inflict serious injuries, or even kill human hunters. These courageous animals have also been known to kill dogs and even leopards.

When they are closely pursued, bushbuck will readily take to water and swim to safety, even over long distances. They are good swimmers, being difficult to catch in the water. They have been known to hide in the shallows when placed under severe stress.

Bushbuck rams engage in serious fighting when contesting the ownership of a ewe. It is thought than many more bushbuck rams are killed in these skirmishes than any other African antelope species, as they will often fight to the death.

Bushbuck breed throughout the year and a single lamb, weighing between 3,5 and 4,5 kg, is born after a gestation period of some 180 days. The female hides her little 'Bambi' in dense undergrowth and returns to suckle it periodically until it is strong enough to move around freely with her. Hidden bushbuck babies remain very still when spotted, but will suddenly bolt off at lightning speed when approached more closely.

Bushbuck are predominantly browsers, but also eat young, green grass of species such as buffalo grass, *Panicum maximum*, and couch grass ("kweek"), *Cynodon dactylon*, when it is available. They are selective feeders, eating mainly leaves but also fine twigs and the flowers and fruit of preferred types of trees and shrubs. The species of browse plants which are preferred vary in different parts of the bushbuck's territorial range but include genera such as *Acacia, Combretum, Kigelia, Zimenia* and *Ziziphus*. Bushbuck can cause damage to gardens on game farms where they like to eat shrubs and roses, in particular, especially during the dry season, when green browse is scarce.

Bushbuck are popular with hunters and photographic enthusiasts alike, posing a special challenge to them to capture that elusive trophy. They are very difficult to catch alive for relocation purposes and this is why they fetch high prices at game auctions when they are offered for sale.

NYALA
Tragelaphus angasii

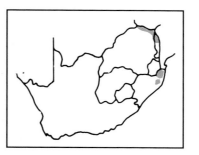

Photograph: Koos Delport

GENERAL INFORMATION

Natural distribution (S.A.): Natal/Zululand, Northern Kruger National Park, Limpopo Valley up to Swartwater in the West.
Conservation status: Fairly abundant in Zululand, otherwise rare.
Limiting factors: Destruction of natural habitat.
Habitat: Prefers thick bush.
Preferred food types: Predominantly browsers. Fond of green grass.
Mating season: Mostly in autumn.
Gestation period: 220 days.
Lambing season: Mostly in spring.

Number of young: One.
Body weight (adults): 55 — 127 kg (122 — 282 lb.).
Shoulder height (adults): 97 — 112 cm (38 — 44 in.).
Horns: Only the bulls have horns.

This beautiful antelope is fairly common in Natal and Zululand but is rare in the rest of its natural distribution area. In the Transvaal, the original distribution area stretches westward, along the Limpopo valley to the Swartwater area. It is claimed that nyalas once occurred in the region of the Matlabas river in the North-Western Transvaal.

The nyala belongs to the same family as the kudu, bushbuck and sitatunga, and like these antelope it prefers dense bush. When nyala are caught and translocated to a new area it is important that these animals are released in or near thick bush on the new farm. They will instinctively bolt for the nearest cover on being released and, if this is a long way off, they tend to become exhausted and collapse. Allowing for possible over-exertion during capture and transport, this may indicate that nyala, which normally make use of thick cover when fleeing, are not accustomed to sudden bursts of speed over a long distance.

The difference in appearance and size between nyala bulls and ewes is very marked. The bull stands considerably higher at the shoulder and may weigh almost twice as much as the female. Zoologists use the nyala as a point of reference to clarify the confusing terminology relating to 'bulls' and 'rams', 'cows' and 'ewes'. However odd it may sound, we speak of a nyala bull and a nyala ewe. Male animals of species larger than the nyala are known as bulls and any male animal smaller than a nyala bull is referred to as a ram. Likewise, any female animal larger than a nyala ewe is called a cow and those smaller than a nyala ewe are known as ewes.

In contrast to the blackish colour of subadult and adult nyala bulls, the ewes and youngsters are reddish brown in colour. Normally only the bulls have horns. Dr Jeremy Anderson gauges the age of a nyala by the length of its horns. When the horns are shorter than the animal's ears, the animal is normally under 14 months of age. When the horns are one to two times as long as the ears, the animal is between 14 months and 2 years of age. Bulls which are not fully grown, and with horns which are more than twice the length of the ears, but have not yet formed a second curve, are about 2 to 3 years old.

There are few sights in nature as awe-inspiring as a nyala bull warning off a rival with a magnificent display. With the long, snow-white hair on the neck, back and loins standing erect, their backs arched and heads held high, the two bulls walk towards each other with exaggerated slowness and on stiff legs. The long, brush-like tails are spread open like a fan and the long, white hair makes the overall spectacle even more impressive. They slowly circle each other in this trance-like state, until one of the animals' nerve fails him and he breaks away. Occasionally, a vicious fight may ensue and one of the bulls may succeed in plunging his sharp horns into the supple body of his opponent, thus ensuring that only the strongest and fittest animals survive to breed and multiply.

Unlike many other wildlife species, the nyala does not have a fixed territorium which it will defend against other nyalas. Their living areas, which are about a half to four square kilometres in size, overlap and they move freely amongst one another.

Animals of the same family group (on average about 5 to 6 animals per group) tend to remain together for a considerable period of time. Because of the constantly changing composition of nyala herds, it is very difficult to identify a particular herd for census or research purposes. The older bulls are more inclined to become loners or join up with other bulls, but they never form actual bull herds as is the case with impala, for instance. Although nyala are usually seen alone or in small herds of about twenty animals, there have been instances when more than 100 animals were counted in a group. If larger herds are encountered this is usually at a waterhole or in an area where they concentrate because of a favourite feeding site.

Nyala feed predominantly on leaves and twigs, as well as the flowers, fruit and pods of trees and shrubs. They have a particular liking for the buffalo-thorn tree. According to available information, nyala utilise more than one hundred different edible trees. They will even, on occasion, eat bits of bark from baobab trees when these have been stripped by elephant. Nyala are also selective grazers and are especially fond of juicy, green grass. In spite of the wide variety of plant material utilised by nyala, they are very selective feeders.

Because nyala bulls, in particular, can reach the last remaining leaves and pods on high branches during severe droughts, and because of other factors still being researched, nyalas are relatively drought-resistant. The theory that nyala will drive off or compete so fiercely with bushbuck for available food that the latter move out of an area is not acceptable to me. I have often seen nyala and bushbuck peacefully feeding side by side during serious droughts, without any significant interference by the nyala. Where these animals are found on mountains, in valleys

and along rivers, it sometimes happens that bushbuck do move off in search of areas with more food. Bushbuck occasionally die in large numbers when the first rains of the season, accompanied by cold and wind, fall in late winter or early spring. However, this is also the case, to a lesser degree, with nyala, impala and a few other game species.

Nyala are generally found near water. They drink often, during the hot parts of the day. In exceptional cases, they are found far from water. It is suspected that the high moisture content of their diet enables them to go for long periods without drinking water.

Nyala lamb throughout the year, but particularly in spring. The peak lambing season in Natal/Zululand is during October. Many nyala lambs are also born during May. The newborn lamb is hidden in thick scrub for the first 10 to 18 days of its life. The ewe visits the lamb at frequent intervals to suckle it and to lick it clean. Nyala which are hand-reared must be regularly massaged with a soft, wet cloth (as a substitute for the tongue of the mother) in order to stimulate them to urinate and defecate. If this is not done, the nyala lamb can die in a very short time of obstipation and/or urine retention and the resultant poisoning of the system .

As is the case with most other game species, nyala feed actively during the early mornings and late afternoons. At night they remain fairly active until about midnight. When they become aware of danger, they warn one another with a characteristic short bark. Although nyala may seem clumsy and vulnerable to predators, they fare surprisingly well in areas where there are many leopards, caracal and jackal. However, they may be easily caught by these predators shortly after release into a new area.

Nyala may appear evasive, particularly in areas where they are constantly disturbed. In fact, they are of the tamest wild animals I know. Nyala lambs which are hand-reared become wonderful pets. Even adult nyala will quickly become quite tame if kept in small camps. If they are treated with care, they may take food from their keeper's hands within a few days. However, nyala bulls can be dangerous and should rather not be hand-reared.

In areas where bush encroachment is a problem, the presence of nyala and other browsing species can be an advantage. Moreover, the nyala with its aesthetic appeal, tame nature, rarity, and consequent high value, is a great favourite among game farmers. In spite of warnings by doom prophets, nyala have been successfully introduced in large numbers on game farms in the dense bushveld areas of the Northern and North-Western Transvaal. Nyala are not truly abundant anywhere and these new breeding nuclei can only be beneficial to the continued existence of nyala in the distant future. In the meanwhile, their presence on these farms means that game farms are significantly better utilised, and the sight of these beautiful, placid antelope browsing around rest camps is a great asset to any ranch.

SPRINGBOK
Antidorcas marsupialis

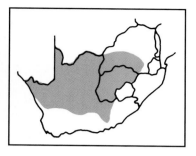

Photograph: Lorna Stanton, S.A. National Parks Board

GENERAL INFORMATION

Natural distribution (S.A.): Southern and western Transvaal, Orange Free State, northern and western Cape.
Conservation status: Abundant.
Limiting factors: Carnivores, drought, heartwater disease.
Habitat: Short grassveld, shrub and thornveld.
Preferred food types: Grass and leaves.
Sexual maturity: Rams 11 months, ewes 6 months.
Mating season: March to May. October.
Lambing season: August to November. March to April.
Gestation period: 165 — 180 days.
First lamb born: Ewe 12 months.
Lambing interval: One year. Occasionally more than one year.
Number of lambs: One. Twins unusual.
Longevity: 10+ years.
Body weight (adults): 18 — 36 kg (40 — 80 lb.).
Shoulder height (adults): 78 — 84 cm (31 — 33 in.).

Apart from the South African springbok, known as *Antidorcas marsupialis marsupialis*, there is a subspecies known as *A.m. angolensis*, which is found in southern Angola and the northern parts of Namibia. These animals are said to have longer ears and longer and heavier horns and are slightly different in colour from the former. The subspecies *A.m. hofmeyri* occurs in the southern parts of Namibia and Botswana. South African springbok are said to be smaller than the springbok found further north.

Colour variation is an interesting occurrence in the springbok. It seems that the black springbok generally has longer horns than the ordinary springbok. Both white and black springbok will reproduce young of the same colour as the parents if animals of the same colour are specifically selected for mating purposes.

Springbok ewes also have horns but they are thinner, shorter and less curved than those of the rams.

A well-known characteristic of the springbok is the skin folds which are present along the length of the back. When the animal is excited, anxious, playful or dying, these skin folds open up and form a ridge of snow-white hair. When springbok leap prancing, stiff-legged into the air, the white hair adds to the overall beauty of this agile animal.

Years ago springbok were found in Natal. They also occurred in the north-western, northern and eastern Transvaal. These days the tick-borne stock disease, heartwater, makes it almost impossible for springbok to survive in these areas.

Springbok favour the drier regions of the country. Desert, semi-desert and open grass plains are their preferred habitat. They do particularly well on mixed karoo grassveld and Karoo and Kalahari thornveld. They are fond of pans but no not thrive in low-lying coastal areas or hilly country.

Short green grass and even the new growth of longer grass species are utilised during the growing season. Springbok do not normally compete significantly with domestic stock for available food since they do not feed on long grass. Furthermore, they eat only about half as much grass per animal as domestic sheep. During the winter months in shrubveld, springbok eat mostly karoo shrub or sheep-bush, several species of which are poisonous to sheep.

Springbok are generally very drought resistant. In desert areas they obtain moisture by digging up tubers and bulbs with their front hooves.

Springbok become sexually mature at a very young age. Between 20 and 50 per cent of the ewes lamb when they are only a year old. However, the majority lamb for the first time when they are 2 years old. Some 70 to 95 per cent of the adult ewes lamb every year. If a ewe should lose her lamb, she may soon become pregnant again and even lamb twice in the same year. It is claimed that the spingbok lamb yield is as high as 140 per cent per year.

Young rams are able to mate at 18 months of age but they are kept away from the ewes by the bigger rams until they are big enough to defend themselves and claim their own ewes.

The number of ewes that can be served by a mature ram can vary considerably, according to available information, and seems to depend on circumstances. In nature, the ratio is approximately two ewes per ram. Aggressiveness in breeding rams, which results in a higher mortality amongst the male sector of the springbok population, definitely contributes to the natural ratio of two ewes per ram. Seven to fifteen breeding ewes per adult ram appears to be the ideal ratio for breeding purposes, while two adult rams per sixty ewes in camps of 150 hectares have been reported to yield good results.

The significance of the bachelor herds should not be under-estimated. Since they constitute pools of diverse genetic material, provision should be made in practice for sufficient additional rams. If too many lone rams or rams from the bachelor herds are hunted, in-breeding can eventually become a problem in certain circumstances.

In-breeding has in the past occurred where springbok were kept for long periods in small numbers in limited areas. Apart from deformities in new-born lambs, other detrimental effects of in-breeding can also arise under these conditions.

Much can surely be said about the introduction of new genetic material ("new blood"). While certain zoologists would like to prevent mixing of antelope of the mentioned subspecies, I feel that the utilisation of rams from Namibia could contribute to improving our own springbok herds. A sufficient number of rams would, however, have to replace rams from the local population in order to have any significant effect of the physical size and productivity of our antelope.

Lambs may be born during any time of the year. After a gestation period of some 5½ months, most of the lambs are born from August to November. There is another lambing peak during March to April.

During the first ten days of their lives, springbok lambs sleep for 90 per cent of the time. They suckle nearly every hour during the first day of life. The ewes usually graze close to their lambs, but the youngsters are sometimes left alone for fairly long periods and they then fall easy prey to black-backed jackals, other carnivores and even baboons.

During hot, dry weather, when the available green feed becomes dry and unpalatable, a considerable number of lambs die because their mothers cannot produce enough milk. In spite of these limiting factors, many lambs reach maturity and farmers are able to harvest between 25 and 40 per cent of their springbok population annually.

According to Dr Liversidge springbok prefer short green grass, especially in summer, and even the new growth of longer grass types is grazed. Otherwise the latter types are generally avoided. Because mature grasses are not usually eaten in the flowering or seed-bearing stages, these grasses are afforded a good chance of propagation. Many karoo-bush types such as, for instance, sheep-bush (*Pentzia spp.*), karee (*Rhus spp.*), olienhout/Olive (*Olea sp.*) and buffalo-thorn (*Ziziphus sp.*) are especially also browsed in winter. Two species that are poisonous to sheep, namely Christmas berry (*Chrysocoma sp.*) and *Geigeria sp.*, also feature on the springbok's menu.

According to Dr Liversidge the springbok should not compete significantly with domestic stock for available sources of fodder. Long grassveld, which is grazed by cattle, is not used to any significant degree by springbok, as was mentioned earlier. Leaf fodder is also not browsed up to the same height as by domestic goats. Short grassveld is only grazed for short periods after the rain, while it is in any case estimated that the springbok consumes only about half as much grass as a sheep.

An interesting habit of the springbok is that of grazing alongside each other over a broad front, allegedly in order to contribute less to the formation of erosion paths. Sheep, however, tend to move from place to place in single file, using the same path.

Carrying capacity is a relative term when applied to game. In contrast to stock, herd habits and species-specific behaviour patterns play an important role in the spacing of game and available grazing and water is therefore not the only important criterion. Taking all of this into consideration, Dr Liversidge calculates that at least as many springbok as sheep can be kept on the same grazing. In mixed scrub it is even possible to farm with a greater number of springbok than sheep. However, in the case of springbok the ratio of male to female animals plays an important role. Because only a certain number of territorial rams can occur per surface area, a relatively large number of ewes would therefore necessarily contribute to a greater number of productive springbok inhabiting a limited space.

In contrast to domestic stock, it is not always so easy to implement rotational grazing with springbok. The territorial behaviour of springbok rams can give rise to difficulties if they should have to be moved from one enclosure to another in accordance with any rotational grazing system, particularly during the mating season. Hunting of territorial rams during the mating season could also have detrimental effects, although one might expect rams from the bachelor herds to replace breeding rams that are shot.

However, in spite of assertions that game cannot be physically moved from one camp to another, methods for doing just this are described in Chapter 16. It is true that difficulties may be experienced when springbok rams who have already demarcated their breeding areas are moved during the mating season. But what is as discouraging to me as having to fight for a new breeding territory in a different camp is to a springbok ram, is the tendency of game farmers to throw in the towel as soon as signs of so-called insurmountable management problems are encountered. Some farmers are all too inclined to condemn game farming out of hand without making even a token effort to address these problems.

Although springbok are particularly hardy when it comes to drought, and can manage well without any water at all in certain circumstances, the provision of water is nevertheless recommended. Like bulbs and tubers, green grazing to a large degree satisfies the springbok's moisture requirements. Springbok herds have been observed to remain for long periods in the vicinity of fountains where water and green grass are available for the greater part of the year. In such cases a herd of springbok may spend long periods in a limited area of approximately 2 square kilometres.

Mention has already been made of the particular susceptibility of springbok to heartwater, as well as losses that can be incurred if such animals are relocated to heartwater regions. Some years ago we managed, with sporadic success, to immunise springbok against this disease, so one cannot exclude the possibility that further experimental immunisation and re-establishment projects will lead to the re-introduction of springbok to their historical distribution areas in the northern parts of the Transvaal. (See immunisation of springbok using Doximplant in Chapter 18).

A small, hidden nucleus of springbok which appear to be immune to heartwater still occurs in a small area of the north-western Transvaal, and the efficient distribution of these animals could also promote the continued existence of this species in heartwater regions where springbok have been eliminated over the years.

Apart from the heartwater problem, internal parasites such as lungworm, wireworm, bankrupt worm and nodular worm can also to a certain extent be harmful to springbok under certain conditions. Particularly when the condition of the animals is poor, scabies and heavy infestations of lice can crop up sporadically and in exceptional cases scabies can even be fatal. Animals that are noticeably infected with scabies should preferably be removed from the herd, since they can infect the other animals.

Treatment with amitras (Triatix; Coopers) or other effective and safe parasiticides can also contribute to fighting scabies in infected wild animals.

These diseases and parasties are in most regions, and particularly under normal, natural conditions, of greater academic than practical interest, and the springbok's exceptional immunity to disease is therefore a particular advantage for farming purposes. Nevertheless, the appropriate precautions should be taken and springbok should be treated under more intensive conditions. It remains a good policy, when game has to be transported from one area to another, to immunise animals and rid them of parasites as far as is practically possible.

In summary, the springbok is an excellent species of game for farming and production purposes in suitable areas. The outstanding breeding and growth rate of springbok and the relatively high annual percentage yield of harvestable surplus animals also count in the springbok's favour. In addition to the sought-after carcass size for export purposes, preliminary research shows that the carcass composition of springbok lambs also compares very favourably with that of sheep lambs. The fact that springbok can be contained by lower fences than most other types of game, their limited competition with stock for grazing and water and their utilisation of vegetation that is poisonous to sheep, all contribute to the springbok's popularity in drier short grass and scrubveld regions. The springbok is furthermore as popular amongst sporting hunters as it is for its good quality meat. Finally, the springbok will always be one of our most beautiful antelope, and every farmer who is still privileged to have these agile creatures adorning his farm should feel justifiably proud.

IMPALA
Aepyceros melampus

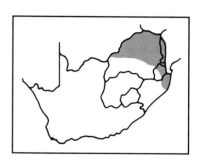

Photograph: Koos Delport

GENERAL INFORMATION

Natural distribution (S.A.): North-western, northern, north-eastern and eastern Transvaal, north-eastern Natal.
Conservation status: Abundant.
Limiting factors: Carnivores, extreme drought, very cold, wet weather.
Habitat: Bushveld and savanna, near water.
Preferred food types: Green grass (summer), leaves and pods (winter).
Sexual maturity: Rams 18 months, ewes 18 months.
Mating season: April to June/July.
Lambing season: November to January.
Gestation period: 195 — 200 days.
First lamb born: Ewe 24 months.
Lambing interval: One year. Occasionally two years.

Number of lambs: One. Twins unusual.
Longevity: 14 years.
Body weight (adults): 40 — 78 kg (88 — 173 lb.).
Shoulder height (adults): 82 — 93 cm (32 — 37 in.).

The impala is surely the most common game farm animal in South Africa and also one of the most suitable species to farm with in the bushveld regions of the country.

The black-faced impala, a separate subspecies with a blackish face, as the name implies, is found in the northern parts of Namibia.

Only the rams carry the lyre-shaped horns. Impala found further north in East Africa have considerably longer horns than those found in our region. The shape of the horns can help to determine the age of the animal. At six months of age, for example, the young rams have short, straight horns. At 18 months, the horns are slightly curved outwards. When animals are 3 years or more old, it becomes very difficult to estimate their age by the shape and length of their horns. When culling impala, farmers are inclined to shoot the big rams with beautifully shaped, long horns first. This practice should be avoided, and these animals saved for breeding purposes and for the highly selective trophy market.

Although it is logical that the hunting of too many rams could be detrimental to the breeding process, excessive numbers of rams on a farm can also place an unnecessary burden on the available grazing and be responsible for a relatively unproductive impala population.

It is an unfortunate fact that the hunting and game capture season coincides with the mating season of impala. Although this can disturb the mating animals, I do not subscribe to the theory that hunting and game capture activities during this period (provided that these are within reasonable limits) will lead to lowered lamb yields. What is important in practice, however, is correct selection of the rams to be removed, and the best time for harvesting game. Various other considerations are also relevant here.

Breeding rams who have already selected their herds of ewes should preferably be left alone. Rather hunt from the bachelor herds, but also not excessively. Furthermore, in my opinion, a start should be made with culling the rams as early as possible, and preferably before the mating season. The reason for this is that the carcass mass of the animals is then still considerably higher than after the rutting time later in the year, while considerably fewer carcasses have to be rejected or given a lower grading owing to horn injuries and wounds resulting from fights.

In East Africa impala breed and lamb throughout the year. In South Africa they normally mate from late April to June or July. Abnormal weather conditions and rainfall patterns can influence this breeding pattern considerably.

A very interesting observation is that impala ewes allegedly lamb later if the rains are late, and vice versa. There appears to be at least a reasonable measure of accuracy in these allegations. However, from a physiological perspective the contention that the impala ewe holds back the lamb when the rains are later than usual is not acceptable. It is common knowledge that varying daylight hours prevailing during different seasons can influence the breeding cycles of horses, sheep and certain other animals. Is it not perhaps possible that solar radiation effects which precede rainfall cycles and which cannot be measured with the instruments currently at our disposal could stimulate the hormone systems of the impala to mate earlier or later and thus cause the ewes to lamb earlier or later during the subsequent rainy season? Although this is admittedly a very contentious speculation, this possibility is an intriguing one!

During the mating season the rams are very noisy and aggressive towards each other. The bigger rams gather a herd of females together and defend them vigorously against rivals. These harems are kept in small areas of some 0,8 to 0,9 square kilometres. The breeding rams often become very thin and are driven off by stronger animals after vicious fighting. This ensures that the strongest, most vigorous animals breed and produce offspring with a good chance of survival.

In the absence of older rams, rams of 18 months can breed successfully. They are normally kept away from the ewes by bigger rams and only actively participate in the breeding process when they are about 2½ years old. Impala rams are at their prime when they are between 4½ and 6½ years old.

Only some 60 — 80 per cent of the young ewes lamb when they are two years old. The remaining ewes lamb from their third year. About 90 — 100 per cent of the adult ewes lamb each year.

No one can say with certainty what the greatest number of ewes is that can satisfactorily be served by a ram. Although approximately equal numbers of ram and ewe lambs are born, it appears that somewhat more natural deaths occur in the case of rams, and the natural sex ratios of the older antelope usually favour the ewes. This minute difference can, however, to great advantage be increased even further for production purposes, with a view to retaining the highest possible percentage of breeding animals in the herd. I suspect that one breeding ram for every ten sexually mature ewes should be adequate and that a ram who is worth his salt should manage rather more than that.

Shortly after birth, a group of lambs may be looked after by a single ewe, while the other animals go to drink, for example. Very young lambs are slightly unco-ordinated and have to remain close to adult impala.

An impala herd only moves about 3 kilometres in any 24-hour period and are very territorial. The same herds are often seen in the same small area year after year. The average area utilised by impala during a day is rarely larger than 0,84 square kilometres. Impala are an advantage on bushveld cattle farms, and the farmers usually protect their impala herds enthusiastically. Even on farms with ordinary cattle fencing, free-ranging impala which have settled in an area are likely to remain there, provided they are not unduly disturbed. If a farmer wishes to enclose his farm with game fencing, the minimum height should be 2,4 metres. Unless a prefabricated type of fencing is used, it is recommended that 21 horizontal strands of wire are used to construct the fence.

The carcass yield of an impala is about 58 per cent of its live weight, in comparison with the lower figure of 44 to 50 per cent for domestic stock. The dressed carcass weights for six-month-old impala is 12 kilograms, on average. In the case of 18-month-old animals, the ewes weigh 19 kg and the rams 23 kg. Adult impala ram carcasses weigh an average of 36 kilograms and those of adult ewes 24 kilograms. These figures may differ considerably from area to area. A very big impala ram can even exceed 45 kilograms.

The impala is particularly drought-resistant. Impala are often still fat and healthy in areas where cattle can no longer survive. During the winter months, impala feed predominantly on leaves and pods and do not compete significantly with domestic stock for available grass.

It is possible to farm with 500 to 750 impala per 1 000 ha in prime impala country for many years in succession. However, in times of extreme drought, there may be large-scale mortalities. It is said that impala will move as far as 40 kilometres in search of water during a drought. In the Kruger National Park, however, most of the impala are not found further than one kilometre from water. Overgrazing, particularly around waterholes, may be a problem if impala numbers are not kept under control.

Since impala do not graze far from water, it is important that water is freely available throughout their grazing areas. This will ensure optimum utilisation of the veld.

I was able to ferret out the following few statistics relating to impala:

Kariba (Zimbabwe) — 0.3 impala/hectare (300 impala/1 000 hectare)

Kruger National Park — 0.1 impala/hectare (100 impala/1 000 hectare)

Timbavati (Eastern Transvaal) — 0.5 impala/hectare (500 impala/1 000 hectare)

Mkuzi (Natal) — 0.75 impala/hectare (750 impala/1 000)

Thabazimbi (Transvaal) — 0.6 impala/hectare (600 impala/1 000 hectare)

These figures should be carefully evaluated before being summarily applied to farming conditions. Some of the above-mentioned locations cover large areas which inevitably include parts which are not suitable for impala or which, owing to a limited water supply, cannot be optimally utilised by impala. Greater numbers may also have been kept in some cases if large numbers of other rival game species had not occurred in the same region.

Conversely, it should be borne in mind that overgrazing has occurred in certain of the areas mentioned and that large-scale game losses have been reported there during droughts. Estimated conservatively, however, it would seem that approximately 2 to 3 hectares per impala would suffice under normal conditions and on farms with suitable and adequate food.

However, in my opinion the most important criteria for the carrying capacity of veld for game remains the satisfactory preservation of the veld and species of plant fodder, as well as the condition of the game during the dry winter months. When the condition of the impala begins to cause concern during a specific winter period and good rainfall does not follow, provision should be made early on in the next hunting and game capture season for the removal of surplus animals. The development of bare patches under popular feeding trees and the absence of edible twigs and leaves within the impala's browse line can also be early indications of overgrazing. The carrying capacity of the veld is discussed more fully in Chapter 16 .

The judicious burning of veld near the impala's overgrazed territory, the supply of water in underutilised parts of the farm and the efficient provision of salt licks and highly prized feeding supplements just beyond the normal grazing boundaries of the impala can solve the problem to a certain extent. Keeping numbers in check and the possible implementation of rotational grazing systems should, however, offer more satisfactory and permanent solutions. Although the practical feasibility of applying rotational grazing principles to game by means of enclosures requires more research, efforts on a game farm have recently succeeded in luring large numbers of game, amongst which almost all the impala (more than three hundred), from one enclosure of 1 000 hectares to a reserve enclosure, within 6 weeks. The erection of subdividing fences for purposes of rotational grazing can, in the case of impala, kudu and other jumping game, be a very costly undertaking, since these fences must be at least 2,4 metres high.

A variety of natural and unnatural factors control impala numbers. During droughts the older animals, and especially some of the pregnant ewes, can become very thin and even die. Continuous and heavy rain, during and shortly after the lambing season, can also contribute to a lower survival rate amongst young impala. Rain, accompanied by cold winds during August to October can, in particular, be responsible for heavy impala losses and appears to be a very important natural factor limiting game populations, especially on poor and overgrazed veld. In the Eastern Transvaal, where numerous impala are infected with lungworm, a considerable number of the infected animals can develop pneumonia during the cold winter months. In the same region, foot-and-mouth disease and sarcoptic mange can also, in exceptional cases, be responsible for deaths amongst impala. Problems with internal parasites can crop up on poor grazing and in moist areas, while old and diseased animals are especially vulnerable to heavy infestations with lice and parasites. Although the impala can therefore be infected with some diseases, this antelope is normally, in my opinion, surely one of the animal species that is least plagued and harmed by infections. In fact, for me the impala remains the epitome of health, vitality and productivity!

Depending on circumstances, predators can also to a certain extent limit impala numbers. On game farms, leopard, black-backed jackal and caracal learn to corner and catch antelope against fences and in smaller enclosures. During the late winter, considerably more antelope are caught and it is usually the old and thin animals that are taken first. In this manner Mother Nature applies her selection principles and the stronger and healthier animals are given a better chance of reproduction. On enclosed farms where predators are strictly controlled, population explosions amongst impala are usually unavoidable and farmers must take active steps to prevent overcrowding and overgrazing.

Next to the kudu and other predominantly browsing game, the impala remains one of the most suitable game species to keep in our bushveld regions together with cattle or other species of grazing game such as zebra or wildebeest. I can only trust that the potential of farming with impala for production pruposes will eventually be realised and utilised to the full.

REEDBUCK
Redunca arundinum

GENERAL INFORMATION

Natural distribution (S.A.): Central Transvaal, Golden Gate National Park in the Orange Free State, Natal (below 2 100m) and the eastern Cape Province, northern Botswana, Zimbabwe and Mozambique.
Conservation status: Rare to fairly abundant.
Limiting factors: Shrinking habitat.
Habitat: Vleis, reedbeds and open grassland close to permanent water.
Preferred food types: Grass.
Mating season: Throughout the year.
Lambing season: Throughout the year.
Gestation period: 235 — 240 days.
Number of lambs: One.
Longevity: 9 years.

Body weight (adults): 40 — 80 kg (88 — 176 lb.).
Shoulder height (adults): 80 — 90 cm (32 — 36 in.).
Horns: Only the males carry horns.

Reedbuck have very particular habitat requirements, requiring cover such as long, dense grass or reeds with permanent water. They are not found in dense bush and will leave an area which becomes overgrown with trees. They will also leave an area if the grass cover is burned down.

During the heat of the day, reedbuck lie up in the thick reeds or grass, usually near the water. They tend to remain immobile for some time after being spotted and even when they are approached. Then they may suddenly leap from cover and bounce off with short, jerky bounds, fanning their bushy tails and kicking up the hind legs high. Each bound is accompanied by a loud but dull 'dub' sound, thought to be caused by the sudden

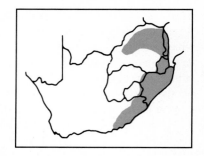

opening of the inguinal gland-pouches which are situated in the groin region. Others believe this sound to be caused by the buck hitting its abdomen with the inner thighs.

When food and water are plentiful, reedbuck may become nocturnal. However, during the dry season, they spend more time grazing during the day, to compensate for the less nutritious grass that is available at that time of the year.

They tend to continually use the same trails leading to the water. The females allow the males and young to approach the water first, while they hang back. Reedbuck do not like getting their feet wet and will frequent spots where they do not have to enter the water to drink. They will drink more frequently on hot days. At watering points, some animals keep a look-out while the others drink.

Before lying down to hide in cover, they will trample the grass to make a bed. They lie several metres apart, usually facing in different directions. When it is very windy, they tend to spend more time lying down in cover.

Reedbuck are not gregarious animals, but will form temporary herds of between 15 and 20 animals during the cold months. They live in family groups of a few animals and are often seen singly or in pairs.

Reedbuck are almost exclusively grazers, but in some areas they will eat small quantities of herbs when the nutritional value of the grass becomes low.

Males are territorial and will defend their territories by chasing off intruding rams. They announce their presence in the long grass habitat by whistling in a shrill voice and by moving about their territory in a rocking canter, displaying the white throat band.

When a territorial ram is challenged by a rival, the animals stand close together, presenting their horns to each other. They may then lock horns and push each other around in a duel of strength. Sometimes this leads to fighting, when they will lunge forward with ears held back and clash their horns together. Fighting between rams is never so intense as to cause serious injury. When the supremacy of one of the rams has been established, he may adopt the display attitude and defecate, but will rarely chase off his rival.

Reedbuck do not breed strictly seasonally. Young may be born during any time of the year, after a gestation period of about 7 months. The young reedbuck hides itself and is only visited once a day by its mother to be suckled and cleaned. The female approaches her lamb very inconspicuously and, when she leaves, the lamb usually leaves to hide in a new spot. It will join its mother to graze when it is about two months old.

MOUNTAIN REEDBUCK
Redunca fulvorufula

GENERAL INFORMATION

Natural distribution (S.A.): Occurs widely in the Transvaal, except the north-eastern and western parts, Natal, eastern and southern Orange Free State, and the extreme eastern and north-eastern parts of the Cape Province, south-eastern Botswana, and south-western Mozambique.
Conservation status: Fairly abundant.
Habitat: Dry, grassy hills and mountain slopes.
Preferred food types: Grass.
Sexual maturity: Females between 12 and 14 months.
Mating season: Throughout the year. Peak in April/May.

Lambing season: Throughout the year. Peak in summer.
Gestation period: 236 — 251 days.
Number of lambs: One.
Period between lambs: 12 — 14 months.
Longevity: 10 — 12 years.
Body weight (adults): 22 — 38 kg (48 — 84 lb.).
Shoulder height (adults): 75 cm (30 in.).
Horns: Only the males carry horns.

This species is closely related to the reedbuck but is somewhat smaller. Furthermore it is found in mountainous areas or in rocky hills, while the reedbuck is a grassland species.

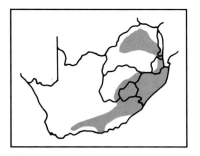

close together. When they are alarmed they emit a shrill alarm whistle, which is similar to that of the reedbuck. They flee along the side of the hill in typical rocking-horse fashion, with upright tails. After running for some four hundred metres, they will stop to turn and look at the source of the disturbance. Sometimes, one can stop them in mid-flight by whistling sharply.

Mountain reedbuck are almost exclusively grazers, preferring the softer, greenest grass, which they eat for as long as this lasts. They avoid eating the grass stems. They feed on flat ground at night and also go down to drink then, as they are dependent on water. They drink more often during the drier months.

Rams are territorial and the ranges of the female herds are larger than those of the males. Females will move from one ram's territory to another.

Mountain reedbuck breed throughout the year. When a courting ram approaches a female, he does so with his head outstretched. If she is willing to accept him, she indicates this by lowering her head in a submissive posture. A single lamb is born after a gestation period of about 8 months. The baby weighs about 3 kilograms at birth.

When the female is ready to give birth, she leaves the herd. As with the reedbuck, mountain reedbuck lambs hide themselves in cover without prompting from the mother. The mother visits her lamb to clean and suckle it once or twice a day, approaching it very carefully in a roundabout way. When she leaves, the baby will move to a new hiding place. The lamb continues to hide for two to three months, after which it will join its mother to graze.

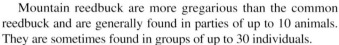

Mountain reedbuck are more gregarious than the common reedbuck and are generally found in parties of up to 10 animals. They are sometimes found in groups of up to 30 individuals.

They are most active during the early mornings, late afternoons and at night. During the hot parts of the day they lie up

GREY RHEBOK
Pelea capreolus

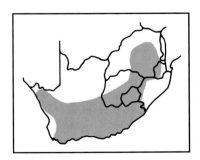

Photograph: Natal Parks Board

GENERAL INFORMATION

Natural distribution (S.A.): Occurs only in South Africa, Swaziland and Lesotho. Found in the Cape province, eastern Orange Free State, Natal (above 1 400 m) and the central and southern parts of the Transvaal.
Conservation status: Fairly abundant.
Habitat: Grassy hills and mountains, mainly on flattish tops.
Preferred food types: Grass.
Limiting factors: Shrinking habitat, poaching and predation by stray dogs.
Sexual maturity: Rams 18 — 20 months.
Mating seaoson: April.
Lambing season: November/December.
Gestation period: 261 days.
Number of lambs: One.
Longevity: 8 — 9 years.
Body weight (adults): 18 — 25 kg (40 — 55 lb.).
Shoulder height (adults): 75 cm (30 in.).
Horns: Only the males carry horns.

Grey rhebok are truly South African antelope and only occur within our borders. Both grey rhebok and mountain reedbuck live in mountains and are sometimes confused. The grey rhebok is more slender than the mountain reedbuck and has a relatively longer and thinner neck with very long and narrow ears. The horns are straighter and thinner at the base. The hair is soft and woolly, affording it the warmth it needs during cold spells, living as it does at high altitudes.

These graceful antelope are very agile and, being very wary, they are difficult to approach. Both males and females emit a warning snort when becoming aware of danger, and may continue to snort in alarm for long periods when they are not sure of the situation. When they flee, they do so swiftly, in the same 'rocking-horse' fashion as the mountain reedbuck.

Grey rhebok live in small family groups of some 12 individuals. These family groups may temporarily join up to form herds of up to 30 animals. Grey rhebok rams do not form bachelor herds as is the case with most other species. Family groups consist of a herd ram, with his females and their young, while solitary males are also seen.

Rams are territorial and a rhebok family group remains in a defined home range throughout the year. The territorial ram will defend his territory against trespassing males and is very active during the rutting season in April. If the herd ram becomes aware of an intruding male he approaches the rival with exaggerated, slow movements, snorting and stamping his feet. If this does not have the desired effect of scaring off the intruder, fierce fighting may result. It has been reported that fighting rams have even attacked and killed mountain reedbuck, domestic sheep and goats.

The courting ram approaches a female in oestrus by tapping the insides of her hindlegs with his forelegs, after which mating may follow. After a gestation period of about 8 months, a single lamb is born in the wet season, when it is warmer.

Grey rhebok are exclusively grazers, feeding very selectively. They are independent of a water supply. They rest during the hot parts of the day, actively grazing during the cooler hours when they rest for short periods. They move over greater distances in winter to forage than they do in summer.

During the dry season, grey rhebok are plagued by bot-fly, which burrow under the skin and make the flesh unpalatable to most people.

TSESSEBE
Damaliscus lunatus

GENERAL INFORMATION

Natural distribution (Southern Africa): Kruger National Park and bordering private reserves, isolated groups in the Waterberg, north-eastern Namibia, eastern Botswana, the Caprivi Strip and north-western Zimbabwe.
Conservation status: Rare.
Limiting factors: Drought. Overshooting. Destruction of habitat.
Habitat: Grassveld and open woodland.
Preferred food type: Grass.
Sexual maturity: Bulls at 40 — 42 months old.
Gestation period: 235 to 245 days.
Mating season: Summer.
Calving season: October to December.
Calves born: One. Twins not recorded.
Body weight (adults): 120 — 150 kg (264 — 330 lb.).
Shoulder height (adults): About 120 cm (48 in.).
Longevity: 15 years.
Horns: Both sexes.

Tsessebe are related to the bontebok and the blesbok, all of which belong to the genus *Damaliscus*. Both bulls and cows carry lyre-shaped horns, which are thinner and smaller on the female. They are fairly large antelope, standing about 120 cm at the shoulder and are a rich chestnut brown colour with a purplish sheen. The newborn calves are a lightish brown colour.

Tsessebe are gregarious animals, living in smallish herds of about 20 individuals. However, large herds of between 120 and 190 animals have been observed at favourite feeding places during the dry winter months. The herd composition is made up of breeding animals, smaller bachelor herds and a dominant territorial bull. These territorial bulls actively patrol their territories, which are estimated to be between 2 and 4 square kilometres in size in the Kruger National Park, according to Dr Joubert.

The territorial bull constantly marks his territory in different ways. One method is to defecate regularly as he walks along the boundaries of his territory. His physical presence on these frequent patrols also advertises his ownership of the territory to other bulls. A territorial bull furthermore scent-marks his territory by means of secretions from the pre-orbital glands on the sides of the face. This is done by inserting grass stalks into the opening of the gland so these are covered with the sticky secretion.

Tsessebe may be seen standing on their knees and rubbing the sides of their faces on a sandy patch of ground, or on a termite mound. Both bulls and cows resort to this behaviour to deposit secretions from the pre-orbital glands, but the bulls are particularly active in doing so.

Furthermore, and frequently after a rainstorm, the territorial bull will drop to his knees and rip the wet earth with his horns to

Photograph: Koos Delport

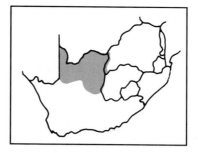

enhance his ownership of the area and so warn other bulls to keep away. It is a characteristic sight to see a tsessebe bull standing statue-like on a termite mound with head held high and ears erect, surveying his territory and keeping a look-out for intruders.

They can often be seen pawing or scraping the ground with their hooves. This is yet another form of scent-marking using the interdigital glands on their feet.

When sighting an intruding bull, the territorial bull will approach the rival while throwing his head up and down, or even by rearing up. The trespassing bull may respond in a similar manner or will retreat. If the bulls continue the challenge, they circle each other and may then drop to their knees and clash their horns in a battle for supremacy. However, serious fights are un-usual. Sometimes during such horn clashing the two bulls may in-terlock their horns and raise clouds of dust around them as they push each other across the ground. After some time the stronger bull emerges as the victor from the encounter and chases off the rival.

A territorial bull will gather together the females in his territory to form a harem. According to Dr Joubert, a bull collecting his cows will show off his dominance over the herd by putting on a ritual display. He walks with exaggerated slowness while lifting his legs high at the knees with every step. His head is raised and pointed forward, with the ears held tightly against the neck and pointing to the ground.

The harem which the territorial bull gathers in this manner remains with him for life. This may sometimes create problems if the territorial bull should become infertile for some or other reason. Farmers who suspect that this is the case with a herd on their property should take steps to replace the bull.

Young bulls born during the previous season are evicted from the herd soon after the cows calve during the following season. These young males then join up to form bachelor herds and do not themselves have a fixed territorium, but remain on the boundary of the territory of the herd bull.

Tsessebe calves are born mostly in October, but some calves are born during November and December. The newborn calf is not hidden by the mother as is the case with many other species. Soon after birth the calves join their mothers in the herd. Small groups of calves may form a nursery herd and will lie down in a safe place, while the adult cows move about to graze. One or more females usually remain close to the youngsters while the rest of the breeding herd will join up with them at the first indication of danger.

Despite its somewhat clumsy appearance, with its long legs and sloping hindquarters, the tsessebe is considered to be the fastest antelope in southern Africa. The tsessebe can truly be considered the racehorse of the African plains, as it is capable of reaching high speeds, which can be maintained over a considerable distance.

Great care must be taken when capturing these fleet-footed animals, as this species is very prone to overstraining disease when chased at high speed over long distances during capture operations. They should never be pursued for long, especially when they are in prime physical condition.

In spite of its agility and speed the tsessebe is very vulnerable to hunters because of its innate curiosity. When approached, these animals will run off for a short distance only, before stopping to turn around and look back inquisitively. They have even been known to remain motionless in the immediate vicinity where several members of the herd have been shot.

Tsessebe are almost exclusively grazers. They utilise long grassveld in the drier regions of the country, but show a pre-ference for newly burnt veld.

They are dependent on water and will drink regularly, although they can go without water for short periods if they are forced to do so. They are extremely wary when approaching a waterhole to drink. They have excellent eyesight, and because they are so cautious when they go to drink, they usually become aware of hidden carnivores waiting at the waterhole long before other animals sense any danger. Observations have been made of tsessebe spotting hidden lions at a waterhole, snorting warningly and staring intently at the lions, while other species such as zebra, wildebeest, sable antelope and warthog tried in vain to spot the carnivores.

Although tsessebe are very observant and quickly become aware of hidden carnivores or other danger at a waterhole, they will normally stand and stare intently at the danger instead of fleeing immediately. In this manner they often expose them-selves to unnecessary risks and are then sometimes surrounded by the predators and caught.

BLESBOK AND BONTEBOK
Damaliscus dorcas

Photograph: Koos Delport   **Blesbok**

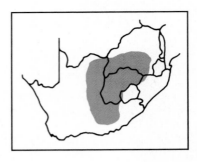

Lambing interval: First lamb is usually born when the female is 3 years (exceptionally 2 years) old. Average lambing interval is about one year.

Mating season: Blesbok March to May (peak March to April). Bontebok January to mid-March.

Lambing season: Blesbok November to February (peak period around late November, exceptionally until February.

Number of young: Usually one.

Longevity: Up to 16 years.

Body mass (adults): Blesbok about 60 to 80 kg (133 — 177 lb.). Bontebok about 70 to 90 kg (155 — 200 lb.).

Shoulder height (adults): Blesbok about 95 cm. (38 in.) Bontebok about 90 cm. (36 in.)

Subspecies

The blesbok, *D.d. phillipsi*, and bontebok, *D.d. dorcas*, are merely subspecies of the same species, *Damaliscus dorcas*. In their natural range blesbok live on the highveld regions of the Transvaal and the Orange Free State, and in parts of the north-eastern Cape and western Natal. By contrast, bontebok have always been native to the southern Cape.

Bontebok numbers dropped to less than 100 individuals during the previous century.There are now about one thousand bontebok in the south-western Cape.

As described in Chapter I, the Van der Byls, Van Bredas and Albertyns played a major role in saving the bontebok from extinction. The animals they protected on their farms served as breeding stock when, in 1931, the Bontebok National Park was proclaimed near Swellendam. The National Parks Board eventually made surplus bontebok available to farmers and to other nature reserves.

The bontebok differs from the blesbok in the following respects: the bontebok's neck and sides are darker brown; it has a purplish sheen on its back; the rump above the tail is snow-white; the blaze is not sub-divided from top to bottom, but is generally continuous from the horns downwards (in the blesbok the blaze is divided by a narrow, brown band between the eyes); the legs are white from the knees downwards; the horns are more black in colour than in the blesbok.

Albinism occurs not infrequently in blesbok. Some farmers breed white or whitish blesbok selectively.

Unique to South Africa

Like the Cape mountain zebra and the black wildebeest, blesbok and bontebok are naturally restricted to South Africa. Foreign hunters have to come to our country if they want to see and hunt any of these species in their natural environment.

GENERAL INFORMATION

Natural distribution (Southern Africa): A truly South African antelope, the blesbok has never been recorded, in its natural state, outside the southern and western Transvaal, the Orange Free State and parts of western Natal, Griqualand West and the north-eastern Cape. Bontebok are naturally restricted to the southern Cape.

Conservation status: Blesbok common. Bontebok still relatively rare.

Limiting factors: Predation, poaching, unsuitable habitat, wrong sex ratios, too small holding camps, poor management, predation and some, as yet, unknown factors.

Habitat: Blesbok prefer flat to gently undulating open grassveld. In their natural environment they are mainly found on short grass in sour and mixed sourveld. Bontebok are naturally found on open fynbosveld in the southern Cape.

Preferred food types: Grass, preferably of good quality.

Sexual maturity: Blesbok at about 18 — 28 months. Mostly at the latter age. Bontebok after 24 months.

Gestation period: Blesbok 225 to 270 days (average 225 days). Bontebok 238 to 254 days.

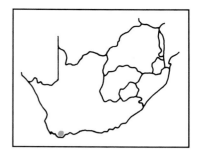

Photograph: National Parks Board

Bontebok

How to differentiate between different sex and age classes

Blesbok can be sexed using the following characteristics: mature males are darker in colour, have heavier necks and thicker, more prominently ridged horns. The penis sheath of the ram can be seen from the side, while the scrotum of the male and the udder of the heavily pregnant female is sometimes noticeable, particularly from the back. The hair of the male's tail is longer (sometimes whiter) and the hair cover, present below the male's anus, is absent between the female's vulva and udder, leaving the bare dark skin exposed.

Different age classes can be identified in blesbok by the following characteristics. During the first two months the hair coat is of a lighter golden-brown colour. The blaze on the face is black. The horns become noticeable at about two months of age. At six to seven months the animal assumes a darker colour. The blaze becomes lighter, assuming a speckled whitish colour. The horns grow to about two-thirds the length of the ears, but are still straight and smooth. At eight months, ridges begin to appear on the horn base and at nine months the horns are as long as the animal's ears. From 12 to 14 months the general colour is still lighter than that of the adult but the blaze has now become whitish. The horns start to curve. At 16 to 18 months the blaze is white. At 21 to 24 months the body colour is very much like that of the adult, but has a reddish tint. The testes of the ram are still small. At 30 to 36 months the animal looks like an adult, except that the testes are still smaller than those of older males. (Rowe-Rowe and Bigalke, 1972).

Social grouping and territorial behaviour

Blesbok live in herds which may number up to several hundred animals. Territorial blesbok rams sometimes leave the breeding herds to live in separate territories, particularly from around February to May. Territorial bontebok males are said to occupy their territories on a year-round basis. New territories are established in a vacant area, or by deposing an existing territorial male from his territory.

Blesbok males become territorial when they reach the age of about four years. Each territorial ram establishes itself in its own territory, on average about 0,02 square kilometre in size, according to Dr Novellie (1975). Termite mounds frequently serve as beacons or central points of territories. Adjoining blesbok territories are from about 30 metres to 1,5 kilometres apart. Blesbok territories are, on average, about 4 to 28 hectares in size.

The ram's pre-orbital glands (situated at the bare patches, in front of and below the eyes) secrete a sticky, yellowish substance which the territorial ram rubs off against grass stems and onto other plant material, as part of his message to intruder rams to stay clear of his territory.

Rams of adjoining territories frequently approach each other, and after some smelling and threatening behaviour, either separate or challenge each other by fighting. Occasionally a ram may be killed in these contests.

Pre-orbital glands are less prominently developed in the females. They also rub the yellowish secretion of the glands off on grass stems and other objects but do not scent-mark as intensively as the territorial rams do. Interdigital, or pedal glands, situated between the hooves of the forefeet, also secrete a yellowish substance. By trampling repeatedly on the termite mound that marks the centre of its territory, the territorial ram also uses these secretions to demarcate his domain. Defecation usually takes place on established dung heaps next to the termite mound and may also have a territorial marking function.

Territorial bontebok males are believed to rely more on their presence in their respective territories and on 'body talk' to keep possible intruders away, than on defecation and urination or other marking methods, employed by some other species. Fighting between territorial males is seldom serious or fatal, and usually lasts for a short while, until one of the contestants gives up and retires.

Bigger blesbok herds usually break up into smaller herds from about January to February, i.e. just prior to the mating season. During the advance of the mating season the territorial blesbok rams move around in characteristic, stiff-legged fashion, with the necks extended and the tails held straight. Females encountered in a ram's territory, or on the periphery, are herded together in harems of up to 30 females or more. Somehow, the females in a specific breeding herd seem to show some preference and attachment to a particular territorial male.

Continuous chasing by the rams sometimes results in the female harems being scattered and a specific group of females may only stay in a particular territory for a short time, before moving into the territory of another male. The young of the year usually accompany their mothers during the mating season and are rarely molested by the adult animals.

Bontebok females gather in herds of about eight animals. During the breeding season they are covered by the males in whose territories they may find themselves at the time.

The newborn blesbok lamb weighs about 6,4 kg and the first year of life is characterised by a rapid growth rate. After that the animals grow more slowly to reach a maximum weight of about 68 kg (females) or 79 kg (males) after four years.

The warning snort of the blesbok ewes and lambs calling to each other, is about the only vocal communication recorded for the blesbok.

Feeding habits

During the summer blesbok may be seen feeding at any time of the day. During winter they are more active in the early morning and late afternoon.

Marchant (1986) maintains that, at low to moderate densities, blesbok can maintain themselves on sourveld which cannot support domestic stock in winter. On sour and mixed sourveld, burning of the veld in spring will cause blesbok to concentrate on the newly burnt veld. They are site-selective grazers, sometimes over-utilising parts of the veld.

Everything possible should be done by the farmer or reserve manager to encourage the more even utilisation of the available grazing. Well planned burning of sourveld, in particular, can contribute to achieving this ideal. Shorter grassveld conditions can also be created by the grazing of mixed veld by cattle during the summer months.

Carrying capacity

The carrying capacity of a specific farm for blesbok is determined by the area covered by old lands and suitable grazing habitat rather than by the total area of the farm. Meissner (1982) suggests that about four to six adult blesbok will require the same amount of grazing as one large animal unit. Dr Peter Novellie suggests a stocking rate of about one adult blesbok per three to six hectares.

Blesbok drink water daily if this is readily available, but can stay without for as long as a week before losing weight.

Adaptable farm animals

Blesbok have adapted very well in many parts of South Africa to which they have been introduced and are now found almost throughout the RSA. In some parts of the Republic, however, including certain farms on the Transvaal Highveld, blesbok numbers are dwindling. The reasons for the decline are not always clear, although predation and poaching seem to be important limiting factors.

Marchant (1986) suggests a camp size of at least 90 to 100 ha if a farmer wants to breed blesbok. In camps which are too small, males may corner each other in the rutting season, resulting in

casualties. It is suggested that farmers should start with at least ten animals.

Some wildlife biologists (Mentis and Collinson, 1980) suggest a sex ratio of one ram to three ewes. In practice more females than males are kept on game farms because the farmer usually strives for the highest possible productivity. However, in extreme cases this may lead to inbreeding and the eventual shortage of trophy rams.

Interbreeding with other species

Red hartebeest bulls sometimes interbreed with blesbok, particularly if there are no hartebeest cows in the area. The offspring are believed to be sterile.

Bontebok and blesbok hybrids are found throughout southern Africa. This is a matter of grave concern as it threatens the existence of pure strains of both the bontebok and the blesbok subspecies. Horn trophies of hybrids are sometimes longer than those of pure bontebok, and many recorded trophies are involved.

Safari Club International consequently requested criteria for the identification of pure bontebok trophies. Fabricius et al (1989) developed a method based on measurements of the white rump patch from photographs of animals in doubt.

Culling and capture

Culling of surplus blesbok should preferably be done in early winter before the animals lose too much weight. The dressed carcass weights of adult blesbok and bontebok are approximately 32 to 44 kg and 37 to 48 kg respectively. In calculating the annual harvestable surplusses, farmers should not be misled by the high breeding rate of blesbok. Mortalities could be high, particularly during the first year of life. Regular total and differential counts for different sex and age groups should be used as a basis for determining culling rates. As a general rule the obviously superior animals should not be culled. Territorial rams should be saved as far as possible. Farmers should remember, however, that out of the breeding season, i.e. in winter when most culling is done, many of the territorial males will have joined the mixed 'breeding herds'.

On game farms blesbok can be caught by the use of funnel, corral or drop nets or by chasing them into plastic corrals. Overstraining disease may be responsible for mortalities in blesbok that have been excessively chased. Affected animals become paralysed within a few days and generally don't recover.

Drug darting of blesbok is time-consuming and expensive but can be successfully applied in the capture of limited numbers. Once captured, blesbok can be easily handled by their horns. Pipes should be fitted over the horns of rams and aggressive individuals before transporting them.

The blesbok's ability to flourish in sourveld areas, its general resistance to diseases and parasites, its high reproductive rate and the relatively cheap fencing required to keep it in, make the blesbok a suitable farm game species in many parts of the country.

RED HARTEBEEST

Alcelaphus buselaphus

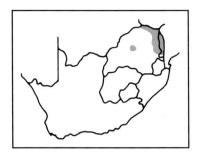

GENERAL INFORMATION

Natural distribution (Southern Africa): Western Transvaal, western Natal, northern Cape, northern and eastern Namibia, Botswana south of the Okavango Delta.

Conservation status: Fairly abundant.

Limiting factors: Overshooting in the past, predation, fighting and shrinking habitat.

Habitat: Savanna and open grassveld.

Preferred food type: Grass. Also roots and tubers.

Sexual maturity: Bulls mate at 3 years. Cows at 2 years.

Gestation period: 238 — 242 days.

Mating season: February to March.

Calving season: October to November.

Calves born: One.

First calf born: Cow 3 years old.

Body weight (adults): 105 — 182 kg (231 — 400 lb.).

Shoulder height (adults): 125 cm (50 in.).

Longevity: 15 years.

Horns: Both sexes.

Red hartebeest are gregarious animals and are usually found in herds of about 20 animals, but sometimes as many as 300 animals are seen together. In Botswana, during November and December, and to a lesser extent from August to May, aggregations of 10 000 animals may be found. These aggregations are made up of a number of herds which are normally separate from each other. The reason for this gathering of red hartebeest is not clear, but it is thought to be due to their movement to preferred feeding grounds after good rains have fallen.

Red hartebeest prefer open country and are found on open grassland of various types. These include floodplains, vlei areas, semi-desert savanna, and open woodland, the latter being less popular. They are not normally found in denser bush, except when they are moving to areas of better grazing.

They are predominantly grazers and utilise grass species such as rooigras (*Themeda triandra*), the *eragrostis* species, and couch grass (*Cynodon dactylon*). Where they have been re-introduced in the S.A. Lombard Nature Reserve in the Western Transvaal, their diet was found to consist of 56,5 per cent grass and 44,4 per cent browse (Van Zyl, 1965).

They are independent of surface water, digging up moisture-rich roots and tubers with their hooves, while they also obtain moisture by eating dew-laden grass. However, they will drink water regularly when it is available. Hartebeest drink in the morning and especially in the late afternoon. When moving to the water to drink, a cow will often take the lead and drink first, while the rest of the herd follows her in single file. They do not remain at the waterhole for long periods because of the danger of hidden predators, and usually drink as quickly as possible. Some animals go down onto their knees to drink, but most of them remain standing and then they will only lower their heads once or twice to drink before moving away. Red hartebeest are most active during the early morning and late afternoons, when they move about actively and graze intensively. Prevailing weather conditions and temperature play an important role in the behaviour of hartebeest. During cool weather they may remain active for most of the day, but in hot weather they will seek shade, where they will stand or lie under a tree and ruminate.

However, during the cooler winter months, hartebeest may be seen lying in the open, in direct sunlight. The individual animals tend to lie scattered over a wide area and not together in a compact group.

Their senses of smell and hearing are very acute, but they appear to have rather poor vision. Like the tsessebe, red hartebeest are inquisitive animals and will stand and stare at an unfamiliar object approaching. If startled, they rapidly swing around, circling in a confused and bewildered way for a second or two before taking off in a bounding gallop at great speed, frequently bouncing stiff-legged and running in a zig-zag fashion. They possess considerable stamina and may keep up a fast pace over a long distance.

Hartebeest herds consist of a territorial bull, females with their offspring and young bulls, and may remain unchanged for up to three years. Bachelor herds consist of male animals of all ages and they have to make do with less suitable grazing, as the harem herd occupies the best areas.

Territorial bulls actively defend their harems against rival bulls and vicious fighting may take place, particularly during the breeding season. The dominant bull is sometimes driven off by the rival, but has been known to reclaim his position. When the herd is temporarily without a dominant bull, an adult cow may take over as leader of the herd. Lone bulls are not often encountered.

Territorial bulls mark the boundaries of their territories by defecating and urinating on the same places and often lie down on such dung heaps to impregnate their skins with their odour. They can often be seen standing on raised ground, such as an anthill or termite mound, from where they survey their territory, and keep a look-out for possible intruders.

Hartebeest have pre-orbital glands on the lower sides of their faces, below their eyes and territorial bulls often drop to their knees and horn the ground, particularly after rain has fallen. In this way the oily secretion from these glands is rubbed off on the ground to act as a further deterrent to rival bulls. Hartebeest bulls also paw and scrape the ground with their forehooves, depositing secretions from interdigital glands between their hooves on the ground. This serves both as a visual and an olfactory warning to intruder bulls.

The rutting season of the red hartebeest starts at the beginning of March and continues to the end of April. Most of the calves are born in October and November.

Just before giving birth, the red hartebeest cow becomes restless and leaves the herd to have her calf in a secluded place. The newborn calf is light in colour and is hidden by the mother for the first few days of life. The mother grazes some distance away, or even rejoins the herd but returns often to suckle her calf and to lick it clean.

If a concealed calf is approached, even to within a few metres, it remains very still, with its head flat on the ground. When the calf, which can recognise it's mother over a distance of 300 metres, is stronger, it joins up with the herd and its mother protects it against other members of the herd. The youngster may begin to nibble grass from two weeks of age, but is only weaned when it is about seven months old.

WATERBUCK
Kobus ellipsiprymnus

GENERAL INFORMATION

Natural distribution (Southern Africa): Northern, eastern and western Transvaal, the Hluhluwe and Umfolozi game reserves in Natal, eastern Caprivi, northern and south-eastern Botswana, northern and southern Zimbabwe and central Mozambique.
Conservation status: Rare to fairly abundant.
Limiting factors: Drought, predation, overshooting on crop farms.
Habitat: Savanna, near water and swamps.
Preferred food type: Grass.
Gestation period: 235 to 250 days.
Mating season: Throughout the year.
Calves born: One, exceptionally twins.
Body weight (adults): 204 — 270 kg (448 — 594 lb.).
Shoulder height (adults): About 125 cm (50 in.).
Longevity: 16 years.

The waterbuck (Afrikaans: Waterbok or Kringgat) species has four subspecies, of which only *Kobus ellipsiprymnus* occurs naturally in southern Africa.

It is closely related to the Defassa waterbuck, which is almost indistinguishable from the common waterbuck except that it has a white rump instead of the white ring around the tail region which characterises the common waterbuck. The two species have been recorded as interbreeding in areas where both are found (e.g. Zambia, Kenya and north-eastern Tanzania.)

Other members of the same family found in southern Africa include the red lechwe, Kobus lechwe, and the puku, *Kobus vardonii*. The red lechwe (Afrikaans: rooilechwe or basterwaterbok) is common in parts of the Okavango delta in northern Botswana, and is also found in the vicinity of swamps and flood plains along the Chobe river (Botswana) and the eastern Caprivi strip.

The puku (Afrikaans: Poekoe), rarely found south of the Zambezi river, is restricted to a small area south of the Chobe river in north-eastern Botswana.

Very popular with trophy hunters and fetching about R2 200 (S.A.) per animal at live game auctions, waterbuck are much sought after in South Africa by game ranchers and hunters alike.

The sharp, forward sweeping, ridged horns are formidable weapons, used to establish dominance in the waterbuck hierarchy, and to fend off predators.

Waterbuck bulls are vicious fighters, intolerant of competitors

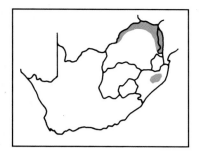

when there are cows in demand. I know of one bull that killed two other adult bulls living on the same game farm, during one season.

When wounded and cornered by the human hunter, the otherwise elusive waterbuck can become very aggressive, attacking fiercely. Even young calves, when captured by hand, are of the most determined fighters known among the antelope species.

Breeding herds may number up to 30 or even more animals. The dominant bull lives with the cows, the others being found singly or in separate bull herds. As the breeding bull becomes old, sick or weak, it is replaced by another, stronger bull, ensuring that the strongest animals breed and produce healthy, strong offspring.

The bulls only start to establish their own territories when five to six years old. Other bulls are then frightened away from the breeding herds by the herd bull, who displays its dominance in an intimidating manner. Vicious fights may result, with the intruder or the patriarchal bull being killed in these skirmishes.

The size of waterbuck territories varies from one herd to another and from place to place, but seems to be quite small, with a diameter of between one and three kilometres.

Experienced hunters can detect a waterbuck, sometimes from a distance of several hundred metres, by its very potent and characteristic smell. While arguing about the significance of this powerful smell, particularly in relation to the ability of predators to locate the buck, the interesting theory was forwarded that its overwhelming smell holds greater benefits than disadvantages for the waterbuck. It seems logical to reason that this smell

would make it easier for a lion or hyena to find a hidden calf. However, the explanation was given that if the whole area smelled of waterbuck, it would be more difficult for a predator to locate the calf.

Old hunters advise one to remove a newly shot waterbuck bull's testicles immediately, in order to remove the waterbuck smell from the meat. In fact, the smell comes from the skin. Therefore, avoid touching the meat after touching the outside of the skin without washing your hands.

Waterbuck are strong swimmers. Even small calves will take to water when threatened, and swim to safety.

Usually found near water, where they live on their preferred diet of succulent, sweet grass, it may come as a surprise to see them, far away from rivers, and equally at home in arid bush-veld, and even on the slopes of rocky kopjes. On game farms they usually thrive where there is suitable habitat (preferably open bushveld).

Waterbuck are fairly prone to external parasites when sick or suffering from a shortage of food. Heavy tick infestations can aggravate the situation. Heavy lice infestations are usually characterised by the appearance of bare, black patches on the necks of the parasitised animals. Farmers who buy waterbuck for their farms will benefit from spraying their animals with Triatix cattle spray (Coopers) (Amitraz, active ingredient) at the recommended concentration. Deca-spot (Coopers) holds some promise as an effective tick, fly and louse-controlling insecticide and could be used on an experimental basis, particularly for the treatment of louse-infested waterbuck.

At one stage, biologists believed waterbuck were the preferred prey species of lion. Despite this, and depending on ever-changing environmental factors (e.g. availability of shelter and alternative water sources), waterbuck can hold their own even in areas with many lion, leopard and other predators.

Like the kudu, nyala, eland and impala, the waterbuck is one of the farm game species that can easily clear a 1,8 metre high fence. As is the case for the other species mentioned, a 2,4 metre high fence is recommended.

Never, *but never*, disturb waterbuck unnecessarily when they are kept in a smallish game camp, as they are then inclined to run in a bewildered fashion into fences they would normally avoid, and could easily break their necks or be seriously injured.

Counting waterbuck is not an easy task. Even aerial counts are not always reliable as waterbuck, like nyala, can hide effectively, and are therefore usually undercounted. Drug darting waterbuck presents another problem to the game captor/farmer, as it does not react too well to the commonly used capture drugs. M99 alone, at a fairly high dosage level, followed by the prompt administration of the antidote, seems to give the best results. Always consult an expert veterinarian with experience of capturing wild animals who will be able to give emergency treatment, when necessary.

Unlike blesbok, wildebeest and impala, which frequently concentrate on overgrazed or trampled veld, waterbuck make good use of long grassveld. They prefer sweet grass species such as *Panicum, Setaria* and *Digitaria*. Although they are predominantly grazers, they also eat some leaves from trees and shrubs. Under drought conditions waterbuck make good use of *Cynodon* grass (kweek), which usually sprouts early in the season and before most other grasses.

Waterbuck breed throughout the year, but have calving peaks around spring and autumn. About eight months after mating, the brownish-coloured, long-haired calf is born and hidden in dense grass or reeds near the water's edge. It is visited periodically, particularly at dawn, by its mother, who then cleans the baby and lets it suckle.

Young waterbuck, weaned at about nine months of age, frequently join up to form calf herds, consisting of up to 10, sometimes more, small to half-grown individuals. These 'teenagers' are occasionally found quite far away from the adults, even in lion country.

The heifers are inclined to stay with the breeding herds, while the young bull calves eventually join the bachelor herds of adult males.

BLACK WILDEBEEST
Connochaetes gnu

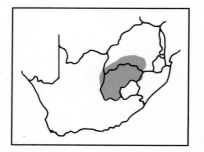

Gestation period: 240 — 260 days.
Number of calves: One.
Period between calves: 1 year. Sometimes 2 years.
Longevity: 20 years.
Body weight (adults): 90 — 160 kg (198 — 352 lb.).
Shoulder height (adults): 120 cm (48 in.).
Horns: Both males and females have horns.

Black wildebeest are gregarious animals, living in herds of up to 60 animals. Solitary bulls as well as bachelor herds and breeding herds make up the social organisation. Bulls become territorial when they are about 4 years old and may gain control over a territory either by ousting an existing territorial bull or by establishing their own territory in a vacant area.

They advertise their occupation of a territory by different means, including scent-marking with interdigital and pre-orbital glands and by urinating and defecating. Before defecating, they paw the ground energetically and also kneel to horn the ground, which is interpreted by rival bulls as a threatening gesture. They are very vocal in advertising their presence and emit a loud, repeated 'ge-nu' sound.

Territorial bulls adopt a 'show-off' attitude and they gallop, bucking and kicking, across the plains at high speed, tossing their heads up and down and swishing their long tails in a rather comical fashion. This has led to them being called the 'clowns of the veld'.

However, they are unexpectedly fierce animals and captive black wildebeest are untrustworthy and dangerous. On a certain game farm a bull became very aggressive and killed several cattle, horses and ostriches. There are several known instances where black wildebeest have killed people. Under certain circumstances, they sometimes attack and kill their own calves and even cows in the herd.

The breeding herd, consisting of females and their calves or even a subadult bull, move freely over their territories and are generally ignored by the territorial bull outside the breeding

GENERAL INFORMATION

Natural distribution (S.A.): Occurs only in South Africa. Central, northern and north-eastern Cape province, the Orange Free State, Natal and southern and south-western Transvaal.
Conservation status: Rare to fairly abundant.
Habitat: Open plains and grassland.
Preferred food types: Grass, but also karoo shrubs.
Limiting factors: Overshooting in the past. Agricultural development. Shrinking habitat.
Sexual maturity: Bulls and cows 16 months.
First calf: Cow 24 (or 36) months.
Mating season: March to April, and even up to July.
Calving season: November to early January.

season. At the start of the rutting season, however, the cows are herded together into groups by the bull.

Black wildebeest are seasonal breeders and most of the calves are born during December and January, after a gestation period of about 8 months. When the cow is ready to calve, she does not leave the herd, but becomes restless and repeatedly lies down and gets up until she eventually gives birth lying down. The calf, which shares a very strong bond with its mother, is able to move about with her shortly after birth.

When the calves are born, the females drive off their calves of the previous season. The female yearlings remain with the female herd, but keep their distance from the mother and her new calf. The male yearlings join up with the bachelor herds, which then consist of adult, subadult and yearling males.

Young black wildebeest grow surprisingly quickly. When they are a year old, their body weight is already some 71 per cent of their adult weight. At 17 months of age they have reached 89,5 per cent of their adult weight and they are fully grown when they are two years old.

The breeding rate is also very high. It is not unusual for more than 90 per cent of the cows to be pregnant at the same time. On farms where small numbers of black wildebeest were introduced, the results are disappointing. It is recommended that farmers begin with at least 12, but preferably 20, wildebeest when establishing this species on their farms.

The female herds and the bachelor herds rest during the heat of the day during summer. They are active in the early mornings and late afternoons, and also before sunrise and after sunset. They do not always lie up in the shade when resting, and when they rest in direct sunlight, they turn their hindquarters towards the sun. When the weather is cooler in winter, they remain active during the day for longer periods and may thus remain active for most of the day. The territorial bulls do not behave in the same way, since they constantly have to look after their territories.

When danger threatens, the animals stand close together, in an alert attitude, to glare at the disturbance. Their heads are held high while they snort and stamp the ground threateningly, their horse-like tails twitching. If they are uncertain of the danger, they wheel about while waving their tails, in an effort to locate the problem. When they are confronted, they suddenly gallop off with great display, tossing their ugly heads and kicking up their hindlegs as they buck and cavort over the plains.

Black wildebeest are predominantly grazers, preferring short grass, although they browse on karroid bushes during the cold winter months. They are dependent on water and drink regularly, usually during the late afternoons but seldom during the hot hours of the day.

Black and blue wildebeest can interbreed and farmers are strongly advised not to keep these two species on the same farm, where they may bastardise.

BLUE WILDEBEEST
Connochaetes taurinus

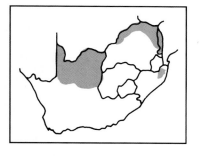

GENERAL INFORMATION

Natural distribution (S.A.): North-western, northern and eastern Transvaal, northern and eastern Natal, Zululand and northern Cape.
Conservation status: Fairly abundant. Becoming scarcer.
Limiting factors: Carnivores, disease and disease control.
Habitat: Savanna and open grassveld.
Preferred food types: Grass.
Sexual maturity: Bull 24 months, cow 15 months.
Mating season: Autumn and winter.
Calving season: November to January.
Gestation period: 225 — 260 days
First lamb born: Bull 2 — 3 years, cow 15 months.
Calving interval: 1 — 2 years.
Number of calves: One. Twins unusual.
Longevity: 20 years
Body weight (adults): 180 — 270 kg (400 — 600 lb.).
Shoulder height (adults): 130 — 145 cm (52 — 58 in.).

The blue wildebeest is one of the larger African game species which, until recently, still occurred in large numbers in the bushveld areas of the Transvaal, northern and eastern Natal, Zululand and the northern Cape.

Blue wildebeest not only impart the atmosphere of untamed Africa to a modern game ranch, but they are also very popular with hunters. The wildebeest is one of the toughest wild animals and can be very aggressive when wounded.

The horns of the blue wildebeest may give an indication of the age of the animal. Until six months of age, the horns grow relatively straight, after which they grow towards the sides and then straight up. The horns assume their characteristic bowed shape when the wildebeest is about 2 years old. Both sexes carry horns but the horns of an adult wildebeest bull are considerably thicker and heavier than those of a cow, especially at the horn base.

Some wildebeest bulls are strictly territorial and are often seen in the same small area. If they are forced to migrate because of drought conditions, they usually return during the following rainy season to their old home area and the same old antheap or marula tree.

During the mating season, the bulls fight amongst each other and the younger bulls are viciously driven from the herd. The calves are born in the rainy season, when there is abundant green grass and water. The newborn calf is a yellowish brown colour, in contrast to the blackish colour of the adult animals. They get to their feet shortly after birth and can run very fast within the first five minutes of life. It is claimed that young calves a few weeks old can reach speeds of up to 72 kilometres per hour, in comparison with the top speed of 48 kilometres per hour of the adult animals. This is probably the natural defence of the youngsters against predators.

Blue wildebeest fall easy prey to lions. At waterholes, wildebeest behave very foolishly, even though they are well aware of the presence of lions. I have often seen zebra walk towards a waterhole beside which lions are concealed, until the wildebeest follow. The wildebeest then continue walking towards the water, as though they have forgotten the hidden danger, while the zebra trot back to a safe distance, from where they watch the age-old death scene of a lion kill. I recall how lions once caught three wildebeest in succession in this manner on a single day in the Kruger National Park. However, during the eleven years I worked and lived in the Kruger Park, I only once saw a zebra being caught at a waterhole in this manner.

It is claimed that wildebeest are more easily caught by lions during years of high rainfall when the bush is thick. I have always found that wildebeest are more easily caught at waterholes during the dry winter months.

The claim that wildebeest calves are preyed upon by hyenas, particularly during the calving season, may be accurate, but I cannot support the claim that hyenas often prey on adult wildebeest. I suspect that I am one of only a few people in the Kruger Park who have had the doubtful privilege of witnessing such a kill. The battle lasted six hours and it was only in the early hours of the morning, after many attempts and hard work by seven adult hyenas, that they succeeded in killing an adult wildebeest bull.

The inquisitive nature of the wildebeest often makes him an easy target for his pursuers. A trick used by experienced hunters, particularly at dusk, when the wildebeest are no longer able to see very well, is to imitate their warning snort and move away from the herd on all fours. Before long these inquisitive animals will follow at an ever shorter distance for a closer look, until they are a mere stone's throw away from the hunter!

In East Africa thousands of wildebeest migrate annually between their summer and winter grazing areas. These plucky animals may walk hundreds of kilometres to their winter grazing areas. On a smaller scale and over shorter distances, wildebeest in the Kruger Park also seasonally migrate to better grazing areas. Zebra and blue wildebeest often migrate together and are in turn followed by prides of lions and hyenas.

The blue wildebeest prefers short grassveld and is particularly fond of the new green growth which sprouts after veld-fires or after the first rains. During the winter months an adult wildebeest of average size drinks up to 16.3 liters of water every second day. They graze about 7 kilometres from the nearest water, but move considerably further when grazing becomes scarce.

During the summer, when food and water are plentiful, they move only half as far and their grazing areas are also considerably smaller.

Although wildebeest and zebra are often seen together, mainly because they prefer the same habitat, there are considerable differences in the behaviour of the two species. One of these is the inability, on a hot day, of the black-skinned wildebeest, to excrete the same amount of sweat as a zebra to keep its body temperature low. Early on a hot day the wildebeest can be observed lazily seeking out the shade of the trees, while the zebra continue to move about, grazing unconcernedly, quite unaffected by the heat.

Some ten to twenty years ago it was not unusual to see herds of up to 500 wildebeest in the Kruger Park. The largest herd which I myself counted consisted of between 900 and 1 000 animals. From 1969 to 1977 the wildebeest numbers in the Park declined drastically from some 16 000 to 6 400 animals. Various factors contributed to this decline. According to the most recent game count in the Kruger Park, the wildebeest now number some 13 673 animals.

In the Etosha National Park, Mr Hugh Berry found that 62 per cent of all wildebeest mortalities in that reserve were due to anthrax. Wildebeest numbers in Etosha have also declined drastically. However, anthrax was not responsible for significant mortalities in the central and southern parts of the Kruger National Park.

Preliminary findings of research conducted in the Kruger Park some years ago, indicated the presence of a viral disease (IBR) which can cause abortion and death among cattle. The same findings were made elsewhere in Africa where wildebeest numbers have declined, and it is possible that this and other limiting factors may be responsible for the natural control of wildlife populations.

It is tragic that the large-scale decline of wildebeest numbers in two of the largest wildlife reserves in southern Africa, namely the Kruger National Park and Etosha National Park, had to be followed by strict cattle disease control measures which led to the killing of wildebeest on private farms. I am referring to the strict control measures regulating the translocation of wildebeest, which severely limit the demand for surplus wildebeest and which leave farmers with no option but to shoot the surplus animals.

It is particularly ironic when one considers that wildebeest are being restricted in order to safeguard cattle against a disease affecting wildebeest, when the wildebeest itself is the only source of the vaccine presently used to inoculate cattle against elephant skin disease!

Research has shown that blue wildebeest can contribute significantly to the control and reduction of tick numbers on game or cattle farms.

The wildebeest has a particular charm for me — it is as much a part of the bushveld scene as the thorn trees, and, without the wildebeest, no bushveld farm is truly complete.

ELEPHANT
Loxodonta africana

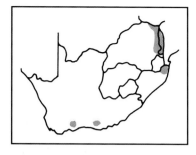

GENERAL INFORMATION

Natural distribution (S.A.): Northern and north-eastern Namibia, northern and eastern Botswana, Zimbabwe (absent from the whole of the central plateau) throughout Mozambique, the Kruger National Park, Addo National Park and the Knysna forest. Recently these animals have been reintroduced to other wilderness areas, such as the Pilanesberg National Park, and private game ranches in the Transvaal and Natal.

Conservation status: Fairly abundant in areas where they still occur.

Habitat: Very adaptable. Found in dense bush, grassland, semi-desert and plains.

Preferred food types: Grass, bark, fruit and leaves.

Sexual maturity: Cows at 11 years of age and bulls about 10 years. (Only breed later).

Mating season: Throughout the year.

Calving season: Throughout the year.

Gestation period: 660 days (22 months).

Number of calves: One. Occasionally twins.

Longevity: 70 years.

Body weight (adults): Up to 6 669 kg (14 452 lb.).

Shoulder height (adults): 400+ cm (160+ in.).

Research done in the Kruger National Park proved that elephants do not transmit foot-and-mouth disease and this has led to elephant recently being relocated to private farms and game reserves where they are contained by electric fencing.

Elephants are intelligent animals and are gregarious, living in family groups which may join up to form herds numbering hundreds of animals. The family groups consist of an adult female and her progeny and closely related females and their offspring. The bulls live together in groups and only join the female herds when a female is in oestrus. The bull herds constantly change as herd members join the herd or leave it at will. Very old bulls often lead solitary lives.

Elephants are normally placid animals but individual animals, particularly if ill or injured, can become aggressive and are very dangerous. Cows with calves are especially unpredictable. An angry elephant will display threatening behaviour by raising its head and trunk, which it shakes vigorously, and spreading its ears. They often trumpet furiously while kicking up dust with their forefeet and may initiate a mock charge, stopping just before reaching the enemy. Bulls are more likely to make mock charges, while the cows are more serious when they attack, especially if there are small calves close by.

Elephant bulls who fight for the favours of a cow in oestrus usually establish supremacy by pushing each other with their huge heads and tusking one another. However, if an intense fight develops, they inflict serious wounds with their tusks, sometimes resulting in the death of one of the bulls.

Elephants sometimes kill hippo and rhino, as they are less tolerant of them than of other species. During droughts when there is a shortage of water at a waterhole they have been known to drive off or kill animals of other species such as sable antelope and zebra.

Elephants are active during both the day and night. They will rest in the shade during the hot hours of the day, when they stand fanning themselves with their huge ears or sleeping.

They feed on a wide range of plants, being both grazers and browsers. They pull up clumps of grass with their trunks and knock the dirt off the roots by hitting the grass clump against a tree trunk or parts of their bodies before eating it. They can be very destructive in areas where there is not enough food to support them, rapidly causing utter devastation of the habitat. They strip the bark from certain trees, favouring the umbrella thorn, *Acacia tortilis*, and the knob thorn, *A. nigrescens*. Most of the trees stripped in this manner die. A fully grown bull consumes about 300 kg of plant material in a single day.

They walk in single file, maintaining a steady gait over long distances in search of their favourite food, and when the fruit of trees such as the vegetable ivory, *Hyphaena ventricosa*, or the marula, *Sclerocarya caffra*, becomes ripe, elephants can be observed feeding on them.

They are dependent on a source of clean, sweet water, drinking up to 315 litres at one time, and will cover great distances in search of it. Elephants are fond of bathing in the river, when they spray water over themselves or lie in the water. They cross rivers readily and may submerge themselves completely, with only the tip of the trunk protruding above the water, as they walk along the river bed. They are also fond of wallowing in mud or spraying dust over their bodies to protect their skins from the hot sun and from irritating insects. They regularly rub their bodies against tree trunks in an effort to rid themselves of parasites.

Elephants have a very acute sense of smell, while their senses of hearing and eyesight are relatively poorly developed. They can often be observed standing with raised trunks as they test the wind for any sign of danger. Feeding elephants are very noisy and the sound of breaking branches can be heard from a long way off. They communicate with a soft rumbling sound while feeding and when they suddenly become silent it is a sure sign that they have become aware of trouble.

Elephants breed throughout the year. After a gestation period of 22 months a single calf is born, although twins have been recorded. The baby weighs about 120 kg at birth and is some 90 cm tall at the shoulder. The cow gives birth in a secluded, safe place, usually accompanied by other females who protect her and her calf during this vulnerable period.

The elephant cow looks after her calf intensively for the first two years of life, since it is vulnerable to predation for some time. For the first few months of life, it rarely ventures further than a few metres from its mother, often sheltering under her belly. The calf suckles for a long time, but is usually weaned when it is about two years old.

Young elephants are very playful and groups of youngsters gambol boisterously, with much squealing and ear flapping. If they overstep their limits, the cows reprimand them sharply by smacking them with their trunks. Injured members of the herd are looked after and are assisted to their feet if they are unable to stand by themselves.

Farmers wishing to establish these giants on their properties must make sure that the habitat is suitable. The property must be at least 2 000 ha in size for a breeding nucleus and be enclosed by a strong, electrified game fence. (See Chapter 15 for fencing specifications.)

WHITE RHINOCEROS
Ceratotherium simum

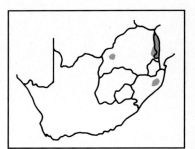

Photograaaph: Koos Delport

GENERAL INFORMATION

Natural distribution (Southern Africa): The white rhinoceros was originally distributed widely throughout Southern Africa.
Conservation status: Previously almost extinct.Now locally common and doing well in nature reserves and on game farms in South Africa. Very much threatened elsewhere in Africa.
Limiting factors: Poaching, fighting, accidental injuries, drought and drowning in floods.
Habitat: Savanna and grasslands within reach of open water and dense bush.

Preferred food types: Short grass, but is well adapted to feeding on long grass.
Sexual maturity: At about 4 to 5 years of age.
Gestation period: Approximately 480 — 490 days.
Calving interval: About 2 to 3 years.
Mating season: Throughout the year.
Calving peaks: Not well defined. March and July in Natal. Breeding throughout the year.
Number of young: A single calf at a time. Twins have been recorded but are very exceptional.
Longevity: 40 years.

Body weight (adults): Bull 2 000 to 2 300 kg (4 400 to 5 060 lb.); cow 1 400 to 1 600 kg (3 080 to 3 520 lb.)

Shoulder height (adults): 180 cm (72 in.).

Horns: Both sexes carry horns which are generally longer and thinner in the female.

At the turn of the century, the white rhino was almost extinct in South Africa. Its numbers were estimated at the time to have been as low as 10 or 20. In 1896 it disappeared completely from the area now covered by the Kruger National Park. Helped by strict and successful conservation measures introduced by the Natal Parks Board, their numbers have increased and there are now an estimated 2 000 white rhino in Natal's reserves. The numbers of white rhino re-introduced to the Kruger Park from the Natal reserves have now increased to 1 565 animals. The South African population currently stands at over 4 000 animals.

In contrast to the above success stories, the future seems bleak in most other African countries for the survival of this impressive pachyderm.

Rhino horn and products have been traded and used for more than 2 000 years. The popularity of rhino horn, used for making dagger handles and for its reputed aphrodisiac and fever-reducing properties, has largely been responsible for the large-scale slaughter and extermination of rhino in many parts of Africa. It is hoped that the stricter control measures imposed internationally to curb the illegal trade in rhino horn will be more successful than in the past.

The Natal Parks Board has, as part of its highly successful 'operation rhino' project, relocated more than 3 000 white rhino to other areas within Africa and throughout the world.

White rhino breed well in captivity. In 1983 there were already 637 individuals in more than 200 zoological collections.

Next to the elephant and the hippo, the white rhino is the largest land mammal in Africa. The name 'white' rhinoceros may be confusing as it originally referred to the shape of the species' mouth (wide mouth) and not to the colour of the animal. The name square-lipped rhinoceros is probably more appropriate for the white rhinoceos and the name hook-lipped rhinoceros more descriptive of the black rhino as the white rhino is not really white and the black rhino not really black.

The white rhino's wide lips are used for grazing grass while the prehensile upper lip of the black rhino enables this predominantly browsing species to strip leaves from the trees and to break off smaller twigs and branches. Apart from the shape of its mouth, the white rhino can also be distinguished from the black rhino by its longer head, which is carried lower, and by the prominent hump on the upper part of the neck.

The two horns on the rhino's nose grow continuously at a rate of about 0,5 cm per month, and if broken off accidentally, will usually be replaced from the underlying skin. The horns are not part of the skull and consist of compact hair-like material. The front horn is usually the longer. The very longest horn recorded for the southern African region is stated to have been almost two metres in length. The front horn usually has a flattened and polished surface because of regular contact with the ground during feeding. Exceptionally, the front horn is used for digging roots and tubers.

The rhinoceros spoor is characterised by the marks left by three toes on each foot. The spoor of the front foot is slightly larger than that of the hind foot. The indentation on the posterior side of the white rhino's spoor distinguishes it from that of the black rhino, whose spoor is more rounded at the back.

Apart from man, the white rhino has few enemies to fear. Lions may prey on the calves and are known to have seriously wounded a fully grown cow. An exceptional case of a rhino being killed by an elephant at a waterhole has also been reported by Dr Tol Pienaar.

The rhino can hear and smell very well, but has poor eyesight. It can hardly see further than about 25 metres and finds it difficult to spot a non-moving object. Acknowledged rhino expert, Dr Norman Owen-Smith estimates that a rhino could smell a human as far as 800 metres when the wind carries the smell towards the animal.

Although of a more patient nature than the easily provoked black rhino, the white rhinoceros can be dangerous, particularly when molested, and has been known to seriously injure and even kill people.

Rhino communicate vocally, by 'body talk' and by scent marking. The strange, squeaking call of the rhino, when perfectly imitated, can lure even wild rhino to within a very short distance.

White rhino are frequently accompanied by red-billed oxpeckers, which usually warn the rhino of approaching humans. When first alarmed, the animals will immediately react by raising their heads, the ears erect. With their buttocks touching, and facing in opposite directions, they will quietly wait until they have established the direction from which danger threatens before breaking away at a fast gallop.

Although a rhino, when forced to do so, can run at about 40 km/h, they normally walk very slowly, with the heads held very low.

Preferred food and feeding behaviour

Being animals of habit, they tend to use the same footpaths over and over. They sometimes move over high ridges and through dense forests to get to water or suitable grazing.

In Natal, Dr Owen-Smith found that four grass species, viz *Themeda triandra, Panicum maximum, P. coloratum* and *Urochloa mosambicensis* constitute 74 per cent of the white rhino's total food intake. *Cynodon dactylon* ('kweek') is very well utilised, when available. In general, the white rhinoceros prefers short, sweet grass and will give preference to new growth.

It is almost unbelievable how selective the white rhino, with its huge mouth, can be when feeding. The big nostrils are used to scan the vegetation and unpalatable grasses and herbs are avoided.

Dr Owen-Smith found that white rhino spend about 48 per cent of daylight hours grazing. The food is partially chewed, but not regurgitated and rechewed, since the rhino is not a ruminant. While feeding, the head is moved in semi-circles, to and fro, and all edible grasses are cut to very short lengths. Then it moves forward a step and the whole process is repeated.

When water is readily available, white rhino will drink regularly. During water shortages, they may go without water for as long as three to four days. They visit watering places most frequently during the late afternoon and early evenings, but may drink at any time of the day or night.

Territoriality and social grouping

White rhino are found singly, or in small groups usually consisting of a single dominant bull, cows and calves. White rhino bulls are strongly territorial and will fight bulls entering their territories. Each territory is about 0,75 to 2,6 square kilometres in size, according to Dr Owen-Smith, which is smaller than the average territory for black rhino. The bulls adhere strictly to their particular territories and will only leave their domain to drink water or when they are defeated by an intruder.

The sexually mature, territorial breeding bulls mark their territories in various ways to indicate their presence to other bulls. Territorial dung piles are established throughout the territory, at a density of up to 15 per square kilometre. Only the territorial bulls kick their dung heaps apart and undisturbed dung piles along regularly used tracks between feeding areas and waterholes are therefore most probably deposited by cows, juveniles and non-territorial rhino.

Urine spraying by territorial males, another form of scent marking, is restricted to the boundaries of the territory. When patrolling his boundaries, the territorial bull frequently emits short bursts of urine spray to continually remind possible male rivals to 'stay out'.

Fighting does not always occur when bulls of adjacent territories meet, as the rights of the owner of a particular territory are usually respected by others that may accidentally trespass. When attending to a cow in oestrus, however, vicious fighting may ensue.

Bruising of the face due to fighting can cause excessive bone growth in the vicinity of the naso-lacrimal duct, i.e. the duct draining the tears from the animal's eye to its nasal passages. When the duct becomes obstructed by the bony obliteration, the tears will run down the animal's cheek, resulting in cancerous growths which may occlude the eye and even lead to blindness and the eventual death of the unfortunate animal.

In confined areas with high rhino density, adult males which do not possess a territory and which are not strong enough to acquire one by active fighting may be found living in another bull's territory. As long as the socially inferior bull behaves in a submissive way, and as long as there is no female in oestrus around, the inferior bull will be tolerated as a subsidiary in the other male's territory.

The territorial bull has a few preferred resting places within his territory where he can usually be found. While resting, the rhino will either stand or lie on his brisket or side.

According to Dr Owen-Smith, the cows have definite home ranges, from 6 to 20 square kilometres in size. Their home ranges overlap, and the living area of a single cow may span the territories of up to seven different territorial bulls. This largely precludes inbreeding in extensive, natural areas and contributes to competition among bulls, favouring the stronger bulls to breed and to produce more vital offspring.

Breeding data

Mating and calving may take place at any time of the year, with peak calving times in March and July, as recorded for Natal.

While moving through male territories a cow on heat will advertise her availability and whereabouts by frequently squirting a mist of urine as she wanders along.

A cow on heat will obviously be much in demand by the bulls of the area. A territorial bull will do everything possible to prevent her from straying from his territory.

Mating is a lengthy affair. With his feet firmly placed on the cow's back, the bull may stay mounted for over an hour.

When a female in oestrus is accompanied by a calf, the latter may occasionally be killed by the bull. Before the cow has her calf, she drives off her previous calf, which then usually joins up with one or more other subadults. Although already weaned at the age of about 12 months, it only leaves its mother when about two years old.

Shortly before calving, the cow will leave the herd. The newly born calf, weighing about 40 kilograms, is rather unsteady on its feet for the first three days. Thereafter it will go where mother goes, or is it the other way around ? The white rhino calf usually leads the way, with the cow directing it gently with her horns. It is interesting to note that in the case of the black rhino, the mother usually takes the lead, with the calf following when they are on the move.

A calf is born every 2 to 4 years and about 10 calves can be produced by a single cow.

White rhino seem to increase at a rate of about 4 to 9 per cent each year, and suitable habitats seem to hold an average of one rhino per 97 hectares, according to Dr Owen-Smith.

A rhino-proof fence can be constructed by sinking strong metal posts used in railway tracks into the ground, which should protrude some 1,5 metres above ground level. With these posts spaced at 10 metre intervals, with two steel cables, stretched between them, 60cm and 120cm above ground level and kept parallel by treated timber droppers every 3 metres, few rhino would ever succeed in crossing the fence. Nowadays, game fences are made rhino-deterrent by the incorporation of electrified fencing. (See chapter 15 on fencing specifications.)

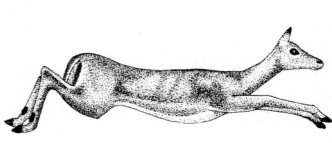

ZEBRAS

Burchell's zebra
Equus burchelli

Photograph: Koos Delport

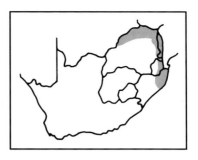

GENERAL INFORMATION

Natural distribution: North-western, northern and eastern Transvaal, northern Natal, northern Namibia.
Conservation status: Abundant.
Limiting factors: Predation, disease and shrinking habitat.
Habitat: Savanna and grassveld.
Preferred food types: Grass.
Sexual maturity: Stallion 2 — 4 years, mare 2 — 3 years.
Mating season: October to March.
Gestation period: 375 days.
First foal born: Mare 3 — 4 years.
Foaling interval: 13 months or more.
Number of foals: One.
Longevity: 22 years.
Body weight (adults): 276 — 430 kg (613 — 955 lb.).
Shoulder height (adults): 127 — 147 cm (50 — 58 in.).

Cape mountain zebra
Equus zebra zebra

Photograph: Koos Delport

Natural distribution: Southern Cape.
Conservation status: Rare. Protected.
Limiting factors: Overshooting (earlier).
Habitat: Mountainous areas.
Preferred food types: Grass.
Sexual maturity: Stallion 7 years, mare 4 years.
First foal: Mare 3 — 4 years.
Mating season: Throughout the year, especially in summer.
Gestation period: ± 364 days.
First foal born: Mare 3 — 4 years.
Foaling interval: 24 months on average.
Number of foals: One.
Longevity: 24 + years.
Body weight (adults): 204 — 260 kg (453 — 577 lb.).
Shoulder height (adults): 116 — 128 cm (46 — 51 in.).

Hartmann's mountain zebra
Equus zebra hartmannae

GENERAL INFORMATION

Natural distribution: Western Namibia.
Conservation status: Quite abundant.
Limiting factors: Mainly droughts.
Habitat: Mountainous terrain.
Preferred food types: Grass.
Sexual maturity: Stallion ± 12 months, mare ± 12 months.
Mating season: Throughout the year.
Gestation period: ± 362 days.
First foal born: Mare 3 years.
Foaling interval: ± 14 months.
Number of foals: One.
Longevity: Unknown.
Body weight (adults): 276 — 336 kg (613 — 746 lb.).
Shoulder height (adults): 150 cm (60 in.).

Two of the three zebra species and several subspecies, which occur worldwide, are found in South Africa. One is the well-known Burchell's zebra *(Equus burchelli)*, which occurs in large numbers in the Transvaal and Natal. The other is the Cape Mountain Zebra *(Equus zebra zebra)* which is found in smaller numbers in the Cape Province.

Burchell's zebra prefer open grassveld or savannaveld. They are even found in fairly dense bush and are surprisingly at home in mountainous or hilly terrain.

The Cape mountain zebra is one of the rarest mammals in the world. This zebra species has shorter legs, is plumper and differs in colour pattern from the Burchell's zebra. The white hair between the black stripes of the Cape mountain zebra is snow-white, while the Burchell's zebra has a darkish stripe (shadow stripe) in the white hair between its black stripes. The Cape mountain zebra has a grid-like pattern on its rump, which is absent in the Burchell's zebra. The black stripes, which on the Burchell's zebra run down over the stomach, end higher up on the body of the Cape mountain zebra, so that the latter animal's stomach is whiter. The black stripes over the rump of the Cape mountain zebra are normally very wide. Over the rest of the body and on the face, the stripes are narrower, so that the Cape mountain zebra has more stripes than the Burchell's zebra. The Cape mountain zebra has longer ears, a donkey-like face and a dewlap, which the Burchell's zebra lacks. The mountain zebra's

nose is a rusty brown colour, while the Burchell's zebra has a black nose. The Cape mountain zebra is the smallest of the zebra species and subspecies which occur in South Africa.

The Hartmann's mountain zebra *(Equus zebra hartmannae)* which is found in Namibia and the south-western parts of Angola is a subspecies of the Cape mountain zebra. Apart from a difference in the colour pattern (the black stripes of the Hartmann's zebra are noticeably narrower) and the fact that the Cape Mountain zebra is smaller than its Namibian counterpart, these two subspecies appear to be identical.

Mountain zebras are particularly well adapted to scrambling along steep mountain slopes. Apart from their muscular physique, their hooves are specially adapted to these conditions. Not only are they very tough, but they also grow considerably faster than those of the Burchell's zebra. Consequently, hoof tissue which is damaged by the rough terrain they live in is quickly replaced by new tissue. When mountain zebras are kept on soft surfaces, such as on sandy soil in a zoo for example, their hooves soon grow disproportionately long. The animals have to be caught on a regular basis and their hooves trimmed.

The colour pattern differs from one zebra to another, even within the same species. Individual animals can be identified by the pattern of their stripes. It is interesting to note that the colour pattern on the left and right sides of the same animal may also differ.

It is fairly common to see a zebra with a short tail. These are normally stallions which have had their tails bitten off by rival stallions during a fight. Zebras can be very ill-tempered and may attack other animals, mutilating them for no obvious reason. They are particularly inclined to do so at waterholes or feeding sites, where they will maim or kill young animals of other species or even of their own kind.

Cape mountain zebra mares only reach maturity at 4 years of age and stallions when they are about 7 years old. For the first few weeks of the young zebra's life, it remains close to its mother and suckles often. Other zebras are kept at a respectful distance by the mother. Zebra foals are weaned when they are between 9 and 16 months old.

In contrast to some other game species, zebras are not territorial and will not drive other zebras out of a particular area. However, the herd stallion will fight to retain his herd of mares when challenged by a rival stallion.

A zebra stallion will gallantly defend and protect his family group. When the herd approaches a waterhole where lions may be lying in wait, the stallion will take the lead, and when the herd flees from danger, the stallion will hang back to assume a defensive position.

The social behaviour and family life of zebras is very interesting. Although zebras may be found in large herds of more than a hundred animals, particularly at waterholes, or when they migrate, this seemingly huge herd of homogeneous animals comprises many smaller family units. The animals in these family groups usually remain together for life. As the animals move away from a waterhole and begin to spread out, one can clearly see how the same group of animals remains together in a small herd. This phenomenon is more easily noticed when the animals are marked.

A family group is formed when a stallion musters a few mares to form his harem. This usually happens when the stallion is between 4 and 6 years old. The members of such a family group become very attached to one another and the mares will normally remain with their stallion until he dies or is driven off by another, stronger stallion. It is known that a zebra stallion may keep his breeding herd for as long as 15 years.

Burchell's zebra family groups normally consist of a stallion and two to three (sometimes as many as six) mares and young foals. Breeding herds of mountain zebra usually consist of between 4 and 7 animals (sometimes as many as 13). The family groups are rarely larger than this, as the foals leave the "closed" family group when they are about one to two years old. Young mares are sometimes driven out of the herd by older mares or are coaxed away by other stallions when the mares are old enough to breed. The young stallions form stallion herds until they are big and strong enough to form their own harems.

The unique family composition of zebras has several advantages for the production of healthy and viable offspring: In the first instance, only the strongest and most vital stallions gather a herd for themselves. Weaker stallions would therefore not normally be given the opportunity to produce foals which may be inferior. In contrast to most other species, zebras do not normally mate with their own offspring and consequently the problems of inbreeding are limited. The possibility of inbreeding is further limited because more stallions are given the opportunity to breed and there is a larger genetic pool than would have been the case if a single stallion were to mate with all the mares in a single group. The phenomenon that large herds split up into smaller groups when the animals graze also contributes to a more even distribution, which holds many obvious ecological advantages.

Burchell's zebra may live up to a maximum age of 22 years under normal, natural conditions. Dr Penzhorn has ascertained that the Cape mountain zebra can live somewhat longer and that mares are still capable of breeding at 21 years of age.

Although Burchell's zebra are particularly close-knit as a family group, they mix readily with other animals of the same and different species. Various interesting theories have been proffered to explain the fact that zebra and wildebeest are often found together. The claim that this is because zebras have keen eyesight and a good sense of hearing and wildebeest have a good sense of smell is not acceptable to me. It is true, however, that zebras will stand and watch intently while wildebeest go down to a waterhole to drink. If a lion should attack the wildebeest from the bushes next to the water, the zebra can flee from a safe distance. However, if it seems safe, the zebra will follow the wildebeest to the water.

Cape mountain zebra are less inclined to mix with animals of other species and graze with them.

Dr Eugene Joubert's research in Namibia has shown that Hartmann's zebra do not normally move over long distances. When they graze they walk between one and three kilometres per day, and a little further when they go to drink.

Hartmann's zebra and Burchell's zebra sometimes use their forehooves to dig for water to a depth of one metre under the sand. In this way they also provide water for other animals in dry regions.

Mountain zebras drink at any time during the day. In regions where they are disturbed or hunted they usually drink at night. In the Kruger National Park, Burchell's zebra normally drink during the day and, in the hot summer months, in the mornings, particularly. They can go without water for as long as three days at a stretch, but in the Kruger, on average, they will usually drink every 35 hours. A zebra ordinarily drinks 21 litres at a time, so that each zebra drinks approximately 14,4 litres of water per day. In the winter months in the Kruger National Park, Burchell's zebra are generally found closer than 2 kilometres from the nearest water during the day. However, they graze about 7 kilometres and further from the water. On an average day in the winter they walk twice as far as they would in summer because waterholes are few and far between at this time of the year.

According to Dr Butch Smuts, the home range of Burchell's zebra in the Kruger Park is approximately 100 to 260 square kilometres in size. Dr Eugene Joubert calculates the Hartmann's zebra's home range to be between 6 and 20 square kilometres in the winter and even smaller during the summer months. As it becomes drier in the winter, zebra will migrate for long distances to find water. After the early rains in spring they will move back to their preferred summer grazing areas. In the Kruger Park these treks are 75 kilometres long and further. In Etosha, according to Dr Hymie Ebedes, they migrate between 100 and 160 kilometres and in the Serengeti, in East Africa, as far as 200 kilometres and further. When zebras migrate, they are often accompanied by blue wildebeest and are usually followed by prides of lion, hyenas and other carnivores to their new grazing areas. While they are on the move, they may walk up to 40 kilometres in a single day.

Lions can be counted amongst the natural enemies of the zebra. Young zebra sometimes fall prey to leopards and are sometimes caught by cheetahs and spotted hyenas. There have been instances where hyenas have been maimed and even killed by zebras.

In recent years Burchell's zebra have been relocated in large numbers on many farms in the Republic.

Zebras are grazers and are amongst the few game species which make good use of long grassveld. In areas where zebras occur in large numbers, these animals often create more favourable grazing conditions for other game species, such as blesbok, which prefer shorter grass. According to Dr Smuts, they show a particular fondness for couch grass (Cynodon dactylon) and are also partial to recently burnt grass and areas where there is new growth after the spring rains. Occasionally they will eat leaves from trees such as the mopane and apple-leaf.

Dr Meissner, who calculated the grazing requirements of game species in terms of large stock units, equates one large animal unit (one cow of 450 kilograms) with 1.3 to 1.7 adult zebras. Accordingly, the grazing requirements of 3 adult zebras can roughly be compared with that of 2 cows.

A sturdy fence 1,8 m high will usually adequately confine zebra to a farm. As zebra are not jumpers, a fence of 2,4 m, which is required to keep in species such as kudu, impala, eland and waterbuck, is not necessary.

Although it is common knowledge that horses as well as donkeys can interbreed with zebras, there has not yet been a case of interbreeding between Burchell's and mountain zebras. These two species do not interbreed even when kept in close confinement, such as in zoos, or on farms. In spite of this, certain nature conservation departments do not allow farmers to farm with both zebra species on the same farm. It could be beneficial on some farms to farm simultaneously with Burchell's and Hartmann's zebra and, in my opinion, this restriction is both unnecessary and unfair. Researchers (e.g. Ansell) claim that the chromosome make-up differs significantly between the two zebra species. This totally precludes the possiblity of a hybrid zebra race being produced. Burchell's and Hartmann's zebra have co-existed for many years in Otjovasando, a beautiful nature reserve in Namibia, without there ever having been a case of interbreeding, according to Dr Eugene Joubert.

Zebras are generally heavily infested with internal parasites, but this does not normally have any significant effect on them. They are also susceptible to some infectious diseases. Dr Hymie Ebedes reports that zebra succumb to anthrax in Namibia.

Research on a number of Cape mountain zebra has indicated that a fairly large percentage of these animals are infested with biliary fever parasites, without showing any symptoms of the disease. This parasite is found in healthy horses and it may cause biliary fever when these animals are subjected to severe stress.

AFRICAN BUFFALO
Syncerus caffer

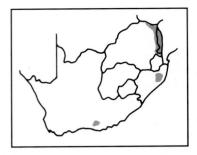

GENERAL INFORMATION

Natural distribution (Southern Africa): Botswana, northern, north-eastern and south-eastern Zimbabwe, eastern Transvaal, Addo National Park, Hluhluwe and Umfolozi game reserves and their immediate vicinity.

Conservation status: Fairly abundant.

Limiting factors: Drought, unsuitable habitat, predation (mainly lion) and, sporadically, disease.

Habitat: Forest, savanna and open grassland. Bulls, in particular, show a strong preference for riverine reedbeds.

Preferred food type: Grass.

Sexual maturity: Heifers 4 — 5 years, bulls 4½ — 6 years.

Estrous cycle: 23 days.

Gestation period: 330 to 346 days.

Calving interval: 13 — 18 months.

Mating season: Mostly at the end of the rainy season. (Kruger Park: peak in January and February).

Calves born: Single. Twins not reported, but possible.

Body weight (adults): up to 800 kg (1 760 lb.).

Shoulder height (adults): 140 cm (56 in.).

Buffalo differ in horn shape, body form, facial characteristics, and colour, even within the same herd. Zoologists were in the past misled by these variations in physical appearance, and hence no fewer than 92 zoological names have been given to African

buffalo which were believed to belong to different species and subspecies. Nowadays, only two separate subspecies are recognized, i.e. *Syncerus caffer*, the Cape buffalo and *Syncerus caffer nanus*, the dwarf or forest buffalo from western Africa.

Dwarf or forest buffalo are smaller than the Cape buffalo that we know in southern Africa. Their horns are smaller, relative to body size, and the hair is usually light to dark reddish brown in colour. They are found further north in Africa, in Chad, Uganda and Nigeria, for example.

The Addo buffalo, found in the Addo National Park near Port Elizabeth (South Africa), can be considered to be a forest-living remnant population of *S. caffer caffer,* thus being of the same species and subspecies as buffalo found in Natal/Kwazulu and in the Kruger National Park.

In South Africa, the major buffalo populations are found in the Kruger National Park and adjoining nature reserves (about 30 000 animals) and in the Natal/Kwazulu parks (about 2 000 buffalo). In the Kruger National Park, despite the culling and removal of some 36 000 buffalo over the past few years, the population is flourishing. In Addo, however, the buffalo population dropped from about 150 to fewer than 50 animals. Buffalo previously distributed from Addo to provincial nature reserves and to game farms fared from unsatisfactorily to outstandingly well. In general the principle of not 'putting all one's eggs in one basket' seems to have been successfully and timeously applied. It's a pity, however, that stock diseases such as foot-and-mouth and corridor disease, carried by buffalo in other regions, prohibit the distribution of live buffalo from places like the Kruger National Park.

Towards the turn of the previous century the dreaded stock disease, rinderpest, swept the subcontinent and killed all but a dozen buffalo in the Kruger National Park. Isolated populations elsewhere in South Africa also survived. Recent blood analyses revealed a high degree of inbreeding in buffalo in the Kruger National Park, most probably as a consequence of the rinderpest epizootic. Visitors to the Park have probably wondered about the frequent occurrence of abnormally short and kinked tails in buffalo. These are but some of the signs of inbreeding.

Buffalo live in herds of up to a few thousand animals. Lone bulls and bull herds, lingering in the vicinity of breeding herds, spend much of their time cooling down in mudholes or in riverbeds.

Herds tend to split up, drifting widely apart to unite again at frequently used grazing grounds or waterholes. Generally moving slowly, about 5 kilometres in 12 hours during daylight or 2,9 kilometres at night in summer, buffalo have to move over longer distances in winter to go to drink. Research in the Kruger

National Park has shown that they travel, on average, about 11,2 kilometres in 24 hours in winter and that they graze up to about 7,8 kilometres from water during the dry season. Longer distances are travelled over a shorter span of time when water gets really scarce, or when the buffalo are disturbed by lion.

Birds feeding on ticks and skin debris of buffalo or on grasshoppers and insects flushed by the grazing animals frequently give an indication of the buffalos' whereabouts. Be on the lookout for circling cattle egrets in buffalo country, or listen for the shrill warning sound when the oxpeckers suddenly rise from the thickets.

When on the move, big herds are quite noisy and can be heard from far away. Old and sick individuals and cows with very small calves usually trail behind. Lions, which may follow a herd for days on end, find the weaklings at the rear of herds easy prey, thereby removing the weaker ones to ensure the survival of the fittest.

Hyenas, leopards and wild dogs are seldom successful in catching buffalo, even calves, from the herds. Crocodiles, although not considered an important enemy, are known to have captured and drowned fully grown buffalo bulls on occasion. Lions are more important natural enemies of buffalo.

Fights between buffalo and lion are amongst the most spectacular combats to be witnessed in nature. The lions' intermittent attacks may last for hours, the big cats repeatedly approaching from different directions, attempting to catch the buffalo by surprise. Sometimes the lions come off second best. Many a lion has been seriously wounded or even killed by buffalo.

When surprised and pursued by lions, the herd usually stampedes. A little later the buffalo may stop, tightly huddled together with the small calves hidden in the centre and with the big bulls frequently reversing the charge.

Buffalo spend about eight to eleven hours every 24 hours grazing. After a long rest during the hottest hours of the day, the animals usually become active from about 16h00.

Long grass is grazed shorter by buffalo and the veld thus opened up for zebra, wildebeest, impala and other game that prefer shorter grassveld. Primarily grazers, buffalo do exceptionally browse. In the Addo Elephant National Park, a lack of grass and an overabundance of browse forced the Addo buffalo to adopt a browsing diet.

In the wilds, buffalo herds can be found in the same home ranges for prolonged periods. Despite the continual splitting up and fusing of fragmented herds, experienced hunters will confirm that buffalo have quite fixed living and grazing areas and drinking places which they utilise, depending, of course, on prevailing rains, wind and the availability of food and water.

The average living area of buffalo studied in the Kruger National Park varied, for their daily movements, from 5,4 X 2,9 square kilometres in summer to 5,9 X 1,8 square kilometres in winter. Over a more prolonged period, Mark Mloszewski, who studied buffalo behaviour in Kenya, Zambia and Zimbabwe, found their home ranges to vary in size from 126 to 1 075 square kilometres. Average buffalo population densities within home ranges varied from about one buffalo per five square kilometres to almost four buffalo per single square kilometre.

Buffalo drink an average of 21 litres of water per day. During summer, when water is readily available, they move from one watering place to another, visiting as many as 5 waterholes and mudpools per day, not only for drinking but also for wallowing and cooling themselves. During the dry winter months they only visit drinking places, on average, every 38 hours.

Buffalo establish natural pools and pans which eventually constitute important waterholes. These holes in the ground are formed and enlarged where buffalo continuously have their mudbaths and carry away large quantities of mud, stuck to their hair, leaving behind ever-growing natural water reservoirs. These 'buffalo pans' have a definite influence on buffalo movement patterns, as the well-trodden and frequently used footpaths lead from one pan to another. These pans are often visited by buffalo, particularly during the warm, rainy season.

Buffalo are quite different from cattle in their behaviour. Calves suckle from behind, poking their heads between the cows' hindlegs.

For such ferocious looking beasts, buffalo are quite unexpectedly, 'friendly' animals. Even when competing for a cow on heat, the bulls, unlike domestic bulls, seldomly indulge in serious fighting.

It is not unusual to see resting buffalo lying on their sides, which is quite an unnatural posture for resting cattle.

As robust and as tough as they may seem, buffalo are susceptible to exposure. During cold, windy days the animals usually move into thick bush for protection. A case has been recorded in the Kruger National Park where a number of buffalo, including adult animals, died from exposure during an exceptionally cold night.

Few calves survive during very dry winters. During the sixties one herd of over a thousand buffalo reared only one calf during a very dry season in the Kruger National Park. Weakened by a shortage of food and exhausted by travelling over long distances, the calves tended to lag behind the herds and fell easy prey to lions following the herds.

Buffalo are in great demand by game farmers. Prices of up to R22 000 have been paid for individual animals at game auctions. Intensive research is being undertaken in order to attempt the rapid multiplication of disease-free buffalo by means of embryo transplants, but so far without much success. Some progress has been made however, as it has been found, by using sophisticated techniques, that between 20 and 30 embryos can be obtained per year from a single buffalo cow for transplant into surrogate mothers.

Heifers reach 'pubertal age' at about 3½ years, but only really start breeding when between 4 and 5 years old. Bulls reach sexual maturity when between 4½ and 6 years old.

The overall percentage of adult females pregnant at a given time can be as high as 75 per cent. This means that 10 adult cows can produce about 8 calves per year.

Newborn calves are black or dark olive-brown in colour and weigh about 35 to 50 kilograms at birth. Their colour darkens with age. They are weaned when about 7 months old.

Buffalo calves can be successfully reared and domesticated. Hand-reared animals should always be approached and handled with caution as a moody individual may unexpectedly turn on its master.

At two years of age, the young bulls develop a noticeable enlargement of the horns at the base, called the 'boss'. As the boss spreads inwards towards the middle of the head, skin and hair progressively disappear and the boss becomes hardened. At three to five years there is still some skin and hair between the horn base on the forehead. It is only at the age of about five to seven years that the two hardened horn-like halves of the boss nearly meet at the centre and that most hair in between has disappeared. At about eight to ten years of age, prominent ridges develop on the boss. After ten years the horn tips start to wear and even break off. These old bulls usually show signs of scarring and loss of hair on the face and body.

GIRAFFE
Giraffa camelopardalis

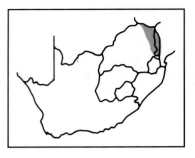

GENERAL INFORMATION

Natural distribution (S.A.): Northern and eastern Transvaal.
Conservation status: Rare to relatively abundant.
Limiting factors: Carnivores (National Parks), shrinking natural habitat.
Habitat: Bushveld.
Preferred food types: Leaves, twigs and pods.
Sexual maturity: Bull 32 — 40 months, cow 56 months.
Mating season: Throughout the year.
Calving season: Throughout the year.
Gestation period: 457 days.
First calf born: Cow 71+ months.
Number of calves: One. Twins unusual.
Body weight (adults): Bull 973 — 1395 kg. Cow 703 — 950 kg. (Bull 2 162 — 3 100 lb. Cow 1 562 — 2 111 lb.)
Head height (adults): Bull 500 — 588 cm. Cow 430 — 460 cm. (Bull 200 — 235 in. Cow 172 — 184 in.)

The Giraffe family (Fam.: Giraffidae) is made up of two species, namely the giraffe and the okapi. Giraffe are classified into 9 subspecies, mainly according to their colour patterns, and these are all found only in Africa, where they occur naturally.

The neck and legs of the okapi are shorter than those of the giraffe and they have white marks on the rump and limbs. There is a similarity between the okapi and a short-necked type of giraffe which occurred in Europe and Asia some 10 million years ago. Okapi are found in the dense equatorial forests of Zaire.

Mammals usually have seven vertebrae in the neck. The giraffe is no exception. Its individual vertebrae are merely very much longer than those of most other mammals.

Although zoologists attach much value to the colour patterns of giraffe as a method of subdividing the animals into sub-species, there may be a great variation in colour patterns even within the same herd. In some instances the dark, block-shaped blotches may even be star-shaped, as in the Masai giraffe of East Africa. Some animals are almost altogether white, particularly over the hindquarters and, in old bulls in particular, the dark brown blotches may be completely black.

Giraffe bulls have a distinct, unpleasant smell which can be detected over a long distance. This smell apparently originates from glands in the skin. The skin is exceptionally thick and makes good leather. Some tribesmen use the leather from the tail to make quivers for their arrows, while the bushy part of the tail is prized as a fly-swatter.

The horns of the giraffe are in actual fact bony growths covered with skin. The horns of the bulls are usually longer and thicker than those of the cows. In exceptional cases, a second pair of horns may be present behind the main horns. In the bulls, a bump-like thickening on the forehead may appear to be a third (or fifth !) horn. This is the origin of the mythical three-horned giraffe.

Giraffe have excellent hearing and eyesight. In areas where they are constantly disturbed it is very difficult to approach them closely. In spite of its size, a wounded giraffe can hide very successfully in a thicket and it may be very difficult to spot such an animal from a searching aircraft.

A giraffe has a very long and mobile tongue, about 45 cm in length. It uses this "handy" tongue to strip even the thorniest branches of their leaves.

In theory, the giraffe should have serious difficulty in regulating its blood pressure when suddenly raising its long neck from a bending position. However, nature has compensated for this in the form of increased elasticity of those arteries and valves in the neck, which supply blood to the head. This mechanism prevents the giraffe from collapsing from dizziness when it suddenly raises its head high. It is interesting to note that valves are normally found only in veins, but that these are also present in some arteries in the giraffe.

Cattle, goats and most other four-legged mammals normally move the opposite front and hindlegs simultaneously when they walk. The giraffe, however, moves the front and hindlegs on the same side simultaneously. A galloping giraffe can reach speeds of between 50 and 60 kilometres per hour.

Giraffe which have been reared on a cattle farm may be successfully confined to a camp by an ordinary cattle fence, even though they are tall enough to be able to climb over such a fence. Some giraffe may learn to climb over such fences, and they then constantly break strands of wire. A standard game fence of 2,4 m high is adequate to confine giraffe to a game farm. Newly released individuals may break through such fences or fall over them when frightened.

In recent years, giraffe have been successfully relocated to many game farms in the Republic. They do not normally compete with domestic stock for available fodder and are a definite asset on any bushveld game farm. The biggest concentration of giraffe in the world is found on private game ranches bordering on the Kruger National Park. Browsing giraffe move over a large area and often browse far away from other members of the herd. The big bulls are not bound to one herd and move freely from one herd to another. Giraffe cows with suckling calves often move far away from their young and it is surprising that many more of these calves do not fall prey to roaming lions.

A giraffe will not cross water readily. Even relatively shallow rivers may confine giraffe to an area. The home range of giraffe bulls comprises some 60 square kilometres, and that of cows, some 80 to 90 square kilometres.

Giraffe take relatively long to become sexually mature. A cow will calve for the first time when she is between 5 and 6 years old. Thereafter, a calf may be born every 16½ months. For the first few weeks after birth, the young calves are hidden by their mothers. In large game reserves, some 50 to 70 per cent of giraffe calves do not survive their first year. On game farms, where large carnivores do not occur, nearly all the giraffe calves survive.

Young twigs and leaves with a high nutritional value comprise the major part of the giraffe's diet. During the winter months this vegetation contains considerably more moisture than the dry grass on which most other animals have to live. Research in the Kruger Park has shown that the leaf fodder which is eaten by giraffe in the winter contains about 58 per cent more moisture than dry grass. This enables the giraffe to go without water for longer periods and to need less water than the animals which are dependent on dry grass.

When water is freely available, giraffe will drink often. An adult giraffe drinks between 40 to 54 litres of water at a time.

In some parts of the country giraffe readily utilise salt licks. Dry bones are also often picked up by giraffe and chewed. This practice makes them susceptible to botulism, a paralysing condition of domestic stock which is caused by toxins from the botulinus bacteria. Young, growing giraffe and lactating cows need ample calcium and phosphate, and game farmers are advised to provide balanced salt licks for their animals.

Giraffe usually browse around a waterhole for extended periods before going to drink. In this way, they become aware of predators hiding near the water in good time. When a giraffe stares intently at a thick bush and ignores approaching vehicles or people, it is safe to assume that it has spotted a hidden carnivore.

Sores on the necks of giraffe are sometimes caused by microscopic filaria parasite larvae. They often rub their necks against tree trunks in an attempt to relieve the irritation. Giraffe use their necks in fights, standing shoulder to shoulder while taking swings at their opponents. Giraffe are formidable fighters. Attacking lions must stay well clear of the flailing hooves of the forelegs and the vicious kicks of the hindlegs of a giraffe. Giraffe have been known to kill lions in this manner. Adult giraffe normally pay little attention to lions and may calmly walk between a resting pride of lions on their way to drink.

Hand-reared giraffe may cause problems when they become bigger. In one instance such a giraffe had to be destroyed because it became so aggressive that people's lives were at risk. In another instance a car was attacked and badly damaged. However, giraffe are usually docile animals. Although they can snort warningly, groan softly or even bay quite loudly on being caught, they normally endure pain and fear in silence. A giraffe is one of the few mammals which may actually 'cry' big tears, which run down their cheeks when they are badly treated. Tame giraffe calves often cry when they have to be injected, are hurt or reprimanded. Bear this in mind next time you have to handle one of these gentle giants.

HIPPOPOTAMUS

Hippopotamus amphibius

GENERAL INFORMATION

Natural distribution (Southern Africa): Still occur naturally in extreme north-eastern Namibia, the Okavango Swamps and the Chobe River in northern Botswana, most of Zimbabwe (except in the extreme western area), in the northern and eastern Transvaal, south of the Zambezi river in Mozambique and north-eastern Natal.

Conservation status: Fairly abundant in areas where they still occur.

Habitat: Rivers, swamps and adjoining areas.

Preferred food types: Grass.

Limiting factors: Poaching, severe drought, disease and fighting amongst bulls.

Sexual maturity: Heifers at about 3 years of age and bulls between approximately 4 and 7 years.

First calf: Cow 4 years.

Mating season: Late winter to spring.

Calving season: Throughout the year. Peak in autumn and early winter.

Gestation period: 225 — 257 days.

Number of calves: One.

Period between calves: 3 years. Exceptionally 2 years.

Longevity: 40 years.

Body weight (adults): 971 — 1 999 kg (2 136 — 4 398 lb.).

Shoulder height (adults): 110 — 172 cm (44 — 69 in.).

The hippo, which may weigh more than 2 tons and measure almost four metres in length is, next to the elephant and white rhino, the world's largest land mammal.

The hippo's protruding nostrils, aptly equipped with a constricting valve mechanism, enable it to remain submerged for as long as six minutes, or to float just under the surface, thereby escaping the extreme heat of the tropical and subtropical areas where it occurs.

The reddish colour of the hippo's sweat has wrongly led

Photograph: Dick Wolff

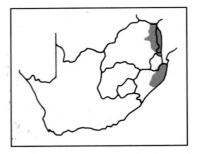

people to believe that the hippo sweats blood. Its skin is prone to severe cracking from the sun when it stays out of the water for too long.

The hippo has the remarkable ability to walk underwater, on the bottom of the river-bed. It is indeed strange to see their characteristic footpaths at the bottom of the river, through the clear water.

Mating, which is quite a noisy affair, takes place in the water and the hippo's gestation period of about eight months is unexpectedly short for such a huge beast.

The baby hippo, weighing from 30 to 60 kg at birth, is born in or near water and has to be protected by its mother against attacks by crocodiles.

Remarkably, the baby suckles underwater, intermittently swimming to the surface to gasp fresh air.

Mother and calf separate from the herd for some months, during which time she is likely to attack anybody approaching her and her calf.

Hippo are infested with leeches — longish, slimy blood-sucking organisms — and it is interesting to see how the fishes which feed on these parasites slide down a hippo's side when the latter suddenly rises above the water level.

Hippo used to occur in all the major river systems of South Africa. As with most other large mammals, their natural distribution range receded as civilization spread through the country. They were extensively killed for their meat and fat (the latter being unexpectedly palatable).

Hippo are not restricted to rivers and lakes. They are frequently encountered in estuaries, and even deeper out to sea, hence the Afrikaans name *seekoei* (sea cow).

Individuals sometimes wander over very long distances. In so doing, some animals in the Kruger Park, for example, frequently end up in earth dams or concrete water troughs, very far from the nearest river. The historic wanderings of a hippo cow named Huberta should be well-known to many readers. She wandered from Lake St. Lucia in Natal to the Cape and covered almost 1 800 km over a period of three years.

Although they may sometimes be responsible for considerable crop damage in agricultural areas, more than 800

hippos are possessively protected by private land-owners outside the Kruger National Park. Since farmers have learnt that hippo can be effectively kept out of their lands and orchards by means of relatively cheap electric fencing, these river giants have now found a safe home on many farms in the Eastern Transvaal.

Apparently of a mild disposition, hippos may behave like savage monsters. They are quite unpredictable and, on occasion, highly dangerous. People have been mauled to death by ill-tempered or provoked hippos. They may attack canoes or people near the water's edge, particularly if molested, when they have small calves, or when they have had unpleasant encounters with people in the past.

These clumsy-looking animals can move unbelievably fast on land and in shallow water. Anyone who thinks that he can outrun a charging hippo is in for an unpleasant surprise. They are also able to climb very steep banks and once a hippo decides to charge, there is very little except a well-placed bullet that will stop the enraged beast.

Vicious fights between bulls, accompanied by hair-raising screams of anger and fear, may last for days on end. They fight more fiercely than most other animals. The sharp canines and long, spear-like incisors of solid ivory serve as formidable weapons, inflicting ghastly and often fatal wounds, turning the river's water red to mark victory and defeat for the fighting giants.

Lions and crocodiles occasionally prey on young hippo. According to Dr U de V Pienaar's research in the Kruger Park, the mortality rate in very young calves is about 16 to 17 per cent. After the first year of life natural mortality becomes insignificant under normal, natural conditions.

Hippo cows calve throughout the year, although in the Kruger Park the autumn/winter period seems to be the prime time for the birth of the little hippos.

Dr Pienaar made an interesting, hypothetical calculation: Assuming that a hippo female becomes sexually mature at 3 years, and calves every third year after her first baby is born when she is 4 years old, one couple could theoretically produce 24 — 38 hippo (of six generations) in 20 years.

Calves are suckled for a long period and, according to Dr Pienaar, calves born during the previous season still suckle periodically. Bull calves are driven from the herd by the herd bull when they become sexually mature at about 4 — 7 years of age.

Herd size may vary from 2 to several hundred individuals. The average herd consists of about 10 to 15 animals. Hippo play an extremely important role in the ecology of rivers and swamps. Not only do they keep the water channels in sludgy marshes open to promote water flow and the movement of fish and other aquatic animals, but they fertilise the water with their faeces and urine, providing a nutrient medium for aquatic insects and micro-organisms.

The hippo spends most of its day in or near water. At night it may wander ponderously for 30 km and more away from water, to consume up to 130 kg of green grass. It has been calculated that a hippo with an average body mass of 1 100 kg eats about 27 kg of food (dry weight) in 24 hours, which is about three times as much as that which a domestic cow would eat. In captivity, the daily ration of an adult hippo constitutes about 40 to 45 kg of lucerne together with some concentrates (e.g. antelope cubes).

Although hippos normally graze at night, odd individuals may periodically be seen feeding during late afternoons or on cool, cloudy days.

When walking through the veld, hippos leave their typical double-tracked footpaths as evidence of their presence in an area.

Dung is scattered along their frequently-used footpaths with rapid side-to-side switching movements of the short, flat tail.

Hippos are efficient 'lawn-mowers'. The wide lips are used to pluck the grass in such a way that they leave behind a perfectly trimmed lawn-like grass cover on the river banks where they frequently feed. Grass is their staple diet; aquatic vegetation is utilised to a varying extent.

The hippo is not a ruminant like cattle, sheep and antelope. Unlike the horse, rhino, pig and other non-ruminating animals which have a single stomach, the hippo has a three-chambered stomach which possibly aids in the digestion of its fibrous, grassy diet.

In parks and reserves where overpopulations of hippo and other game occur, the animal numbers may result in severe trampling and overgrazing of the veld, causing erosion of the river banks and adjoining areas.

During extreme drought, hundreds of hippo may be forced to share the remaining pools, and the water eventually turns into a stinking mess, exposing the animals to the risk of disease.

Not unlike humans, hippo are subject to stress caused by high population densities and, more often than not, insufficient habitat is more of a limiting factor where too many hippos concentrate than any actual lack of food.

6. NATURAL DISTRIBUTION AREAS, HABITAT REQUIREMENTS AND FEEDING PREFERENCES OF SOUTH AFRICAN GAME

As climate, landscape and the nature of the soil vary from region to region, so does the vegetation, and together with this, the distribution of game and other animal species from one region to another, in accordance with their needs. Although the habitat requirements of our different species of game have not basically changed, man has changed the environments of these animals to such an extent that certain species have disappeared from certain regions. With imagination, ingenuity and a sufficiently enterprising spirit, farmers can in some cases adapt parts of their farms in such a way that they create a more natural and acceptable home for the wild animals in their vicinity.

THE NATURAL DISTRIBUTION OF SOUTH AFRICAN GAME

Protracted droughts, disease, predators and numerous other limiting factors, together with each species's free choice of the area most to its liking, have caused certain game species to settle in specific geographic regions over a period of centuries. However, owing to the historical development of our country, the present distribution patterns of game differ from those that prevailed a century or two ago. The establishment of breeding herds of certain types of game outside of their historical distribution areas has also contributed to the difficulty of providing an accurate and comprehensive indication of each species's historical and natural distribution areas. The table on p. 65 , which has been collated from different publications, does however offer a reasonably reliable indication of the natural homes of most of the indigenous game in South Africa.

Certain game can be found in areas not specified in the table. In most cases, these are probably isolated populations, or game imported to the area and released some years ago.The steenbok, duiker, klipspringer, mountain reedbuck and grey rhebok are some of the species that are distributed most widely throughout the country. The last three are, however, mainly restricted to mountains and rocky outcrops in the distribution areas given for them.

DIVERSITY OF GAME IN THE DIFFERENT PROVINCES

As far as diversity is concerned, the northern and eastern Transvaal are way ahead, with north-eastern Natal close behind. Then follow the western Transvaal and the northern Cape, and finally the rest of the country. This comparison is not necessarily valid for the numbers of game found, although in this respect the Transvaal once again beats the other provinces.

Some species of game were originally restricted to a single province. Thus the giraffe, tsessebe, sable antelope and roan antelope are characteristic of the Transvaal, while the Cape mountain zebra and bontebok are unique to the Cape. Other species do occur in more than one province, but can be concentrated chiefly in one province. Nyala, red duiker and blue duiker are, for example, especially common in Natal, while the Free State is predominantly the home of the black wildebeest.

The Cape mountain zebra is unique to the Cape Province, but also does well in mountainous areas elsewhere in the country.

SHRINKING DISTRIBUTION AREAS

The original distribution areas of most game species have shown an alarming decrease over the past few centuries. Eland and springbok have already been cited as species which can no longer even be successfully re-established in their original distribution areas, because adverse and limiting factors have been introduced into these areas which were apparently either absent previously or, at least, did not impose the same restrictions on these species in these areas. Buffalo that were previously found in the northern, eastern and southern Cape, must now, like the Addo elephants confined to the limited space of the Addo Elephant National Park, be protected because these larger animal species had to make way for agricultural and other development projects in adjacent areas. These few examples typify the fate of most of our other game species.

THE NATURAL DISTRIBUTION OF SOUTH AFRICAN ANTELOPE AND OTHER LARGER MAMMALS

SPECIES	TRANSVAAL				ORANGE FREE STATE				NATAL				CAPE PROVINCE			
	N.	E.	S.	W.	N.	E.	S.	W.	N.	E.	S.	W.	N.	E.	S.	W.
ANTELOPE																
Sable antelope	+	+														
Roan	+	+														
Gemsbok	+												+			
Eland	+	+						+				+	+			
Kudu (greater)	+	+		+					+	+			+	+	+	
Bushbuck	+	+		+					+	+	+	+		+	+	
Nyala	+	+							+	+						
Springbok			+	+	+	+	+	+					+	+		+
Impala	+	+		+					+	+						
Klipspringer	+	+		+			+	+	+		+	+	+	+	+	+
Suni		+							+	+						
Steenbok	+	+	+	+	+	+	+	+	+	+	+	+	+	+	+	+
Oribi		+	+				+		+	+	+	+	+	+		
Cape grysbok														+	+	
Sharpe's grysbok	+	+							+							
Common duiker	+	+	+	+	+	+	+	+	+	+	+	+	+	+	+	+
Red duiker		+								+						
Blue duiker										+				+		
Mountain reedbuck	+	+	+	+	+	+	+		+	+	+	+	+	+	+	+
Reedbuck	+	+		+					+	+	+	+				
Grey rhebok	+	+	+		+	+	+		+	+	+	+	+	+	+	+
Tsessebe	+	+														
Blesbok		+			+	+	+	+				+		+		
Bontebok															+	
Red hartebeest				+								+	+			
Waterbuck	+	+		+					+	+						
Black wildebeest			+	+	+	+	+	+					+			
Blue wildebeest	+	+		+					+	+			+			
CARNIVORES																
Cheetah	+	+		+					+	+			+			
Leopard	+	+		+					+	+			+	+	+	+
Lion	+	+							+	+			+			
Caracal	+	+	+	+	+	+	+	+	+	+	+	+	+	+	+	+
Serval	+	+		+								+				
African civet	+	+							+	+						
Aardwolf	+	+	+	+	+	+	+	+	+	+	+	+	+	+	+	+
Spotted hyena	+	+							+	+			+			
Brown hyena	+	+	+	+	+	+	+	+					+	+	+	
Wild dog	+	+							+	+			+			
Bat-eared fox	+		+	+	+	+	+	+					+	+	+	+
Cape fox			+	+	+	+	+	+				+	+	+		+
Side-striped jackal		+														
Black-backed jackal	+	+	+	+	+	+	+	+	+	+	+	+	+	+	+	+
OTHER LARGE MAMMALS																
African elephant	+	+		+					+	+				+		
Black rhinoceros		+							+	+				+		
White rhinoceros		+		+					+	+						
Burchell's zebra	+	+		+					+	+			+			
Cape mountain zebra														+	+	
African buffalo	+	+							+	+				+		
Giraffe	+	+							+	+						
Bushpig	+	+		+					+	+				+		
Warthog	+	+		+					+	+			+			
Antbear	+	+	+	+	+	+	+	+	+	+	+	+	+	+	+	+
Chacma baboon	+	+	+	+	+	+	+	+	+	+	+	+	+	+	+	+
Hippopotamus	+	+							+	+						

THE PREFERRED HABITAT AND FOOD TYPES OF SOUTH AFRICAN ANTELOPE

SPECIES	HABITAT	PREFERRED FOOD TYPES
ANTELOPE		
Sable antelope	Mixed savanna and grassveld. Near water.	Grass.
Roan	Savanna and grassveld. Near water.	Grass. (Feeds selectively.)
Gemsbok	Semi desert. Shrub and grassveld.	Grass. Also tsamma, bulbs and tubers.
Eland	Bushveld, savanna and grasslands.	Grass and leaves. Also fruit, bulbs and tubers.
Kudu (greater)	Bush and mountainous areas.	Leaves, twigs, pods and veld fruit.
Bushbuck	Thick bush, especially near water.	Leaves, twigs, pods and veld fruit.
Nyala	Thick bush and open bushveld. Near water.	Leaves, twigs, pods and veld fruit.
Springbok	Dry flats. Short grass, brush and thornveld.	Grass and leaves.
Impala	Bushveld and savanna. Near water.	Green grass (summer). Leaves and pods (winter).
Klipspringer	Rocky mountains and kopjes.	Grass and leaves.
Suni	Dry, densely vegetated areas. Sometimes along rivers.	Leaves.
Steenbok	Open grasslands. Independent of water.	Grass. Also leaves, roots and tubers.
Oribi	Short and open grassveld.	Grass.
Cape grysbok	Macchia, especially at the foothills of mountains.	Leaves and grass. Also veld fruit.
Sharpe's grysbok	Undulating veld and Acacia thickets.	Leaves and grass. Also veld fruit.
Common duiker	Open savanna.	Leaves, twigs and veld fruit.
Red duiker	Dense forests.	Leaves, twigs and veld fruit.
Blue duiker	Dense forests.	Leaves and veld fruit.
Mountain reedbuck	Mountain slopes and kopjes.	Grass and leaves.
Reedbuck	Grassveld, marshes and reed thickets. Near water.	Grass.
Grey rhebok	Mountain slopes and plateaus.	Grass.
Tsessebe	Savanna and open grassveld.	Grass.
Blesbok	Open grassveld.	Grass.
Bontebok	Macchia.	Grass.
Red hartebeest	Savanna and open grassveld.	Grass.
Waterbuck	Savanna and swamps. Near water.	Grass.
Black wildebeest	Open grassveld.	Grass. Prefers short grassveld.
Blue wildebeest	Savanna and open grasslands.	Grass. Prefers short grassveld.
OTHER LARGE MAMMALS		
African elephant	Varied, from deserts to forests.	Grass and leafy branches.
Black rhinoceros	Varied but prefers bushy areas.	Leaves of trees and shrubs.
White rhinoceros	Savanna and grassveld.	Grass. Preference for short grassveld.
Burchell's zebra	Savanna and open grasslands.	Grass. Also long grassveld.
Cape mountain zebra	Mountains. Near water.	Grass. Also long grassveld.
African buffalo	Bushveld, savanna and grasslands. Near water.	Grass. Also long grassveld.
Giraffe	Dry bushveld and savanna.	Leaves. Also twigs and pods.
Bushpig	Thickets, preferably near water.	Grass, leaves, roots and tubers.
Warthog	Open grass- and savanna-veld.	Grass.
Antbear	Varied, preferring sandy areas with termites.	Termites and ants.
Chacma baboon	Mountainous areas. Not very selective.	Varied plant and animal diet.
Hippopotamus	Suitable hippo pools near adequate grazing.	Grass.

In contrast to the shrinking distribution areas of most game species, game farmers, and in some cases certain conservation bodies, have with their enthusiastic efforts to distribute game proved that species such as the blesbok, impala and giraffe do particularly well when released in areas other than their historical distribution areas. One of the most surprising and illuminating findings continues to be the successful establishment of the lechwe, a semi-tropical water-loving antelope which is not even indigenous to the Republic, on a game farm in the vicinity of Harrismith in the Free State! As mentioned earlier, on game-proof farms it may for production reasons be necessary to abandon the policy of certain nature conservation departments of discouraging the reintroduction of game into areas other than their alleged historical distribution areas. Meaningful criteria should instead be based on more practical considerations, such as the ability of the species concerned to survive in a particular habitat and to make a contribution to animal production, the beneficial or detrimental effects that such an animal may have on its new environment and on other animal species occurring there, and last but not least, the animals' natural preferences as regards habitat.

THE HABITAT REQUIREMENTS AND FEEDING PREFERENCES OF GAME

Whereas the above-mentioned table and discussion refer to the geographical distribution areas of the different game species, an animal's habitat preferences have to do with the choice of the species concerned of a suitable type of environment (for example, bush, open grassveld, rocky outcrops or vlei areas) within the geographical area in which an animal finds itself. A suitable habitat satisfies all the animal's vital needs and should at all times offer adequate shelter, food and water and places and opportunities for all the animal's life functions.

The grazing and feeding habits of an animal and its disposition are usually reflected in its choice of habitat. Thus the timid bushbuck, which is predominantly a browser, will be found in well wooded areas, while wildebeest and Burchell's zebra, which are almost exclusively grazers and are of a more sociable disposition, will be found in herds on open grassveld.

The table on page 66 summarises the habitat preferences of the different game species and their principal sources of food.

ANTELOPE FOUND IN DENSE BUSH

Kudu, nyala, bushbuck, suni, red duiker and blue duiker are antelope that favour thickets. In suitable areas, farmers could do much to improve conditions for these antelope by saving dense bush near rivers and ravines and against mountain slopes, which are in any case generally inaccessible, from the bulldozers. It is almost unbelievable how much game still exists on certain farms in Natal in the "islands" of natural bush in between the sugar plantations. In the bushveld regions of our country, where bush encroachment creates considerable difficulties, great benefit can also be derived from keeping giraffe, kudu, nyala and bushbuck. Nyala generally thrive even in the dry bushveld areas of the north-western Transvaal, well beyond their natural distribution areas!

GAME SPECIES OF THE OPEN GRASSVELD

Just as the springbok, blesbok, black wildebeest and oribi are generally associated with the open grassveld of the higher-lying central and southern parts of the country, so the blue wildebeest

The common duiker occurs throughout the country in suitable habitats. Other species of antelope which are abundant in South Africa include the mountain reedbuck and grey rhebok, the steenbok and the klipspringer.

and Burchell's zebra and, to a certain extent, the tsessebe and roan antelope, are found on open grassveld in the denser parts of particularly the northern and eastern Transvaal and/or of North-eastern Natal. When game that prefers open grassveld is kept on predominantly densely wooded farms, one finds that the open parts of such farms are usually utilised more intensively. Blesbok and wildebeest, especially, are known to concentrate on small patches of short grassveld and gradually overgraze and trample these spots, while the rest of the farm is left relatively underutilised. Deforestation on suitable areas of the farm, mowing grass to create short grassveld conditions and the judicious burning of surplus grazing can assist in spreading the game out over a larger grazing area. Alternatively the over-grazed areas can in some cases be fenced off and used as capture corrals for surplus game. In cases where grazing game cannot efficiently utilise long grassveld and keep it short, the possibility of grazing cattle on surplus veld could also be considered.

INHABITANTS OF THE MOUNTAINS AND ROCKY OUTCROPS

Mountains and rocky terrain are excellently suited to mountain reedbuck and grey rhebok, klipspringer, kudu and mountain zebra. Impala, bushbuck, nyala and even waterbuck and Bur-chell's zebra also make good use of rocky territory.

In bushveld regions where kudu and other browsing game may become very thin and die from a shortage of adequate leaf fodder during the dry winter months, these animals generally do much better on farms that incorporate some mountains or rocky outcrops, or a section of river front, where they are able to have a source of green leaf fodder until quite late in the winter. Pros-pective game farmers would therefore be well advised to make the extra effort and, where possible, allow their game fences to run across the top of the mountain rather than exclude the moun-tain when fencing in the new farm. Farmers who are able to produce lucerne or other podplants, should also bear in mind that old antelope enjoy green leaves. During the dry winter months this important source of supplementary fodder can be very useful and may even save lives.

GAME FOUND IN TALL GRASSVELD

Game species that are readily found on tall grassveld and which utilise such veld are appropriately referred to as "bulk roughage feeders". Elephant, buffalo and zebra are examples of wild ani-mals which, like cattle, can thrive on tall grassveld. When sweet grassveld is available, these animals will give preference to it. Giraffe, hartebeest, eland, kudu, waterbuck, reedbuck, sable antelope, roan antelope, steenbok and oribi may also often be found on tall grassveld, but this does not mean that all of these species use the tall grassveld, as such. Game farms with large areas of tall sour grassveld are unsuitable for most species of game, and where game is nevertheless kept in such areas, the veld should be burnt judiciously, in accordance with a rotational system, or, where possible, mown. On such farms supplement-ary feeding will have to be considered during the dry winter months.

DESERT ANIMALS

The last category of game species which should be mentioned is animals such as the gemsbok, springbok, eland and red hartebeest, which are characteristic of the drier western parts of the country. These animals are remarkably resistant to drought and to varying degrees utilize veld fruits such as tsammas, and also dig for roots, bulbs and tubers to meet their moisture re-quirements. Whereas the red hartebeest generally manages to thrive, no matter where in the country it is established, erratic results are occasionally achieved with the re-establishment of eland, springbok and, to a certain extent, gemsbok. Farmers are therefore advised to make enquiries in their particular areas regarding the survival success of the mentioned animals before acquiring large numbers of these animals and releasing them on their farms. Alternatively, smaller breeding herds could initially be acquired on a trial basis.

In the Transvaal the Nature Conservation Division currently stipulates that a game farm must be at least 200 hectares in size, if a farmer wishes to keep eland or gemsbok on his farm. In the case of most other species, the restriction is 50 hectares per game species.

This does not, however, imply that some of the animal species could not, under favourable conditions, survive on smaller game farms, nor that the policy of the Nature Conservation Division in this regard might not, in time, be modified.

The above should give some indication of the game species that may occur in your area or which may be suited to it. Because conditions can vary from farm to farm in the same region, however, I should like to emphasize that it would be well worth the effort and expenditure to obtain expert advice concerning the suitability of each specific farm for specific game species before acquiring and releasing game on the farm.

ESTABLISHMENT OF ELEPHANT ON PRIVATE PROPERTY

The policy of the Chief Directorate for Nature Conservation regarding the establishment of elephant on private property is the following:

1. An electric fence, which complies with regulations, will be accepted for confining elephant to a farm.
2. Such an electric fence shall consist of at least 2 electrified wires with a diameter of not less than 2,44 mm and with a voltage of 6 000 volts or more.
3. The bottom wire must be placed at ground level and the other at the very top of the fence.
4. A standard game fence to which the electrified wires are attached will be acceptable.
5. The minimum size of the property shall be 2 000 ha. However, depending on individual circumstances, a smaller property may be acceptable, while a larger surface area may be required in other cases.
6. No permits will be issued for the release of elephant unless the following conditions are complied with:
    (a) The owner of the property shall take out an insurance policy to indemnify the public against damage caused by the elephants.
    (b) The owner accepts responsibility, in writing, for any possible damage which escaped elephants may cause.
    (c) If the farm is sold, the new owner must be notified of the particular conditions and must confirm, in writing, to the Administrator that he accepts these conditions.
    (d) The owner shall provide annual proof of his insurance policy.
    (e) If the insurance policy expires, or the new owner of the

property refuses to accept the conditions of ownership, he shall forfeit all rights to the animals and the fate of the elephants then rests with the Administrator.

In addition to the above stipulations, it is further required that:

7. (a) The Chief Directorate shall inspect the property to ascertain whether it is suitable for keeping elephant.

(b) At least two elephants, which have already been weaned, and in a sex ratio of one to one, shall be released on the property.

(c) The number of elephant allowed on the farm will depend on the carrying capacity of the property as decided by the Chief Directorate.

(d) It shall be decided, in consultation with the Chief Directorate, whether elephants may be replaced or new elephants be introduced after losses, providing that animals are not culled to keep young animals only.

(e) Owners must be aware that they will be held liable for escaped elephants as well as any damage caused by such animals.

(f) It is acceptable to keep elephant in smaller camps during the adaptation phase of their introduction to a new property.

Relocation permits will only be issued to those property owners who comply with the stipulations as laid down in paragraphs 6 (a - e) and 7 (a - f) and accept these in writing.

7. HERD BEHAVIOUR, MATING AND BREEDING SEASONS OF FARM GAME

The herd behaviour, mating times and lambing seasons of game varies from species to species. A synopsis of the social grouping, gestation periods, breeding seasons and life expectancies of our major game species is given and discussed in this chapter.

Information concerning our indigenous game species is readily available in a wide variety of books, theses and other scientific publications. When collating and summarising this information, one gradually comes to the conclusion that a great gap still exists for further and more reliable statistics relating to farm game. Much of the available information is unfortunately contradictory and possibly even unreliable. As far as possible, only the most reliable sources were used when compiling the table, and this information should therefore offer at least a reasonably representative overview of the relevant differences between species.

In the first place, it is important for the game farmer to know the mating season of a particular game species and when the calf or lamb harvest is due. These are the times of the year when the breeding herds should be disturbed as little as possible. The presence of lone bulls or rams or the size of bachelor herds during the mating season can, in the case of certain species, give an indication of relevant sex ratios and even sometimes offer a good opportunity for the removal of surplus bulls or rams from male herds when the mating season of the species concerned and the hunting season happen to coincide.

The social grouping and herd composition of the different game species change continuously from season to season. Impala, for example, will drive surplus rams from breeding herds during the mating season, while a greater degree of tolerance amongst the adult rams will be observed during the rest of the year. By contrast, the composition of the zebra's family group is more permanent, and a particular stallion may keep the same mares in his group for long periods. Some animals, such as the steenbok, the duiker species, the bushbuck and the klipspringer, are definite loners and prefer to live singly or, at the most, in pairs or in small groups. Impala, springbok, blesbok, hartebeest, gemsbok, wildebeest, zebra and numerous other species are herd animals, are usually observed together in large groups and are easier to keep in large numbers on game farms.

Notwithstanding the differences that may occur from time to time and from place to place, even amongst animals of the same species, the table on page 71 gives an indication of the general social grouping, approximate mating seasons, gestation periods and calving and lambing seasons of 37 species of game.

According to the table, twins may be born to impala, springbok, the common duiker and even the giraffe. This is an exceptional occurrence with most of our indigenous game species, and although it is not always indicated in the literature and hence not in the table either, other animals may also produce twins.

HERD FORMATION

Although it is not justified to draw generalised conclusions, a basic correlation does seem to exist between the social habits of the larger and more sociable animals, on the one hand, and the smaller and/or more timid and individualistic antelope on the other.

In the case of herd animals of the larger species, one usually finds breeding herds consisting mainly of female animals and lone bulls or rams, or bachelor herds. This social grouping is, for example, reasonably characteristic of impala, springbok, blesbok, bontebok, hartebeest, wildebeest and many other species.

Steenbok, grysbok, oribi, suni, klipspringer and the duiker — in other words the very small antelope — as well as some of the other antelope, such as the bushbuck, reedbuck and rhebok, tend to live alone, and especially during the mating season, to form pairs. When groups are formed, particularly by the last three species, the groups are usually very small.

INTERMIXING OF SPECIES

Although most game species do not readily mix with other species (except at waterholes), most people are familiar with the peculiar affinity wildebeest and zebra have for each other's company. Lone eland and roan antelope bulls also often join herds of other game, while red hartebeest bulls display a tendency to drive out blesbok rams and even to interbreed with blesbok.

NURSERIES

An interesting phenomenon is the nurseries formed by young members of certain antelope species. Up to thirty and more young impala lambs can, for example, be left in the care of one or two impala ewes while the other ewes go to drink water. Waterbuck calves often also form groups once they are weaned. Sometimes, when a herd of eland is being pursued through dense bush, the calves will suddenly and imperceptibly separate from the herd and hide together in a thicket, while the rest of the herd will continue to flee, to all appearances quite unconcerned.

INTOLERANCE IN BULLS AND RAMS

The aggressiveness of bulls and rams of some game species in particular can occasionally cause problems on game farms. Waterbuck and gemsbok bulls are examples of animals which are extremely intolerant towards other bulls of the same species, and which could try to eliminate rivals, especially on small game farms.

Mutual intolerance seems to become particularly problematic when too many animals are kept on a small farm area. Under such conditions, for example, a tendency has been noted amongst blue and black wildebeest to attack and kill calves and weaker individuals, even from their own herds.

SEXUAL MATURITY

Reliable information concerning the age at which game animals become sexually mature is not generally available.

A blesbok ram can alledgedly mate successfully from the age of one-and-a-half to two-and-a-half years. Blesbok ewes become sexually mature at approximately the same age. Red hartebeest bulls actively participate in breeding activities from the age of three years, while the heifers become sexually mature during their second year. An eland heifer should start calving round about her second or third year, and is theoretically able to produce a calf every subsequent year. Blue wildebeest bulls can serve cows when they are two-and-a-half years old, but only begin to participate actively in mating activities from their third year. Most blue wildebeest heifers are sexually mature at the age of 15 months, and begin to calve from their second year. The giraffe develops somewhat more slowly, and the heifers are only reported to be sexually mature at the age of 3 to 4 years.

MATING AND BREEDING SEASONS

The mating seasons of game are seldom specified in the literature. Taking into consideration the lambing and calving seasons of the different game species and their respective gestation periods, mating seasons have been estimated and for convenience included in the table. Mating seasons can vary from year to year and from area to area in the case of certain species.

Some game species, such as the impala, blesbok and blue wildebeest, have relatively easily defined mating and lambing or calving seasons. Species such as the steenbok, reedbuck and giraffe lamb or calve throughout the year, while the small antelope can lamb at any time of the year, but nevertheless seem to produce their young during certain peak seasons. In the case of the waterbuck and the springbok, there even appears to be a tendency to breed during two different seasons, namely spring and autumn. Most other animals calve or lamb in spring or summer, when sufficient water and grazing are generally available.

The gestation periods of game vary considerably. A glance at the table reveals a tendency for the smaller species to have shorter gestation periods, and the larger ones to have longer gestation periods. Most small antelope, up to the size of an impala or a bushbuck, have gestation periods of approximately 6 to 7 months. The springbok's gestation period of about five-and-a-half to six months is particularly short for an antelope of this

THE SOCIAL GROUPING AND BREEDING DATA OF SOUTH AFRICAN GAME SPECIES					
SPECIES	**SOCIAL GROUPING**	**MATING SEASON**	**GESTATION (DAYS)**	**BREEDING SEASON**	**NO OF YOUNG**
ANTELOPE Sable antelope	Single bulls. Male herds. Breeding herds.	Autumn and winter.	261-281	Peak in summer.	1
Roan	Single bulls or herds.	Autumn and winter.	268-280	Peak in summer.	1
Gemsbok	Single or herds.	Mainly autumn.	261-275	Peak in summer.	1
Eland	Single or herds.	Esp. Dec - Jan.	254-277	Peak in spring.	1
Kudu (greater)	Single bulls. Male herds. Breeding herds.	Esp. winter.	210-240	Mainly late summer.	1
Bushbuck	Single, pairs or females with lambs.	Esp. winter.	180	Peak in summer.	1
Nyala	Single or small herds.	Esp. summer and autumn.	252	Peak in spring.	1
Springbok	Single rams. Male and breeding herds.	March - May, Oct.	165-180	Aug. - Nov., April.	1 (2)
Impala	Single rams. Male herds. Breeding herds.	End April - July.	195-200	Nov. - Jan.	1 (2)
Klipspringer	Single, pairs or small groups.	Esp. winter.	210-215	Peak in summer.	1
Suni	Single, pairs or small groups.	Winter to spring.	130-180	Peak in summer.	1

SPECIES	SOCIAL GROUPING	MATING SEASON	GESTATION (DAYS)	BREEDING SEASON	NO OF YOUNG
Steenbok	Single, pairs (mating season) or female with lamb.	All year.	170	All year.	1
Oribi	Single, pairs or small groups.	Esp. winter.	195-210	Peak in summer.	1
Cape grysbok	Single, pairs (mating season) or female with lamb.	Autumn.	175-185	Spring.	1
Sharpe's grysbok	Single, pairs (mating season) or female with lamb.	Esp. winter.	175-185	Peak in summer.	1
Common duiker	Single or pairs.	Esp. winter.	210	Peak in summer.	1 (2)
Red duiker	Single, pairs or small groups.	—	—	Peak in summer.	1
Blue duiker	Single, pairs or small groups.	All year. (Captivity)	± 153	Peak in summer.	1
Mountain reedbuck	Single or small herds.	Autumn and winter.	223-240	Peak in summer.	1
Reedbuck	Single, pairs or small herds.	All year.	235-240	All year.	1
Grey rhebok	Single or small herds.	Esp. summer.	245-260	Peak in spring.	1
Tsessebe	Single bulls. Herds.	Summer.	235-245	Peak in spring.	1
Blesbok	Single rams. Male herds. Breeding herds.	March - April.	270	Nov. - Dec.	1
Bontebok	Single rams. Male herds. Breeding herds.	Dec. - Feb.	235	Aug. - Oct.	1
Red hartebeest	Single bulls. Male herds. Breeding herds.	Esp. Feb. - March.	238-242	Esp. Oct - Nov.	1
Waterbuck	Single or herds.	All year.	235-250	Peak in spring and autumn.	1
Black wildebeest	Single bulls or herds.	Autumn and winter.	240-260	Peak in summer.	1
Blue wildebeest	Single bulls or herds.	Autumn and winter.	255-260	Summer.	1

SPECIES	SOCIAL GROUPING	MATING SEASON	GESTATION (DAYS)	BREEDING SEASON	NO OF YOUNG
OTHER LARGE MAMMALS					
African elephant	Solitary bulls. Bull and breeding herds.	Throughout year.	660-720	Throughout year.	1 (2)
White rhinoceros	Solitary. Small groups.	Throughout year.	480-490	Throughout year.	1
Burchell's zebra	One or more stallions. Family groups.	Esp. Jan - March.	371	Esp. Jan - March.	1
Cape mountain zebra	One or more stallions. Family groups.	Esp. Sept. — Feb.	364	Esp. Sept. — Feb.	1
African buffalo	One or more bulls. Breeding herds.	Esp. March — May.	320-330	Esp. Jan — April.	1
Giraffe	Single or groups.	All year.	450	All year.	1 (2)
Bushpig	Solitary. Groups.	—	—	Mainly in summer.	Up to 8 (Av. 3-4)
Warthog	Solitary. Family groups.	Round about winter.	167-175	Mainly September to December.	Up to 8 (Av. 3)
Hippopotamus	Sociable.	Throughout year.	225-257	Throughout year.	1

size. In the case of antelope large than those mentioned above, for example the reedbuck, kudu, waterbuck and hartebeest, the gestation period is approximately 7 to 8 months, and the very large antelope, such as the eland and roan antelope have gestation periods of approximately 9 months. In the case of the larger hoofed animals the gestation periods are even longer, namely 11 months for the buffalo and approximately 15 months for the giraffe. The elephant cow, as might be expected, has to wait the longest for her calf — anything between 22 and 24 months! Exceptions do occur, however, and gestation periods do not always increase proportionally to the size of the animal. For example, the hippopotamus has a gestation period of only 8 months.

LIFE SPAN OF DIFFERENT GAME SPECIES

Finally, a few statistics indicating the estimated life span of the different game species. The following ages have been recorded for individual animals: steenbok and blue duiker — 6 years; klipspringer and grey duiker — 8 years; grey rhebok and reedbuck — 9 years; springbok — 10 years; blesbok, bontebok, bushbuck, mountain reedbuck and common duiker — 12 years; oribi — 13 years; impala — 14 years; tsessebe, red hartebeest, kudu, nyala and red duiker — 15 years; waterbuck — 16 years; eland and sable antelope — 18 years; roan antelope — 19 years; gemsbok, blue wildebeest and black wildebeest — 20 years; Burchell's zebra — 22 years; giraffe 24 years; and buffalo 25 years. These life spans have mostly been recorded in zoos or for tame animals, and do not mean that animals may not live to be much older. However, in nature animals generally do not survive as long as in captivity. Diseases and predators ensure that the maximum average ages of veld animals are considerably lower than those of animals that have been cared for and protected in captivity.

8. GAME CAPTURE TECHNIQUES — CROSSBOWS, DART GUNS AND GAME CAPTURE DRUGS

It is usually the ideal of every game farmer to own a dart gun. All dart guns are not, however, equally suited to capturing farm game. The basic requirements for a suitable dart gun and the different types of darts that can be used are discussed below.

Dart syringes can be fired or projected by means of a variety of crossbows, dart guns, dart pistols and even specially designed blow pipes.

THE CROSSBOW

The Van Rooyen crossbow with a tension of 100+ kilograms on the string and a remarkably accurate aperture sight has been used for many years, and is definitely one of the most suitable crossbows for the capture of large game, in particular. This crossbow is drawn by means of a special lever, while a safety catch ensures the safe transport of the drawn bow.

The long range and silent manner in which the darts are launched, together with the resulting reduced disturbance to the animals, are just a few of the advantages of the crossbow. Cartridge-type detonators are also not required to fire the darts or to activate the syringe mechanism, which makes the use of the crossbow very economical. Furthermore, a firearm license is not a prerequisite for owning a crossbow.

Although with a good crossbow it is possible to shoot very accurately up to a distance of approximately 80 to 100 metres,

the distance must be measured beforehand using a special optic range finder, and the sight adjusted accordingly. Thus valuable time is lost and the animal often flees before the dart can be fired.

Although the dart travels at approximately 90 metres per second, this is occasionally not fast enough to hit an animal leaping out of its path. It is claimed that gemsbok have even in a few instances shielded their bodies from the darts with a slashing movement of their horns. The crossbow is furthermore much clumsier to handle than a rifle and can only with considerable difficulty be fired through the window of a vehicle or from a helicopter. The trajectory of the dart is particularly high, and in densely wooded areas the dart can quite easily end up in a branch.

Special long darts are used in conjunction with the crossbow. The Van Rooyen bow darts are perfectly balanced and a very interesting technique is used to inject the drug into the animal once the target has been hit. Diluted acetic acid and a bicarbonate-of-soda solution, placed in separate compartments in the tail end of the dart during the loading process, mix when the movable valve separating the two fluids opens from the impact of the dart striking the animal. Carbon dioxide, formed when the bicarbonate of soda and acetic acid mix, causes sufficient pressure behind the rubber plunger of the syringe to inject all the drug contained in the cylinder in front of the plunger into the animal within a fraction of a second.

All crossbows and dart guns are not equally suitable for game capture. A good crossbow may be very accurate, but a suitable dart gun is often a better option.

South Africa is a leader in the development of new game capture equipment and techniques. With the exception of the imported Palmer Cap-chur gun (third from the top), which is commercially available, the dart guns on the photograph were all developed by Mr Gert van Rooyen.

The crossbow has largely fallen into disuse and has been replaced by improved dart guns, and all sorts of dart syringes have been developed and perfected for the capture, inoculation, culling or marking of game. Once again, Mr van Rooyen, who was employed by the National Parks Board, has been responsible for the greatest progress in producing suitable dart guns and syringes.

DART GUNS AND PISTOLS

Dart guns developed and manufactured by the National Parks Board for its own use are unfortunately not available commercially. Certain other types are less well known and are sometimes hard to find. Let us review the basic requirements that must be met by a good dart gun or pistol:

1. Range: When game must be darted under veld conditions, the dart must be capable of hitting the animal over the longest possible distance. It is unfortunately true that a gun with excessive impact can cause great damage over long distances. Over shorter distances or with smaller game, the dart can penetrate too deeply, with the dart even penetrating right into the animal's body. Fractures, severe wounding and even death can be the result. I know of a farmer who fired the first dart from his new dart gun right through his expensive race horse. Check with your firearms dealer, therefore, that the dart gun you are buying is suited to your purpose. Most good dart guns will hit an average-sized antelope over approximately 30 to 70 metres. Elephant, rhino, buffalo and other large animals with thick hides can be darted efficiently up to a distance of approximately 100 metres.

2. Adjustability: Special cylindrical metal adaptors can be made to fit into the back of the dart gun's barrel to increase or decrease the impact of the gun. The same effect can be

achieved by using blank cartridges with stronger or weaker charges. Unfortunately the charges of commercial cartridge-type detonators, even those of the same size, are not always exactly the same, with resulting lower accuracy in the poorer quality cartridges. Good blank cartridges are available from either Ramset Tools or from Swartklip Products (Pty) (Ltd) in Cape Town. A permit may be required to purchase these cartridges.

3. Gas or powder charge: Dart guns and pistols which operate by means of compressed air are usually highly suitable for use on captive animals. The possibility of the dart penetrating the animal's body is normally reduced, and gas rifles and pistols are therefore especially suitable for use on smaller animals and animals with thin skins. The gas pistol is particularly easy to handle and is recommended when an animal must be darted through the bars of a cage. Unfortunately the accuracy of gas rifles and pistols is affected by the ambient temperature. On a very hot day, the gas pressure, and consequently also impact, is increased. On a cold day, the opposite effect occurs, and the dart may occasionally be shot into the ground a few metres from the gun. With the exception of smaller game such as steenbok and oribi, which can coincidentally be shot from close by, or fleeing animals such as rhino which can be darted from a pursuing vehicle over a very short distance, the use of weapons of this type is rather limited in the veld.

Dart guns using cartridge-type detonators to fire darts are more commonly used under veld conditions. The Palmer 32-bore Cap-chur gun, which is imported from America and can be

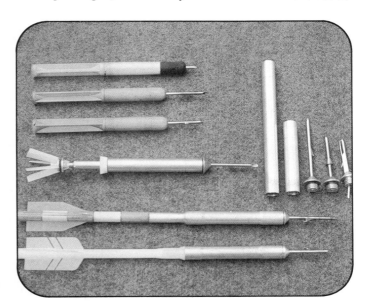

Different types of dart syringes: The top three darts are made of durable plastic. The topmost one has a coloured stain in the rubber bulb around the needle which can be used to mark an animal that has been hit. The bottom two are for use with a crossbow.

Mr Gert van Rooyen, veteran designer and manufacturer of game capture equipment with one of his dart guns that can hold several darts in the magazine.

obtained from Photo Agencies in Johannesburg, serves as a good example. Once again it may be necessary to fit the gun with the necessary adaptors to allow equally safe functioning over short as well as long distances.

The Sabi 32-bore semi-automatic dart gun represents a further development in the perfection of game capture apparatus. This gun does not only have an adjustable telescopic sight, but has also been equipped with an adjustable gas chamber which can allow accurate firing over between 5 and 100 metres, without the usual risk of the dart syringe fatally injuring an animal that has to be darted over a short distance. Darts can be fired in rapid succession and on a wind-calm day this unique gun can achieve a dart grouping of 150 millimetres over a distance of 75 metres. This gun, as well as the Sabi plastic darts, can be obtained from Dr Blackie Swart at Box 3930, Nelspruit, 1200.

A good dart gun can presently be purchased for approximately R2 500 to R3 500. Shotguns can also be modified and converted to dart guns, but the results achieved are often erratic. Although this may, therefore, seem to be the cheapest way of obtaining a dart gun, an inferior product and unsatisfactory results, such as the loss of a single animal, may eventually prove this to be false economy. It remains the responsibility of the firearms dealer to prove the effectiveness of any rifle he is selling, and with some guarantee from him it is unlikely that you will make an unnecessary and expensive error.

IMMOBILISING DARTS

Different dart types are available for the 32-bore drug dart guns and pistols. Cap-chur metal syringes, also obtainable from Photo Agencies, are normally suitable, especially if the animals have to be darted over average and short distances and provided that the needles of the dart syringes have been reinforced where these meet the syringe cylinder. All darts should satisfy the following requirements:

1. Accuracy: The stability of a loaded dart syringe, the type of tailpiece used (flax plumes, tail-fins, etc,) and various other factors determine the accuracy of a specific type of dart. Naturally the rifle or pistol from which the dart is fired can also influence the directional accuracy of a dart. For the layman, the best criterion will probably always be the end result, and therefore a satisfactory demonstration of a rifle or pistol and darts should precede the purchase of any equipment.

2. Capacity: Modern game capture drugs are exceptionally powerful and the necessary doses can be administered in incredibly small volumes of liquid solutions, even in the case of elephants and other large animals. For most game, a dart syringe with a capacity of 1 to 2 millilitres is adequate. When capturing medium-sized game and small game, and for inoculating game using the dart syringe method, a 1 millilitre dart syringe is generally big enough. Dart syringes with a capacity of 20 millilitres of fluid and more may also be used, but not without sacrificing range and accuracy. These large darts are used especially where large doses of medicine have to be administered to sick animals in captivity or where physical handling of the animals should best be avoided.

3. Durability: Even metal syringes can become so damaged after repeated use that they have to be discarded. Modern dart syringes, made from high-tensile plastic, are remarkably durable. Although most types of dart syringe are re-usable, a cheaper disposable vaccination dart is made by the National Parks Board for inoculation purposes. The price of metal game capture darts with a capacity of 1 to 3 millilitres is currently in the region of R50,00 to R80,00 per dart.

4. Injecting mechanism: In some dart syringes the syringe plunger is still, like in crossbow darts, activated by means of compressed carbon dioxide. The plungers of Cap-chur darts and certain other types of dart are, however, activated by the explosion of a detonator placed in the hollow part at the back of the rubber plunger. A loose weight which is normally held in place by a small spring in the back section of the detonator is impelled forward by the impact of the dart hitting the animal. This metal weight then strikes the powder charge in the front section of the detonator, which explodes and causes the drug to be injected. Detonators with different charges are obtainable from Photo Agencies. The "5 through 10" detonators should be used for syringes larger than 5 millilitres. For syringes smaller than 3 millilitres the "1 through 3" detonators are recommended. The more powerful charge can also be used when a smaller self-ejecting ("uitval") syringe with retractable barbs is used for inoculation purposes, for example. The smaller syringes are, however, incapable of withstanding repeated use together with the more powerful detonators and the syringe cylinders will consequently begin to become distended and unusable.

5. Needles: The dart syringe strikes the animal so hard that a dart with a smooth needle usually bounces back and drops to the ground immediately. This may even happen before the full dose has been injected. In the case of elephant and other

thick-skinned animals, a dart with a smooth needle can occasionally remain in the animal for a short while.

A sophisticated syringe designed by Mr Gert van Rooyen has retractable barbs which fold into the needle once the injection has been completed. The dart syringe thus automatically drops off immediately after the injection. Animals struck by a self-ejecting dart usually do not run very far after the injection, since they are not constantly irritated by a dart that they can see and feel.

Non-retractable barbs or metal ridges on the needle shaft of the dart may ensure that the dart syringe remains in position long enough for the drug to be injected fully. Barbs are more effective for use on most game species than ridges on the needle shaft, and are generally used in cases where the darts have to be repeatedly retrieved and re-used.

For thin-skinned animals such as impala and zebra the barbs are welded to the needle shaft close to the tip so that the tip of the dart can withdraw slightly once the drug has been administered. Thus the running animal is subsequently hurt less by the suspended, swinging dart.

For thick-skinned animals such as elephant and rhino only a ridge is required on the needle shaft to ensure that the dart syringe does not fall out on its own and that all the fluid is injected sufficiently deeply under the skin, into a muscle. In the past barbs were used for these animals, but removal of the dart syringes was considerably hampered as a result.

The length of the dart needle is naturally very important. A needle that is too long could unnecessarily and fatally injure smaller game, while a needle that is too short may be incapable of penetrating the skin of larger species. For small and medium game, dart needles with lengths ranging from approximately 3,0 to 3,5 centimetres are preferred, depending on the species and size of the animal. For buffalo the needles must be at least 4,5 cm and for elephant 6,5 cm in length.

In the case of certain species such as zebra, a needle with an opening at the front end is occasionally plugged by skin when the dart needle penetrates the skin. When this happens the drug cannot be injected and the dart syringe may even explode owing to the high pressure in the syringe's cylinder. To overcome this problem the front tip can be welded closed and small holes drilled along the shaft and near the tip of the needle. Alternatively the needle opening at the tip can be slightly compressed into an oval shape or a round piece of metal welded into the opening so as to prevent bits of skin from entering but without hindering the injection of the drug.

HOW TO USE YOUR DART GUN

The dart gun can be a dangerous weapon in the hands of an inexperienced or negligent operator. Some capture drugs are highly poisonous and extreme caution should therefore be exercised in order to prevent accidents. This section has been included for the convenience of those who do not know how to operate a dart gun, e.g. new farmers, students and farm managers, but it must be stressed that game capture with a dart gun is a highly specialised form of animal anaesthesia and should only be attempted under the direct supervision of a qualified veterinarian.

Although some of the following recommendations may seem so commonsensical that they might not even be considered worth mentioning, they should all be strictly adhered to if you want to make the best use of your new dart gun. Instructions and precautions, listed, are explained with diagrams. The powder charged Palmer Cap-chur gun and Cap-chur dart syringes are used as examples for the purpose of this discussion:

FILLING AND HANDLING OF THE DARTS

The different parts of the dart syringe, stored separately in suitable containers, are assembled as follows: lubricate the rubber plunger (no. 3) around its perimeter with silicone grease. Then push it with a suitable (preferably glass) rod through the barrel of the syringe (no. 2) a few times until it slips through smoothly and easily. Push the plunger into the dart cylinder with its concave opening protruding slightly at one end of the cylinder. Insert a 'one through 3 cc' detonator (no. 4) for small (up to 3 ml) or a 'one through 10 cc' detonator for larger syringes, into the hollow part of the plunger. Screw the tailpiece (no. 5) on, rest the syringe upright in a suitable container and prepare to fill it with the necessary drugs. Wear disposable plastic gloves when handling the capture drugs, as they may be absorbed through unprotected skin with fatal results.

Calculate the correct dosage (s) of the drug (s) to be used, and use a clean, disposable 1 ml tuberculin syringe (marked in hundred 0,01 graduations) to accurately measure the required quantities. Dosages are usually indicated in milligrams (mg) but measured in millilitres (ml). If a buffalo bull would, for instance, require 60mg of Fentanyl (Janssen Pharm.) and the Fentanyl has been dissolved at a concentration of 40mg/ml, 1,5ml of Fentanyl (100 + 50 graduations on the tuberculin syringe) would be required. If 100 mg xylazine hydrochloride (Rompun, Bayer), at a concentration of 200 mg/ml, has to be used to adequately calm the animal, 0,5 ml (50 graduations of the tuberculin syringe) must be added.

Never leave empty bottles or bottles containing drugs within reach of children or uninformed persons. Keep remaining stocks of drugs safely locked away in a cool place.

Destroy or properly clean used syringes. A contaminated syringe could be a highly dangerous tool in the hands of, for instance, children who might like to play with it.

Always fill the empty space in the dart syringe with sterile water or a suitable solvent of one of the drugs used. The dart syringe must be full to stabilise its flight.

Screw the needle (no. 1) on. A bit of silicone grease, used to seal the needle opening, can later serve as a useful indication of possible leakage of drugs through the needle's end — a problem of particular importance on hot days.

Never point a filled dart at anybody and keep and transport it in a suitable, closed container, well padded to prevent the detonating mechanism in the dart from going off whilst driving over bumpy roads and rough terrain. Keep the dart box and drugs in a cool place at all times.

LOADING THE GUN

Depending on circumstances, the dart (s) may only be filled with drugs after the capture site is reached and the size and condition of the particular animal to be darted has been evaluated.

A dart should only be placed in the barrel once you are reasonably sure that you will use it within the next minute or so.

The correct adaptor (long, medium or short distance type) should then be placed into the barrel, behind the dart.

Fit a blank cartridge with the correct charge into the tailpiece of the adaptor. Too powerful a charge may project the dart over or right into the animal's body while a weak charge may not even be adequate to allow the dart to reach its target. It is strongly recommended that you practise using your dart gun and become familiar with it before you attempt to dart a wild animal.

The blank cartridges, used to propel the dart syringes, and the detonators, placed into the dart syringes to expel the drug on impact, may fail to function at a critical stage of your operation. This is usually due to dampness of the explosive. Try to prevent such failures by always storing the detonating cartridges in tightly closed containers, containing desiccated silica gel granules or some other suitable hygroscopic or moisture absorbing chemical. Leaving the detonators in the hot sun, shortly before use, may also help to overcome this problem.

Don't cock the dart gun before you are ready to fire the shot and never, but never point a loaded dart gun at anybody !

If the animal runs away too soon, as so often happens, don't forget to uncock the gun immediately.

Preferably remove the dart by gently pushing it out from behind with a ramrod. Obviously, the dart should not be allowed to drop out of the barrel onto the ground as the detonating mechanism may go off, squirting the contents of the dart all over the place.

GETTING CLOSE ENOUGH

As the markman has to get pretty close to the animal, dart gun hunting demands exceptional hunting skill. Hiding at a preselected spot, or driving slowly closer to relatively tame animals with a vehicle that they are used to, may also enable you to get to the correct distance.

In a smallish camp the marksman may hide close to a fence or a corner of the camp and wait for the animal(s) to be slowly moved towards him. It is generally advisable to hide in such a position so that you will eventually not have to shoot towards the fence. Because of the relatively slow travelling speed of the dart, an animal moving past you along the fence, will too often be hit behind the aiming point. It is better to hide closer to the fence so that you are able to dart the approaching animal from the front, in the neck or brisket. It is, however, generally not advisable to try to dart a moving animal. A low pitched whistle, or a handkerchief hidden in the grass in the animal's pathway, may stop it for a second or two, presenting you with a better opportunity and an easier target.

Loaded and used dart syringes must be handled with extreme care. The lethal contents of a loaded dart can explode in someone's face if the dart accidentally falls or knocks against something. The barrel of the dart gun must be cleaned regularly in between shots and damaged darts should not be used under any circumstances. When an animal is darted from a moving vehicle and the dart becomes lodged in the barrel, some of the drug may escape from the barrel in the form of a fine mist and be inhaled by the passengers, possibly with fatal consequences.

After many hours of stalking, hiding, sweating and really working hard for your animal, one becomes terribly desperate to pull that trigger. Never do it before you are absolutely certain that you will hit the animal in the right place.

WHERE TO AIM

It is very important to know where to dart an animal. Always go for thick muscle and avoid the animal's head, thorax, abdomen, the perineal area (below the tail) and other parts of the body with superficial bones, nerves or bloodvessels, as illustrated. Larger

animals such as buffalo or giraffe can be darted in the neck. The thick muscle of the upper thighs offer an ideal target from behind, especially when fleeing buffalo or rhino have to be darted from a pursuing vehicle. Ideal darting sites are indicated in dark red on the diagram. Parts of the animal's body to be avoided (marked in light red) are:

From the front: the head (1), trachea or windpipe (2), jugular veins and underlying carotid arteries (3) and the heart (4) of small animals in particular or when long needles are used.

From the side: the head (1), vertebral column in the upper neck (2), superficial bony spine of the scapula (3), heart (4), thorax (5), abdomen (6), flanks (7) or limbs (8).

From behind: the tail or perineal region. Zebra should never be darted from behind as the dart may penetrate too deeply. In addition dart syringes are often deflected when striking the rounded, outer (lateral) parts of the buttocks.

REMOVAL OF THE DART

Gently pull the dart to slightly raise the skin directly above the needle barb. Carefully make a 1 cm long incision over the raised area to release the barb and remove the dart.

Dangerous amounts of capture drugs may stick to the dart and needle. It is therefore advisable to handle the dart carefully, to wrap it in a plastic bag and to put it in a safe place until it can be washed and packed away. At this stage all the attention is usually focused on the animal and the game catcher too often leaves the dart lying about, where inquisitive people are tempted to pick it up for a closer look.

When the target is missed, a dart syringe which lands on soft ground or in grass may still contain all of the drug. It is advisable to discard the contents and to keep these darts in a safe place as well.

Dart syringes seem to have a special affinity for trees. Some marksmen seem to find it much easier to stick a dart into a tree trunk instead of the real target. Never attempt to pull a syringe from a tree before unscrewing the tailpiece and releasing the built-up pressure, caused by the detonating mechanism behind the plunger. If not, a syringe full of deadly drugs may explode in your face !

When dismantling darts for cleaning, it is also a good and safe practice to unscrew the tailpieces of the darts first, before removing the needle ends. A needle plugged with animal skin and bone, could also result in built-up pressure in the syringe and the drugs may squirt out if the needle is taken off first.

AFTER A SUCCESSFUL DAY

Use disposable plastic gloves when washing the darts and do not attempt to blow through blocked needles.

Paper towelling is very useful for the cleaning and drying of darts. A thin roll of paper towel, pulled through the dart cylinder, is particularly useful to remove remaining dirt and to dry the cylinder.

Clean your dart gun in the same way that you would clean any other rifle.

Dart guns and pistols are considered to be firearms by law, and the same rules and regulations regarding safe keeping are applicable.

OTHER APPARATUS AND TECHNIQUES

For drugging wild animals in cages or in very small enclosures, a home-made type of dart syringe can be fired by means of a blow-pipe.

Animals in transporting crates and in trucks can also be injected by means of a specially extended hand-held pole syringe. The syringe can be mounted on the end of a long handle or, alternatively, the syringe's needle can be especially lengthened and reinforced by a metal tube. These manual syringes are useful for administering worm remedies and medication, but they are usually not accurate enough for injecting precise doses of drugs.

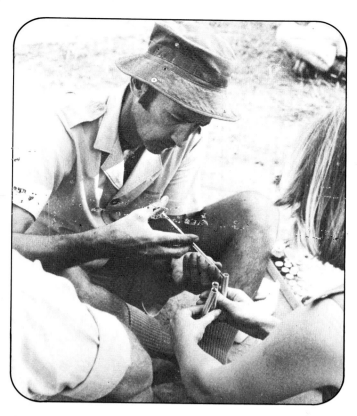

Game capture drugs must be measured out very accurately using small tuberculin syringes.

GAME CAPTURE DRUGS

Ten milligrams — approximately one four hundredth of the contents of a teaspoon — of a certain game capture drug, dissolved in a quarter teaspoon of water, is sufficient to immobilise a seven-ton elephant for two hours. Less than a drop of this substance can be fatal to humans if it is absorbed through the skin. Certain other drugs are addictive to humans and therefore stringent legal control is exercised over these. The uses of the most important game capture drugs will now be discussed briefly.

DOSAGES OF THE MOST IMPORTANT GAME CAPTURE DRUGS
(Dosages in milligram)

Species	M 99	Fentanyl	Rompun	Azaperone	Acetyl-promazine	M285	M5050	Lethidrone	Narcan
Impala	0,4 - 1,0	8 - 10	20 - 30	25 - 40	5 - 10	1 - 2	1	50	1 - 2
Springbok	0,4 - 1,0	8 - 10	20	25	5 - 10	1 - 2	1	50	1 - 2
Blesbok	1,0 - 2,0	15 - 30	—	25 - 50	—	3 - 5	2 - 5	50	2 - 4
Bontebok	1,0 - 2,0	15 - 30	—	25 - 50	—	3 - 5	2 - 5	50	2 - 4
Common duiker	0,3 - 0,6	5 - 7	15	25	5	1 - 2	0,6 - 0,8	25	1
Tsessebe	2,0 - 4,0	30 - 40	20 - 30	100	—	3 - 5	5 - 8	50 - 75	5
Red hartebeest	2,0 - 4,0	30 - 40	15 - 30	100	—	5 - 6	4 - 6	75 - 100	5
Eland	4,0 - 8,0	50 - 90	100 - 300	200 - 300	—	10 - 15	8 - 15	150 - 250	10
Gemsbok	3,0 - 5,0	—	20 - 40	50 - 100	—	10 - 12	6 - 8	100 - 150	6 - 10
Kudu	3,0 - 5,0	20 - 60	50 - 100	50 - 100	—	5 - 10	6 - 8	100 - 150	5 - 6
Bushbuck	0,8 - 2,0	8 - 20	10 - 20	50	—	3 - 4	1 - 2	50 - 75	3 - 5
Nyala	1,0 - 3,0	10 - 30	15 - 30	75	—	3 - 4	2 - 3	50 - 75	2 - 3
Waterbuck	3,0 - 6,0	—	30 - 50	100 - 150	3 - 5	6 - 12	6 - 8	100 - 150	5 - 7
Reedbuck	1,0 - 2,0	10 - 25	20	50	—	2 - 3	1 - 2	50	2 - 4
Mountain reedbuck	0,3 - 1,0	8 - 15	15	30	—	1 - 2	1	50	1 - 2
Grey rhebok	0,3 - 0,8	8 - 10	12	30	—	1 - 2	1	50	1 - 2
Blue wildebeest	2,0 - 3,0	20 - 30	—	50	20	6 - 8	5 - 6	100	5
Black wildebeest	1,5 - 2,0	15 - 25	—	50	15	5 - 6	3 - 5	75 - 100	2 - 4
Burchell's zebra	2,0 - 4,0	—	—	200	20	7 - 10	6	150 - 200	3 - 5
Cape mountain zebra	2,0 - 3,0	—	—	200	20	4 - 6	3	150 - 200	3 - 5
Buffalo	4,0 - 8,0	50 - 80	100	100 - 150	20 - 40	10 - 15	10 - 20	200 - 450	10
Giraffe (adult)	3,0 - 5,0	30 - 50	—	200	30	10 - 15	—	300 - 400	—
Giraffe (young)	2,0 - 3,0	20 - 30	—	150 - 180	20	10	6	200	5 - 6
Sable antelope	2,0 - 4,0	30 - 50	20 - 25	50 - 100	—	8 - 10	4 - 9	100 - 150	5 - 6
Roan	3,0 - 5,0	40 - 60	25 - 30	50 - 100	—	10 - 12	6 - 8	100 - 150	5 - 10

FOOTNOTE: Lower dosage levels are recommended for young, very old, thin and sick animals. Dosages for animals which have been in captivity for a long time, are also considerably lower. When catching zebras and giraffe, 5 to 10 mg hyoscine can be added to the above drugs. Young giraffe weigh about 300 - 550 kg and have a head height of about 3 - 4 m. Phenergan (promethazine-hydrochloride) can be added to the capture drugs for catching tsessebe (25 mg) and waterbuck (50 mg).

Game capture drugs can be divided into two basic groups. The more potent game capture drugs, of which the most important are currently M99 or Etorphine (oripavine hydrochloride, Reckitt), Fentanyl (fentanyl citrate, Janssen Pharm.) and Superfentanyl (R33799, Janssen Pharm.), will be dealt with first.

These preparations literally provide the immobilising potential of the combination of game capture drugs placed in the dart syringe. Even without the addition of other drugs, M99, Fentanyl and Superfentanyl can usually affect an animal severely. Elephant and rhino, for example, can be captured using only M99 or Superfentanyl.

Because animals generally fight the soporific effect of these drugs and may try to run away when approached or handled, certain adjuvants, or tranquillisers, are added to the game capture drug. Animals captured using Fentanyl are especially inclined to continue moving even when half asleep. Without the addition of Rompun (xylazine hydrochloride, Bayer), Azaperone (flupyridol, Janssen Pharm.), Acetylpromazine (acetylpromazine maleate, Boots) or another suitable tranquilliser to the drug mixture, the successful capture and handling of most game species is impossible.

The effects of M99, Fentanyl and Superfentanyl can be reversed by antagonists such as M285 (Ciprenorphine hydrochloride, Reckitt), M5050 (diprenorphine hydrochloride, Reckitt), Lethidrone (nalorphine hydrobromide, Burroughs Wellcome & Co.) or Narcan (naloxone hydrochloride, Endo Labs). For a rapid reviving effect these drugs should be administered intravenously. There are no antidotes for the tranquillisers, however, which means that animals treated with a tranquilliser remain drowsy for quite some time. Where animals have to be transported immediately after capture, this lasting sedating effect is a definite advantage.

If an animal has been sedated too deeply, is breathing very slowly or heavily, its heart functions are not satisfactory or a good response to the antidote is not achieved, a variety of veterinary analeptics can be used. Of the different drugs available commercially and which should preferably be administered by a qualified vet, the cortisone preparations and Dopram (doxapram hydrochloride, A H Robbins & Co) are of particular value.

Animals that have not been captured by means of game capture drugs can nevertheless be treated with certain tranquillisers in order to calm them for transporting and handling. In addition to the above-mentioned tranquillisers, Serenace (haloperidol, G D Searle & Co.) is also particularly suitable for this purpose.

Anaesthesia can also be induced and maintained with drugs such as chloral hydrate or with barbiturates or even with the above-mentioned capture drugs, and the animals transported in this condition. Constant supervision by a vet is, however, necessary to monitor the condition of the animals continuously and, depending on circumstances, to administer more narcotic or analeptic and to carry out emergency treatment.

Anaesthetising wild animals is by no means less complicated or less dangerous than it is with domestic animals, or even humans. The process is made even more complex by the fact that the wild animal that has to be captured has not necessarily abstained from food or water the previous day. Initially the drug is often not administered in strict accordance with the prescribed dose, owing to technical problems associated with the dart syringes. The patient also frequently decides to bolt after the drug has been administered and all sorts of physiological complications can develop before veterinary assistance arrives to save the life of the half-asleep, half-dead animal. Anyone who really cares for the safety of his valuable animals and who does not possess sufficient practical experience is therefore strongly advised to make use of a vet's assistance. Even a vet who does not have much experience in capturing game will have the necessary basic training to enable him to understand the effects of the drugs and to apply the correct emergency treatment.

The lower doses in the table are intended for female and young adult animals, and the higher doses for large bulls and rams. Please note that either Fentanyl alone or M99 alone should be used, and that only one tranquilliser, preferably the one most suited to the game species in question, should be mixed together in the dart syringe. After that the dart should be filled up with distilled water. Doses of antidotes are also given. These doses may not be exceeded.

When choosing the above-mentioned drugs for specific uses it is essential to know the most important properties and effects of each drug. Some of the most important will now be discussed briefly:

Fentanyl and M99, the two most important drugs used for the capture of farm game, act in very similar ways. M99 is particularly useful for dangerous animals such as buffalo, where the immobilising effect should be rapid and complete. The dose of M99 is usually approximately one tenth that of Fentanyl. The latter is a better choice when animals have to stay on their feet. Giraffe that have to be led into crates while drugged are a good example here.

Fentanyl is not very effective for waterbuck, gemsbok, elephant and zebra, and M99 should be used on these animals instead. Superfentanyl is less well known, and can be difficult to obtain.

For interest it may be mentioned that Fentanyl and M99 are not suitable for carnivores such as lion or cheetah, or for anaesthetising monkeys and baboons. Sernylan (phencyclidine hydrochloride, Park-Davis & Co.) or Ketamine (ketamine hydrochloride, Park-Davis & Co.) are used in conjunction with the above-mentioned tranquillisers to capture these animals. The former drug has unfortunately been withdrawn from the market because of its highly addictive effect in humans. Zoletil, a drug currently being used in place of Sernylan, is said to be very effective and is becoming popular.

Tranquillisers are generally much safer in the event of accidental overdoses. Detrimental effects of this group of drugs is the tendency of animals to develop heat stroke when they are treated on a hot day with, for example, acetylpromazine. These and closely related drugs of the phenothiazine group can also cause animals to die of heat stroke if they run long distances or move around very actively during or after capture.

In the case of waterbuck, an overdose of acetylpromazine can furthermore cause spasms of the neck muscles and death, while even a small overdose can put elephants to sleep for a very long time. In other respects, it is a very valuable drug.

Rompun, an excellent tranquilliser for game, has the tendency to slow down breathing rate and heart beat considerably. Symptomatic treatment with Dopram usually adequately relieves respiratory distress and also has a general stimulating effect. When an animal has been treated with Rompun its tongue usually protrudes from its mouth. This makes Rompun the ideal drug to use when the mouth and throat of an animal have to be examined for foot-and-mouth lesions, for example.

Anaesthetised animals or animals whose throat muscles are relaxed from the effect of drugs should not be dosed with water or medication, since they can easily choke and thus get fluid into their lungs.

With the exception of Narcan, antidotes should normally not be given in doses exceeding those prescribed. The reason for this is that overdoses of certain antidotes have a similar depressive effect on animals as narcotics.

I regularly encounter game captors who don't know exactly how to prepare, mix and correctly administer drugs. First, there is confusion regarding the different basic units of measurement:

Doses are generally not given in volume measures (millilitre = cubic centimetre), but in mass units (usually in milligrams). These drugs are made up by a pharmacist or vet into a suitable concentration (a certain number of milligrams (mg) of a drug in powder form per millilitre (ml) of solvent). When the dose is given in milligrams, the concentration (mg/ml) indicated on the bottle or container should therefore first be ascertained. Example: If the dose of M99 for a buffalo is 6 mg and the concentration of M99 in the container is 4 mg/ml, 1½ ml of the solution is required. If the M99 concentration should be 10 mg/ml, 6/10 of a millilitre would contain the correct amount of M99. The game capture drugs should be very accurately measured out in a suitable small syringe, such as a tuberculin syringe.

At all times, even in the veld, all drugs should be kept as cool as possible. Although most game capture drugs, even in solution form, can be kept for more than a year, provided of course that they are kept cool, fresh stock and freshly prepared drugs should be used whenever possible. Drugs prepared in a dart syringe should preferably be discarded if these are not used the same day.

Owing to the dangerous properties of game capture drugs and also because certain drugs can lead to addiction, the acquisition, possession and use of substances such as M99, Fentanyl and others are subject to strict control. These substances may only be used by a vet or under his direct supervision. In exceptional cases other persons may obtain a permit from the Department of Health to possess and use these drugs. Legal requirements regarding the locking up of these substances and the keeping of a register must be strictly observed.

Control over the acquisition and use of tranquillisers is less strict. In all cases it should, however, be ascertained that legal requirements are being met and all drugs should be kept locked up out of reach of children.

Although chemical game capture drugs continue to fulfil an important function in the game farming industry, the use of game nets and capture corrals offer a better alternative in most cases.

9. CAPTURING GAME BY MEANS OF MOVABLE CAPTURE CORRALS

Whereas the dart gun is particularly suitable for capturing big game such as elephant, rhino and buffalo, and smaller numbers of rarer animals, the movable capture corrals play a more significant role in the large-scale capture and handling of game. More than 8 000 head of game can be captured by a game capture team in one season.

20 years ago, doom prophets and opponents of the developing game farming industry claimed that successful farming with game would prove impossible. One of their arguments was that game could not be handled in sufficiently large numbers in a practical, acceptable manner. Nonetheless the ostrich industry had been established years earlier, and some critics conveniently overlooked the fact that these large birds had once also only occurred wild in nature.

Ideals are realised through judicious forethought and determined action, and, thanks to the knowledge and experience of men such as Jan Oelofse, and the ingenuity of our pioneer game farmers, this new industry developed overnight into a giant. Although remaining practical difficulties, especially with regard to the control of grazing and disease, the harvesting of surplus game in our bushveld regions and also, especially, with the marketing of game products, continue to pose challenges to farmers, agricultural unions, co-operatives and the government bodies concerned, game farmers have over a relatively short period come a long way and achieved incredible success. The perfection of mass capture techniques has made game farming possible even without the need to tame the wild animals, as in the case of the ostrich. This does not mean, however, that tame or hand-reared animals cannot make an equally important contribution to the industry.

Pop-up corrals and the use of permanent capture corral systems enable a farmer to handle large numbers of game with only a few assistants. Modern pit trapping methods and the innovative use of game capture nets have now made it possible to capture elusive species which could not be caught successfully in the past. In this chapter, only the use of movable capture corrals will be discussed.

THE OELOFSE CAPTURE CORRAL

The success achieved using capture corrals fabricated from a type of plastic material (woven high-density polyethylene plastic) arose from an interesting observation made by game captors. Most wild animals perceive the opaque walls of the capture corrals as solid and impenetrable and can effectively be restrained by these plastic walls, even though the animals would in some cases have the strength to break through the plastic. Even rhino have already been held successfully in plastic corrals for a length of time.

Game species that can successfully be herded into and caught in plastic corrals include kudu, waterbuck, gemsbok, red hartebeest, eland, blue wildebeest, zebra, impala and nyala. Problems are still to a certain extent experienced with springbok, but most other farm game species can be captured in plastic corrals. In the case of high-leaping game such as kudu, waterbuck, eland and impala, the height of the plastic walls of the capture corral is very important.

Capture corrals vary in size and shape, but generally consist of five basic compartments, namely a capture funnel (A), a catching camp (B), a holding camp (C), loading funnel (D) and loading ramp (E). Examples of a few designs are illustrated schematically below.

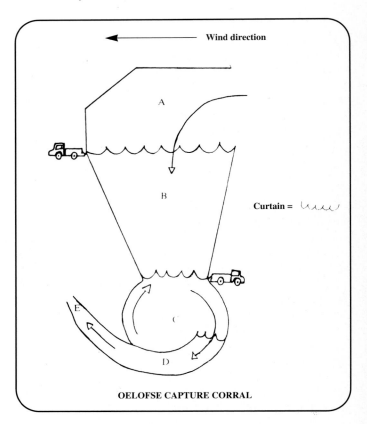

OELOFSE CAPTURE CORRAL

The Oelofse capture corral requires the prevailing wind direction to be taken into account during erection of the corral. At all times the game must remain upwind of the corral while being herded into the capture funnel, to prevent the animals from scenting the corral.

Curtains separating the capture funnel and the catching and holding camps were initially attached to cables and buried in shallow furrows in the ground, and covered with sand and leaves. The cables from which the curtains were suspended were anchored to a tree on one side and the other side was attached to a tractor or powerful vehicle. As soon as the animals had passed over the hidden curtain, the cables were quickly drawn taught by means of a tractor or four-wheel-drive vehicle, and the walls that were thus raised instantaneously behind the animals prevented them from escaping from the corral. Subsequently these pop-up curtains were replaced by curtains that could be drawn shut by hand from the sides.

The observation that captured animals usually run in circles along the sides of the capture corral in their efforts to escape led to the successful circular design of the holding camp, which leads into the curved junction of the loading ramp leading from it.

The Oelofse capture corral has since been modified quite considerably, but still serves as a suitable model for any other type of movable herding corral.

THE ALEC ROUGH CAPTURE CORRAL FOR BUSHVELD CONDITIONS

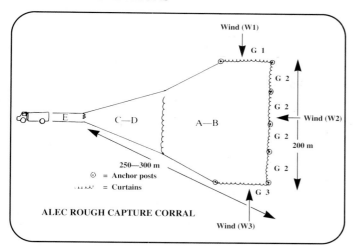

ALEC ROUGH CAPTURE CORRAL

Wind (W1)

G 1
G 2
G 2
Wind (W2)
G 2
200 m
G 2
250—300 m
⊙ = Anchor posts
ﻬﻬﻬ = Curtains
G 3
Wind (W3)

E
C—D
A—B

The Alec Rough capture corral allows the series of curtain segments (C1 — C3) comprising the capture funnel and a part of the catching camp to be controlled in such as manner that the opening through which the animals must be driven can be adapted to the prevailing wind direction. When the wind is blowing from direction W1 towards the corral, the curtain C1 will be opened prior to the catch and curtains C2 and C3 will be kept closed to prevent the animals from running right through the corral system. If the wind is blowing from direction W2, curtain C2 is kept closed and C1 and C3 opened, and so on.

Each curtain is 50 metres long and is suspended from sliding wire rings on a tightly strung cable which spans the entrances at a height of approximately 2 to 2,4 metres. The cables from which the curtains are suspended are concealed as thoroughly as possible amongst the foliage of the trees. The entire corral system is erected in dense bush and hidden so that the animals cannot see it until they are right inside the corral.

Curtains opened prior to the catch are rolled up tightly close to the supporting poles and covered with leafy branches. Each curtain is manned by two assistants, who conceal themselves in the rolled-up curtains. As soon as the helicopter has herded the game into the corral, the curtains are quickly closed behind the animals. The curtain between A-B and C-D is also opened prior to capture, and after the animals have been caught, is used to separate the herd or to trap the captured animals in C-D, so that more animals can be herded from the veld and driven into A-B. After they have been captured, the animals can be kept in camps A-D, or driven onto the truck immediately after capture by means of the helicopter.

The capture funnel of the Alec Rough capture corral is approximately 200 metres wide at the point furthest away from the loading ramp, while the sides of the corral are each 250 to 300 metres in length. The capture corral must be sufficiently deep, and the curtains and sides adequately concealed, to ensure that the herded game will not realise that they have entered a corral until the curtains have closed behind them.

SPECIAL MODIFICATION FOR OPEN GRASSVELD AREAS

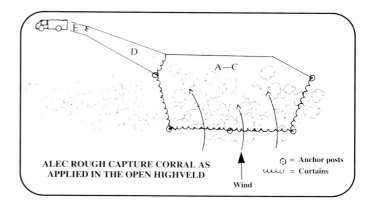

ALEC ROUGH CAPTURE CORRAL AS APPLIED IN THE OPEN HIGHVELD

E
D
A—C
○ = Anchor posts
ﻬﻬﻬ = Curtains
Wind

Where shelter is scarce and it happens that only a strip of dense bush occurs on a part of a farm, the Alec Rough capture corral can be modified and adapted in several ways in order to make optimum use of the available shelter. The above illustration serves as an example:

The supporting poles for the curtains are hidden at the edge of the bush and the rest of the capture corral is erected behind the bush, out of sight of the fleeing animals.

SUITABLE SITES FOR ERECTING CAPTURE CORRALS

In addition to dense bush, footpaths leading to watering points and the normal routes followed by game through small ravines and relatively open paths through otherwise dense forest all offer suitable spots for erecting capture corrals. A thorough knowledge of animal behaviour and the movement patterns of game in a specific area therefore contributes a great deal to the successful positioning of a capture corral.

Although the capture corrals must necessarily be erected in areas where game occur abundantly, care should be taken not to place the corrals close to game watering points or in the middle of the animals' grazing areas. The reason for this is that the disturbance caused by clearing the bush and erecting the corral may cause the animals to leave the area. If they spot the corral beforehand it will also be much more difficult later to herd them in the direction of the capture corral. It is consequently advisable, with due consideration of the prevailing wind direction, to erect the capture system in thickets in the immediate vicinity of the largest concentration of game. Preferably the corral should be within a kilometre or two of the animals' grazing area. An experienced helicopter pilot can slowly herd the animals towards the capture corral for as much as 5 or 6 kilometres without ill effects to the animals.

PRECAUTIONS

The corral should be erected as quietly as possible, smoking should be avoided and every care should be taken not to leave traces of human scent or to disturb the environment unduly. At the entrance to the capture funnel, especially, the minimum number of branches should be removed, the grass should not be trodden unnecessarily and driving around with vehicles should be limited as far as possible. No papers, tin cans or other strange objects should be left behind, and, in contrast to other curtains, those at the entrance to the capture corral should not have a lower cable. A cable lying on the ground frightens the animals and hinders efforts to herd the animals inside. If the wind should begin to blow once the animals are inside, the curtain must simply be held in place by hand, or anchored on the ground by means of logs and rocks.

Immediately after capture, the animals often mill around in the corral in confusion for a while, and it is therefore vital to remove logs, sharp branches, large rocks and other objects against which the running animals may injure themselves. Sawn-off branches lower than two metres can, in particular, be the cause of broken ribs and serious injuries. However, large shady trees and thickets in which the animals can seek shelter hold obvious advantages and should not be removed unnecessarily from the catching and holding camps.

ERECTING THE CAPTURE CORRAL

Like hanging the sliding curtains, constructing the walls of the capture corral is an enormous and time-consuming job. It takes an experienced team of workers approximately a day to erect the 600 to 900 metres of plastic walls and curtains.

Normal, non-reinforced plastic is not suitable because it reflects light, flutters and makes a noise in the wind, tears easily and can only be used once. Woven high-density polypropalene plastic is excellent (obtainable from Cape Bag and Twine, Cape Town), since it is lightweight and durable and also particularly resistant to the sun. The recommended honey-coloured plastic

blends well with the beige winter grass and vegetation and makes concealment of the capture corral considerably easier. This plastic is available in rolls with a width of 2,95 metres, which, when erected, makes it high enough for high-leaping game. This material currently costs R15 per metre and is sufficiently thick to keep in most types of game without additional support from game capture nets. However, when capturing zebra, supporting nets are always recommended, especially on the outside of the plastic walls of the loading funnel, since an agitated animal may succeed in breaking through the plastic. Waterbuck bulls sometimes also tend to tear the plastic with their horns. Holes in the plastic should be repaired without delay, since the animals will attempt to escape through any gap which allows them to see out.

Hessian can also be used, provided that it is not transparent. Old hessian tears easily and is not considered suitable. During experimental efforts to obtain a cheap and more durable material for erecting permanent capture corrals, hessian has been treated with various chemicals. So far a rubbery paint has yielded the best results. Game captors and game farmers are still waiting for the perfection of a type of material which will be opaque, durable and economical, and which will be able to withstand the destructive effects of solar radiation, wind and the elements for several years.

The plastic sides of the capture corral are suspended from two tightly strung steel cables. The cables are 9 millimetres thick, have a breaking strain of 1,5 tons and are strung between trees by means of a one-ton cable pulley. The upper cable is strung at a height of 3 metres, while the lower cable must be directly above the ground. These cables are pre-cut in lengths of 250 metres (maximum). Home-made cable reels are used to facilitate transport and handling of the cables. The cables are secured to the trees by means of metal clamps.

Where there is a lack of suitable trees — a common problem, especially on the bare grass plains of the Transvaal Highveld, as well as the Kalahari, Karoo and the Orange Free State — lightweight metal rods can be used to keep the cable and plastic upright between the anchoring poles or trees. Probably the most suitable rods for this purpose are the peg-and-rod type used by Mr Alec Rough's capture team: a 1 m long boring rod (diameter of 25 millimetres), of which both ends have been slightly sharpened, is driven into the ground. A 3 m long thick-walled steam-pipe with a diameter of 30 mm is slid over the boring rod. At ground level and at 2,4 metres above the ground, metal rings are welded to the steam-pipes; the cables are guided through these rings and thus held in position. A thin chain, 4 m in length, is attached to the top of the steam-pipe. On the outside of the capture corral, the chain is attached to a 0,5 m long anchoring peg, to hold the rods and plastic walls upright. At the narrow end of the loading funnel, where animals continuously press against the plastic walls from the inside, the tops of the rods are also connected by means of thin chains across the capture funnel, in order to achieve the necessary stability. The rods of the capture funnel and catching camp are spaced at intervals of approximately 15 m, those of the holding camp at intervals of 10 m and those of the loading funnel at intervals of 3 m.

The plastic is transported in rolls. While it is being unrolled and erected, thorny branches should be avoided as far as possible, since these can damage the plastic, particularly on windy days. Lightweight aluminium step-ladders considerably facilitate erection of the plastic walls. The plastic or hessian sides should be secured firmly. Steel wire pins, 20 cm in length and which have been sharpened at one end and bent around in a circular shape at the other, are used to fasten the plastic over the top and bottom cables. When the corral subsequently has to be dismantled, the wire pins are easily removed by means of the circular handles and threaded together in bundles for re-use. Hessian can also be secured in the same manner using these pins, or attached to the cable by means of strong twine and a sail-needle.

Erecting a curtain entails fastening two thick cables of 6,4 mm, cut into lengths of 50 m, to an anchoring pole or tree at one end, with one cable on the level of the ground and the other higher up. The curtain, which has circular wire sliding rings at the top and at the bottom (except those used in the catching funnel), is then unrolled in the direction in which it is to be closed. The loose ends of the cable are threaded through the sliding rings and drawn taught by means of a half-ton cable pulley, and secured to an anchoring pole or tree at the other end by means of clamps. Except at the catching funnel, where the cable is suspended at a height of approximately 4,5 m, the uppermost cable of the curtains is usually suspended 3 m above the ground. The bottom cable must be strung and kept as low as possible above the ground, to prevent the animals from tripping over it when the curtain is opened. When the curtains are closed, they should present an obstruction 2,7 m high. In exceptional cases, single impala or kudu may succeed in clearing this height. Curtains that tend to sag in the middle can be supported and held upright from behind by means of forked poles.

The shape of the loading funnel is important. When the animals are loaded, they should never feel that they are being trapped in a dead-end passage, since this will cause them to break free continuously and run back. Good results have been obtained using a funnel curved in a crescent shape, which keeps the animals moving forward in the hope that the next bend will offer an opportunity for escape. When the animals are able to see daylight through the roof slats of the truck, they also seem more willing to mount the loading ramp.

Adjustable loading ramps with sturdy wooden floors and shallow cross-bars at floor level, covered with a layer of soil, are commonly used. Using these adjustable ramps, the necessary adjustments can be made to load animals onto trucks with floor levels of different heights and with doors of different sizes. The loading ramp is usually about 1 m wide, 2,4 m high and covered overhead with plastic to form a tunnel when high-leaping game has to be loaded. The ramps are sturdy but constructed of lightweight material, and can be assembled and dismantled quickly. Some loading ramps are equipped with a sliding or swing-door on the side of the loading funnel, which helps to confine the animals to the loading ramp and facilitates handling of the animals during the loading process.

THE CAPTURE PROCESS

Although the animals, specifically from small game camps, can be herded into the capture corrals on foot or by means of Landrovers and horses and various other methods, the success of this capture technique depends largely on the use of helicopters. The success of the capture is determined to a great extent by the experience and skill of the helicopter pilot.

Moments after these impala arrived at the water, a plastic enclosure shot up from the ground, instantaneously surrounding them. The RIVSCO capture corral, designed by Mr Koos Gilliomee, has since been considerably modified. For example, it is now possible for a game captor to capture the animals over a distance of kilometres, simply by activating a radio-controlled trigger mechanism.

An expert helicopter pilot will know that noticeably wild, agitated and aggressive animals, as well as ewes with young lambs, should preferably be left behind in the veld. Driving ram herds of species such as impala into the corral together with breeding herds, especially during the mating season, is simply inviting trouble. When game has to be chased over long distances, a pace no faster than a trot should be maintained, and the animals should not exert themselves at any cost! Some species flee readily ahead of the helicopter. Others, such as impala and bushbuck, can be very perverse, tending to head in a direction diametrically opposite to the one you would like them to take. Sometimes it helps to muddle these animals up a little by chasing them to one side and then another for a short while before heading in the direction of the corral. Although game is generally quite willing to move through stock fences and open farm gates, they are sometimes less inclined to do so when being pursued, and a fair amount of patience may be required in these instances.

Once the animals arrive at the corral, all fun and games are at an end! Taking wind direction into account, the pilot guides the animals towards the centre of the funnel opening. This is where the pilot's skill is put severely to the test! Frequently at his own peril, the pilot must dodge tall trees and fight against gusts of wind, while creating as much noise as possible right on the heels of the animals, ready to dart right or left at a moment's notice to head off a wayward animal. At this stage it is sometimes useful to fire a shot or two from the helicopter's open door and even to use hooters and sirens to create the necessary noise behind the animals, who often stop in their tracks at the entrance to the funnel. Once the animals are far enough into the corral, the helicopter pilot signals to the ground team to close the curtains. The battle is far from over, however, since the herd often has to be split up by the capture team before the animals can be loaded. Aggressive bulls or rams must also sometimes be speedily removed, before they injure the other animals.

When the animals must be herded directly onto the truck by means of the helicopter, they must be chased on immediately, before they begin to run in circles around the capture corral. When the animals are very tired, it is desirable, especially on hot days, to allow them to rest and cool down before loading them. Except during the loading procedure, talking next to or near the corral should be avoided, and any form of disturbance limited to the absolute minimum.

ADVANTAGES AND DISADVANTAGES OF CAPTURING GAME IN CAPTURE CORRALS

Capturing game in plastic corrals certainly has its disadvantages, risks and dangers. The acquisition and replacement of equipment is a fairly costly undertaking, while the use of a helicopter also increases the capture cost per animal considerably. When the game has become aware of the presence of a capture corral on a certain part of the farm, the corral must usually be moved to another location. The successful use of this capture technique is also limited to a great extent in regions where the veld does not offer sufficient bush or natural cover for a capture corral. Without the support of an experienced ground team, capture efforts can also be doomed to repeated failure.

Mention has already been made of the important influence of wind when capturing game. A few additional observations in this respect: When the wind is particularly strong, this can render the use of a helicopter unsafe and even impossible. In addition to scent, the noise of plastic fluttering in strong wind may also frighten the animals and cause them to flee from the corral or, if already caught, to mill around in the corral. Gusts of wind can also lift the plastic and allow the animals to escape.

In areas where large predators occur, lions have in the past crept under the plastic and injured and killed game left in the corral overnight. Losses due to overstraining disease can also be suffered if an inexperienced pilot chases the animals too far or for too long. Wildebeest that are herded into the corral together with zebra or kudu may also attack and injure the other animals.

Movable capture corrals allow the largest numbers of game to be captured in the shortest space of time. More than 100 zebra or 150 impala have on occasion been caught in single capture operations. In general it remains a good policy to capture different herds or family groups separately. In this manner fighting and injuries are minimised.

All things considered, the use of movable capture corrals offers the quickest and most efficient method of capturing large numbers of game. The few disadvantages of this capture method can largely be eliminated by observing the above precautions.

In the following chapters, other capture techniques are discussed, and attention is given, in particular, to cheaper methods that farmers can use themselves to capture and cull the surplus game on their farms.

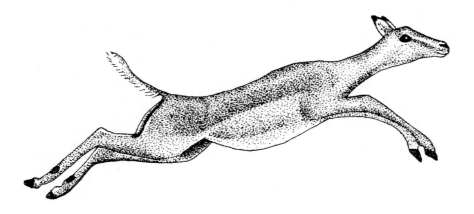

10. CAPTURE METHODS PARTICULARLY SUITED TO THE GAME FARM

Game farmers can choose from quite a wide variety of game capture techniques. In this chapter, special attention is given to methods which the farmer can implement himself on his farm at a relatively low cost.

POP-UP CORRALS

Mr Koos Gilliomee of Hoedspruit achieved a remarkable breakthrough in the perfection of game capture techniques when he tested and proved the practical feasibility of his conception of a pop-up corral. His so-called RIVSCO capture corral, which has since been patented, consists mainly of a large plastic corral which is concealed in a shallow furrow around a waterhole or some other point frequented by game, and which, when activated by a trigger, shoots up from the ground at a specific moment to surround the animals.

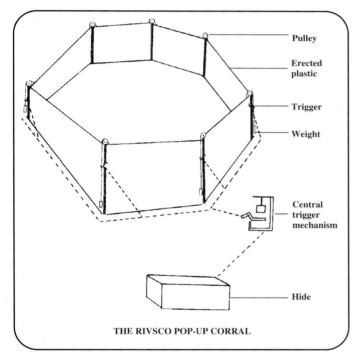

THE RIVSCO POP-UP CORRAL

The initial pop-up mechanism of the RIVSCO capture corral is very interesting and testifies to the ingenuity of the designer. First, a shallow furrow was dug around the watering point. A series of pipes were set upright approximately 5 m apart, next to the furrow and all around the watering point. A reasonably heavy weight was placed next to each pipe and tied to a thin but strong rope running across a reel affixed to the top of the pole. The weights would be used later, to pull the plastic wall up out of the furrow.

A roll of game capture plastic was then unrolled alongside the furrow, folded carefully and placed in the furrow. A light cable was fastened to the upper edge of the plastic along its entire length and concealed in the furrow together with the plastic. At each pipe, this cable was connected to the weights on the other side of the pipe by means of the ropes over the reels. The weights were held in a suspended position by means of hooks which had also been attached to the tops of the pipes, so that no

force would be exerted on the ropes running from the weights to the concealed cable and plastic. The hooks from which the weights were suspended could, however, be released simultaneously by means of remote control, upon which the weights would, naturally, drop. This would pull the ropes taught over the pulleys and cause the plastic wall to shoot up, thus surrounding and capturing the animals at the waterhole.

To prevent the animals from spotting the plastic in the furrow when approaching the water, the plastic and cable were concealed by means of a thin layer of sand, dry grass and leaves and left for a few days.

When Mr Gilliomee wished to capture some of his game, he would watch the animals from a hide near the capture site. As soon as the animals entered the sphere of the capture corral, he would activate the central triggering mechanism using a long wire. At a spot near the capture corral, a heavy weight would initiate a levering action, which would in turn release all the hooks on the poles instantaneously and simultaneously. The weights next to the poles would then all fall simultaneously and the plastic rise up in a flash, to form a perfect plastic wall around the astounded animals.

This method obviates the need to herd the animals towards a capture corral and thus eliminates over-exertion of the game. The game captor furthermore has better control over the number of animals and the composition of the herds he wishes to capture.

Considerable modifications to this system were subsequently effected by Mr Gilliomee, the National Parks Board, the National Zoo in Pretoria and private game farmers. The wire triggering mechanism was, for example, replaced by radio-controlled triggers which enable a game captor to catch the animals at a distance of several kilometres simply by activating a switch.

This system can be implemented to good effect on game farms by combining the pop-up corral principle with a permanent capture funnel and holding camp system. A permanent hide for the game captor, in the form of a tree-house or a watchtower erected near a capture site, considerably simplifies the capturing process. The example illustrated and described below was perfected by Mr Z J Young of Northam (see p. 88):

The basic idea is to place the pop-up part of the capture system near to or around a waterhole or salt lick frequented by game, with a funnel leading to a permanent holding system. Like the funnel, the latter could be constructed using treated split poles or reeds. Reeds are recommended since the animals sometimes injure themselves against the sturdier split poles. If the animals do not need to be held captive for long, the funnel can lead to a plastic capture corral, from where the animals can be loaded onto the trucks by means of a permanent loading ramp.

The advantage of this system is that the animals become accustomed to the permanent structures (watchtower, funnel and holding camps) at the waterholes or salt licks and that they even learn to move into the permanent funnel section on a daily basis to drink water or use the salt licks. The only portion of the system that has to be erected especially prior to the catch is the plastic wall section at the entrance to the capture funnel.

This capture method requires very little labour, as one person can catch the animals single-handed and only a few assistants are required to load up the animals. Costs are also considerably reduced, since the same relatively cheap structures and materials can be re-used for a number of years.

Some disadvantages: As one has to wait for the animals at the capture site, this method can be very time-consuming. The necessary precautions must also be taken to prevent termites from damaging the wooden or reed walls of the permanent structures. Using treated poles and building a low concrete embankment under the wooden or reed walls can, however, help to overcome this problem, particularly if the poles or reeds do not extend down to more than 5 cm above this embankment.

game farm, this system allows the game to be caught in a smaller catching camp as time passes. A permanent capture funnel and corral 3 m high, which, like the fence of the capture corral, is constructed using approximately 21 strands of steel wire, form part of the capture system.

After the animals have been kept in the smaller catching camp for some time, and they have become accustomed to moving through the capture funnel and capture corral, plastic or hessian sheeting is hung over the fences comprising the funnel and capture corral, and the animals are immediately moved through the

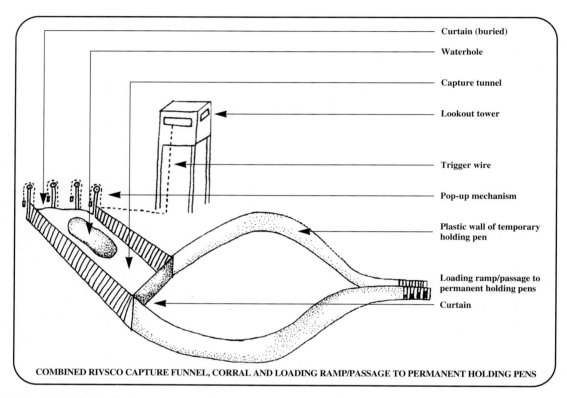

- Curtain (buried)
- Waterhole
- Capture tunnel
- Lookout tower
- Trigger wire
- Pop-up mechanism
- Plastic wall of temporary holding pen
- Loading ramp/passage to permanent holding pens
- Curtain

COMBINED RIVSCO CAPTURE FUNNEL, CORRAL AND LOADING RAMP/PASSAGE TO PERMANENT HOLDING PENS

PERMANENT CAPTURE CORRALS

The use of permanent capture corrals and catching funnels, a practice developed by my late father approximately 28 years ago, remains one of the most economical and effective game capture techniques for the game farmer, in my opinion.

Because it is difficult to herd and capture game on a large

capture funnel into the capture corral on foot or using Landrovers and/or horses, and shut in there. Then they are loaded onto trucks as soon as possible and transported to their new destinations.

Two catching and holding camps can preferably be erected next to each other, so that game can be caught in one camp and periodically be moved through to the second holding camp.

As soon as the animals from the large game camp have been

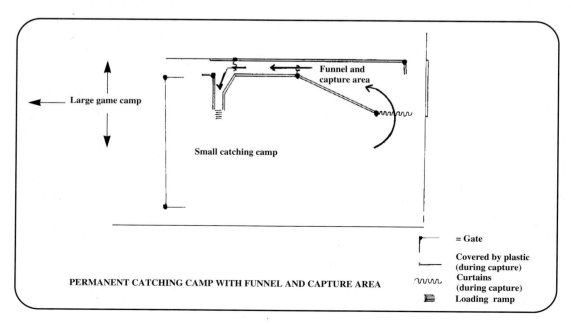

- Large game camp
- Funnel and capture area
- Small catching camp

PERMANENT CATCHING CAMP WITH FUNNEL AND CAPTURE AREA

- = Gate
- Covered by plastic (during capture)
- Curtains (during capture)
- Loading ramp

caught in the first catching camp, the gates separating these two camps are shut, those leading to the holding camp are opened and the game moved through a little later. This process is repeated until sufficient animals have been caught.

The catching and holding camps can each comprise an area of approximately 20 ha, and should offer the game adequate shelter, otherwise the animals may injure themselves against the fences in their attempts to escape. The positioning of the camps is also

It is important not to attempt to force the animals through a gate which has been kept closed prior to the capture operation. By leaving the gates separating the two camps open for a day or two, considerable time can be saved when the animals have to be moved through. At no stage should the animals be subjected to undue pressure, and care should be taken to prevent them from jumping against the fences and injuring themselves.

Except that the smaller capture funnels and corrals in the

important. Brackish hollows and preferred grazing areas with permanent watering points are usually suitable spots for these camps. During the summer, the grazing in these camps should be saved for the capture season.

A well planned network of narrow farm roads in these camps facilitates counting and moving the animals. The gates should be erected in the corners of the camps, to simplify herding the game through them and also to prevent young animals from staying behind on the wrong side of the fence when the other animals are moved through.

above-mentioned catching camps require less plastic sheeting than the larger, movable capture corrals discussed earlier, and that a helicopter is not needed to herd the game, this system basically functions according to the same principles as the movable capture corral. In addition to savings in terms of helicopter flying time and materials, the permanent fencing structures also facilitate hanging of the plastic, and moving the game into the corral is also easier, as they are accustomed to moving through the capture system. Gates can also be covered with plastic as a substitute for plastic curtains, to save time hanging the curtains.

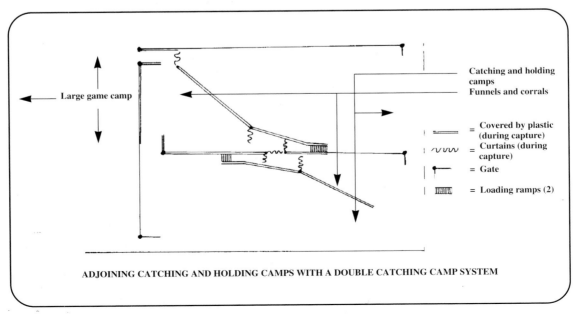

ADJOINING CATCHING AND HOLDING CAMPS WITH A DOUBLE CATCHING CAMP SYSTEM

On large game farms, several capture corrals can be erected at strategic spots. If the watering points for the farm's game are incorporated as far as possible into these systems, the game will be caught relatively quickly. Unfortunately predators such as leopard, caracal and jackal soon learn to trap the game against the fences of these small camps. Alternative watering points should therefore preferably also be available.

When two adjacent smallish game capture camps both have their own capture funnel and corral with their own loading ramp, and the two capture systems are sub-divided and joined by means of sorting gates, groups of animals of different species can be captured in short succession and held apart until they have to be loaded. This combined system also allows herds to be divided and animals to be separated more easily if this becomes necessary due to fighting or for other reasons.

Dr Tony Harthoorn adapted the principle described above further in an attempt to limit over-exertion of the animals during capture. His method makes provision for the permanent coverage of the capture funnel(s) and capture corrals(s) with plastic walls, so that the animals become accustomed to this and can be driven through the system regularly, thus also becoming used to the capture process. His objective with this technique was to accustom the animals to a slow herding process, while simultaneously increasing their fitness with this regular exercise, so that the animals would be better prepared physiologically when they were eventually captured.

Apart from the considerable time involved, this method is rendered impractical for general use by the large expenditures required to replace the plastic, which does not withstand the effects of wind and weather very well. As mentioned earlier, the development of a type of material that can be left in the veld for years without deterioration would contribute enormously to

allowing game to be captured economically in such permanent capture corrals.

As soon as this ideal is realised, it would be advisable to lure the animals into the capture corrals with lucerne, salt licks or water and then simply to shut the gates behind them, rather than chase them repeatedly through the system beforehand. Optic detectors at the capture gates, similar to those used at the doors of certain shops and pharmacies, could warn the game captor some distance away that animals have entered the corral. Automatic or remote-controlled closing mechanisms could also, in these advanced technological times, contribute to the perfection of this capture procedure.

GAME CAPTURE NETS

Game capture nets have in the past played an important role in the capture of wild animals. For nyala, bushbuck, and other elusive bush-dwelling animals, as well as the smaller antelope such as duiker, oribi and steenbok, the use of nets continues to be one of the principal capture methods.

The nets, which are usually 2,5 m high when suspended, are available in lengths of 50 m or more. For the smaller antelope, nets with a mesh of 10 cm are used, and, for the larger species, nets with a mesh of 15 cm are ideal. The breaking strain of these nets is 520 kg. The cost of 100 m of game capture net currently varies between R4 934 and R5 215.

Nets can be employed in different ways. When secured to cables at the top and bottom and rigged tightly in an upright position, they can be used as capture corrals. Although the animals do, to a certain extent, become entangled, the nets do not fall onto them, as is the case with drop nets.

The upper edge of drop nets is loosely secured by means of

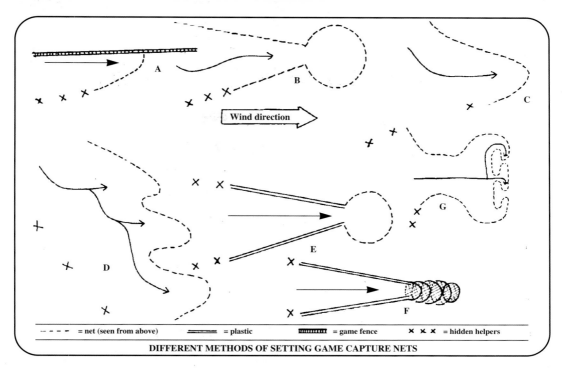

- - - - = net (seen from above)	═══ = plastic	▓▓▓ = game fence	x x x = hidden helpers

DIFFERENT METHODS OF SETTING GAME CAPTURE NETS

biltong hooks or thin twine to a cable or even to overhanging branches. The net is not drawn tight, but is nevertheless positioned sufficiently high to prevent animals from jumping over it. The best results are obtained when the lower edge of a loosely hung net is pulled back slightly and laid flat on the ground in the direction from which the animals will approach. A little distance above the animals' heads, the net can preferably hang over slightly in the same direction. A few loose logs on the bottom edge of the net will prevent the running animals from lifting the net from the ground and running right through. Rocks, sharp branches, metal poles and other objects which may injure the animals should, however, never be used anywhere near the nets.

The net corrals or drop nets are suspended across the footpaths or flight paths of the game, or next to a fence along which the animals usually run. A thorough knowledge of the movement patterns of timid antelope such as bushbuck and duiker in a specific area will, to a large extent, determine the success of the capture effort. Naturally wind direction must also be taken into account, so that the animals can, as far as possible, be moved downwind.

When antelope such as oribi, which prefer open plains, have to be caught, the nets must sometimes unavoidably be rigged up in open grassveld. In these cases it is especially vital that the nets should be of approximately the same colour as the veld, and be camouflaged as well as possible. Generally speaking, straw-coloured nets are recommended.

As shown in the sketches, the nets can be set up in a straight line and join up with a game fence at a slightly bent angle (Sketch A) if the animals are to be chased alongside the fence into the nets. The nets can also be erected in the shape — seen from above — of a corral (Sketch B) or a loop (Sketch C), or in a wavy line (Sketch D), in order to trap the animals in the nets more easily. A plastic funnel can also be used to herd the animals into the nets (Sketch E). These plastic strips can either be laid on the ground or erected similarly to the walls of plastic corrals. Smaller antelope can sometimes be caught more easily if the capture net is arranged at the end of the funnel in the shape of a closed-ended tunnel (Sketch F). Bushbuck, nyala, and duiker, who are inclined to walk all along the net looking for a bolt-hole, soon become discouraged when a net structure such as

the one shown in Sketch G is used, and eventually jump into one of the loops of the nets.

While the nets are being rigged, the minimum of noise should be made, smoking should be avoided and all the other precautions pertaining to movable capture corrals should be observed.

As soon as the nets are ready, a few assistants are hidden near the nets, as indicated on the sketches.

Too many animals should not be chased into the nets simultaneously, since injuries and over-exertion commonly result in such circumstances. When very young lambs or calves are included in the herd, the animals should also not be captured using nets. If a helicopter is used to herd the animals, special care must be taken during the capture process.

In open bushveld or grassveld, suitable vehicles and experienced riders on horseback can be used very effectively to move capricious animals such as blesbok and springbok along. A long line of people moving on foot in the direction of the nets and making a great deal of accompanying noise usually succeed best in flushing concealed antelope such as oribi from their hiding-places and chasing them towards the nets. Co-ordinated teamwork is crucial here!

The assistants hiding near the nets must help to guide the running animals into the nets and should be on hand quickly to attend to trapped animals. It is especially important that sufficient assistants are ready to restrain the captured animals at once, to prevent them from struggling in the nets, thus possibly injuring muscles or ligaments or hitting their heads against the ground. The animals' legs should be held firmly and their heads kept up to prevent injuries to their eyes and mouths.

Sufficient blindfolds should be available to cover the animals' eyes. Tranquillisers such as Rompun, Azaperone, Acetylpromazine, Combelen or Serenace can also contribute considerably to the easier and safer handling of the animals, provided of course that these drugs are administered correctly!

Occasionally the nets or ropes may constrict the neck or limbs of an animal, and will need to be cut. A pocket knife for this purpose, some disinfectants and ointments for possible injuries, and flat ropes to tie the animals' legs together should also be within reach.

Nets can furthermore be used to catch animals in zoos or in cages for the purpose of collecting blood samples or treating or moving individual animals to other cages. In these cases it is suggested that animals be moved to an adjacent cage, in which the net has been set up in advance. The net should be erected sufficiently far from the fence, to prevent the running animals from dragging the net along and injuring themselves against the fence.

Game capture nets should never be left in the veld overnight or remain unguarded. Wild animals can easily become ensnared in such nets, sustaining injuries and even dying if they are not freed in time. Dassies, squirrels and termites can also cause extensive damage to the nets, while rain can cause mildew on the nets if they are rolled up while wet. Rats and mice have also been known to cause great damage to expensive nets which were not stored safely. Petrol drums with metal lids in rodent-proof store-rooms are probably the best way to store game capture nets.

Nets can also be used in numerous other ways to catch game. A large square net of approximately 20 x 20 square metres can be suspended above the animals' feeding place and dropped over the animals when they are grouped together under the net. A remote-controlled triggering device can be used to drop the net at the right moment. Similarly, the gate of a net corral erected around a feeding place can be shut behind the animals once they are in the desired spot.

CANNON NETS AND NET GUNS

So-called cannon nets have been used for many years to capture animals at feeding sites. A large net is folded up next to the feeding site and fastened to ball weights, which are loaded into cannon barrels and fired at a given time. The cannons are fired simultaneously by means of an electrical circuit activated by someone concealed near to the capture site. As soon as this happens, the ball weights carry the net over the animals, trapping them under the net.

The net gun represents one of the most modern pieces of game capturing equipment available. It consists of a gun with three barrels, each of which is loaded with .308 blank cartridges, and can simultaneously fire three weights, each with a diameter of 20 mm. Attached to these weights is a light net, approximately 4 to 5 m wide and 6 m long, which can be fired from a helicopter or a moving vehicle to catch a running animal. Oribi, springbok, impala, reedbuck and even young kudu, waterbuck and ostriches have been captured successfully by means of net guns.

PIT NETS

Everyone is probably familiar with the custom of primitive hunters of catching game in pit traps. Well, a modified version of the pit trap capture technique appears to be one of the cheapest and most efficient methods to date of capturing reedbuck.

As indicated in the sketch, a rectangular pit is dug in the

footpaths of the reedbuck. The pit is approximately 4 m long, 2 m wide and 2 m deep, and dug within the confines of the narrow end of a capture funnel. A capture funnel, consisting of tightly rigged game fencing 2,4 m in height and with 21 steel wires, incorporates the reedbuck's watering point or favourite grazing site in its broad end, and narrows in the direction of the pit trap. The animals are left for a few weeks to grow accustomed to moving through the capture funnel. They then leave the narrow end of the funnel via a gate near the pit trap.

On the afternoon preceding the night on which the reedbuck are to be captured, the gate is closed in such a manner that the antelope running through the funnel will have no choice but to jump into the pit trap. At the same time, a 15 cm mesh net is rigged tightly in a horizontal position across the opening of the pit. The sides of the net are secured to the bottom wires of the fence, to ensure that the net has the necessary elasticity. The net is then camouflaged with dry grass and leaves.

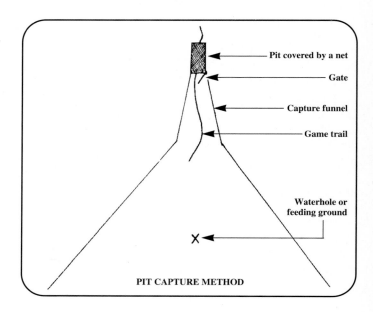

PIT CAPTURE METHOD

Later that evening, when the antelope are chased through the funnel with vehicles and spotlights, they usually hesitate in front of the pit trap. When the game captors approach them from behind, they leap into the net and remain suspended helplessly until they are freed and loaded into the transport truck. Using this method, my late father succeeded in capturing a large number of reedbuck without suffering any significant losses.

POLE-LASSOS

Today the technique of capturing wild animals from a pursuing vehicle using a pole and a noose is no longer widely used. In the past this method was restricted mainly to open veld, with one light truck or more generally being used to chase the animals. The game captors stood on the back of the trucks or were strapped to the bumpers of the vehicles. Sable antelope and

black wildebeest, in particular, could often be captured quite easily after a long chase, when the exhausted animals turned to defend themselves. The noose was then thrown over the animal's horns and pulled tight until the fighting and struggling animal was brought up against the side of the vehicle. Owing to the danger of over-exertion and the damage caused to the vehicles, this method is no longer recommended. The use of horses for the same purpose is also strongly discouraged.

Similarly, the use of wire snares and trained dogs is not advised for capturing game. Although I have been told of several cases where these capture methods were successfully employed, there are certainly safer and better techniques available today.

Earth dams have already been used in the capture of game in various ways. For reasons of completeness, mainly, it is interesting to recall cases where black wildebeest were chased into such a dam and driven by means of motor boats towards a cable spanned slightly above the surface of the water. When the black wildebeest swam into the cable, the captors in the boat would seize them and use the boat to drag them to the shallow end, where they would be immobilised with ropes. This was in the good old days, before the advent of dart guns and helicopters.

SPOTLIGHTS

Impala, blesbok, reedbuck and steenbok are still captured regularly and successfully at night with the help of powerful, blinding spotlights. Usually, the game is located by driving across the game farm on an open vehicle and searching with a spotlight. A few fit and fleet-footed captors, dressed in dark clothes, stand on the vehicle ready to jump off. As soon as the animals are spotted, the vehicle rapidly closes in on the animals while they are blinded by the spotlight. The captors jump down from the vehicle in the darkness behind the spotlight beam and run towards the animals as quickly and quietly as possible. The best place to grab the animal is just above the ankle. The antelope should preferably be grasped firmly and held down on the ground. It is very important to keep the animal's head well above the ground, to prevent injuries to the eyes and mouth. The antelope should be treated as gently as possible. Bruised flanks and broken ribs are most often the result of careless handling during capture. Care should be taken, in particular, not to pin down a struggling animal with one's knees as this may easily lead to broken ribs and other injuries.

Game captors are sometimes very preoccupied with the success of capture techniques, but neglect to pay the necessary attention to the well-being of the captured animals. Inadequate knowledge is often the cause. The following chapter discusses the correct handling and treatment of newly captured game.

Captured game should not be over-exerted and animals entangled in nets should be grasped firmly and freed as quickly as possible to prevent injuries.

11. THE CORRECT HANDLING AND TREATMENT OF NEWLY CAPTURED WILD ANIMALS

Once the animals have been captured, the game captor's knowledge of and experience in the handling of wild animals and the application of veterinary treatment methods are thoroughly put to the test.

Thorough training in animal husbandry, physiology, pharmacology and veterinary medicine are important prerequisites for anyone intending to master all aspects of the game captor's profession. Although capturing game by means of capture corrals and nets can be mastered without much theoretical training, the use of dart guns and drugs should preferably be practised under the guidance of a vet.

The application of game capture drugs, as well as the associated veterinary treatment methods, has been described in detail in books such as "The Capture and Care of Wild Animals" (Ed. E Young, 1973) and "Chemical Capture" (Dr A M Harthoorn, 1976). In this chapter brief reference is made to physiological disturbances and disease/pathological phenomena that may occur in captured game. Appropriate treatment methods are also shortly outlined, while the emphasis is placed on preventive measures.

ANIMALS CAPTURED IN CORRALS

By the time the animals are safely inside the capture corral, they are usually very tired, frightened and bewildered, often continuing to run around and exert themselves even further. Sufficient shelter within the capture corral and the prevention of noise and unnecessary disturbance by curious observers will enable the animals to settle down and recover sooner.

It may sometimes be necessary to separate animals of different species, or to isolate bulls and rams of the more aggressive game species, as this will assist in preventing injuries.

Blue wildebeest confined in the same capture corral with waterbuck, kudu or impala may, for example, fatally injure individuals of the other species. Mature and young impala rams should also be removed before they injure ewes and younger animals.

Aggressive animals can be separated from the rest by means of sliding curtains which divide the capture corral, removed by darting, or, for example, shooting surplus impala rams using a small calibre rifle. Capricious individuals should, as far as possible, be separated from the rest of the herd by the helicopter pilot and left behind in the veld before the animals are driven into the capture corral.

Animals that are exhausted after a chase should be left in the capture corral to recover and to cool down before being loaded onto trucks that may possibly have poor ventilation, especially on hot days. Experienced game captors will, however, be able to discern when the animals are ready to be loaded straight after capture. Kudu, impala and some of the other species can be driven directly into the truck by an experienced helicopter pilot. Unruly impala rams can thereafter be removed from the truck one by one and released.

Where circumstances require animals to remain in a plastic capture corral for a day or more, sufficient shelter and shade, grazing and water should be available in the corral. Activities in the vicinity of the corral should proceed as silently as possible,

and adequate precautions should be taken to prevent dogs or predators from entering the capture corrals.

GAME CAPTURED IN NETS

Nets should never be used to catch large numbers of animals at the same time. When too many animals arrive at the nets simultaneously, they can injure themselves by falling over and on top of each other.

Prior to the catch, a sufficient number of experienced assistants should hide near the nets, ready to attend to the captured animals at once. In the case of smaller species, such as steenbok and duiker, one person per animal is adequate. For larger and more aggressive species, provision should be made for more assistants.

Animals that have become entangled in capture nets run the risk of injuring themselves in various ways. To prevent this, sharp and hard objects such as stones and logs should be removed from the capture site beforehand. As far as possible, the use of iron posts to suspend the nets should be kept to a minimum.

As soon as the animals arrive at the nets, the concealed assistants must attend to the animals without delay to prevent them from escaping or becoming too entangled in the nets. Each animal's head must be freed from the net immediately to prevent it from suffocating. The head must then be held up high to prevent the animal from hitting its head against the ground and injuring itself. Fractured skulls and other head injuries can easily occur if assistance is not given soon enough. The limbs must also be removed from the net as quickly as possible. Delays in this respect may lead to injured muscles and joints.

It is furthermore important to calm the captured animals as speedily as possible and to secure the limbs in a satisfactory manner. Covering the eyes with a soft blindfold often has almost the same calming effect as administering tranquillisers. When animals have to be handled for any length of time or transported over long distances, the use of suitable tranquillisers as well as blindfolds is recommended.

Round, hard ropes should preferably not be used for binding the limbs. These chafe and hurt the limbs and can even cause permanent damage. Flat, soft canvas ropes or leather straps, and even old nylon stockings in the case of the smaller antelope species, are recommended instead. These straps or ropes should be checked regularly to ensure that they are not too tight. They should be able to move freely along the limb. Regularly massaging the limbs will also enable the animal to stand up and use its limbs normally when it is released.

The correct way to hold an antelope to prevent it from being injured, bloating or suffocating will be described in detail later.

ANIMALS CAPTURED OR TREATED WITH GAME CAPTURE DRUGS OR TRANQUILLIZERS

Animals that have been captured using narcotic drugs should not be chased, allowed to exert themselves or become distressed in any other way. The combined effect of the capture drugs, fear and exhaustion can quite easily cause the animal to die.

Animals that are under the influence of narcotic drugs or tranquillizers require special attention and care. Such animals should preferably be handled and treated under the constant supervision of a veterinarian. The level of sedation and the animal's heart and lung functions must be monitored continuously, and appropriate treatment given where necessary.

Correct handling of the animal: Particularly on very hot days, anaesthetised animals should be moved into the shade without delay. If suitable cover is not provided by trees, branches and other means can be used to provide the necessary shade.

Ruminants such as buffalo, giraffe and antelope must be kept and transported in their natural recumbent position, i.e. on their briskets. If these animals are allowed to lie on their sides, the fluid level in the rumen rises above the opening to the oesophagus and the gases accumulated in the rumen, unable to escape, cause the animal to become bloated. The resulting increased pressure in the abdomen can cause the diaphragm to become so distended that the animal cannot breathe normally. Fluid may also be forced up into the mouth through the oesophagus. As the animal is under sedation, it cannot swallow normally and these stomach contents may accidentally be inhaled. If the animal does not die immediately from impaired breathing or suffocation, the partially digested food particles entering the lungs may cause pneumonia after a day or two.

To prevent all these complications, the animal's limbs should be neatly tucked beneath its body and it should be lifted onto its brisket. The head and neck must held higher than the chest so that the stomach gases can escape freely through the oesophagus. If the abdomen continues to swell and the animal becomes too bloated, the forequarters must be lifted even higher in the case of the smaller antelope species, and the animal rocked gently to and fro until the gases escape. When this happens, one usually hears and smells the escaping gases. If the animal is large and heavy, it is sometimes helpful simply to hold the neck and head up high and to roll the animal from one side to the other.

Even when anaesthetised, an animal may groan and attempt to change its position when it becomes bloated or when its limbs have been folded underneath it in an uncomfortable position. This is a sign that the animal requires immediate assistance!

Since the animal is unable to swallow normally, saliva may flow into the trachea and cause suffocation. Consequently the neck should be kept sloping downwards, so that excessive saliva can drain from the mouth.

The animal's respiratory tract must constantly be kept open so that it can breathe freely. The person holding the animal's head should, for example, ensure that its neck is not bent downwards or sideways, and that the animal's throat and neck are not resting on anything that may obstruct the airway. Anaesthetised antelope often die when the assistant responsible for holding the animal's head tires and allows the animal's throat to rest on his knee. An animal that has been transported over a long distance with its neck remaining in an unnatural position for too long must sometimes be destroyed once it is finally released, because its stiffened neck falls to one side in a permanently bent position.

In contrast with the ruminants, elephant, rhinoceros and zebra mostly digest grass and other plant matter further back in the digestive system. Gas accumulation therefore does not lead to bloating in these animals, since the gases are able to escape through the anus. These species can therefore be transported lying on their sides. Elephant must in any case be rolled over onto their sides if they go down on their briskets, since they are unable to breathe freely in this unnatural position and may die as a result.

Hard metal floors inside transport trucks and sharp and hard objects against which the animals may kick during transport can cause permanent injuries to the limbs. When an animal is transported lying down, the floor should be covered with a layer of soft material such as hay, sackcloth or a mattress, and precautions must be taken to prevent the animal from kicking against the sharp edges of the truck.

Animals under anaesthesia are not able to blink their eyes or to avert their heads in order to protect their eyes against the sun, wind and elements. The eyes should therefore be covered with a soft cloth and preferably also be treated with a suitable eye ointment. Terramycin ointment can, amongst others, be used for this purpose.

Disturbances of the nervous system: Increased stimulation by certain drugs can lead to muscular movements and even cramps and convulsions. Drugs such as phencyclidine hydrochloride (Sernylan, Park-Davis & Co.) that were previously used for game capture, cause severe convulsions. Diazepam (Valium, Roche) or xylazine hydrochloride (Rompun, Bayer) are very valuable in counteracting these convulsions.

Problems arising from excessive sedation are more common and generally more severe than those caused by overstimulation of the central nervous system. Overdoses of capture drugs or tranquillizers, or sensitivity to these drugs in the case of old, debilitated, thin or sick animals, can cause fatal over-reactions. Animals that have been confined in cages for some time are also unusually sensitive to narcotic drugs and as little as half of the normal dose of capture drug can in some cases be quite adequate to immobilise a captive animal. The drug doses prescribed for free-ranging animals can therefore constitute a fatal overdose to captive animals of the same species.

Narcotic drugs and tranquillisers do not simply cause proportionally higher levels of sedation as doses increase. The control centres in the brain responsible for regulating blood pressure and body temperature can also be severely disrupted by overdoses of these drugs.

It is therefore imperative to avoid drug overdoses, and to administer the correct antidote to any animal showing signs of poisoning without delay.

If other factors responsible for a deterioration in the animal's condition, such as exertion or heat fatigue, are not also effectively counteracted, an animal may fail to respond positively or satisfactorily to the antidote given. Various analeptic drugs which stimulate the central nervous system have in the past been used with varying degrees of success to revive such cases. Methylphenidate hydrochloride (Ritalin, Ciba) serves as an example here. Doxapram hydrochloride (Dopram, A H Robins & Co.) is also particularly effective and should definitely be included in the game captor's standard medical equipment. It should, however, be stressed once again that very limited benefit will be achieved through the use of stimulants if the true causes of the deterioration in the animal's condition and loss of consciousness are not first eliminated successfully.

The use of antidotes and supportive treatment: In Chapter 8, which deals with game capture drugs, specific antidotes and their recommended doses are given. If these drugs are given intravenously, most animals respond within approximately two minutes, or soon after.

If, for some good reason, the drug cannot be administered intravenously, an intramuscular injection can also be given. The results obtained in the latter case are usually unpredictable and the animal will take longer to react because, as a rule, drugs are absorbed more slowly through the muscles.

If an animal does not appear to be responding satisfactorily to the antidote, it is important to remember that, in the case of nearly all antidotes, the administration of additional doses can weaken the animal even further! Within limits, however, supportive treatment with naloxone hydrochloride (Narcan, Endo Labs Inc.) may in certain cases help to tide the animal over.

Glucoronic acid (Guronsan, Chugai Pharm. Co.) is a valuable aid in cases where the animal just does not seem to be able to recover. This detoxification preparation is available in the form of an injectable solution. Although immediate results cannot be guaranteed, this remedy can help to counteract fatigue and listness in debilitated animals.

An animal which is not responding well to an antidote should not be disturbed continuously, since further demands on an already weakened system can precipitate the animal's death. Specialised emergency care is required in such cases. Possible physiological complications, such as those discussed below, should also receive attention.

Circulatory and blood pressure problems: If the heart does not continue to beat fast and strongly enough, or if the blood vessels dilate excessively, the animal's blood pressure may drop dangerously low.

The cardiac functions are regulated by a control centre in the animal's brain, as well as by the heart muscle itself. Excessive doses of game capture drugs can have a deleterious effect on the regulating centre in the brain as well as on the heart muscle.

Far more often than is generally realised, stress, fear, exertion and heat fatigue can contribute as much to the death of an animal as an overdose of capture drugs. Pursuing game over great distances, particularly on hot days, as well as any behaviour on the part of the capture team that is likely to frighten the animals unnecessarily, should therefore be avoided wherever possible. A considerable percentage of captured animals that die during the capture process for ostensibly no reason are victims of fear, stress and exertion! When capture drugs or tranquillisers are used, special care must be taken not to subject the animals needlessly to fear and stress.

Terminology relating to circulatory and blood pressure problems which may confuse the layman are briefly defined and clarified below.

Low blood pressure (hypotension): Poisoning or weakening of the heart muscle which leads to a slower and/or weaker heartbeat can, like dilation of the blood vessels, cause lowered blood pressure. Aggravating factors have been described earlier. This condition is common amongst newly captured wild animals, and in its advanced stages can lead to fatal complications.

Shock: In contrast to the layman's conception of "shock" as a psychological reaction to bad news, this term in a physiological context refers to the progressive collapse of the body's ability to regulate blood pressure. Although severe haemorrhages can be responsible for shock, factors such as the following are more often implicated in game capture:

Fright, fear and pain can, similarly to the abnormally increased body temperature resulting from excessive chasing of game, play a role in the development of shock. Capture drugs and tranquillisers can also, in certain circumstances, poison the regulating mechanisms in the brain, and/or the heart muscle, and this in turn can cause blood pressure to drop even further. Drugs which suppress the animal's respiration can also lead indirectly to shock.

Shock is a complex physiological condition which, to put it simply, ultimately causes an insufficient blood supply and the resulting oxygen starvation in the tissues. Not only is this syndrome precipitated or aggravated by a variety of factors, but it also in itself initiates a series of physiological reactions which can eventually culminate in the death of the animal.

Symptoms of shock include the usual signs of lowered blood pressure. Blood vessels which are normally prominent on the animal's face and other parts of the body collapse and become less noticeable. It may even prove difficult to find a vein for intravenous injections. The pulse is rapid but faint. Breathing and heart rate, which may initially have accelerated, become slower and weaker and the blood turns a darker blue. Finally the animal lapses into a coma. In acute cases, the animal may die suddenly; sometimes death comes more slowly.

Post-mortem examinations reveal non-specific lesions and may also point to other causes of death. Blood vessels that are filled with darkish blood and are prominently visible, the accumulation of fluid and froth in the lungs and small haemorrhages in the heart walls and elsewhere in the body are, inter alia, noticeable in animals that have died as a result of shock.

The treatment of the shock syndrome is complicated and should be left to a veterinarian. Stimulants and preparations which act on the heart and promote the contraction/dilation and/or thickening of the blood vessel walls are sometimes used. High doses of corticosteroids can prove particularly valuable.

Although oxygen therapy and the intravenous administration of fluids such as blood, serum, plasma or commercial saline solutions are more difficult under veld conditions, they remain the method of choice for treating shock.

Oxygen therapy under field conditions.

96

Preventing the development of shock as far as possible is of paramount importance. Once again, sufficient emphasis cannot be laid on the compelling necessity of protecting captured animals from exertion and fear as far as is humanly possible!

Heart failure or cardiac arrest: An overdose of capture drugs, or any of the above-mentioned factors, can eventually lead to heart failure. Symptoms are self-evident and post-mortem lesions are very similar to those described above. Heart massage and oxygen and fluid therapy, if these are provided timeously, can be beneficial. A cardiac stimulant such as heptaminol (Cortensor, A Wander Ltd) can also be used to boost the weakened heart function.

Irreversible brain damage usually ensues when the heart stops functioning for three to four minutes, or longer.

Once again, it is imperative to eliminate all contributing factors and especially to ensure that only game capture techniques that do not risk the animals' lives needlessly be employed.

Impaired respiration: It has already been stressed that the animal's respiratory tract should at all times be kept clear and open. Impaired breathing due to bloating (p. 95) should also be corrected.

If, in spite of the proposed treatment procedures, an animal continues to breathe in a laboured and gasping manner, other causes should be sought. Spasmodic contractions of the throat muscles or terminal airways are encountered in exceptional circumstances. In these cases the animal's breathing is accompanied by a wheezing sound. Fits of coughing also occur, and the animal may finally cease breathing altogether. The inhalation of stomach contents can be the cause of this condition. Occasionally the animal recovers spontaneously. If, however, this condition persists or occurs repeatedly, treatment with pethidine hydrochloride or aminophylline can be considered. The administration of oxygen and follow-up treatment with an antibiotic are also advised.

Shallow and weak breathing is commonly observed in animals that have been treated with narcotic drugs or tranquillisers. These drugs can, particularly in excessive doses, affect the breathing centre in the brain or the muscles of the respiratory system. Although mildly impaired breathing should not give rise to undue concern, insufficient ventilation of the lungs can lead to the accumulation of carbon dioxide and acidosis of the blood. When an animal experiences an advanced stage of oxygen starvation, the mucosa of, for example, the mouth and eyes, which are normally pale pink, assume a dark blue tinge. The detrimental effects of acidosis are discussed in more detail later.

Respiration can cease altogether if the above-mentioned situation is not corrected in time. Overdoses of capture drugs and tranquillisers, as well as fear, shock, exhaustion and excessive pressure on the animal's chest cavity, abdomen or trachea, can severally or collectively contribute to total respiratory failure. Old, debilitated and sick animals, in particular, are unusually susceptible to the toxic effect of capture drugs and tranquillisers.

Artificial respiration can be applied to animals in various ways. If no special facilities are available, the animal can be rolled onto its side and the chest cavity compressed manually.

If oxygen supply equipment is available, compressed air can be used to assist respiration. Oxygen can be administered using the same equipment, or even by means of a naso-tracheal tube or a self-made oxygen tent. Pure oxygen can irritate the mucous linings of the respiratory system and should, when administered in this form, first be filtered through water in the form of bubbles.

Respiratory stimulants such as picrotoxin, caffeine and doxapram hydrochloride (Dopram, A H Robins & Co.) can also be used to assist impaired breathing. Debilitated animals injected with Dopram generally not only breathe more quickly and deeply, but also tend to recover faster from their stupor. In animals experiencing severe respiratory distress, follow-up treatment with stimulants may be required. These drugs should be injected intravenously if a sufficiently rapid reviving effect is to be achieved.

The blood and mucosa of an animal with impaired breathing will turn dark blue in the advanced stages. When an animal dies as a consequence of an inadequate air supply, swollen blood vessels and dark blue discoloration of the blood, haemorrhages in the muscles and organs and the accumulation of fluid and froth in the respiratory tract will, once again, be observed during a post-mortem examination.

OVERSTRAINING DISEASE (CAPTURE MYOPATHY, WHITE MUSCLE DISEASE)

This is undoubtedly the most important disease with which a game captor will have to contend. Since being identified, it has been established that more than 20 species of game are susceptible to death from overstraining disease. These include rare species such as the roan antelope, sable antelope, tsessebe, bontebok and black rhino. Elephant, blesbok, springbok, impala, buffalo, blue wildebeest, kudu, nyala, red hartebeest, eland, gemsbok, giraffe, steenbok, red duiker, oribi, Damaraland mountain zebra and Burchell's zebra also feature amongst the species that can die from overstraining disease. Of these species, the roan antelope, sable antelope, tsessebe, red hartebeest, nyala and oribi are particularly vulnerable. The buffalo, blue wildebeest, kudu, eland and impala are only affected in exceptional cases.

Overstraining disease is particularly prevalent amongst animals that have been chased excessively or exerted in any other way during capture. Fear and stress can also contribute to the development of this disease. Abnormally high body temperatures, impaired heart and lung functions and certain capture drugs can also predispose animals to overstraining disease.

The disease arises when muscular glycogen is broken down chemically to form lactic acid which cannot be assimilated and excreted by the animal's body fast enough. The resulting acidosis can lead to severe damage to the muscle fibre and organs.

Affected muscles become pale and dull and usually have a striated appearance. In fact, the affected parts closely resemble the flesh of fish, and haemorrhages in the muscles are usually observed. Although it is mainly the muscle groups that have been most severely overstrained that show prominent lesions, any muscle, even the heart muscle, can be affected.

Animals with extensive lesions rarely recover. In exceptional cases the acute lesions do, however, heal, and white scars are left on the heart muscle. White scars several centimetres in diameter can, for example, be present in the heart muscle. When such an animal subsequently gets a sudden fright, or is again overexerted, it may quite unexpectedly drop dead from heart failure, even months later.

In addition to the muscular system, the liver and kidneys are also affected. The muscle pigment (myoglobin) released into the blood by damaged muscle tissue is excreted by the kidneys. As a result, the urine turns a reddish brown colour. These pigments can occlude and damage the renal tubes to such an extent that renal failure ensues. The lungs of an animal that succumbed to overstraining disease usually contain fluid and froth and such cases are often incorrectly diagnosed by laymen as heartwater disease.

The symptoms of overstraining disease are variable. Animals that have been acutely overexerted can die suddenly from heart failure. In such cases post-mortem examinations generally reveal prominent blood vessels filled with darkish blood. Traces of blood are present in the heart and other muscles, while the lungs may contain a considerable amount of froth.

In less acute cases, the animals may appear perfectly normal after capture. At any subsequent stage, even two to four weeks after the animals have been overexerted, symptoms may, however, begin to develop. Some animals may even then die suddenly of heart failure. Others may become weak and develop paralysis. Paralysed animals that remain lying down can appear healthy in all other respects, and may even feed and drink normally if food and water are within reach. After a while the animals become weaker and the neck may bend over to one side permanently. Advanced cases such as these hardly ever recover!

If an animal suddenly dies long after it has been captured or overexerted, the possibility of delayed heart failure due to lesions in the heart muscle should certainly not be discounted.

Animals that have been overexerted can recover if they receive intravenous doses of sodium bicarbonate immediately after capture. No satisfactory treatment exists, however, for advanced cases of overstraining disease.

Overstraining disease in game closely resembles a pathological condition found in horses, known as paralytic myoglobinuria ("Monday morning disease"). Horses fed on high-energy rations and subjected to strenuous exercise after a few days' rest, as would be the case, for example, on a Monday morning following a weekend, can suffer such severe effects to their muscular systems that they are unable to run any more. Associated symptoms, as well as the post-mortem lesions of these two diseases, show marked similarities.

Nutritional deficiencies in domestic stock can also lead to the development of similar lesions. A shortage of Vitamin E in the young of cattle and sheep can, for example, be the cause of muscular lesions similar to those characterising overstraining disease. It has not been proved, however, that nutritional deficiencies in the grazing render game from specific areas more susceptible to overstraining disease.

Overstraining disease is responsible for the death of large numbers of game and huge financial losses every year. The loss of valuable animal lives can only be prevented by less callous handling of helpless and terrified wild animals. Exposing game to overexertion, pain and fear during capture and handling should therefore be avoided at all costs, not only for civilised, humane reasons, but also in the interest of the animals' survival.

HEAT STROKE

Body temperature is kept within normal limits by a regulating mechanism in the animal's brain. The functioning of this mechanism can be hindered by the action of certain tranquillisers. Drugs of the phenothiazine groups such as acetylpromazine maleate (Acetylpromazine, Boots Pure Drug Co.) and chlorpromazine hydrochloride (Largactil, Maybaker) serve as examples here.

Heat stroke develops when body temperature is forced above its normal limits as a result of chasing the animal too hard or too far or subjecting it to any other excessive exertion. When animals are captured during hot or humid conditions the risk of heat stroke is at its maximum. Animals that are allowed to lie in the sun immediately after having been captured with capture drugs, or loaded directly into bags or hot crates or transport trailers, and especially those treated with the above-mentioned tranquillisers, have a very good chance of contracting heat stroke!

Heat stroke can develop quite suddenly. High body temperatures (up to 43°C and even higher), rapid breathing and even panting, an accelerated and weak pulse, signs of exhaustion, in some cases a neck which falls back limply against the body, excessive perspiration (not observed in all game species) and, in severe cases, eventual loss of consciousness, generally precede death.

To prevent heat stroke animals should not be captured or transported in hot weather. Every sensible precaution should be taken to prevent overheating, for example by using well ventilated transport trailers. On hot days, game captors should refrain from using drugs that are known to predispose animals to heat stroke. Captured animals should be cooled down as quickly as possible in the shade and not be subjected to any further struggling and strenuous activity.

The practice of transporting game species such as springbok and blesbok in grain-bags is strongly discouraged. Transport trailers should, wherever possible, be kept in the shade before the animals are loaded and should start moving as soon as possible after loading, to improve the circulation of air through the loading compartment. All trailers should be designed and constructed in such a way that sufficient ventilation will be provided to prevent overheating of the animals even if the vehicle carrying game should break down and be forced to stand in the sun.

Animals already showing signs of overheating can be hosed down with water and cooled down further by fanning them with branches and sacks. It is important to note that animals that are hosed down in enclosed spaces may suffer further adverse effects if the air does not circulate sufficiently to induce cooling through evaporation. As a matter of fact, excessive humidity in a hot, confined space can interfere with the animal's normal cooling processes, and the use of electric fans in transport trailers is recommended by wildlife experts such as the late Dr Ian Hofmeyr of Namibia to overcome this problem.

Consideration can be given to treating individual cases with intravenous fluids and oxygen and drugs which help to lower body temperature, but this should be left to suitably trained veterinarians. The application of cold water through a gastric tube can also be useful in lowering an animal's body temperature to within normal limits.

The post-mortem lesions of an animal that succumbed to heat stroke do not differ notably from those of animals that died of the other physiological disturbances discussed above. Quite often one complication in any case leads to another and the animal usually dies from a complex combination of causes. Example: Overexertion on a hot day in an animal that has been caught using capture drugs which impair the animal's breathing may, for example, lead to heat stroke, while impaired respiration may lead to acute oxygen starvation, which can in turn cause the animal to die of cardiac arrest. If such an animal were to survive for longer, overstraining disease may develop, and the animal may succumb much later to yet another complication, such as renal failure.

Nonetheless, post-mortem lesions usually associated with heat stroke include the following: prominent blood vessels filled with dark blood, damage to and haemorrhages in the muscles and organs and fluid and froth in the lungs. In some cases the right-hand heart chamber is abnormally relaxed and dilated. The carcass also decomposes more rapidly than usual.

HYPOTHERMIA

Animals captured at night or on very cold days, or which are exposed to very low temperatures after treatment with drugs known to affect the temperature regulating mechanism in the brain, can experience an abnormal drop in body temperature. Such animals can lapse into a coma and do not easily recover. Good nursing and treatment aimed at raising the body temperature of such animals may, however, bring about positive results.

PREVENTION OF INFECTIONS AND CONTAGIOUS DISEASES

Overexertion, injuries, exposure to excessive variations in ambient temperature and other stress factors can contribute to pneumonia, festering of damaged tissue, and even to the development of clinical manifestations of diseases or parasite infestations that may have been dormant or even contracted at the time of capture or transportation. It is therefore most strongly recommended that, especially in cases where it is possible to handle animals individually, the opportunity be used to administer the necessary preventive treatment. This basically entails the following:

Ointment containing a broad-spectrum antibiotic, or a suitable mastitis ointment such as Terramycin (oxytetracycline) or Orbenin (cloxacillin), can be used to treat dart and other smallish wounds. The contents of a small tube of mastitis ointment can be squeezed into a dart wound.

Larger, open wounds can be cleaned thoroughly and treated with the same ointments or with Tr. chloramphenicol , Tr. merthiolate (mercurochrome), or, in the case of animals with thick hides such as rhino and elephant, with Stockholm tar. Numerous other remedies which can be applied with good results are also available.

The injection of long-acting, broad-spectrum antibiotics such as Liquamycin/L.A. or Terramycin/L.A. (oxytetracycline) or similar preparations are particularly useful in preventing pneumonia, general infections resulting from bruises and injuries, as well as diseases caused by bacterial infections.

Depending on the species concerned and the contagious diseases prevalent in that particular area, the local veterinarian may also prescribe other specific treatments. The immunisation and treatment of game to prevent contagious diseases and combat parasite infestations is discussed in Chapter 18 .

It is the responsibility of everyone who captures and transports game to do everything possible to prevent the unnecessary spreading of diseases and parasites and to afford the animals in their care the best possible protection against disease and parasites. If game captors and their staff do not possess the necessary knowledge to meet these requirements, the assistance and supervision of a veterinarian should be sought.

HARMFUL SIDE EFFECTS OF CERTAIN DRUGS

Cortisone treatment is quite widely used by people who do not always understand the pharmacological action and side effects of this drug. Corticosteroids lower an animal's resistance to disease, and antibiotics should as a rule be given in conjunction with this drug. When corticosteroids are given in large doses during late pregnancy, abnormalities can also result.

Like corticosteroids, other drugs can also have adverse side effects. It is therefore imperative for anyone wishing to treat animals to be thoroughly conversant with the pharmacological action and toxic properties of the drugs used.

The game captor should also satisfy himself that animals that have been treated with capture drugs or tranquillisers and subsequently released do not later suffer the rebound or delayed effect of the drugs. When an insufficient dose of antidote has been administered, an animal may, after a period of apparent recovery, revert to a deep sleep. If such an animal remains lying in the hot sun or rolls over onto its side, it may die as a result of overheating, bloating or suffocation. Animals under the prolonged influence of narcotic drugs, or drugs such as hyoscine hydrobromide which causes temporary loss of vision, may fatally injure themselves against trees and logs or, for example, as a consequence of falling down cliffs or the steep walls of ravines. It is therefore essential to keep treated animals under surveillance until they have fully recovered.

It has been observed that many game captors appear to prefer the more exciting part of the capturing process, that is until the animals have been chased into the nets or capture corrals and caught, or until darted animals have been immobilised. When this is done, however, care of the captured animals is all too often left in the hands of inexperienced assistants with inadequate or non-existent training. As may be deduced from the preceding paragraphs, it is precisely at this point that specialised care and treatment of the newly captured animals, based on thorough background knowledge, is needed most to prevent unnecessary losses. The diagnosis and treatment of physiological disturbances in captured game is a complex task which rightly belongs in the hands of a qualified veterinarian. Nature conservation departments and organisations which capture and handle game on a large scale should therefore have the services of an experienced veterinarian at their disposal. Farmers who capture game themselves, and particularly those who use game capture drugs, should also avail themselves of professional services, since insufficient knowledge and inadequate precautions are no excuse for causing the death of captured game.

12. THE NUTRITION AND CARE OF CAPTIVE GAME

Since game must often remain in captivity for short periods following capture, or even be quarantined for a month or longer, it is vital that every game farmer and professional game captor should possess a thorough knowledge concerning the feeding and care of captive game. Training and practical experience at a zoo are strongly recommended.

MINIMUM REQUIREMENTS

These can be summarised as follows:

— effective accommodation in terms of space, shelter, ventilation and drainage;
— satisfactory facilities for separating animals of different species, sex and behaviour;
— suitable taming procedures dictated by the behaviour of each species and individual concerned;
— direct supervision by responsible and correctly trained personnel;
— scrupulous hygiene measures;
— compliance with veterinarian's directions regarding special rations, parasite control and treatment;
— regular inspections and, where necessary, treatment by a veterinarian.

HAND-REARING BABY ANIMALS

Anyone hoping to hand-rear a young wild animal must be prepared to devote considerable time and attention to his little charge. It is a task which requires certain sacrifices and, most specifically, a lot of patience!

All animal species react differently, and the approach to each should therefore to a certain extent vary accordingly. Characteristic behaviour traits of the various species are exhibited at a very early age by the little individuals in the kindergarten, and offer the animal lover a unique opportunity to study animal behaviour.

Suitable cage or pen: First, it is important to provide the young animal with the right type of cage or pen. Initially, foster-animals tend to feel very frightened and insecure in a human environment and therefore need a sheltered place to hide. This is particularly true of animals such as the kudu, nyala, bushbuck, steenbok, the duiker family and other species of which it is characteristic for the mother to leave her baby on its own, hidden in dense bush, between feeds.

A small sleeping area which can be closed off separately and which adjoins an exercise pen offers the ideal solution to the problem of providing suitable accommodation.

Sleeping quarters with a roof and a well drained floor are essential for protecting the young animal against sun, wind and inclement weather. The floor of the sleeping quarters should preferably consist of a rough or lightly grooved concrete floor, covered with a thick layer of grass-hay or straw. If windows are present, these should be sufficiently high up and covered, so as not to encourage attempts to escape. The walls may initially be padded with bales of hay or straw-filled sacks, to prevent injuries if the animal jumps against them.

A smallish exercise pen, the size of an average room in a house, is usually quite adequate. An open wire cage is not suitable, since the wary little creature can spot people, dogs and other strange beings approaching and may, in an effort to escape, run into the wire fence and injure itself. For this reason, the pen should be closed off on the inside of the fence with densely packed reeds, firmly stretched game capture plastic or any other suitable opaque material.

The exercise pen may have an earth floor, from which manure and left-over food should regularly be removed. Animals such as steenbok may refuse to urinate or defecate unless they are able to dig a small hole in the ground. If these animals have to be kept on a concrete floor for any length of time, the floor should therefore be covered with a thick layer of earth.

It is recommended that the new arrival be shut quietly in its darkened sleeping quarters for a few days, to accustom it to its new surroundings and keeper. The door of the sleeping quarters can thereafter be left open and the young animal allowed to explore its exercise pen at its own pace. Since it will by then have learnt to regard its sleeping quarters as a place of safety, it will flee back to its sleeping quarters at the first signs of danger to hide.

The taming process: Especially during the first few days, the keeper should spend as much time as possible with his new fosterling in order to win its trust and accustom it to the conditions of captivity.

The value of certain tranquillisers to tame animals is still not widely recognised. When a wild animal has been treated with one of the following drugs and is handled and stroked by his keeper in peaceful and quiet surroundings for an hour or more, such an animal may within a very short time come to accept his new foster-parent and become completely tame. The following drugs have already been used successfully for this purpose: chlorpromazine hydrochloride (Largactil, Maybaker), acetylpromazine maleate (Acetylpromazine, Boots Pure Drug Co.), chlordiazepoxide (Librium, Roche), diazepam (Valium, Roche) and xylazine hydrochloride (Rompun, Bayer).

Although animals adapt better to others of the same species, it is possible to keep and rear different species together. Individuals who object to other animals should, however, be removed without delay in order to prevent injuries. Young animals belonging to game species such as steenbok and duiker, which are classified as solitary animals, may be kept singly. Animals that generally form herds, such as impala, zebra and wildebeest, fare better in captivity when they have company. Baby elephants, buffalo and zebra foals, in particular, should be kept together with other hand-reared animals, or even together with a tame domestic calf or lamb, otherwise they may feel lonely, and even languish and die.

Although newly captured wild animals grow tame more quickly and adapt better when they have the companionship of other animals, problems are sometimes encountered when hand-reared animals are kept together. They may, for example, develop the habit of licking and sucking each other's ears and tails. Hair loss and even skin infections can be the result. As soon as these tendencies are noticed, the animals should be separated, especially during and shortly after feeding times. If this is not done, they may ingest so much hair that their digestive systems may become obstructed.

Baby elephants and buffalo calves are usually very aggressive at first. However, they soon learn to accept their keeper as a surrogate parent and subsequently grow extremely attached to him or her.

Certain species such as giraffe, eland, kudu and rhebok become remarkably tame and enjoy being fondled. Others, such as the impala, become quite tame but do not tolerate being touched and handled. Newborn animals usually become tamer than young animals that have lived for a while in the veld with wild animals prior to capture.

Colostrum and surrogate parents: Newborn animals should ideally receive colostrum from the mother animal within 24 hours of birth. Colostrum is rich in antibodies against diseases to which that particular species is susceptible and to which the mother has already developed a measure of immunity. Its vitamin A content is also high and the ingestion of colostrum shortly after birth can increase the young animal's resistance to disease.

If a newborn animal who has not had colostrum has to be hand-reared, it may be useful to give it fresh blood serum from the same species, either orally or intravenously. Intravenous infusions should be carried out under sterile conditions, while the oral administration of serum will only be useful within the first 24 hours after birth. The importance of colostrum may have been exaggerated, however, since antelope have already been hand-reared successfully without it.

Domestic surrogate parents can be used to help raise young wild animals. Dairy cows and goats as well as sheep have been successful foster-parents to various game species. Domestic dogs and cats have also on occasion been roped in to help raise the cubs of lions, leopards, cheetah and wild cat species. Unfortunately the latter foster-mothers tend to be rather heartless towards their strange babies.

Milk surrogates: Research has been conducted for years and numerous articles published on suitable milk surrogates for hand-rearing wild animals. Efforts were nearly always directed at formulating a substitute having approximately the same chemical composition as the milk of the species concerned. The fat content of cow's or domestic goat milk was, for example, increased by adding fresh or powdered cream or egg-yolk, or decreased by diluting the milk with water. The carbohydrate quality was supplemented by the addition of lactose or glucose to the milk, while the protein value was raised to the required levels by the addition of hydrolysed protein preparations. Vitamins were even added in some instances.

Experience with hand-rearing nearly all the South African game species has, however, taught me that, regardless of whether the milk of the black rhino cow contains virtually no fat and that of an elephant cow more than 20 per cent fat, it is quite possible to use cow's milk, goatsmilk or any good powdered milk with the same beneficial results to raise any of the animal species. The secret remains scrupulous hygiene and care, and the implementation of satisfactory measures to prevent disease.

In addition to cow's and goatsmilk, good results were also obtained using Nespray's full-cream powdered milk, as well as with a milk surrogate constituted as follows:

Skim milk powder:	80%
Whey powder:	8%
Fine Kaffir corn meal:	8,5%
Brewer's yeast:	2%
Dicalcium phosphate:	1%
Sodium chloride:	0,5%
Vitamin A:	8,8 g/100 kg milk powder
Vitamin D3:	1,1 g/100 kg milk powder

The milk powder referred to directly above is prepared by mixing 1 kg of powder in 9 litres of water. Other full-cream milk powders are prepared in accordance with the manufacturer's directions for use. The powder milk can be made up in a stronger concentration for the feeding of very young or very thin animals. In such cases two to four raw hen's eggs can also be mixed in a litre of milk to boost the nutritional value of the milk.

Special precautions: The milk should never be too cold or too hot, since the animal may then refuse to drink it. When the milk is dripped onto the hand, and it neither burns the hand nor feels too cold, it should be more or less at body temperature and ready to use.

Limewater is essential for counteracting the development of gastro-enteritis and diarrhoea. Limewater is prepared by adding a few teaspoons of slaked lime powder (calcium hydroxide) to a clean bottle of water. The powder is shaken up and the bottle left to stand until the white sediment leaves a clear liquid at the top of the bottle. This clear liquid is known as limewater and can be poured into a separate container. One part limewater to seven parts milk will prevent excessive acid formation in the digestive system and thus contribute to the successful nutrition and raising of the young animal.

Since the animal's system requires time to grow accustomed to the new type of milk or milk surrogate, preventive treatment should be given each time the type of milk is changed. Obviously the same type of milk should be used throughout, if this is at all possible.

Young wild animals can be taught to drink milk from a bowl or a bucket. Milk splashing onto the animal's face may, however, attract flies and even lead to dermatitis and hair loss. My personal preference is to use a glass or plastic bottle and a teat.

Once an animal has grown used to his bottle, it may refuse to drink from any other. The correct size teat should be used and the opening at the tip should not be too large, as fast flowing milk may cause the animal to choke. Likewise, the opening should not be too small, either, since the little creature may become discouraged when it has to work too hard to suck the milk from the bottle.

It may take a day or longer before a newly captured young animal will drink from a bottle of its own accord. Especially in the beginning, no drinking water should be provided. When the baby becomes thirsty, it is more amenable to accepting the bottle as an alternative to his mother's teat.

In the early stages only the young animal's keeper should be present during feeding times. In the quiet of its hiding place, where its attention is not diverted by people or any other distractions, the baby animal will relax sooner and take the bottle. It can be coaxed a little by moving the teat slowly towards its nose, and even by dripping a little of the milk onto its nose so that it can catch its smell. This process requires a lot of time and considerable patience!

If the newcomer cannot be persuaded within a day to accept the bottle, consideration may be given to getting an assistant to catch and hold it. Every effort should be made throughout, however, not to frighten the animal unnecessarily, and to try to gain its trust instead.

When the teat is placed inside the animal's mouth and it refuses to swallow, the teat can gently be moved in and out of the mouth. The tongue should remain under the teat. If it still refuses to swallow, the tongue may carefully be moved forwards and backwards with one's finger, while the milk flows into its mouth. After a while the baby may begin to suck on its own. Under no circumstances may the animal's nose be occluded in an effort to force it to drink.

Feeding times and quantities of milk feed: It is usually not necessary to feed precisely measured quantities of milk. Approximately one tenth of the animal's body weight represents the mass of milk required daily by the young animal for sustenance. An animal weighing 10 kg will therefore require about 1 kg, or 1 litre, of milk daily. This amount is divided up between feeds. With the exception of some greedy individuals, most baby animals know their limits and will spontaneously stop drinking once sufficient milk has been taken. The animal's appetite, condition and the extent to which the abdomen fills out during a feed serve as criteria for the amount of milk required.

Drinking regularity varies from animal to animal. It is, however, wise to introduce a specific routine and to keep to it. Very young animals can initially be fed 4 to 6 times a day, with the first feed early in the morning and the last late at night. Later, older animals can be fed 3 times daily and eventually only twice daily. By this time they should be taking in adequate solid food and drinking water.

Solid food and weaning age: Solid food in the form of green fodder, lucerne leaves, etc., can be provided from the age of approximately 3 weeks. At this age, most wild animals begin to nibble on solid food. The food should be easily digestible and of a good quality.

The age at which an animal is weaned varies from one species to another and from individual to individual. With a few exceptions, the period from birth to weaning in most species is approximately as long as the corresponding gestation period. Smaller animal species with shorter gestation periods therefore usually wean their young at an earlier age. Some animals suddenly stop drinking on their own, and thereby wean themselves. When an animal has to be weaned artificially, however, this should be done gradually and care should be taken to ensure that it takes in enough solid food to prevent weight loss. Ruminants which are weaned too early develop a paunch and generally do not grow to a normal size.

Bottle-fed babies who refuse to drink: When a bottle-fed baby refuses to drink its milk, something is amiss! If the animal appears to be listless and out-of-sorts, and especially if it is feverish, it is probably ill and should receive proper treatment.

The injection of a broad-spectrum antibiotic, for example oxytetracycline (Terramycin, Pfizer Labs) may be of value if the precise cause of the illness cannot be determined. Treatment with A.C.T.H., cortisone and vitamin B complex generally helps to stimulate the animal's appetite. If necessary the assistance and advice of a veterinarian should be used, since incorrect treatment may have a severely adverse effect on the young animal.

Before concluding that the animal must be sick, it should be established whether it is not refusing to drink for any other reason. The presence of strangers, a new teat or one with too small a hole, a new type of milk or milk which is too hot or too cold, milk made up using old and rancid milk powder and numerous other factors can also discourage the animal from drinking.

Gastro-enteritis: Gastro-enteritis and diarrhoea count amongst the most common and often the most serious illnesses that may occur. Signs of abdominal pain, discomfort, a poor appetite and abnormally loose and smelly stools can all be indications of gastro-enteritis. Inadequate hygiene is all too often the cause! Bottles, teats and milk containers which were not routinely cleaned and disinfected have frequently caused the death of hand-reared animals. After every use, all utensils should be washed thoroughly with clean water. No milk particles which may turn sour should remain in the bottles, milk jugs or teats. All utensils should furthermore be disinfected in boiling water daily.

Preventive as well as therapeutic treatment of diarrhoea consists of administering a suitable antibiotic or sulfonamide, in conjunction with kaolin. The sulfonamide, phthalylsulphathiazole (Thalazole, Maybaker) is particularly effective! Various other treatment methods can be used. The most sensible approach is to consult a veterinarian regarding the best treatment. Diarrhoea can be caused, inter alia, by a range of parasite infections and disease-causing organisms and may thus require specific treatment, about which a veterinarian is best qualified to make a decision.

Parasites: Infestations with internal and external parasites ought to be controlled by treating the newcomer with safe and effective parasiticides. Bland deworming medicines, such as thiabendazole (Thibenzole, MSD) for roundworm and niclosamide (Lintex, Bayer) for tapeworm can be administered in the milk. Superficial spraying of the skin and hair with Amitras (Triatrix, Coopers) or any other suitable preparation, is also considered necessary to control tick infestations and diseases transmitted by ticks. Mange and contagious scabies can also be treated with similar parasiticides.

As will be indicated later (Chapter 18), some parasiticides can cause symptoms of toxicity in certain circumstances, and this unfortunately leaves the owner of a wild animal no alternative but to use unfamiliar medicines at his own risk.

Obstipation: Obstipation of the digestive system occurs quite commonly in young giraffe and elephant. A poor appetite, unsuccessful attempts to defecate and chafe marks around the animal's tail can indicate obstipation. Treatment with purgatives can lead to diarrhoea which is difficult to control. Consequently an enema is the preferred treatment. Lukewarm soapy water or a mixture of water and glycerine or liquid paraffin can carefully be introduced into the rectum by means of a rubber or plastic tube and kept there for a while, after which the animal will often relieve himself quite normally.

Animals which have been hand-reared are easily handled and transported and generally adapt better to new areas.

Obstipation, or the absence of normal bowel and bladder functions, often gives rise to serious problems in young steenbok, duiker, reedbuck, nyala and other animal species where the mothers hide the babies in between feeds. In the case of these species, the babies usually only defecate and urinate during feeding times when they are licked by their mothers. The mother instinctively laps up the soft stool and urine and swallows it, so that the hiding place of her baby is not soiled and the scent will not lead predators to the little creature. When these young animals are cared for by humans, the necessary stimulus for bowel and bladder motion is absent, and a distended abdomen, listlessness and anorexia could indicate the above-mentioned condition. This problem can effectively be prevented and even overcome by massaging the young animal with a damp cloth or cottonwool. Usually urine is excreted every time, but faeces only once a day or every other day. A face cloth soaked in lukewarm water and which is then carefully and gently wiped over the genitals and perineal area repeatedly is recommended in particular. Massage should specifically be applied during or directly after feeding times. The face cloth should be thoroughly washed after every use. In cases of severe obstipation it may be necessary to apply an enema. The excessive accumulation of faeces and urine in the system can lead to symptoms of toxicity which would necessitate treatment by a veterinarian.

In very young hippo calves, normal bowel functions and urination can be induced by allowing them to swim regularly, or by emptying a few buckets of water over the animal's back during feeding times. If this is not done, all efforts at raising a hippo calf may be doomed to failure!

THE NUTRITION AND CARE OF ADULT WILD ANIMALS

As has been explained with regard to hand-reared animals, adult wild animals must also be handled carefully and kept in suitable holding facilities in order to prevent injuries.

Holding facilities: These should preferably consist of a night shelter and an adjacent exercise pen.

A suitable night shelter, similar to that described for hand-reared young aniamls, is recommended. The night shelter and exercise pen should preferably by separated by a sliding door. This door should be able to be opened and closed by means of a long handle or by means of a cable and pulley system from outside the night room.

Since older animals are able to jump higher than hand-reared young animals and are wilder, it is important to cover the fence of the exercise pen carefully with game capture plastic, densely packed reeds or any other suitable soft opaque material. This will prevent them from seeing out and continuously jumping against the sides of the pen in fruitless efforts to escape.

When the animals are kept isolated for the first few days in the night shelter section, in which sufficient bedding, food and water have been placed in advance, they calm down sooner and can be released into the exercise camp after a few days with a greater degree of safety. The tranquillisers mentioned on p. 101 can likewise be used to tame adult wild animals sooner.

When newly captured animals are kept in the same pen or cage with animals that are already tame, they also tend to calm down sooner. Belligerent animals and bulls or rams of the more aggressive game species, in particular, should be housed separately.

Feeding procedures: It may take a few days for wild animals from the veld to start eating in captivity. Green grass and the branches of palatable trees occurring in the veld may speed up the process.

Elephant, rhino, hippo, zebra and giraffe can be fed the same types of fodder in captivity, just like buffalo and the different antelope species. Grazing species can survive on good quality hay and a concentrated feed mixture, while the fodder of browsers such as the black rhino, giraffe, kudu, nyala and bushbuck can be supplemented with green leafy branches or other fodder rich in foliage.

Hay must be of a good quality. Maize cobs, thatch or sour grass, or other hay or straw with a high cellulose content, are usually not suitable. Mouldy hay should not be given under any circumstances, since certain types of mould are poisonous and can have fatal consequences. Animals fed with mouldy hay can develop colic or diarrhoea, or may simply just die. Rhino and elephant are particularly prone to colic.

Sun-bleached hay usually is nutritionally inferior. Such hay may be deficient in protein, phosphate and vitamins A and E, and could have an adverse effect on the animals' health if given over long periods.

Grass-hay that may contain poisonous plants should also be avoided. Grass cut on road reserves and in gardens may include leaves of the oleander (*Nerium Oleander*), chincherinchee, also known as white violets (*Ornithogalum spp.*), or other poisonous garden plants. Hay cut in vleis or marshes may contain poisonous tulip (*Homeria and Moraea spp.*), which poses a threat to animals feeding on it.

Good quality lucerne hay which has been well dried, and is green and leafy, is still considered the best type of hay to feed game. When lucerne hay is not available, good quality grass hay may be used. This seldom yields the same excellent results, however!

Grass hay can be sprayed with molasses to increase its palatability and nutritional value. Approximately 10 kg molasses diluted in water can be sprayed over approximately 100 kg grass hay. Too much molasses can cause loose bowels and at the first sign of diarrhoea the amount of molasses should be cut back, or preferably be eliminated temporarily from the fodder of affected animals.

The smaller types of game and browsers such as nyala often find it difficult to eat hard hay stalks. When the hay is chopped into smaller pieces in a hammer-mill and mixed with the leaves, these species of game find it easier to manage.

Antelope consume approximately 2 kg hay per 100 kg body mass per day. An elephant can consume more than 100 kg dry hay per day, while approximately 50 kg of hay will satisfy the daily requirements of an adult rhino or hippo.

The hay, or any other fodder, should not be placed on the ground where it can come into contact with the animals' excretions, since this could lead to severe parasite infestations.

The use of hay racks is not recommended for feeding antelope, except when the design specifically precludes the risk of the animals' horns being caught. Shallow concrete feeding troughs are recommended as a better alternative.

Green fodder is extremely valuable in encouraging newly captured and sick animals to eat. As is the case with domestic stock, however, green lucerne may cause wild animals to become bloated, and should therefore be fed in limited quantities.

When such lucerne is mixed with dry hay, or fed in conjunction with it, the risk of bloat is reduced.

Barley, oats, kikuyu grass and cultivated plants which do not cause prussic acid poisoning can also be planted to provide a useful source of green fodder during the dry winter months.

The branches of palatable trees such as the buffalo thorn (*Ziziphus mucronata*) and numerous other species are readily taken by captured game. Green fodder generally stimulates the appetite and provides a natural source of vitamin A and other essential elements. Wilted leaves carry the risk of prussic acid poisoning and must be removed from the animals' cages.

Care should be taken to avoid inadvertent feeding of the branches of poisonous trees to the animals. Poisonous shrubs such as *Lantana camara* growing in small game camps have already caused deaths amongst captive wild animals.

In smaller pens where animals tread on grass planted underfoot, heavy infestations by internal parasites may occur. The regular use of deworming blocks or other parasite control measures play an important role in such cases.

Various concentrates or meal rations can be used to supplement the hay rations. Commercial concentrates such as cow meal can be used, provided that these do not contain ureum or other potentially harmful ingredients.

Epol antelope cubes have been in use for years. Special meal rations can also be mixed as prescribed. Constant attention should be given to ensuring that the mixture contains sufficient quantities of basic ingredients such as protein, energy and minerals. The palatability and acceptability of the concentrate is of overriding importance. Meal mixtures containing certain animal sources of albumin are generally poorly utilised, while appetising food products can be added to improve the palatability of the mixture.

A meal mixture containing the following ingredients has been well utilised by a variety of game species. More than 15 species bred successfully in captivity while fed exclusively on hay and this mixture, of which the ingredients are as follows:

Yellow maize meal	70%
Bran	17%
Sunflour cake meal	5%
"Rumevite" stud concentrate	5%
Mineral lick	3%
The mineral lick consists of:	
Bone meal	30 kg
Salt	15 kg
Manganese sulphate	120 g
Copper sulphate	60 g
Cobalt sulphate	15 g
Sodium iodide	5 g

The meal requirements of game amount to approximately 1 to 2 kg per 100 kg of body weight per day. It is extremely important to note that animals should be introduced to meal rations gradually, since they may otherwise suffer severe gastrointestinal disorders before their digestive systems adapt to the new diet. Start them off on small quantities of concentrates, therefore, and gradually and judiciously increase these quantities.

For economical and other practical reasons, elephant, rhino and hippo can be given smaller quantities of a cheaper meal mixture. Yellow maize meal, wheat bran and lucerne meal can be combined in equal parts, and given to the animals at a daily rate of 14 kg per adult animal. Together with sufficient quantities of good quality hay, this mixture keeps the animals in excellent condition. The meal mixture can preferably be combined with coarsely chopped hay and moistened with molasses and water before being given to the animals. In this form the animals are able to pick up their food with ease. If elephant are given dry meal, they often blow it over their bodies as though enjoying a sand bath.

When the composition of meal rations has to be altered drastically, the animals should once again be started on small amounts of the new mixture. As soon as the animals' digestive systems have adapted to their new diet, the quantity of meal rations can gradually be increased.

Digestive disorders: Severe digestive disorders can occur when an animal eats too much meal. In addition to indigestion and diarrhoea, the animal may as one of various secondary complications develop inflammation of the feet, and animals affected in this way may find it difficult or impossible to move about normally.

Animals that have eaten too much meal and have developed diarrhoea should be given less meal and more hay. The meal can even be eliminated completely from the daily food rations until the animals have recovered. If an animal stops eating altogether, it may be given green fodder to stimulate its appetite.

Stale meal is usually unpalatable and is consequently poorly utilised by animals. Concentrates should preferably be used within two months of being chopped and mixed. Mixtures that are left unused for longer than this are inclined to become rancid. Game pellets tend to crumble after a while and stale rations are also less nutritious.

Toxic fungi can develop in meal mixtures that have been stored in damp conditions. Feed mixtures containing peanut products can also in certain circumstances be contaminated with toxins which can cause game and stock to become sick and die.

Meal rations must be kept in cool and well ventilated storerooms. Sufficient meal for only one day should be placed in the feeding troughs, and the troughs cleaned out thoroughly on a strict daily basis. This is essential! Damp and sour meal mixtures should be discarded, out of reach of the animals. Acid formation due to poor supervision in this regard can cause severe gastro-intestinal ailments in the animals. Preventive and therapeutic treatment in such cases is very similar to that for animals that have eaten too much meal.

Captive animals should at all times have access to sufficient quantities of clean drinking water. Feeding and water troughs which may injure the animals should not be used. Movable troughs which do not have any sharp edges and which can be removed from outside through an opening in the wall to be cleaned and filled with food and water are recommended.

13. THE SAFE TRANSPORTATION AND SUCCESSFUL ESTABLISHMENT OF GAME

Although game capture techniques have been perfected to such an extent that losses are mimimal, the transportation of game still leaves much to be desired. Better transportation facilities and services could sharply reduce game losses during transportation. General requirements and procedures are described in this chapter and special precautions highlighted.

Today most types of game are loaded and transported together, in groups of 5 to more than 100 animals, in specially equipped trucks. Larger numbers of animals can thus be moved more quickly, at a lower cost, and in most cases with fewer losses than when the conventional crate method is used. The practice of transporting individual animals in crates has become somewhat outmoded, but is still an important method of transporting rhino, hippo, young elephant and aggressive bulls and rams. Transporting animals such as impala and springbok in grain-bags is strongly discouraged, while the use of narcotics and tranquillisers can in future play an increasingly important part in the transportation of rare species in particular, and animals which are not easily transported.

GAME TRANSPORT TRUCKS AND TRAILERS

Owing to a lack of knowledge, buyers of game and game transport contractors regularly arrive at game auctions and game farms with trucks that are better suited to housing chickens than transporting game. Comprehensive information sheets distributed by conservation bodies to game traders, farmers, transport contractors and other interested parties could contribute much to the safer and more satisfactory transportation of game and would certainly do much to raise the general standard of game transport services.

Animals newly captured from the wild will often risk life and limb to escape, and therefore the construction of the bodywork must be sturdy and free of sharp objects or openings or grooves which may cause injuries. The back of the truck needs to be dark, adequately ventilated, with a non-slip floor, smooth sides and a sufficiently high roof. Properly functioning sliding doors at the sides and/or back perfectly round off a good game transport truck. Naturally such a vehicle must be absolutely reliable and roadworthy, since any delay on the road, particularly during long journeys, may have fatal consequences.

The space at the back of the truck determines the species and numbers of animals that can be transported. A floor area of approximately 14 square metres ought to be large enough for a consignment of 18 kudu or 50 impala. A large truck and a trailer with a combined floor area of 28 square metres can transport approximately 40 kudu or 100 impala at a time. These numbers merely serve as an aid to planning, and should not be regarded as minimum requirements. It is far more important to note that animals should be loaded in such a manner that they stand reasonably close together, but that there is also enough space for animals to lie down comfortably if they need to rest. Too many animals in one consignment may trample each other, while animals standing too far apart may be thrown about if the vehicle accelerates or stops suddenly or swerves unexpectedly.

Fractured limbs, sprained joints and permanent injuries frequently occur when the surface of the truck's floor is slippery.

Photo at top: Transvaal Division of Nature Conservation

107

When hoofed animals have to be transported, the best results are obtained by welding a flat, low grid to the metal floor of the truck. A rolled-iron grid 1 cm in diameter, with blocks measuring approximately 30 x 30 cm, is ideal. The grid must be covered with a layer of damp, dust-free soil to which a small amount of grass or straw has been added. Damp kraal manure is just as effective. When grass, straw or lucerne is placed on the floor of the truck as a cover or as fodder, it should be spread out evenly, since clumps of plant matter may cause the animals to stumble and fall.

Occasionally the animals may nibble at grass and hay lying on the floor and care should therefore be taken not to use poisonous plants or strange herbs or shrubs as a cover for the truck floor. If the animals have to be treated for ticks while in the truck, a safe product such as Amitras (Triatix, Coopers) should preferably be used and contamination of the grass and straw on the floor should, as far as possible, be avoided. Where tick control during game transport is compulsory, care should be taken that veld hay does not, in fact, become the medium of transport for parasites!

The height of the sides of the transport truck is also important. According to some transporters, very high sides will, to a certain extent, prevent jumping species such as impala, kudu and waterbuck from injuring themselves against the roof. Good results are nevertheless obtained with roofs that are approximately 2 m high. Some game captors assert that gemsbok, which have to bring their long, straight horns forward in order to fight, sustain fewer injuries in vehicles with low roofs. Where a roof is low, however, this should not restrict the animals' normal movements and there should not be any narrow slits or other gaps in the roof in which the animals' horns can get caught and broken.

Good results are obtained with the transport of gemsbok by using a very high, net-covered roof structure. Plastic tubes are placed over the animals' razor-sharp horns through the net roof immediately after capture. The number of fatal wounds inflicted during fights is thus limited.

High transport trucks with double decks have been used successfully to transport red hartebeest. All animals will not, however, find it equally easy to walk up and down the stairs between the two decks.

A closed roof offers the best protection against sun and rain. However, wide slits in the roof facilitate the cooling down of hot, tired animals and provide adequate ventilation during transport. A thick, strong shade net placed over the roof slits not only affords greater protection against the sun, but also appears to deter animals from trying to jump through the roof. There is, nonetheless, no good substitute for a sufficiently high roof! In rain and cold weather a tarpaulin over the roof will afford the animals the necessary protection. It is very important to tie the tarpaulin down firmly, since a loose tarpaulin fluttering against the truck will frighten the animals and may cause them to panic.

The sides of the holding compartment should be free of protruding screws, nails, corner-irons and other sharp objects which may injure the animals. Metal sides must be sturdy and should not rattle and the ideal would be to line them with thick rubber mats (such as used conveyor belts which may be obtained from mines). Next to rubber sides, smoothly finished wooden walls are an equally acceptable alternative against which the animals do not easily injure themselves. In contrast, bars or wire mesh covered from the outside with hessian, plastic, canvas or any other material are unsuitable and dangerous, since the animals generally injure or damage their limbs or horns in such structures.

The sides of the transport compartment must, except for a few narrow ventilation slits, have no openings and should be completely opaque. If slits on or near floor level are unavoidable, these should be of such a nature that the animals' limbs cannot get caught in them. Antelope are especially prone to severe injuries to their hooves if gaps are left just above floor level. Needless to say, the necessary precautions must also be taken to ensure that the exhaust fumes from the vehicle do not enter the transport compartment through low ventilation slits.

Gaps which allow the animals to see outside will prompt most species to attempt to jump out. Injuries to the head and mouth, with the associated complications, are usually the result. From the above it can be deduced that any openings for ventilation purposes should be positioned judiciously, and should preferably be adjustable so as to offer the required air and temperature control in hot as well as in cold weather. On hot days, sufficient cool air should be able to circulate and keep the temperature down, while cold draughts should be eliminated during cold weather, to prevent the risk of pneumonia.

If possible the vehicle must be left in the shade on hot days before the animals are loaded, and a truck loaded with game should not stop in the sun for long periods on hot days. The wind moving through a truck during transport contributes much to lowering the temperature in the transport compartment to a satisfactory level. When game has to be captured and transported on hot days, temperature problems are still best overcome by restricting capture and loading operations to early morning and late afternoon, when temperatures are usually lower. Although it is not generally essential, some transporters are already making use of electric fans and air-conditioners to lower the temperature in their game transport trucks on very hot days.

The use of movable partitions to divide the backs of very large trucks and trailers into different compartments is strongly recommended for various reasons. These partitions can be made of thick, strong boards, must be solid and preferably approximately of the same height as the sides of the transport compartment and can preferably either slide backwards and forwards on rods or be attached to hooks at specific points to change the sizes of the various compartments. To facilitate handling, the partitions should be as sturdy yet as light as possible. Many animals have been seriously injured or even killed when partitions have become loose during transport and fallen on the animals. It is therefore essential to attach all partitions very securely.

Dividing the back of the truck by means of partitions allows easier loading as well as smoother separation and handling of game, and facilitates the separate transport of bulls, rams and aggressive antelope and, in particular, prevents a consignment of animals from bunching up excessively and trampling on and injuring each other if the vehicle has to stop suddenly. In the case of animal species which are not generally easy to off-load, such as gemsbok and waterbuck, a movable partition can be especially useful when the animals have to be persuaded to leave the truck.

An important feature of trucks and trailers is suitable doors leading to the outside as well as in the partitions between the various compartments. Sliding doors are considered more suitable than hinged doors. Once the animals have been loaded, hinged doors cannot, for example, be shut quickly enough in the time that it takes the truck to move sufficiently far away from the platform to allow the doors to be swung closed. By the same token, antelope may jump off the truck too soon during off-loading, when the hinged doors have been opened but the truck has not backed up against the loading ramp. If an antelope were to leap up against a hinged door, anyone opening or closing the door from the other side could be seriously injured.

For the above reasons, hinged doors have been largely replaced by sliding doors in all modern game transport trucks. Most types of sliding doors are suspended from an overhead rod by means of pulley-type wheels, sliding hooks or sliding pipes. At the bottom, the door is usually held in position by pegs which are attached to the sliding door and move to and fro in a track in the floor when the doors are opened or closed. Because the tracks often become blocked by droppings and sand, it is vital to ensure that the doors are able to move freely, before the animals are loaded!

A rolled iron rod running across the doorway just above floor level and over which a saddle-shaped metal fitting mounted to the bottom of the door slides often offers a better solution than the pin and track mechanism.

Sliding doors can be opened and closed quickly, while the truck is parked securely against the loading ramp. Long levers or wire rods can be used to open and close the doors from the outside. Sliding doors built into the partitions between the different compartments are especially handy when animals have to be sorted into groups or aggressive individuals need to be separated from the rest.

The outer doors, in particular, must be fitted with suitable locking mechanisms. I know of several cases where the doors of game transport trucks accidentally opened while the truck was moving, and some of the animals never reached their destination.

SPECIAL PRECAUTIONS DURING MASS TRANSPORTATION OF GAME

If game are not to be in transit for more than a day or two, it is usually unnecessary to have feeding and watering containers in the vehicle. Such containers may cause injuries and are not, as a general rule, recommended. Although it is usually not advisable to feed the animals from the floor, the best compromise here is possibly to place lucerne hay and edible twigs and leaves on the floor.

Different species should, in general, be transported separately. In the case of species where the bulls and rams are inclined to fight, it is essential to remove them from the herd in good time. Where captors have neglected to do so, impala rams have on occasion fatally injured several ewes and lambs. If some of the large rams are inadvertently loaded onto the truck with the ewes and begin to injure the other animals, one may be obliged to go in amongst the animals and remove the rams bodily by the horns. A small sliding or hinged door, approximately 60 cm high, 75 cm wide and placed just above floor level at the side of each compartment, can prove very useful when troublesome or injured animals have to be removed.

It is not advisable to climb into a truck loaded with wild antelope, since this disturbs the animals and may lead to injuries. Where there is some compelling reason to do so, however, it is safer to use a wooden door or a similar shield for protection. Going in amongst gemsbok, sable antelope, wildebeest and many of the other more aggressive species, especially, is taking a deliberate risk!

Buyers are generally unhappy when large impala rams are not off-loaded with the other animals. It should be borne in mind, however, that the younger rams with curving horns are already able to serve ewes. If preferred, large rams can be transported in the same truck in individual crates or in a separate compartment, usually at a higher cost. Such rams cannot, however, be transported together without risk unless they have been tranquillised

beforehand and plastic or rubber tubes have been placed over the sharp horns.

A single large kudu bull can be loaded up and transported together with cows, with minimal risk. In the case of blesbok, the rams can generally be loaded up with the ewes, but then the truck must begin to move as soon as the animals are loaded. It is also sensible to place rubber or plastic tubes over the animals' horns. In general, the sound and sensation of the moving truck has a calming effect on the animals and the engine should be started as soon as the doors are closed behind the animals.

Impala, zebra and blesbok are very difficult to load. They can successfully be prevented from turning and breaking back by means of a tractor equipped with a high nudging board of the same width as the loading ramp. Although the animals are not physically pushed forward with the board, they usually move forward on their own ahead of the tractor, considerably facilitating the loading process. The same results can generally be achieved by a group of assistants fluttering plastic behind the animals. However, the animals should on no account spot anyone ahead of them during any stage of the loading process. Even the person who has to close the sliding door at a given time should conceal himself very well. Once a few antelope have entered the truck, the rest usually follow more willingly. Waterbuck generally climb into the truck without hesitation. Cases are known where the first animals climbed onto the truck while the capture team was still rounding up the rest of the herd a few hundred metres away.

While the animals are on the loading ramp, the opportunity can be used to close doors or gates in front of and behind them and, for example, to place plastic tubes over the sharp horns of gemsbok. Parasiticide sprays can also be used now, although the smell of these substances in this section of the corral may hamper subsequent loading of other animals.

If some of the larger species, in particular, have to be handled individually before being loaded, they may be darted in the capture corral. When they have been treated for internal and external parasites or even immunised or treated with antibiotics, the sleeping animals may be loaded. This procedure also facilitates the separate loading of cows and bulls in different compartments.

The veterinary treatment of game that has to be relocated in a different area is still, in my opinion, not receiving adequate attention. While the animals are in a condition to be handled, one has the ideal opportunity to rid them of parasites in order to avoid the unnecessary introduction of alien infestations in new areas. While it is certainly true that every animal cannot always be sterilised of all parasites, every effort should nevertheless be made to establish clean animals in clean areas, as is the case when domestic stock has to be moved.

Veterinary disease control measures should also not be sidestepped, since these measures are intended to safeguard the country's stock and game populations. Smuggling game from a foot-and-mouth disease area for financial gain, for example, not only endangers the stock industry, but can also be severely detrimental to the game industry and the country's economy!

The necessary veterinary and nature conservation permits must be obtained in advance and should accompany the driver during transportation. This will definitely eliminate unnecessary and irksome embarrassment and delays en route.

As has been mentioned, it is generally the best policy to load and transport the animals as soon as possible after capture. The period during which the animals are subjected to stress and fear is thus reduced and, before they realise it, they are off-loaded at their destination. When the animals are hot from being chased, it is preferable, especially on hot days, to postpone loading until the coolness of the afternoon or at least until the animals have had time to rest and recover.

If the circumstances warrant it, animals such as impala, kudu and waterbuck may be left in the truck overnight with only a slight risk before proceeding with the journey. In the case of gemsbok, wildebeest, sable antelope and roan antelope, however, the journey should be commenced and completed as soon as possible, since these animals remain agitated and restless for a while after capture.

If animals must be kept in captivity for a few days or more before transportation, it is not advisable to move them to their new destination before they have regained their condition. Animals usually lose weight during the first two weeks in captivity, and it is only after this period that they adapt sufficiently to their new diet and surroundings to recover the lost weight.

In the case of nyala that have been captured using nets, post-capture losses due to overstraining are often experienced, especially if the animals have to be loaded directly and transported over a long distance. Here it is better to tame the animals in a pen for approximately 2 to 3 weeks before transporting them. Tame and hand-reared animals can be transported much more easily and safely than animals from the wild, and are especially suited to export.

The decision whether animals are ready to be transported after a period of temporary captivity should be based on the condition of the animals and cannot be rigidly prescribed in terms of a minimum or maximum number of days or weeks following capture.

An experienced and responsible truck driver and well trained assistants to accompany the animals on the trip are essential to the safe transportation of game. The truck should commence moving slowly and should accelerate and decelerate gradually. The driver should also traverse sand-banks and farm roads slowly and should take special care to negotiate sharp bends slowly. Particular caution is required on steep gradients. Large numbers of dead and trampled animals have in the past repeatedly borne witness to incompetence on the part of truck drivers.

Although stopping in towns of cities or other noisy places should be avoided as far as possible, and the truck should preferably keep moving, particularly on hot days, a short stop every hour or two is nevertheless recommended so that the animals can stand up, stretch their legs and relieve themselves. As soon as they become restless, however, the journey should be recommenced without delay. The animals should be inspected at regular intervals and the temperature in the transporting compartment and the well-being of the animals attended to. Every effort should be made to keep the animals as calm and comfortable as possible during transport.

Some time ago a transporter admitted to me that, after 30 hours on the road, he had no idea how the animals in his truck were because he had not stopped to check on them. So, too, on another occasion, a supplier arrived on a farm with 18 dead animals because he had failed to notice that a loose, heavy partition between two compartments fully loaded with animals had been systematically mowing down the animals en route. The sight of several trampled zebra lying dead because some reckless driver had not observed the basic principles of safe driving is surely painfully unacceptable to anyone who has any regard at all for the well-being of innocent animals.

PREPARATIONS AT THE OFF-LOADING POINT

Game traders are delayed almost every day by the ignorance of game buyers who do not see to it that their roads are adequately cleared or, typically, who do not replace stay wires between gate posts with anchor wires in good time so as to allow the sizeable game transport trucks unobstructed access through the gate and to the off-loading point. Some of these trucks are very high and wide, are difficult to manoeuvre on narrow farm roads and, in

A suitable ramp for off-loading should be erected before the consignment of animals arrives at the farm. The truck must be able to reverse tightly up against the vertical wall of the platform. The gradient of the sloping end of the platform, which the animals will use to descend from the truck, should be approximately 45 degrees and should be covered with earth.

particular, can only be backed up against a loading ramp if the surrounding area has been thoroughly cleared of vegetation beforehand. Some farms do not even have a loading ramp, and valuable time is lost trying to improvise a loading ramp with no materials. The height of the truck's floor should therefore be ascertained well in advance, as well as the space required at the off-loading point for turning the truck around, so that the off-loading site can be prepared accordingly in good time.

Every game farm should have a suitable loading point far away from fences and buildings, where the animals can be off-loaded safely. The off-loading ramp should be set up in such a way that even a very large truck would be able to reverse up against it or move sideways alongside it until the sliding door can be opened against it at a safe and comfortable height. A few empty grain-bags, pick-axes and spades as well as a sufficient number of assistants should be on hand to fill in gaps between the truck and the platform which may cause the animals to injure and break their legs. Platforms fashioned from bales of straw and planks do not always function effectively, and a permanent, broad earth platform with a vertical wall at the one end (i.e. against the truck) and a 45 degree gradient at the other is recommended instead.

During the off-loading process, inquisitive and noisy neighbours, labourers, children and dogs, especially, should be kept at a safe distance. Impala and kudu often jump out very quickly and may sustain fatal injuries if they take fright and run into fences near the off-loading point.

Red hartebeest are sometimes unwilling to budge, but can be dragged out by the horns by experienced assistants. Other animals, such as gemsbok, may for hours on end refuse to exchange the shelter of the truck for the wide, open spaces outside. In such cases, attempting to catch these animals with ropes and drag them outside is decidedly risky, and this practice is not recommended. Better results are usually obtained when a movable partition inside the truck or fluttering strips of plastic are used to chase the animals out.

Gemsbok, blue wildebeest and black rhino, especially, are occasionally inclined to go for anything that moves the instant they leave the truck, and it is therefore advisable to keep observers at a safe distance when the more aggressive species are off-loaded.

Sufficient grazing and enough easily reached watering points should be present on the farm on which the animals are to be released. A single dam in the middle of a large game farm may not be discovered in time, and animals which may very well have gone without water for days may thus die of thirst at their new destination. Since, for the first week or two, the animals may move up and down along the fences in their efforts to escape, it is advisable to observe where the animals tend to congregate and then to dig holes at these spots which are capable of holding approximately 200 litres of water. These holes should be kept full of water until it has been confirmed that the animals have located the permanent watering points on the farm.

During this time, the fences should be inspected daily at least, to mend breaks and close up warthog holes, through which antelope such as red hartebeest and gemsbok can escape. Care should, however, be taken to move slowly and cautiously through the game enclosure, since the new arrivals may take fright and run into the fences. After approximately 2 to 3 weeks the animals generally lose the urge to escape and are less inclined to look for bolt holes.

Although it is desirable to release game in the veld as soon as possible, there is some justification in certain cases for keeping game in temporary captivity before releasing them. Veterinary disease control measures in some cases impose an obligatory quarantine period. Thin, debilitated and injured animals should furthermore also receive treatment and special care before being released.

When rhino are kept for a while in a quiet spot near water and are released in small groups, they are more inclined to become established on that part of the farm. Occasionally, animals that have been released in this manner may even return to the holding pen later in search of lucerne and other supplementary feed.

GAME TRANSPORT CRATES

Since game transport crates play an important role in the transportation of game, information concerning suitable crates is essential. These crates are rectangular and sturdy and are usually constructed of strong planks reinforced by flat and corner-irons or hoop-irons. Planks approximately 2 to 3 cm thick usually suffice for the construction of antelope crates. A crate should be reasonably dark when the two sliding doors at the ends are closed, and should not have any holes or large gaps through which the animals may attempt to jump out and thus injure themselves. The sides of the crate, as well as the inner sides of the sliding doors, must be smooth. The floor should be as level as possible, without being so smooth that the animals run the risk of slipping. Shallow transverse planks on the floor covered by a layer of straw usually offer the best solution.

Narrow ventilation slits at the upper ends of the sides and horizontal, narrow but strong wooden handles running along the full length of both sides of the crate at a convenient height are features of most modern transport crates. The roof of the crate must be high enough to allow an animal to stand in a comfortable position and can be made of planks or preferably of a thick, broad rubber mat which will give the roof the necessary elasticity if the animal should attempt to jump out through the top.

The size of transport crates is vital. Antelope crates are usually just large enough to transport one animal at a time. The crate should be slightly longer than the animal and approximately one and a quarter times its width. The animal should thus be able to stand or lie down comfortably in the crate, without being able to turn around. To ensure good balance, most animals are loaded into crates with their heads facing forward. Rhino, however, travel better in the reverse position.

The following specifications have been taken from a textbook on the capture and care of game (Ref.: Hirst S M 1973. In. Young, E (Ed.) The Capture and Care of Wild Animals, Human & Rousseau, Cape Town and Pretoria), and serves as a good indication of suitable crate sizes:

ANIMAL SPECIES	LENGTH cm	WIDTH cm	HEIGHT cm
Eland, kudu bull.	225	75	185
Zebra, roan antelope, water-buck, blue wildebeest bull.	190	64	180
Black wildebeest, blue wildebeest, sable antelope, tsessebe, red hartebeest, nyala bull, waterbuck cow.	175	52	178
Blesbok, reedbuck, nyala ewe.	140	35	127
Giraffe (large).	225	92	200
Giraffe (medium size).	190	82	180
Giraffe (small).	182	80	160

Giraffe crates are open at the top and the front section of the sides are especially extended. Shortly after being darted, these animals are tied up with a special, strong halter, blindfolded and led into the crates using long ropes. Since severe difficulties may arise if a giraffe lies down while in a crate, a special sling is looped loosely under the animal's thorax and abdomen and tied to the sides to prevent this. However, it has become more usual to transport giraffe in large trucks in groups of six, or sometimes more, animals at a time, and crates are no longer generally used.

Specially modified crates are used for rhino and young hippo and elephant. These crates are usually fitted with sledge-like runners and have strong metal rings at the front and at the back by which they can be hauled onto the transport trailer along sloping loading tracks with the aid of winches and ropes.

When crates holding animals are loaded or off-loaded, the crates should not be allowed to tilt in any direction, since this may cause the animals to fall about and injure themselves. The availability of cranes, winches and other loading gear and sufficient assistants is essential for speeding up the loading process and reducing the fear and stress that the animals have to experience.

When crated animals have to be shipped or have to remain in crates for long periods, specially designed food and water containers have to be provided. These containers should have no sharp edges, should not penetrate too deeply into the crate and should be easily removable for cleaning and replenishing. Water containers that can slide into the front of the crate and be clipped into position are generally satisfactory. When these containers need to be removed temporarily, a small panel can be slid across the opening in the wall of the crate.

Newly captured animals tend to jump wildly around and injure themselves when loaded directly into a crate. Injuries can be reduced to a minimum by prohibiting any talking or noise in the vicinity of the crate and, if possible, by injecting the animals beforehand with a suitable tranquilliser. Once again, drugs such as Rompun, Azaperone, Acetylpromazine and Serenace, as well as Largactil, Trilafon and Valium, are well suited to this purpose. The action and side-effects of these drugs should, however, be carefully studied before use, since they may adversely affect the animals in certain circumstances. Too much of any tranquilliser should also not be administered just before loading the animals, since this will render them incapable of maintaining their normal standing or recumbent positions. If, while under the influence of these drugs, they should collapse in the crate, they may die as a result of a wide range of complications. Professional supervision is therefore important if losses are to be avoided.

Crates holding animals should be kept cool and in the shade. Overheating may cause animals to succumb to heat stroke. When the animals in the crate are very hot, they should not be sprayed down with water unless there is sufficient air circulation inside the crate to cool them down. In a crate with restricted air movement, the increased humidity may harm the animal further by hindering its normal cooling processes.

Mass crates are a useful expedient for transporters who only wish to use their trucks for game transportation during certain times of the year. When needed, these large, sturdy wooden crates, each capable of simultaneously holding a group of wild animals and fitting securely on the back of a truck, are loaded onto the truck by means of a crane. These crates must comply with all the basic requirements discussed above.

TRANSPORTING TRANQUILLIZED ANIMALS

When animals have to be transported under the influence of narcotics or tranquillizers, a number of very important requirements must be considered and observed:

Animals that have run far and are suffering from over-exertion, or were chased into a capture corral tired and exhausted, should first be given sufficient opportunity to recover before being darted. Very thin, debilitated and sick animals should preferably not be transported under anaesthetic.

The transportation of sleeping animals should only proceed under the direct supervision of a veterinarian. Assistants should be trained to keep the animals in a position of natural recumbency. Bales of straw or grain-bags filled with grass may be used to prop up the animals so that they do not fall over. A thick layer of straw on the floor of the vehicle can prevent the animals from hurting their limbs on the hard floor.

The animal's head must be kept higher than its body so that gases formed in the stomach can escape freely above the fluid level in the stomach through the opening to the oesophagus. The animal's mouth should hang downwards so that the saliva can drain from the mouth, thus preventing the animal from choking in it. It is also important to avoid exerting pressure on the animal's thorax or abdomen, since this may obstruct respiration.

Blindfolds over the animals' eyes, and nets or ropes rigged over the animals when they are transported on the back of an open truck or by air may help to prevent individuals from suddenly jumping up should they unexpectedly recover from the effects of the drug. As an additional precaution, the limbs may be tied lightly with flat straps. Old nylon stockings are soft and elastic and are particularly useful for securing the limbs of small antelope such as oribi and steenbok.

Naturally the condition of the animal must be monitored continuously and more narcotic or even a little antidote administered periodically to maintain the desired level of sedation. Stimulants and other supportive aids should also be readily available in case the animal's condition deteriorates.

The animal's neck should not be allowed to bend over to one side too sharply or for too long, since this can cause the neck to stiffen; after administration of the antidote, the frightened animal may begin to fall about with a bent neck, resulting in fatal injuries. The limbs should also be massaged regularly and the animal must periodically be rolled from the one side of its thorax to the other, to promote blood circulation to the limbs and to allow gases that have accumulated in the stomach to escape.

Rhino may be kept in temporary holding bomas before being released into the veld.

TRANSPORTATION BY RAIL AND BY AIR

Wild animals are seldom transported by rail, as they generally cannot tolerate the jolting of the trucks and the noise that accompanies this type of transportation. Tame animals may be transported by rail or even by sea with a greater measure of safety.

Game can successfully be transported by air if the cost can be justified and the animals have been tamed earlier and are transported in suitable crates, or if the animals are taken to their destination under sedation and under veterinary supervision. Obviously the latter method is only feasible if the flight lasts no more than a few hours.

The export of game is a specialised undertaking and entails more than can be discussed here. In addition to the import and export permit requirements, note must also be taken of IUCN stipulations and IATA's regulations.

SUITABLE TIMES FOR CAPTURING AND TRANSPORTING GAME

We will now consider the most suitable times of the year for capturing and transporting game. For many years, the colder autumn and winter months of the year were reserved for the capture and culling of game. Because certain species of game calve or lamb mainly in summer, and hot weather is not generally suitable for the handling of game or game products, game capture and culling activities were largely avoided during these times of the year. However, modern mobile cooling facilities and improved game capture methods and transportation facilities have now made it possible to re-evaluate existing practices and to modify these, where necessary.

For example, does it not make sense, in the case of kudu, waterbuck, sable antelope and other species that usually still have young calves in winter, to capture these animals a little later in the season and on cool days, or in the early morning or late afternoon during summer, when the calves are already somewhat older? In summer the animals are usually in a better condition and grazing and water are generally more plentiful in the areas where the animals are to be released. Impala and red hartebeest, however, should possibly be captured in early winter, since these animals are in advanced stages of pregnancy by the end of the winter and the hartebeest begin calving in certain areas by September. In addition to the ambient temperature, special attention should therefore also be given to the breeding seasons of the species concerned, and ewes with young calves and lambs should preferably be captured at other times of the year.

Wildebeest and blesbok, in particular, which tend to run hard during the capture process, should be captured in cool weather. Since it cools down earlier in autumn on the Highveld than in the bushveld regions, these animals can possibly be captured as early as March-April in the cooler areas of the country, provided that the calves and lambs of the previous season are already old enough at that stage.

From the above it should be clear that generalised rules cannot summarily be applied. Like the summer's high temperatures, so too the winter's icy cold can cause mortalities amongst animals during and after transportation, particularly if the animals' condition, the condition of the grazing and the availability of water in the veld leave something to be desired.

THE IMPROVEMENT OF GAME CAPTURE AND TRANSPORTATION SERVICES

In view of repeated allegations and complaints regarding mortalities amongst game during and after transportation, and also regarding duplicated permit control and related matters, attention has been given to the institution of:
— requiring professional game captors and transporters to pass

appropriate examinations and practical tests and issuing them with licenses. All operators should be able to prove that they possess the necessary vehicles and equipment to provide a satisfactory service;

— exempting game farmers from these licensing requirements, as long as they capture game on their own farms and only transport their own game;

— giving preference to candidates with appropriate training when appointing game capture personnel and supervisors;

— restricting the use of narcotics during the capture and transportation of game to veterinarians or experienced persons under the direct supervision of a veterinarian;

— requesting organisations concerned to supply appropriate information sheets to game farmers, game traders and other interested parties containing guidelines regarding basic requirements for acceptable transport facilities and services. The introduction of unnecessary and restrictive measures which could handicap the industry should consistently be avoided, but satisfactory steps should be taken to ensure the well-being and safety of the animals during transport.

— requesting representatives of the relevant government departments (e.g. Departments of Agriculture, Transport, Trade and Industry), provincial authorities, agricultural unions, game farmers' associations, game traders and other interested parties to meet with a view to examining and solving problems relating to the transport of game. In particular, consideration can also be given to the proposed streamlining of permit control and the possibility of a simplified, uniform permit system controlling the transport of game throughout the whole Republic.

THE USE OF LONG-ACTING TRANQUILLIZERS

The use of long-acting neuroleptics (tranquillizers) is a new concept and an important breakthrough in the management and translocation of wildlife.

Over the past few years, the effects of LANs (long-acting neuroleptics) have been evaluated by Drs Ebedes and Burroughs at the National Zoological Gardens in Pretoria because of the difficulties in keeping certain animals in restricted and unfamiliar accommodation following relocation from their original enclosures. Neuroleptics were needed that had a longer duration of effect than the drugs that were currently available. They were also needed to reduce stress factors during long-distance translocation by road or air; for acclimatising or adapting wild, recently captured animals to unnatural situations, enclosures and new habitats and to sedate animals sufficiently to enable them to resist the stressful activities at game auctions.

Under confined situations, some of the horned animals like red hartebeest, blesbok, black wildebeest and gemsbok tend to stab each other indiscriminately, usually with fatal results. This accounts for a significantly high percentage of translocation mortalities in certain species.

A high percentage of mortalities still occur during transportation, notwithstanding advanced transportation methods. Injecting LANs together with a short-acting neuroleptic before transport has proven to be of benefit and a dramatic reduction in mortality has been reported.

EFFECT OF NEUROLEPTICS

The main effect of neuroleptics is the relief of anxiety, and a decrease in motor activity and excitement. In wild animals a modification of mood is noted; they become indifferent to their surroundings and lose their fear of humans.

Many of the newer neuroleptics achieve their effect without causing drowsiness and sedation. Drowsiness is a side-effect of some neuroleptics, especially the older phenothiazine derivatives. This can be a beneficial effect in animals because they appear sedated and the neuroleptic can be seen to be effective.

LANs are Schedule 5 drugs and are obtainable only on prescription. It must be stressed that these drugs should only be used by a veterinarian or by someone under the direct supervision of a veterinarian as there may be certain side-effects which may need treatment. Commonly LANs used in South Africa are Clopixol-acuphase, (Zuclopenthixol acetate in viscoleo) (Lundbeck) 100mg/2ml, Trilafon LA (Perphenazine enanthate in sesame oil) (Sherag) 100/ml and Piportil depot (Pipothiazine palmitate in sesame oil) (Maybaker) 50mg/ml and 100mg/2ml.

Average duration of effect of long-acting neuroleptics

Clopixol-acuphase	50 - 150 mg	1 hour to 3 - 4 days
Trilafon	100 - 200 mg	16 hours to 7 days
Piportil	100 - 200 mg	48 hours to 21 - 28 days (?)

Although LANs should be injected intramuscularly, they are also effective when injected subcutaneously. A pole syringe is used for injecting animals in a crush or transport crate and because of the slightly thick, oily consistency of LANs, a 15 or 16 gauge needle is recommended. Because of the slow breakdown and absorption into the blood, it may take from several hours to a few days before sedation is noted. In the case of Trilafon, calming was usually first noticed from about 12 to 16 hours after injection, but this could vary. The maximum or peak effect of Trilafon was usually noted on the third day after injection. With Piportil the onset of sedation was sometimes delayed for up to 72 hours. Because of this delayed action it is necessary to initiate the sedative process by injecting a short-acting neuroleptic at the same time as the LAN. In small to medium-sized antelope, haloperidol has proved to be an ideal drug when used in combination with a LAN. In larger animals such as kudu and eland, Azaperone was effective. In gemsbok, a combination of Acetylpromazine or Combelen in doses of 5 to 10 mg with 100 mg Trilafon was found to be effective.

A combination of Acuphase and Trilafon has the advantage that the calming effect of Acuphase starts within an hour of injection and by the third day when its effect starts wearing off, the effect of Trilafon LA is reaching its peak.

DOSAGES OF LONG-ACTING NEUROLEPTICS USED IN CAPTIVE ANIMALS AT THE NATIONAL ZOOLOGICAL GARDENS IN PRETORIA

SPECIES	ACUPHASE (mg)	PIPORTIL (mg)	TRILAFON (mg)
Black wildebeest			50 - 100
Blue wildebeest			100
Blesbok		100	100
Burchell's zebra	100	300	100
Bushpig			50
Eland		200	200
Gemsbok		150 - 400	100 - 200
Grey duiker		20 - 50	
Hartmann mountain zebra			200
Impala	50 - 100	50 - 100	50 - 100
Klipspringer		50	50
Kudu	200	200	
Mountain reedbuck	50		100
Nyala		100	50 - 100
Roan Antelope	100		50 - 200
Red hartebeest			100 - 200
Sable antelope	100	150	100 - 200
Springbok		100	50 - 150
Steenbok		25 - 50	20 - 50
Tsessebe			100 - 200
Warthog			50
Waterbuck		50 - 150	100 - 200

Drs Hymie Ebedes and Richard Burroughs are thanked for the information provided in this section on long-acting neuroleptics.

14. GAME AUCTIONS

Game auctions have a definite and a most important role to play in the game industry. Unfortunately buyers are frequently disgusted when many or all of the animals they bought die shortly after the auction.

Here follow suggestions to buyers, with hints of what to watch out for when looking for a good batch of animals, and to sellers for a well-planned, successful auction. A brief comparison between live game auctions and catalogue auctions, regarding the advantages and disadvantages of both is also discussed. Minimum specifications for holding bomas as laid down by conservation departments of the Transvaal and the Cape Province are also set out in this chapter.

ADVICE TO BUYERS

* Preferably only support auctions held by dealers with a good record.
* Take a good look at **each** individual animal in the bomas, **shortly** before the auction, and preferably take a veterinarian or an experienced game farmer with you to help you spot those unmistakable signs of disease or weakness in affected individual animals.
* Look for signs of listnessless, lack of appetite, and ruffled hair coat. The latter, particularly on a hot day, usually indicates that something is wrong. Be careful not to misinterpret the signs of a sedated animal with an ill or injured one. Ascertain whether the particular batch of animals you are interested in have been treated with tranquillizers or not. Nervous or aggressive animals such as black wildebeest, tsessebe, red hartebeest, roan and sable are some of the species likely to be tranquillized.
* Look at the quality of food offered to the animals. If, for instance, only coarse, dry grass hay is fed and the animals look thin, they may be weak. If mouldy lucerne or too many concentrates are fed and there are signs of diarrhoea (look on the floor of the pen and for soiling of the animal's hindquarters), then you may be in for trouble.
* Excessive scarring, fresh poke wounds or bite marks (or other signs of rough handling or fighting between individual animals in the same pens) are ominous signs. Be careful !
* Animals covered with visibly engorged ticks not only indicate that the animal's resistance is down, but it also reflects on the level of care and management of the seller.
* Excessively doped animals, e.g. of the smaller antelope species, may create a false impression as these animals may become unmanageable in captivity once the effect of the tranquillizer has worn off.
* Species such as gemsbok and horned animals of a species that become aggressive when nervous, should have plastic or rubber pipes fitted over their horns so that the sharp horn tips do not protrude.
* Excessively worn or split pipes usually indicate an aggressive or nervous animal that has already used its horns in agitation or in an attempt to escape.
* When animals are crated individually, like gemsbok for instance, look for excessive chafing, particularly below the tail, as these wounds may turn septic.
* Lameness may be due to injury. Try to evaluate how serious it is. Lameness in several animals may mean an infectious condition, such as foot-rot, which can occur if the floor of the boma is allowed to become wet and muddy.
* Animals caught immediately before (or even during the auction) should be viewed with suspicion. Animals should preferably be kept in well-planned, suitable bomas for several weeks before the auction to allow them to regain lost

condition and to enable the seller to spot problem animals before they are offered for sale.

* Overstraining disease is a very common killer ! Animals which have been chased excessively during capture are theoretically at risk. Species which are very susceptible include sable antelope, gemsbok, nyala, oribi, tsessebe, blesbok, bontebok and red hartebeest. Animals may die within a few days or even after a few weeks after delivery.

* In general, go for animals which appear tame, relaxed, in good condition and without signs of stress, disease or injuries. Rather pay a bit more for a better-looking batch of animals and save money in the long run. The game auctions of the Natal Parks Board are a good example of animals offered for sale in prime condition and the prices paid for them are generally considerably higher than those for the rest of the country. They are kept in the holding pens for several weeks and are used to the presence of people by the time the actual sale takes place. The relative tameness of the animals is very noticeable and some species, such as kudu, will even feed out of their keeper's hands. Such animals transport well and have a good chance to adapt well when they are eventually released.

SUGGESTIONS TO SELLERS

* Employ only the very best game captors to catch all the game you wish to sell. Keep the animals in the best possible bomas for a long enough period of time for them to recover from the stress of capture and to regain lost weight.

* It is unbelievable how much money is sometimes spent on impressive, modern auction pens, and how little attention is then given to the care and feeding of the animals. There is no excuse for feeding animals poor quality food.

* Minimum requirements for good holding bomas are discussed later in this chapter. Adequate space (not too little but also not too much), sufficient shelter and hiding places (for secretive species), and floors, walls and troughs that present the minimum risk of injury to the animals, are imperative.

* **Don't** offer any animal on an auction that is not in excellent condition and which presents any risk to the buyer whatsoever.

* Try to arrange good transport and refuse to load animals on vehicles which are not up to standard. (See Chapter 13 on transport of wild animals.)

* If at all possible, give buyers some assurance, for instance, that you guarantee the animals delivered to the buyer's farm will be alive and healthy provided the transport is undertaken by yourself.

AVERAGE PRICES PAID FOR GAME AT AUCTIONS HELD BY VLEISSENTRAAL IN THE TRANSVAAL DURING 1992

Impala R210, kudu R785, blue wildebeest R537, black wildebeest R479, gemsbok R1 094, eland R1 974, red hartebeest R1 241, giraffe R6 019, heartwater springbok R1 200, springbok R102, zebra R1 087, ostrich R914, tsessebe R3 166, nyala R1 853, common duiker R950, blesbok R278, waterbuck R2 035, roan antelope R29 000, sable antelope R18 694, lion R6 300, buffalo R20 500, mountain reedbuck R698, white rhinoceros R32 500, reedbuck R683, steenbok R300.

These prices include the catalogue sale held by the Transvaal Division of Nature Conservation during which 1 937 animals were sold. It can clearly be seen from the prices paid for wildebeest that game farmers are suffering losses when marketing because of the disease threat discussed in Chapter 18.

MINIMUM SPECIFICATIONS FOR HOLDING BOMAS AT GAME AUCTIONS IN THE TRANSVAAL

LOCALITY:
1. Holding pens must be erected in a quiet area, away from noise and the immediate vicinity of roads.
2. Pens must face north and be built away from marshy areas.

PEN STRUCTURE:
1. The walls of the pens must have a mimimum height of 2,5 m.
2. The walls must be built of solid material with openings for ventilation and inspection.
3. Animals may injure themselves against the solid walls and it is recommended that the corners of the pens are padded with grass sheaves or other material tightly packed into hessian sacks.
4. Two spare pens should be available at all times to accommodate animals when their pen is being cleaned, to move sick animals or when pens have to be repaired.
5. Swinging doors which can be used to cordon off passages when moving animals from pen to pen or to a loading ramp are recommended.
6. Animals must be protected against the hot sun, cold, rain and hail. One third of the pen must be covered by a roof. A solid roof is recommended. In instances where pens have already been erected and do not have roofs, 80 per cent shade cloth may be used.
7. Care must be taken to ensure that sharp objects such as nails, bolts or wire, which could possibly harm the animals, do not protrude from the walls of pens or passages or are left lying around in the pens.

SIZE OF PENS:
The minimum size for a pen is calculated at 2m/50 kg live body weight per animal. This excludes elephant, buffalo and rhino, which require bigger pens.

Pens for single animals: The minimum size for animals smaller than a nyala bull must be at least 9 square metres.

Pens for sable antelope, eland, gemsbok and red hartebeest must be at least 15 square metres in size.

The minimum width for a pen should be 3 metres.

The walls of pens for giraffe should not be lower than 2,5 metres high. Special feeding and drinking troughs should be built into these pens. The height of the door must be able to accommodate the largest animal. A third of the pen must be underroof and this should be high enough to enable the animals to move about freely. The pen must allow for 20 square metres space for each giraffe.

PASSAGES:
Passages between the pens must not be wider than 2 metres. The floor of the passages must be covered with sand.

LOADING RAMP:
The floor of the loading ramp must be built of non-slip material. The loading ramp should also have solid walls with smooth sides to prevent injury to the animals during the loading process.

FEEDING OF ANIMALS:

1. Only the best quality fodder, such as lucerne hay, should be fed to the animals and should be available to them at all times.
2. Fodder must be placed in the pens before the animals are introduced to the pens.
3. There must always be sufficient fodder available for the animals for the duration of their stay in the pens.
4. Feeding and drinking troughs must be underroof and should be separate.
5. Keepers should be able to reach feeding troughs from the outside of the pens so that they can easily be cleaned and kept filled.
6. The space available to the animals for feeding should not be less than 10 per cent of the total area of the pen.
7. When natural fodder is given to the animals, these branches should be hung on the walls of the pen. As an alternative to feeding troughs, animals may be fed from a hanging net. The holes in the net should be large enough to allow them to feed.
8. Keepers should take care that they are always visible to the animals when feeding them or when cleaning the pens, so that they do not take fright and injure themselves.

WATER:

1. Drinking troughs should be built approximately 15 cm above ground level and should be accessible from the outside of the pens, to facilitate cleaning.
2. They should have round edges to prevent injury and must have a capacity of at least 50 litres. A ball valve system is recommended for the convenience of the animals and to facilitate the management of the pens.

OVERHEAD PLATFORM FOR VIEWING THE ANIMALS:

It is not recommended that the public be allowed to walk freely along an overhead platform to view the animals, but it is useful to facilitate handling of the animals by the captors and handlers.

HEALTH CONSIDERATIONS:

Good drainage of the area is essential and must be regarded as a priority at the planning stage of the pens. Water must drain out of and away from the pens and must not drain into neighbouring pens or passages. All pens, and particularly those containing rhino, elephant, buffalo or zebras, should be cleaned daily.

Captured animals must be treated for tick infestation when they arrive at the holding bomas and before they are off-loaded into the pens.

Manure and other dirty material which is collected from the pens should be dumped far away from the pens to prevent concentrations of flies from creating a problem for the animals and the public viewing them. Flies must be kept under control by using suitable fly traps or poison.

GENERAL:

1. Animals which are to be auctioned should preferably be kept in the pens for a minimum period of two weeks before the day of the auction.
2. During this period the animals may be sorted out and the weaker or injured animals can be removed and treated. Sex ratios can also be determined during this time.
3. It is imperative that a veterinarian should examine the animals and treat them where necessary.
4. Before transport, tranquillizers should be administered to the animals where possible.

5. Animals must be transported by the shortest route to and from the auction pens.
6. Animals are not to be kept in the transport trucks for long periods of time.
7. A back-up vehicle must be available at all times in case of a break down of the transport truck.
8. Where necessary, rubber or plastic pipes must be fitted over the horns of animals to prevent injuries.

It is important that the animals are transported in as humane a way as possible with the minimum of noise and stress.

MINIMUM REQUIREMENTS FOR THE TRANSPORT OF WILD ANIMALS

1. The transport truck must be roadworthy.
2. The truck must have a sturdy floor and sides.
3. There should be ample room for the animals to stand up or lie down.
4. Provision must be made for different compartments in the truck to transport different species or aggressive individuals.
5. Removable dividers which form compartments must be sturdy and firmly attached. Rubber conveyor belting over an iron frame is suitable.
6. The floor of the truck must be of a non-slip material. A rubber mat is suitable for this purpose but it should be attached to the floor. If this is not done, the mat tends to move during transporting and the animals may trip over the folds in the mat and injure themselves.
7. The sides of the truck must be covered with material through which the animals cannot see and which will not flap in the wind.
8. The truck must have a roof to prevent the animals from attempting to jump out of the top.
9. There should not be any loose articles in the transport compartment.
10. Care must be taken to remove any protruding nails, bolts or wires which can injure the animals, from the walls of the truck.
11. There must be adequate ventilation. Cool air must be able to enter the compartment from the front and warm air allowed to escape at the top. Provision must be made for drainage of urine or water from the truck.
12. Animals should not be transported in a large compartment in small numbers as this allows them to fall about easily when the truck moves and lead to injuries. The compartment should be made smaller by using dividers.
13. The truck should begin moving as soon as possible after the animals are loaded as this tends to have a calming effect on them and may prevent fighting.

MINIMUM SPECIFICATIONS FOR HOLDING BOMAS AT GAME AUCTIONS IN THE CAPE PROVINCE

PENS AND PASSAGES:

1. The walls of the pens must be built from wooden poles, planks, sturdy rubber matting which is supported from the back, reeds, sisal poles or other suitable material.
2. All pens must be connected by a passage to facilitate moving, loading or off-loading of animals. The passage must lead to a loading ramp. If each pen has a separate exit with a suitable loading ramp, the passage is not necessary. The passage must not be wider than 1m.

3. The walls of the pens as well as those of the passages, must be at least 2m high. In the case of kudu, waterbuck and eland, they must be 3m high unless the passage as well as the pen are covered by an opaque material, in which case these must be as least 2,5m high.

4. There may not be any permanent openings in the walls or in the passages, or any objects which may injure the animals.

5. The doors or gates of the pens must preferably be able to form an obstruction in the passage, so that animals can be herded into or out of a pen. If this is not done, a movable wall, preferably made from wood or metal, must be used for this purpose.

6. All gates should be made of the same material as the walls of the pens, with the exception of reeds.

7. Provision must be made for shade in at least one third of the area of the pen. This can be constructed of the same material as the walls, or asbestos sheets, tarpaulins or 70 per cent shade cloth. In pens with a permanent roof, provision must be made for ventilation.

8. The floors of pens in which animals are to be kept for periods exceeding 10 days, shall be built of rough concrete, covered by a layer of sand, with adequate drainage. If roofs are built over such pens, provision must be made for the drainage of storm water. There must be a separate holding pen, in which the animals can be kept while the pen is being cleaned.

9. The pens must have a removable drinking trough, built in such a way that it will not injure the animals. It should be possible to fill and clean the trough from the outside of the pen, except in cases where the animals are moved out of the pen for cleaning purposes.

LOADING AND OFF-LOADING OF ANIMALS:

1. The width of the loading ramp and any loading passage shall not be wider than 1m.

2. The walls of the loading ramp must be the same height as that of the passage and pens. The floor must be made of compacted earth, or rough concrete covered with earth or poles which fit tightly against each other.

3. The exit of the loading ramp must be constructed in such a way that it can be adapted to the height of different trucks. Alternatively, material such as sandbags, or a loose ramp must be available to adjust the height of the surface of the loading ramp to that of different trucks. Care must be taken that the animals' hooves cannot get stuck in any gaps between the loading ramp and the transport truck.

4. Vertical openings between the transport truck and the loading ramp must also be covered with an opaque material during the loading process.

5. There must be a gate or sliding door between the loading ramp and the passage to prevent animals from running back into the passage while the vehicle is being manoeuvered into position and to prevent animals from escaping from the loading ramp. This gate or sliding door must be able to open or close from outside the passage.

6. The walls of any off-loading bomas or sorting bomas which are wider than 20 metres, can be made of woven game capture plastic, backed up by game capture nets.

LIVE GAME AUCTIONS VERSUS CATALOGUE AUCTIONS

Generally, live game auctions are better for the buyer, while catalogue game auctions are better for the animals. Here follow some of the advantages and disadvantages of both types of auction:

When large sums of money are spent, particularly on some of the rarer species, buyers want to see the animals they are paying for. When the animals are standing in the bomas, as with live game sales, the prospective buyer can decide whether or not he is happy with a particular consignment. The sex ratio may be perfect for his needs and the total number of the animals ideal for what he wants or can afford. He can decide there and then whether or not to buy the animals and he can see exactly what he is getting.

Good looking animals, especially when there are not too many of the same species offered for sale, will be more popular than those in a less than perfect condition. Such animals tend to obtain very high prices, to the benefit of the seller and the auctioneer. This is good for the game industry in some ways but tends to create false expectations in others. People tend to forget that the cost of capturing wild animals is extremely high and that there will always be losses. This all has to be accommodated into the final selling price. The farmer buying an animal at an auction often does not take all of this into account. As a result, these high prices become the norm and farmers do not want to sell the animals on their farms at a more reasonable price.

Prices paid for animals at live auctions are generally higher than those paid at catalogue auctions. One of the reasons for this is that the buyer sees what he is getting. The other reason is that there is no waiting period between buying the game and delivery of the animals. Once the animals have been paid for, they are delivered to the new owner after he selects a transporter at the auction. He has the added peace of mind that the animals will travel well after seeing the truck for himself.

This is an area where huge losses often occur. After being captured professionally and treated with care in the bomas, the animals are often loaded onto an unsuitable vehicle, sometimes by the new and inexperienced owner himself. Unless you are well equipped to deal with transporting animals yourself, rather pay the extra money for a good transporter and be sure that your animals arrive in good health.

From the point of view of the seller, bad debts may sometimes be a problem. They may even run into tens of thousands of rands. Although buyers are required to pay on the day of the auction with bank guaranteed cheques, it sometimes happens that the account is not honoured by the buyer. If the buyer takes his animals immediately after the auction, releases them onto his farm and then does not honour his cheque, it can be very difficult for the seller to get his money or his animals back.

If the animals are sold by catalogue auction, they are usually only delivered to the new owner after several days or even after several months. Should payment not be met in this time, the seller will refuse to deliver the animals.

On the other hand, it may sometimes be impossible to capture the correct sex or age ratio of animals as decided upon at the catalogue auction. It may also happen that the animals are not caught at all, while the seller has the buyer's money in the bank and the buyer loses other opportunities to buy the animals he wants. It is possible to put clauses into the contract to compensate for an eventuality like this, but it often leads to dissatisfaction and ill feeling.

If a person buys animals at a live game auction and then discovers shortly thereafter that his farm is unsuitable for keeping the particular species, or finds that it is illegal for him to do so, the animals can be auctioned once again to another buyer. If this should happen after a catalogue auction, it may sometimes become quite a legal tussle, since the seller has lost the opportunity to sell his animals.

From the animals' point of view, there is much less stress on them if they are captured in the veld and moved directly to their new destination with the minimum of fuss and bother, as happens with a catalogue auction. Howere, care must be taken not to push the animals too hard during the capture process because of a feeling of commitment to the buyer and to become reckless. Mortalities due to overstraining disease may result and may only become noticeable several days or even weeks after delivery. It may then be difficult to prove that the animals were in a bad state when they were off-loaded.

Provided a reliable and experienced game captor does the catching for a catalogue auction, this can be avoided. Losses due to stress, fighting, incorrect diet and disease are common when animals have to be kept in the pens for any length of time. When animals are kept in the bomas for a considerable time, this is definitely to the advantage of the buyer since he can see if there are problems with a batch of animals and avoid buying them.

When buying game at a catalogue auction, it is sometimes left up to the buyer to provide or arrange for his own transport. When animals are caught at short notice, this can be a major problem. The buyer may be misled and a totally inexperienced transporter used to transport the valuable animals. A case is known where 20 nyala were bought at a catalogue auction and transported from Natal to the Cape in a cattle truck, covered loosely with tarpaulins. Adult bulls were loaded with the female animals and, needless to say, only one animal survived the journey.

Insurance should always be taken out on the animals at both types of auctions. If the deal is between the buyer and the seller, and an independent transporter transports the animals, there may be serious arguments over who should bear the loss when animals loaded in a good condition are injured during transport, due to carelessness on the part of the transporter. This should be borne in mind when drawing up the contract.

These are the main pros and cons of the two types of auctions, but, no doubt, readers will have experienced others. Some departments of nature conservation, like the Cape Province, for example, prefer catalogue auctions to live game sales. The Transvaal Division of Nature Conservation also held their own catalogue auction during this year and the animals were caught by the Division's own capture teams. The Natal Parks Board, on the other hand, has had several very successful live game auctions, also using their own capture teams. They go to considerable lengths to ensure the animals' well-being and the animals are generally in an excellent condition, posing the minimum risk to the buyer or the animals themselves.

There is always a risk to the animals when they are captured, kept in pens and then translocated. However, losses can be minimised if the stipulations in this chapter are adhered to.

Photograph: H. du Preez Wild

120

15. SPECIFICATIONS FOR GAME FENCES

Game farmers generally tend to be uncertain about game fence specifications. Different standards apply in the different provinces. The type of fence prescribed is furthermore determined by the class of game it must contain.

CAPE PROVINCE

The following basic specifications merely serve as clues. Officials of the Department of Nature and Environmental Conservation exercise sound judgement when evaluating fences, and use the following specifications as guidelines only. For the purpose of the specifications, farm game is divided into the following groups:

Class I: Kudu, impala and nyala.

Class II: Eland, red hartebeest, grey rhebok, bushbuck, zebra and waterbuck.

Class III: Gemsbok, blue wildebeest, black wildebeest, blesbok, bontebok, mountain reedbuck, springbok, reedbuck, roan, sable antelope and all other smaller antelope.

Height and fence types:

Class I: Height 2,4 m. The lower 2 m should preferably be covered with diamond or square mesh.

Class II: Height 1,8 m. The lower 1,5 m should preferably be covered with diamond or square mesh.

Class III: Height 1,4 m. The lower 1,0 m should preferably be covered with diamond or square mesh.

For Classes I and II, steel or barbed wire can be used in conjunction with either or both diamond or square mesh to erect the wire, provided the material is of sufficient strength. For Class III the wire specifications are as for standard jackal mesh.

Mesh sizes for the diamond mesh should be approximately 8 x 9 cm and for the square mesh approximately 6 x 6 cm. Veldspan or Bonnox fences are considered adequate by the Department, provided that these have been sturdily and correctly erected.

Where only steel and barbed wire, or any of the types of wire are used on their own, the individual wires should not be set too far apart. The distance between wires and line posts and droppers should be smaller than is the case when diamond or square mesh is also used.

In all cases fences must be sturdy and free of holes and weak spots. Where steel or barbed wire is used in conjunction with diamond or square mesh, care should be taken to ensure that the horizontal suspension, anchor and supporting wires satisfy the requirements of the fence and that the diamond or square mesh is firmly attached to these wires.

Diameter and spacing of posts:

Classes I and II: Straining, gate and corner posts should, in the case of wooden posts, have a top diameter of at least 12 cm. The prescribed diameter for iron posts is 8 cm.

Straining posts should preferably not be spaced further than 300 m apart. Straining, corner and gate posts should be properly anchored or be supplied with effective angle-supports.

For ordinary line posts the required top diameter for wooden posts is 8 cm and the total diameter for iron posts is 5 cm. The recommended spacing is 18 to 24 m apart.

Semi-rounded wooden droppers must have a diameter of at least 8 cm, and iron droppers a diameter of 3 cm. The droppers are placed 3 to 4 m apart. Where line posts are placed closer together than the required distance, or where vertical wire binding is used, the distance between the droppers can be increased.

Class III: Here, the diameter and spacing of posts must comply with the standard specifications for jackal wire.

In the implementation of the above, if the materials used are supplied in imperial units, conversions can be done in order to meet the Department's requirements in terms of the metric system. In all cases, however, nature conservation officials will give due consideration to requirements imposed by the habitat in relation to the specific types of game that have to be contained by the fences. If, in the opinion of the Department, a farmer has adequately fenced off his farm so as to satisfactorily contain the animals in question, a certificate to this effect will be issued. Holders of such certificates are eligible for special concessions as regards the right to dispose of their game.

TRANSVAAL

The Transvaal Division of Nature Conservation makes provision for two types of fence to restrict the movements of two classes of farm game. The higher type of fence is erected particularly in bushveld regions or on farms where jumping game occurs, while the lower fences are mostly used on the Highveld, in regions where farming activities concentrate on blesbok and springbok. The specifications for the following classes of game are briefly summarised below:

Class I: Kudu, eland, waterbuck, impala, wildebeest, zebra, gemsbok, blesbok, springbok, red hartebeest, giraffe, buffalo, sable antelope, roan, tsessebe, common duiker, ostrich and oribi.

Class II: All the above species, except kudu, waterbuck and eland.

Clas III: All the above species, except kudu, waterbuck, eland, impala and giraffe..

Heights and fence types:

Class I: Height 2,3 m. Provision is made for two basic fence types, viz.

(a) barbed or steel wire fences not incorporating Veldspan or Bonnox wire, and (b) barbed and steel wire fences incorporating Veldspan or Bonnox wire.

(a) **Barbed or steel wire fences without Veldspan or Bonnox wire:** Seventeen strands of barbed or smooth steel wire are laid down as the minimum requirement. From ground level the prescribed spacing for the individual horizontal wires is as follows: The lowest wire is positioned 50 mm from the ground, and thereafter wires are spaced at intervals of 100, 100, 100, 100, 125, 125, 125, 125, 125, 150, 150, 150, 175, 175, 175, and 200 mm. The highest wire is secured 25 mm below the ends of the posts. These horizontal wires are all attached to the inside of the fence. Where wooden posts are used, the Division of Nature Conservation recommends that the wire should be stapled to the posts using 35 mm x 8 S=D galvanised staples.

(b) **Barbed or steel wire fences incorporating Veldspan or Bonnox wire:** Here Veldspan or Bonnox wire 0,94 m high is used for the bottom part of the fence, supplemented by 8 horizontal barbed or steel wires above. All the latter strands may be round steel wire, or every second and third strand smooth steel wire and the rest barbed wire.

In terms of the specifications, the lower edge of the Veldspan or Bonnox wire should be 50 mm above the ground surface. At this height and every 300 mm above that, one individual horizontal strand is added, up to a height of 0,95 m, to support the Veldspan or Bonnox wire. The spacing (in mm) of the individual horizontal strands above the Veldspan or Bonnox wire from bottom to top is as follows: 125, 150, 150, 150, 175, 175, 175 and 200. The topmost strand is secured 25 mm below the ends of the posts.

The Veldspan/Bonnox wire is secured to the other wires by means of 14-gauge galvanised binding wire, in such a manner that all protruding ends are on the outside. Where wooden posts are used, all wire must furthermore be secured to the inside of the posts by means of 40 mm x 8-gauge galvanised staples.

Class II: 1,8m high, with 15 strands of wire.

Class III: Height 1,4 m. Only barbed or steel wire is prescribed and a minimum of 10 horizontal strands is required. The bottom strand must be 75 mm above ground level and thereafter the spacing of strands, in mm, from the bottom to the top strand is as follows: 100, 125, 125, 125, 150, 150, 150, 150 and 175.

Diameter and spacing of posts:

Regardless of whether Veldspan or Bonnox wire is used in conjunction with barbed or steel wire, the Division of Nature Conservation recommends the following: Impregnated wooden posts, 3 m in length and with top diameters of 100 to 125 mm, are recommended. Different thicknesses and lengths are not given for straining and line posts. The posts should be erected 10 m apart and 0,75 m deep. Wooden droppers are placed at intervals of 2 m between the wooden posts.

If iron posts and metal droppers are used instead of their wooden counterparts, the spacing may differ quite considerably, depending on the sturdiness of the posts and droppers. It is recommended that iron Y-posts are placed 8 to 10 m apart and the droppers 2 m apart.

Iron posts or "suitable wooden posts" are acceptable. It is recommended that Y iron posts are placed 10 m apart, for example, with droppers at intervals of 2 m in between.

In cases where the Transvaal Division of Nature Conservation inspects a game fence and finds that a game species occurring on the farm is fenced in in such a manner that it cannot escape from the farm, the owner concerned acquires certain rights in respect of the shooting and disposing of the game species on that game-proof farm.

MINIMUM FARM SIZE FOR DIFFERENT SPECIES LAID DOWN BY THE TRANSVAAL DIVISION OF NATURE CONSERVATION

Game may only be introduced to a farm if it falls within the natural distribution area of the particular species.

If the farm is less than 50 hectares in size, the only species which will be allowed on the property are steenbok, duiker and ostrich.

For species such as blesbok, springbok, impala and free ranging ostrich, only one of these will be allowed on a property of 50 ha. Two of these species will be allowed on 100 ha, three species on 150 ha and all of them on 200 ha.

Species such as wildebeest, zebra, red hartebeest, gemsbok and eland also require at least 200 ha.

Reedbuck, oribi, bushbuck and klipspringer have specific habitat requirements and these must be met before they will be approved for release on a property. It must also be a minimum of 200 ha in size.

When kudu are introduced to a new area, it must be ascertained whether there is sufficient browse to sustain the animals throughout the year, particularly during the dry winter months. The size must also be at least 200 ha.

Giraffe will only be allowed on properties of 400 ha in size and the property must first be evaluated to ascertain whether it is suitable.

Animals such as buffalo, tsessebe, sable antelope, and roan must have a minimum surface area of 400 ha.

The logic of some of the above is rather puzzling. Surely it would be better to have 2 giraffe on a property of 200 ha than 10 giraffe on a farm twice as large ? I feel that, instead of placing limitations on the species, especially if the area is particularly suitable for them, their numbers should rather be restricted. It would be more practical to evaluate each case separately, since farms differ in vegetation, even within the same small area. A smaller farm may offer better habitat to animals than a bigger property. Suitability of habitat and survival of the animals should be more important than the total surface area.

NATAL

The Natal Parks Board makes provision for minimum requirements for a variety of game fences. The requirements described here are those that apply to game-proof fences for commercial nature reserves where the movements of antelope have to be controlled. Where necessary, these fences must be additionally reinforced to contain lion and rhino.

Height of fence and spacing of wire:

Height 2,0 m. Horizontal wires can be attached to the insides of the posts and droppers by means of 3,75 mm galvanised staples or, especially in high rainfall areas, by means of 3 mm galvanised binding wire. The horizontal wires should not be further than 15 cm apart.

Veldspan wire mesh (standard grade 1 483/6), which is obtainable in rolls 2,1 m wide, can be used as an alternative. Binding wire (3 mm galvanised binding wire) is used to secure the Veldspan wire to the posts.

Diameter and spacing of posts:

Straining posts must be firmly anchored. Example: At each straining point, two treated wooden posts with top diameters of 175 to 200 mm are implanted deep in the soil, 1,8 m apart in an upright position. Wooden posts 1,8 m long are fastened horizontally on two levels between the upright posts so as, together with cross-wires 4 mm thick, to lend the necessary reinforcement to the angle-supports. On level ground the straining posts are implanted 250 to 300 m apart. On ridges and depressions additional straining posts are required.

Normal wire or line posts can consist of treated poles (pine poles are not recommended), with top diameters of 125 mm. These poles or standard Y-posts are implanted at intervals of 10 m or even less, sufficiently deep in the ground to impart the necessary sturdiness to the fence.

Droppers can be made of treated poles with top diameters of 75 mm. These or metal droppers are used every 2 m or less.

RHINO PROOF FENCING

The Natal Parks Board supplied the following recommendations regarding rhino proof fencing:

Straining posts

* Poles creosoted (gum, not pine), 2,1 m long with 175 to 200 mm diameter tops.
* Construct anchors in box-like pattern, with transverse pole support between upper tips of poles and diagonal wires.
* Spaced 250 to 300 m apart, as well as in all dips and on all ridges. (For Veldspan fences, 200 m is adequate.)
* Planted 90 cm into the ground (deeper in sandy soil), concreted in except for the lower ends of the poles, which must protrude into the soil to retard rotting.

Poles

* Poles, also creosoted and 2,1 m long, with 175 mm diameter tops.
* Planted, in the same way as the straining posts, 0,9 m deep into the ground (deeper in sand) and spaced 10 m apart.
* Cross-ties on every pole.

Droppers

* Creosoted, only 0,75 m long, with 75 mm diameter tops.
* Placed between upper and lower cables and spaced 1,7 m apart (i.e. five between each pair of poles).

Cables and wires

* Cable, 12,5 mm in diameter, attached to straining posts with strong wire rope clamps and to poles and droppers with 4 mm plain galvanised binding wire.
* Space these cables at 38 cm, 75 cm and 112 cm, respectively, above ground level.

Requirements per kilometre

* 106 poles, 2,1 m long with 175 mm tops (more, if broken terrain).
* 525 droppers, 0,75 m long with 75 mm tops.
* 3 000 m cable, with 12,5 mm diameter.
* 6 rolls of 4 mm plain galvanised binding wire.
* Cement, wire rope clamps and other smaller items.

ORANGE FREE STATE

The approach in this case is very similar to that already being followed in the Transvaal. Different types of fence are also recommended for different species of farm game:

Class I: Kudu, eland, waterbuck, impala, hartebeest, bontebok and other jumping game.

Class II: Blue wildebeest, black wildebeest, zebra, sable antelope, gemsbok, mountain reedbuck and grey rhebuck.

Class III: Blesbok, springbok and bushbuck.

Height and fence types:

Class I: Height 2,4 m. Seventeen strands of barbed or steel wire, 15 cm apart, are suggested.

Class II: Height 1,8 m. Thirteen strands of barbed or steel wire, 15 cm apart, are recommended.

Class III: Height 1,38 m. Thirteen strands of barbed or steel wire, 15 cm apart, are once again recommended. (My calculations suggest that this should probably be **nine** strands, with the recommended spacing.)

Diameter and spacing of posts:

The diameter of posts is not specified. The following types of post and spacing are, however, suggested:

Class I: Straining posts (wood or iron) should be placed at intervals not exceeding 400 m. Anchoring posts (iron) should be used every 5 m and droppers (wood or iron) every 1,5 m.

Class II: Straining posts (wood or iron) should be placed at intervals not exceeding 300 m. Anchoring posts (iron) should be used every 5 m and droppers (wood or iron) every 1,5 m.

Class III: Straining posts (wood or iron) should be placed at intervals not exceeding 500 m. Anchoring posts (iron) should be used every 5 m and droppers (wood or iron) every 1,5 m.

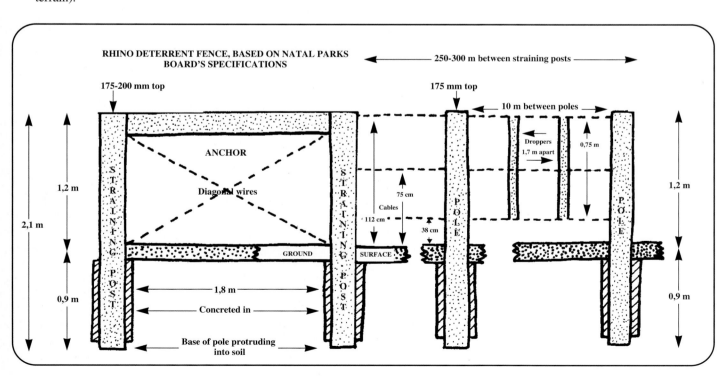

The idea behind these proposals was that, if a game farmer in the Orange Free State satisfactorily met these requirements at some future stage, he could be exempted from certain or all of the stipulations of the Nature Conservation Ordinance in respect of the animal species on his enclosed farm, as is the case in the Transvaal.

It would appear that satisfactory results can be achieved with many disparate types of fence. Although diverging conditions in the different provinces and the requirements of different game species may necessitate different minimum specifications for suitable fences, the diverging nature and standard of prescribed fences in the different provinces are also due to unco-ordinated planning and other factors.

Although each fence described above has considerable merit, experienced conservationists and game farmers would agree that the recommendations will not always produce the best and cheapest game fences in all cases. One or two of the fences specified are even considered inadequate, and will not satisfactorily contain all antelope. The classification of game in accordance with their jumping prowess does also not agree in all cases, and a more uniform method of classification is clearly required for the Republic as a whole.

The following section is an attempt to combine the above and other practical fencing systems in order to suggest a standard fence. Although not necessarily the best fences possible, simplicity, effectiveness and economic considerations have been thoroughly weighed up in planning the standard fences discussed below.

STANDARD FENCES FOR FARM GAME

Depending on the terrain across which the fence must be erected, the local availability and cost of fencing material, the experience of the personnel who have to erect the fence, and, most particularly, the animals that have to be kept inside, modifications to the specifications proposed below may be necessary. These prescriptions are, however, suggested as the minimum requirements in order for fences to be effective in containing antelope and other common species of farm game, with the possible exception of rhino, other large animals and predators.

In contrast to the minimum requirements of the different provinces, the specifications suggested here are an attempt to create a very simple model. The spacing of the horizontal strands of a steel wire fence is the same throughout, and, if it should later become necessary to increase the height of, say, a Class III fence for smaller game so that it can also contain jumping game, this can easily be done by simply implanting longer posts and further increasing the height of the existing fence without changing the spacing between the horizontal strands.

Farm game species are reclassified in accordance with their jumping capability and provision is made for fences with corresponding heights, viz.:

Class I: Kudu, nyala, impala, eland, waterbuck.

Class II: Gemsbok, red hartebeest, wildebeest, zebra, grey rhebuck and mountain reedbuck.

Class III: Springbok, blesbok, bontebok and smaller game.

Height and fence types:

Class I: 2,4 m (21 strands)
Class II: 1,8 m (16 strands)
Class III: 1,4 m (12 strands)

Adequately erected game fences with exemption from the Nature conservation Ordinance will ensure property right to farmers over the game enclosed on such farms.

Provision is made for two basic fence types, viz. (a) barbed/steel wire fences and (b) a combination of barbed/steel wire with a prefabricated game-proof fence such as Veldspan.

(a) **Barbed/steel wire fence:** The vertical spacing of the horizontal strands from ground level to the top strand is 11,4 cm throughout. The lower strand is therefore placed 11,4 cm above ground level and all the subsequent horizontal strands are placed 11,4 cm apart, right up to the top. The number of strands for each class of fence is given above, together with the height.

Except for the uppermost and lowermost strands, the horizontal strands must be galvanised high-tensile steel wire with a minimum (recommended) diameter of 2,24 mm. Barbed wire can be used throughout, although this is not considered necessary.

The top strand should preferably be barbed wire (e.g. Campeon barbed wire), which, with its high visibility and deterrent effect, discourages animals from trying to leap over the fence. The bottom strand can preferably also be barbed wire, in order to deter animals such as warthogs and predators from attempting to crawl underneath the fence.

Binding wire with a mimimum thickness of 2,5 mm must be used to secure the horizontal strands firmly to the posts and droppers. Binding wire of the same thickness should be used for vertical reinforcing strands (see later).

(b) **Combination of barbed/steel wire with prefabricated game-proof fencing (e.g. Veldspan):** The above minimum heights are also applicable here. In cases where prefabricated fencing is not available in the precise heights given, steel wire strands with a barbed wire strand at the top, as specified above, are placed 11,4 cm apart above the prefabricated fencing.

While Veldspan is recommended here, farmers who may

have erected other accepted prefabricated fences on their farms can rest assured that the same good results will be achieved provided that the fence is impenetrable, is sturdy enough and meets the above criteria in other respects.

Diameter and spacing of posts, droppers and supporting wires

It is suggested that iron posts be used wherever possible, since veld fires and weathering may cause the effectiveness of wooden posts to deteriorate over the years.

For straining and corner posts, 22 kg/m ridged iron droppers are recommended. Iron Y-posts and ridgeback iron droppers must comply with Iscor standards with respect to mass and diameter.

If using wooden posts cannot be avoided for economic or other practical reasons, the straining, gate and corner posts should have a top diameter of at least 150 to 200 mm. For normal line posts, the required top diameter is 100 mm. The droppers must be round and have a diameter of at least 50 mm.

Firebreaks must be made on both sides of the fence to prevent wooden posts, droppers and wire from being damaged through exposure to fire.

The spacing of straining posts, in particular, is determined largely by the topography of the terrain. On flat ground the straining posts can be implanted at intervals of 250 to 300 m. When prefabricated game-proof fencing is used, the straining posts should be spaced no more than 200 m apart. In mountainous terrain, sandy soil or on uneven terrain, it may be necessary to place the straining posts even closer together. The straining posts should be sufficiently well anchored to impart the necessary firmness to the fence.

In the case of barbed/steel wire fences, the line posts (e.g. iron Y-posts) should be 15 m apart, and the droppers 3 m apart.

The droppers may be purchased in the correct lengths, or be cut or joined to reach the total height of a barbed/steel wire fence. Greater benefit is derived, however, when two droppers (preferably lightweight metal droppers, such as those described above), each slightly longer than half of the total height of the fence, are secured in such a manner that the top end of the lower dropper and the bottom end of the upper dropper scissor past each other when an animal jumps up against the fence. The main principle here is that, although a fence should be strong, it should simultaneously be sufficiently elastic to prevent broken necks and other injuries when animals jump into the fence.

Between the droppers, vertical support wires, placed 1 m apart, are added by weaving binding wire firmly from one horizontal strand to the next, up the full height of the fence. These vertical wires hold the horizontal strands the desired distance apart, and imparts remarkable resistance and elasticity to the fence.

The horizontal strands of a fence which has its droppers positioned too far apart or which lacks vertical reinforcing wires can easily be wedged open when an animal attempts to jump through it, and this can help game to escape.

In the case of prefabricated game-proof fences droppers are not required and the line posts can be positioned 10 m apart.

THE IMPORTANCE OF EFFECTIVE GAME FENCES

In addition to preventing losses, such as those resulting from the escape of valuable game, a fence which effectively keeps game in also holds further indirect advantages for the game farmer.

During 1991, game farmers were finally granted property rights over their wild animals, provided that the game-proof fencing around their farm subscribes to the specifications laid down by the relevant conservation department and is certified as being adequate. He is then deemed to exercise full control over the animals on his property and they therefore belong to him.

Since the recognition of game farming as a commercial branch of agriculture by the Department of Agriculture, the allocation of subsidies on inner fences is also applicable to game farms. It is therefore very important for game farmers that standard fences, as described above, in the suggested or a modified form, be acknowledged by the authorities for subsidy purposes.

ELECTRIC FENCING

Standard game fences are generally not effective enough to keep species such as buffalo, rhino, hippo, elephant, lions and cheetahs in. The Armstrong fence which is erected around various national parks costs about R90 000 a kilometre and is simply too expensive.

Although supporting cables and/or heavy wire netting could improve the safety of any fence, the mere electrification of well-erected, standard game fences seems to be all that is required.

Elephant, for example, are successfully kept in by electric fence supported barriers in Kruger Park, the Timbavati and Klaserie game reserves, Letaba Ranch and Manyeleti in Gazankulu and on various private farms in the Eastern Transvaal Lowveld and the Cape Province.

The following standard fence is suggested: A 2,4 m high, 21 strand steel wire fence, with the individual wires evenly spaced, on average 11,4 cm apart, from just above the ground to the prescribed height. Carnivores and creepers could be more effectively kept in if say, the lower 1,8 m of the fence consisted of barbed wire or of heavy wire netting, the latter stretching some 60 cm to the inside at the bottom, a few centimetres below the surface of the soil.

The fence described above can generally be accepted to be effective in keeping all antelope and most other game species in. It should preferably be supported with at least four 2,24 mm thick, electric (6 000 + volts) wires, attached to the fence with off-set brackets. The individual electric wires should be spaced just above ground level (for lion and other digging animals), 45 cm and 90 cm above ground level, mainly for lion, cheetah, buffalo, rhino and hippo but also for elephant, testing the fence with their trunks, and with the highest wire some 2,1 to 2,4 metres above ground level, for young elephant. The latter will also prevent baboon, monkeys and carnivores from climbing over the fence, particularly if this wire is placed close enough to the top of the fence.

It must be emphasised that the regular inspection and continuous and meticulous maintenance of the fence is of cardinal importance.

16. VELD MANAGEMENT ON GAME FARMS

As is the case with pasture control on cattle farms, diverging opinions are also held regarding the most suitable forms of veld utilisation and control on game farms. The wide spectrum of game species, each with its own habits and needs, and the development of appropriate field survey techniques and rotational grazing systems, offer unique opportunities to interested researchers. In the meantime, sound management practices are based on practical experience, a thorough knowledge of the nutritional needs and grazing habits of the game species in question and the characteristics of the relevant veld types, as well as the modification of the general veld control principles used in livestock farming.

THE GRAZING HABITS OF GAME

On the basis of their diverse nutritional requirements and grazing patterns, farm game can be classified in different ways. The division of game into grazers and browsers is surely familiar to most people. The grazers are now being subdivided even further on the basis of their size and tendency towards selective grazing. Probably the most useful classification for practical purposes is the following by M T Mentis, which includes domestic stock:

Bulk grazers:
Cattle, buffalo, Burchell's zebra, waterbuck.

Selective or concentrate grazers:
White rhino, blue wildebeest, red hartebeest, gemsbok, black wildebeest, nyala, reedbuck, blesbok, bushpig, sheep, impala, warthog, springbok, mountain reedbuck, grey rhebok, oribi.

Browsers:
Black rhino, giraffe, eland, kudu, domestic goats, bushbuck, common duiker, steenbok.

The bulk grazers are large grazing species which normally do not graze very selectively and, amongst other things, make good use of the longer, less digestible grass types.

The selective grazers are, with a few exceptions, smaller in size (average mass of under 200 kg) and subsist mainly on grass. These species (e.g. white rhino) are, however, highly selective of the specific area they will graze or the types or parts of plant food they will utilise. Because the laws of nature determine that smaller animals require more energy per unit of body mass per day, the feeding requirements of this group of animals theoretically places greater demands on their environment. They do not necessarily consume more food per unit of body mass, but often select the more nutritious parts of available plants. The selective feeding habits of certain of the smaller antelope and the limited availability of their preferred food in the veld is responsible, amongst other things, for the fact that the small species of game never occur in large herds or in great numbers in a particular area.

In addition to leaves, the browsers eat young shoots, herbaceous plants, fruit and even the flowers of veld plants. These food sources are usually high in nutritional value and as a rule also contain more moisture, as we shall see later.

The grazing patterns of the impala and many other species are influenced to a large extent by the availability and distribution of water.

Some farmers believe that the resistance of the eland to ticks is influenced by the plants (e.g. aloe) they consume.

The animals in the above classification have, within each group, been arranged in order of decreasing size. Theoretically these animals should, from the largest to the smallest, consume a greater total amount of plant food, even of a poorer quality, per animal in the case of the larger species, but selective grazing of the more palatable food should increase as more animals belonging to the smaller species occur in a specific area.

Kudu eat very little grass and do not compete significantly with cattle for available grazing.

CORRECT SPECIES RATIOS

In the livestock industry it has been the practice for many years to combine cattle and sheep in a specific ratio (for example 1 head of cattle for every 5 or 6 sheep) in order to achieve optimum veld utilisation. The combination of large and small game also offers several obvious advantages. Buffalo and zebra can, for example, graze tall grassveld sufficiently to make it more accessible to game such as wildebeest and blesbok which

specifically prefer short grassveld. Where suitable large game does not occur on a farm, cattle offer the best alternative. Relevant research is urgently needed to determine the correct ratio of game species that will lead to optimum utilisation of veld in the different vegetation regions without adversely affecting the condition of the grass or the composition of the grazing and browse.

VELD TYPES

A thorough understanding of the veld to be managed as well as of the wild animals on it is essential if sound grazing principles are to be applied. Consequently some of the characteristics of the more important veld types are discussed briefly below.

Acocks, probably one of the greatest experts on South African veld types, classifies the grazing in our country into different grassveld, savanna or bushveld and karoid types. This still, of course, leaves our indigenous forests and the unique Cape fynbos or macchia.

Whereas grassveld, followed by the savannas, represents the most productive types of grazing for livestock, the different species of game thrive on all the above veld types. On close examination, grassveld and trees and shrubs of the savannas constitute the most productive veld for game farming.

Grassveld

For the purpose of this discussion, grassveld is simply divided into sweet, sour and mixed grassveld. The latter incorporates sweet and sourveld components and therefore has characteristic features of both.

Sweet veld, which is characterised by palatable and relatively easily digested grass species, is found mainly in the country's low-lying, frost-free regions. This veld type is equally favoured by all grass eating game and stock and is very susceptible to overgrazing, especially during periods of active growth in spring and summer. Game, like stock, has the unfortunate habit of concentrating on new growth which has been grazed short and thereby exhausting damaged veld even further. On sweet veld, the consequences of overgrazing are low grass cover, the disappearance of the most popular grass species, as well as bush encroachment. Particularly where game has to be supported for years within a single camp system, it is essential to keep animal populations within reasonable limits, especially on vulnerable grazing, if overgrazing is to be prevented.

Sour grassveld occurs in the colder, high-lying regions of the country, against mountain slopes and on well drained sandy soil. In contrast to sweet grassveld, sour veld is found particularly in the higher rainfall areas (>800 mm). This type of veld comprises approximately 13 million hectares of the country's surface area.

Although in the case of cattle the carrying capacity of sourveld and mixed veld is usually higher than that of sweet grassveld, sour grassveld consists mainly of tall sour grass species which are only well utilised by cattle for approximately 6 to 8 months. These grasses are also only significantly grazed by game during the actively growing phase, in spring and early summer. During autumn and winter this grass is long, fibrous and unpalatable to game and stock alike, and its nutritional value drops to very low levels. Although game species such as blesbok, mountain reedbuck, grey rhebok, reedbuck and oribi may continue to survive in such veld, they prefer to eat the newer growth alongside streams and vleis, and some of the more palatable and nutritious plants growing in the area. Most other game fare very poorly on sourveld during winter.

Overgrazing usually does not affect the grass cover to the same extent as on sweetveld. The more palatable vegetation is, however, selectively overgrazed and destroyed, so that unpalatable and pioneer grasses eventually become increasingly abundant. Sour grassveld is usually at its best when red grass (*Themeda triandra*) occurs abundantly in the grazing.

Underutilisation of sour grassveld, which may be more common with game than with livestock, is also detrimental. The veld cover and carrying capacity diminish as the grazing changes and becomes woody. Shrubs grow unchecked, until the underutilised veld eventually develops into a shrub climax stage.

Savanna

Approximately 40 per cent of the country's surface area consists of savanna. This veld type, which includes the Lowveld, bushveld regions and thornveld and shrubveld, is characterised by grass and tree or shrub components, and occurs particularly in warm regions which have variable and low rainfall. Savanna veld is extremely well suited to most game species, providing shelter and food for the shy, bush-dwelling browsers as well for the large herds of grazing plains animals such as zebra and blue wildebeest.

Excessive bush encroachment, a symptom of deterioration in this veld type, is causing increasing management problems on stock farms. An estimated 13 million hectares of savanna veld are already affected by various stages of bush encroachment. Black thorn (*Acacia mellifera subsp. detinens*) and bitter bush (*Chrysocoma tenuifolia*) are already cause for concern in the Kalahari thornveld of the Northern Cape, while sweet thorn (*A. karroo*) and sickle bush (*Dichrostachys cinerea*) are forming excessively dense stands in the dry thornveld of the eastern Cape and the bushveld regions of the northern, western and eastern Transvaal, respectively. It is estimated that grass production in these thickets may be decreased by as much as 40 to 50 per cent. Consequently some farmers have begun spending astronomical sums of money on bush control projects. For the game farmer, however, dense stands of sickle bush and thorn trees, in particular, often hold definite advantages, in that valuable leaf fodder helps to sustain game during droughts. In areas where almost no grass is to be found in winter, impala, kudu and other game thrive on the pods of the sickle bush (*Dichrostachys cinerea*), umbrella thorn (*A. tortilis*) and scented thorn (*A. nilotica*).

In his book on trees of the bushveld and grazing regions ("Bosveldbome en weistreke"), Prof. J Bonsma provides interesting information on the nutritional value of some of our bushveld trees. Expressed as a percentage on a dry basis, the crude protein value of the edible parts of the shepherd's tree (*Boscia albitrunca*), for example, is 13 to 17 per cent; that of camel thorn pods (*A. erioloba*) approximately 12 per cent; of karee (*Rhus lancea*) 12 to 13 per cent; mopane (*Colosphospermum mopane*) 11 to 13 per cent; sickle bush 10 to 11 per cent; and red bushwillow (*Combretum apiculatum*) 7 to 15 per cent. The comparable value for lucerne hay is approximately 15 per cent. Numerous other popular and nutritious edible tree species occur in this veld type.

Karoo

With its varied combination of grass and scrubveld, the Karoo forms part, inter alia, of the natural home of the springbok. This veld type covers a large portion of the interior plateau and incorporates the larger part of the Cape Province. Whereas the protein composition of grass in these areas varies between approximately 3 to 6 per cent, some of the karoid scrub contains from 6 to 9 per cent crude protein on a dry basis. Dr Rudi Bigalke has found that springbok in the Kimberley vicinity utilise no less than 20 species of karoid scrub. This includes the bitter bush, which is poisonous to sheep, with a crude protein value of 8 to 13 per cent.

Good management practices are required to ensure the desired balance between the grass and scrub components of this veld type. As was mentioned in an earlier chapter, springbok predominantly consume scrub during the dry season, and do not compete significantly with sheep for available grazing. Karoo farmers have already shown that game and livestock can be beneficially combined.

Forests

Indigenous forests, which constitute the natural habitat of the red and blue duiker, amongst others, and which host unique plant and bird species, are restricted mainly to the eastern parts of the country. Since these forests are not, from the point of view of grazing, capable of sustaining a significant number of stock or game, and are economically more viable as a source of wood, this priceless habitat has unfortunately been destroyed to a large extent. When grassveld in the vicinity of these forests is burnt, farmers sometimes rely on the forests to halt the fires. Unfortunately extensive damage is inflicted on the trees, and the surface area of isolated forests is continuously shrinking. From the point of view of conservation, our indigenous forests should be excluded from any form of intensive stock or game farming, and the remaining patches of forest be afforded stricter protection.

Cape fynbos

The Cape fynbos, which occurs mainly in the winter rainfall area of the southern and south-western Cape is the last main veld type that will briefly be discussed. Protea and heather dominate this beautiful veld, while grass does not generally occur. Grazing practices over the past three centuries have largely turned the fynbos region into what it is today. In spite of its beauty, this garden-like part of our country does not constitute valuable grazing. Game occurring naturally on this veld type includes the bontebok and the Cape grysbok.

With the grazing habits of game and the different veld types as background, a few important principles relating to veld development and utilisation can be examined before appropriate management practices are discussed.

VELD DEVELOPMENT AND UTILISATION

Rather than present game farmers with a few hypothetical and academic instant formulae for grazing programmes, I prefer to point out a few elementary physiological and ecological principles of which game farmers should take note if they wish to make optimum use of their veld. By observing these basic principles, and planning intelligently and obtaining the expert assistance and advice of agricultural advisers and ecology consultants, detailed programmes can be devised for each farm in accordance with its needs and circumstances. I trust that this short discussion will stimulate further and more specialised self-studies. With this in mind, the excellent book "Veld and Pasture Management in South Africa", edited by Prof. N M Tainton, is highly recommended.

Let us begin with the most important element, namely the plant itself. In addition to soil, rain, and the other vital natural elements over which we have little or no control, each clump of grass and each plant requires from the farmer a reasonable opportunity to grow on protected soil and to produce seed for propagation. After the growing season in autumn, even if this is only possible once every few years, the clump of grass or plant would like to send some of the starch produced as well as other nutrients down to the roots, so that, thus invigorated, it will be able to produce food once again for the animals of the veld during the next season.

By means of photosynthesis the leaves transform energy from the sun into a form that can be used by game and stock. If the green leaves are lightly grazed, the grass plant is not severely affected. If, however, the leaf-producing section at the base of a leaf is removed, that particular leaf stops growing. Whereas light grazing can to a certain extent stimulate growth, heavy and continuous grazing pressure leads to weak growth and lower production. In contrast, the removal of dry blades of grass may in some cases be beneficial, since growing leaves lower down on the stem thus receive greater exposure to the sun.

The response of the grass plant to grazing or damage to the grass tops or ends is equally interesting. Whereas light grazing may, especially in certain species, lead to the development of side shoots and denser growth, excessive grazing of grass tops can hinder growth and seed production. No matter how obvious the above information seems, these elementary principles have been ignored for years, and as a result many farmers have literally allowed their grazing to be grazed and trampled right into the ground.

TRAMPLING OF THE VELD

The effect of trampling of the veld by stock and game is also generally ignored. Bare, dusty patches around corrals and watering points, and footpaths of livestock which form erosion gulleys, bear witness to the fact that animals do not only damage the veld with their mouths! When planning inner fences and camps and deciding on the positioning of watering points, it is therefore important to select concentration points correctly, or, wherever possible, to avoid these altogether. Sloping ground and the sensitivity of certain soils to erosion are important factors to consider here.

Certain grass species with soft, fleshy leaves are more susceptible to damage due to trampling than others. The veld is also

Blue wildebeest, like blesbok, tend to concentrate on short grassveld.

not damaged equally by all animals. In the case of cattle and horses, for example, the static load pressure is calculated at approximately 1,7 kg per square cm, whereas for sheep, by comparison, the pressure is only 0,65 kg per square cm. The grazing and walking patterns are also significant. Where sheep are inclined to tread footpaths, springbok move and graze in a more even distribution across the veld. Large herds of buffalo, which tend to bunch up together when grazing and moving ahead, probably trample the veld to a greater degree than most other game species.

Aside from the damage to grazing, breaking up of the earth crust by, for example, cattle and buffalo also has advantages, in that a suitable seed bed is created for grass and other seeds. On game farms where a layer of hard crust has formed on the surface of trampled veld owing to prolonged exposure to the sun, scoring of the ground surface by hoofs, in conjunction with fertilisation by the animals, may promote renewed growth of grass and other plants.

BUSH ENCROACHMENT

The development of dense stands of sickle bush and other invasive plants may, however, also be encouraged in this manner. Adequate proof of this is supplied by the nearly impenetrable bush around corrals, watering points and other concentration points in the bushveld regions of Transvaal. In my opinion, the so-called problem of bush encroachment in these regions is caused partially by excessive deterioration of the veld and undesirable methods of stock and veld management.

In contrast to cattle and buffalo, impala, rhino and certain other game species prefer to use specific middens. This phenomenon can have important ecological consequences. First, some of the disadvantages: The veld is not evenly fertilised, as is the case with domestic stock. Isolated middens consisting of hard pellets such as those of impala cannot make a meaningful contribution to the circulation of nutrients in nature, and therefore do not promote plant growth.

The advantages do, however, appear to outweigh the disadvantages. The larvae of internal parasites are not transmitted throughout the veld to the same extent as with stock, and have a smaller chance of surviving on such middens and reinfecting animals. The seeds of alien plants such as sickle bush germinate successfully, but are concentrated around these middens.

What is even more significant — on some of these middens, where young sickle bush trees shoot up after the first rains like hair on a dog's back, these seedlings manage to grow only a few centimetres high before dying! This phenomenon has been observed most frequently on impala middens.

The activity of blesbok and certain other species at specific middens, as well as at termitaria, also lead to interesting changes to the composition of the grass. At such spots it is, for example, not at all unusual to find dense stands of couch grass, (kweekgras) which smaller game species find more attractive as forage than the sour grassveld that often occurs in the surrounding areas. It would even appear that certain species of game may create a more favourable habitat for themselves through their specific grazing habits and behaviour.

CATTLE ON A GAME FARM

Since it is often recommended that cattle and game farming be combined, it may be appropriate to examine more closely the role of cattle on a game farm. Apart from the better utilisation of the veld, the distribution of cattle dung on the grazing has further interesting consequences which have not yet been discussed.

Cattle allegedly excrete dung 12 times a day. Approximately 0,04 ha of veld are annually covered by the dung of one animal. For 100 cattle this area therefore becomes 4 ha. Now it is claimed that veld soiled by cattle dung is temporarily unacceptable for grazing, that the grass under and around the dung dies, and that approximately 0,16 ha of pasture are theoretically affected by the dung of a single animal in one year. Only approximately 20 per cent of the nitrogen present in so-called "unprocessed dung" is fed back to the soil, and then it is furthermore claimed that this unrefined dung hinders grass production in its immediate vicinity! And then, as if this dung has not already wreaked sufficient ecological havoc, the parasitologists add that such dung is a source of parasite larvae — as many as 25 000 grub larvae can occur in a teaspoon of cattle dung!

If you have managed to persevere thus far with this execrable tale, you must by now have concluded that I am one of those super-conservationists who cannot contemplate the thought of cattle on a game farm. This is, in fact, not so. The reason: Dung beetles, of which there are approximately 2 000 species in Africa, also favour cattle. When dung beetles process the cattle dung, approximately 90 per cent of the nitrogen in the dung is returned to the soil. And, quite apart from anything else, grass production is thus given a considerable boost, with plants growing near to dung having approximately 11 per cent more crude protein than their less fortunate counterparts.

VELD DETERIORATION

Veld deterioration should not only be viewed and measured in terms of bare veld and erosion gulleys. Otherwise one is conducting a post mortem instead of diagnosing a severe veld disease! The first indications of change are subtle and often elude even an expert's keen eye. Game and stock, especially small livestock, tends to consume the most palatable veld plants first. When the animals concentrate too much or for too long on these palatable species, it is only logical that some of these popular food sources may be exterminated.

On numerous game-proof farms in the Transvaal it has been observed that gemsbok and eland thrive for a few years and breed successfully. After a few years, and in spite of the successful survival of other game on the same farm, these animals begin to lose weight, fewer calves are reared and some of the adult animals begin to die of heavy tick infestations. Some farmers blame the ticks. It is, however, possible that the ticks are merely a part of the complex syndrome of veld deterioration. Numerous farmers believe that aloe (Aloe spp.), when consumed by the animals, help to keep the game free of ticks. When the aloes on a farm have been exhausted, the ticks allegedly take over and cause mortalities amongst the game. This is only one of many theories! The question arises whether excessive selective grazing of essential forage, no matter of which type, is not perhaps the reason why such animals, which are controlled in terms of a single camp grazing system, begin to deteriorate.

Another interesting observation indicates that smaller game such as steenbok and duiker are apparently inclined to occur more commonly on cattle farms than on neighbouring game farms. Is it perhaps possible that competition with other small game for sought after food items is too strong in the game camps, or do the juicy herbaceous plants which are more common on veld which has benefitted from cattle manure offer a more attractive alternative? Although the above observation may be exceptional, and the interpretation of these events has definitely not been confirmed scientifically, farmers should constantly keep a close watch on the condition of the grazing and of the animals on their farms, to prevent permanent damage. Later (p 135) reference will be made to simple botanical survey techniques that can be used to determine veld deterioration.

ERADICATION OF BUSH

On stock ranches, where it should be a specific aim to counteract bush encroachment, it is especially important to ensure a dense grass cover. Grass generally utilises water better than trees and shrubs and bush encroachment can therefore allegedly be most effectively counteracted by a good grass cover. In cases where excessive bush encroachment has already occurred, however, grass development is often excessively undermined by competition, and it may be necessary to thin out some of the trees and bush by mechanical or chemical means.

From an ecological point of view, total eradication of bush on a farm cannot be condoned, since leguminous plants, in particular, can have a very beneficial influence on the grass stratum. Trees with a deep root system also continuously enrich the topsoil. Furthermore, trees and shrubs provide shade and protection for the veld and its animals. It is especially sad when gigantic trees that are centuries old or protected species fall victim to reckless eradication.

UNDERUTILISATION OF GRASSVELD

Some game farmers appear to be unaware that the underutilisation of sour grassveld, in particular, can be extremely detrimental to the veld. Apart from the fact that relatively useless woody shrubs and herbaceous plants increase, some of the tufts of grass begin to die from the centre, and the percentage of living grasses covering the ground drops.

TREES AND SHRUBS

Information concerning the germination success of edible tree species as well as of alien plants, and factors influencing this, is vitally important in pasture management. Seeds of the sweet thorn (A. karroo), like those of many other trees, are enclosed in a thick, protective pod. Under laboratory conditions, these seeds can be kept for more than 50 years, after which they will still germinate. In the veld, only about 5 to 10 per cent of seeds germinate. As is the case with numerous other trees, germination of sweet thorn seeds is stimulated by veld fires. During periods of high rainfall, germination statistics are also generally considerably higher. Seeds that have passed through an animal's digestive system are also said to germinate more readily. Particularly on trampled and burnt veld, where competition from a dense grass cover is negligible, encroachment of sweet thorn can therefore become a problem.

The shoots of sweet thorn, (Acacia karroo), buffalo-thorn (Ziziphus mucronata) and some of the other veld trees are usually long and tender. The growing points at the tips of branches are dominant and it is here that the mentioned growth patterns originate. When the branch-tips of young trees of a particular species become damaged by excessive browsing or veld fires, their growth pattern and shape change considerably, because growing points lower down on the trunk take over and

The black rhino, like the giraffe, kudu, nyala and the bushbuck, is primarily a browser and, to a certain extent, may contribute to the controlling of bush encroachment.

cause the young trees to form bushy lateral growth. This partially explains the dense stands of sweet thorn bush that sometimes occur on grassveld. Although generally a nuisance, this form of growth supplies browsing species with more foliage within reach.

Naturally low-profile trees and shrubs will be used more beneficially by game during this stage of growth than tall trees. In the case of stock, plant fodder from the ground up to a level of 1,5 m (domestic goat) or 2 m (cattle) is considered within reach. Kudu can reach green leaves and shoots higher up, and for giraffe even 6 m is not beyond reach.

Particularly during autumn and winter, when the pods of the sickle bush and thorn trees and the leaves of mopane and many other edible species begin to fall, the taller trees play an increasingly important role in supplying good quality reserve fodder during the dry months.

Even the soft shoots of the cork bush (Mundulea sericea) and other edible species are then increasingly browsed by kudu. During severe droughts kudu will even eat the branches of the candelabra tree (Euphorbia ingens). Records show that kudu have on occasion suffered acute blindness as a result of contact with the toxic sap of the candelabra tree.

Although grass generally provides a greater quantity of edible plant matter than trees and shrubs, a reasonable generalisation would be that trees and shrubs on savanna veld, despite variations in rainfall, usually ensure more fodder of a higher quality to most game for a larger part of the year.

Researchers such as Rutherford, Kelly, Goodman and Aucamp have conducted interesting studies on the production potential of savanna veld. It has been established that veld in Central Africa (rainfall: 500 ml) yields approximately 20 000 kg plant matter per hectare and that about 1 500 kg shoots and leaves are produced per hectare annually. Depending on the type of veld, approximately 33 to 75 per cent of this leaf fodder may be within the reach of stock. Although these statistics cannot summarily be applied to all bushveld regions, they do provide some indication of the productivity and accessibility of fodder from trees and leaves.

Light grazing may stimulate the development and productivity of leaf fodder, while heavy grazing pressure can cause shoots to die and production to drop sharply. It would appear that prolonged and intensive grazing of the larger species of developing edible trees, such as actively growing sickle bush and umbrella thorn, may cause developing shoots within the animals' reach to be permanently damaged. Up to a height of approximately 1,5 to 2 m only the bare, woody trunks are left; slightly higher up, actively growing shoots, leaves and pods remain unaffected, contributing to the animals' food requirements later on in the season, when the trees begin to shed their leaves and pods. Impala, who have to subsist on leaves as well as grass are then forced to consume more grass during the growing season. Young developing shrubs and herbaceous plants which tend to flourish on trodden veld are, however, also subjected to intensive grazing by impala, and bush encroachment can thus, to a certain extent, be suppressed at an early stage on mixed game and stock farms.

CARRYING CAPACITY OF THE VELD

Effective pasture management on a game farm requires a flexible approach. Established concepts relating to carrying capacity, grazing capacity and livestock units that are relevant to the stock farming industry cannot summarily be extrapolated to game farming.

Statistics relating to carrying capacity can be misleading and may even serve as an excuse for overgrazing of farms, unless these are considered and judiciously applied in conjunction with all other relevant information concerning a specific farm.

Owing to the diverse food requirements, social behaviour patterns and, in particular, the different grazing patterns of the individual game species, I feel that the concept of carrying capacity, when applied to game farming, should be replaced with a more realistic approach regarding effective pasture utilisation.

Carrying capacity may, for the purposes of clarification, be defined as the largest number of animals of a particular species that may be kept permanently in a specific area without adverse effects on the animals and without deterioration of the grazing.

When more than one animal species is concerned, technical difficulties arise with the definition of a standard criterion for animal units. In an effort to overcome this problem, a theoretical standard animal size, known as a large stock unit, was created in agricultural circles.

A large stock unit is defined as the equivalent of one head of cattle with a mass of 450 kg that increases its mass by 500 g per day on grass pastures with an average energy digestibility of 55 per cent.

Although it is possible to describe game units in terms of large stock units (see, for example the tables on page 136), such information has limited value when it comes to determining the carrying capacity of veld for game.

The ability of only a few larger species of game to utilise tall grassveld effectively, the highly selective grazing patterns of certain smaller species of game and the limited availability of certain types of plant fodder for the selective game species, as well as many other significant differences in the social behaviour and vital requirements of the various species, simply cannot be satisfactorily measured in terms of animal units or other similar theoretical criteria.

Reference has already been made to the known populations of impala in various regions (p. 36). More research is urgently needed to acquire similar information on this and other species in other parts of the country. Just as important as the maximum populations of game that can be supported for long periods on specific areas without significant deterioration of the veld, is the number of game that can, on average, be harvested annually per unit area in different regions. Good record keeping by farmers with game-fenced farms can assist considerably in the obtaining of this vital information.

Because the game farmer does not farm with a single animal species, the number of animals that can be supported by a specific area is not the only significant information. The proportion of grazers to browsers, and even of the larger bulk grazers to the smaller, more selective species, is also of extreme importance.

The use of cattle or large game to make tall grassveld more accessible to the smaller and more selective species has been discussed. Correct species ratios should be established and applied judiciously. The simultaneous grazing of veld by cattle and sheep offers great advantages. However, these benefits are curtailed by too great a number of sheep. Similarly, waterbuck and nyala are said to complement each other well in Natal and Zululand. Dr M T Mentis of Natal suspects that, as a general rule, two animal units of bulk grazers to every two units of selective browsers and one unit of browsing species should represent an optimum ratio in bushveld regions. Naturally the nature of the veld and of the game species concerned may necessitate certain modifications to this proposed ratio.

The theory that no more than one impala per head of cattle should be kept on the same farm is not acceptable, and research is once again needed in order to establish the optimum species ratios for the different game regions. Owing to the diverse nature of individual farms, care should be taken not to extrapolate grazing standards for a specific region to all farms in that area without thorough consideration of the conditions prevailing on such farms.

DIFFERENT APPROACHES

Thus far, quantitative criteria for optimum pasture utilisation have been considered without examining primary objectives. In practice, however, considerations frequently apply that have little or nothing to do with statistics, or that may not even have maximum production as their primary objective.

The management principles for game farms and for national parks such as the Kruger Park may, for example, differ widely. In conservation areas, the preservation of unique vegetation may in some cases be regarded as more important than the breeding and production of game. Since the natural appearance and survival of all forms of fauna and flora must be ensured, care should be taken, in particular, not to allow excessively large game populations to destroy or disturb the habitat in national parks.

In general one would therefore expect a tendency for larger numbers of game to be kept on game farms. However, the desire to make a profit should never lead to too much game being kept. Especially on farms with a single-camp grazing system, the principal criterion should be the drier rather than average rainfall years, and in theory one should stock no more game than can survive successfully during unusually dry years, with or without supplementary feeding, without permanently damaging the veld.

Some farmers unfortunately tend to be overly protective towards their game. Their love for their animals prevents them from hunting surplus game, and they often lack the facilities or services to have the surplus game taken off timeously. The consequences are usually catastrophic. Almost all the animals have on occasion died on such farms during a single dry winter season! Although great admiration is felt for the conservation efforts of such farmers, the harsh reality is that the culling of game on any game farm eventually becomes a vital necessity.

INSUFFICIENT BROWSE

Statistics relating to carrying capacity and other quantitative criteria are furthermore also meaningless unless a realistic assessment is made of the amount of accessible and usable leaf fodder available, for browsers in particular, at the end of the dry season. For example, thousands of kudu die periodically in different parts of the country, in regions where an abundant supply of leaves was available for the greater part of the year.

During late winter, when the last leaves are blown to the ground by cold winds and winter rains cause the old leaves on the ground to become unpalatable, kudu and other browsers search desperately for alternative green fodder. While large numbers of animals die of hunger on the plains amidst thousands of leafless trees, their peers generally survive on neighbouring farms where montane or riverine veld supplies sufficient edible leafy fodder, and sometimes even new growth. How does one measure carrying capacity in such cases? Counting tree trunks and weighing leaves could never provide the answer. And comparing carrying capacity of the veld for cattle and for kudu, where cattle eat mainly grass and kudu live almost exclusively on leaves, appears to be just as senseless as dividing scraps from the kitchen between the orphan calf in the cowshed and the pet cat, purely on the basis of their respective body mass or energy requirements.

MINERAL DEFICIENCIES

In parts of the Karoo and False Karoo, as in other parts of the country, specific shortages of phosphates, cobalt, copper, manganese and magnesium often occur.

It is said that veld that has deteriorated as a result of excessive selective grazing is no longer able to sustain the same numbers of game successfully. These and many other factors often play an almost imperceptible and unquantifiable role in determining the productivity and carrying capacity of the grazing for game.

Even in the Kruger Park certain areas are relatively deficient in minerals, thus affecting the productivity of the animals. Impala with heavy infestations of internal parasites, and which visibly do not always maintain their condition as well as impala elsewhere in the Park, also proved to have lower reserves of minerals such as iron, cobalt, manganese, zinc and magnesium when analysed. In areas where the impala fare better, higher mineral values were measured during analysis of tissue. Mineral licks can help to supplement poor pastures such as these. This can best be achieved by analysing soil, plant and animal samples from a specific area and the making of a special mineral lick on the basis of this information.

WATER SHORTAGE

In many parts of Africa it is not a shortage of grazing but a lack of water which imposes significant limitations on the utilisation of veld. Even in nature reserves and on large game farms where there is sufficient water, but this is not widely distributed, the carrying capacity of the veld can be decreased.

MANAGEMENT PRINCIPLES

The complex nature of grazing control on game farms necessitates a totally new approach. The game farmer must keep track of every aspect of his farm at all times. In bushveld regions where browsers and grazers share a farm, management techniques are particularly complicated, and utilisation of both grass and bush must be monitored and controlled.

Because sweet grassveld is very susceptible to overgrazing, game populations should be limited so as to ensure that the grass is not utilised to such an extent that it loses the necessary vitality. Savanna veld often also has a sweet grass component which can easily be damaged by overutilisation. Sweet grassveld is usually in a good condition when grass species such as buffalo grass (*Panicum spp.*), finger grass (*Digitaria spp.*) and manna grass (*Setaria spp.*) are present. Bare patches and other noticeable signs of overgrazing such as the increase of pioneer grass species (*e.g. Aristida, Tragus and Chloris spp.*) should, however, be seen as warning signals.

In sour grass areas, bulk grazers should be employed to utilise the veld better and to prevent the selective grazers from causing patchy overgrazing or deterioration of the veld, owing to selective overgrazing of the more palatable and nutritious grass species.

At the same time, care should be taken on mixed veld to ensure that high grazing pressure by large numbers of cattle does not cause undue damage to the sweet grass component of the veld. In areas where the grass can be mown, great benefits often accrue from keeping underutilised sour grassveld short. The grazing is not only made more acceptable to game, but the veld cover may increase in the longer term. In general, mowing of poorly utilised, tall sour grassveld is recommended in preference to burning.

In addition to the few basic principles of tree and shrub utilisation discussed earlier, much remains to be learnt regarding the effective management of savanna veld. It is said that a regular resting period of 6 to 9 months during the growing season may be beneficial. A resting period of a full year, every four years, has also been suggested to afford the grass, trees and shrubs the opportunity to recover from sustained utilisation.

Light grazing in a single-camp system may, in certain circumstances, necessitate no resting periods at all. Conversely, in times of crisis, it may be necessary to chop down tree branches to place leafy branches within reach of the hungry animals. When doing so, it should be borne in mind that wilted leaves of certain trees may cause prussic acid poisoning, and consequently too many branches should not be chopped down simultaneously in a specific area. Flowers of sulphur("blomswael") added to the animals' salt licks can do much to prevent prussic acid poisoning.

Particularly where the grass stratum has been destroyed and the veld is very denuded, branches laid on the ground can offer the necessary protection to the recovering grazing. Branches of which the trunks have not been completely sawn through and which hang over onto the ground at an angle often continue to grow, and, in addition to protecting the grass growing beneath the branches, also provide leafy fodder during subsequent years.

ROTATIONAL GRAZING

Rotational grazing can to a certain extent be successfully applied in large game conservation areas such as the Kruger National Park by burning the veld alternately in different areas. The green grass growing on burnt areas usually entice game from adjacent areas. When an abundant supply of green grazing is in any case to be found in the surrounding regions, newly burnt veld is less attractive. Conversely, game often concentrate to such an extent on newly burnt veld that overgrazing soon ensues.

Furthermore, account should be taken of the fact that, where game such as zebra and blue wildebeest will migrate naturally, even over long distances, to better grazing, animals such as impala who have a small grazing area will not always be influenced in their distribution and movements by rotational burning, unless the burnt and unburnt areas occur close together.

A well planned mosaic of veld which is alternately burnt during different years may therefore generally yield the best results. The numerous advantages and disadvantages of veld fires should naturally be considered in conjunction with the above in order to decide whether veld fires are justified for the purposes of rotational grazing.

The closing off of controlled watering points, such as water troughs situated in large game areas where only isolated waterholes occur naturally, can also cause game to leave certain areas, thus affording the veld a period of rest.

Within the grazing area of a herd of game, the provision of mineral licks at certain points may also contribute to a certain extent to concentrating the game on certain sections of the veld. In some parts of the country, game do not utilise licks, however, and this method of controlling the movements of game is therefore of no practical value.

Planted pasture can also help to alleviate the grazing pressure exerted by game on surrounding, possibly overgrazed, veld, particularly in winter. Sunflowers, lucerne, kikuyu grass and various other cultivated plants are highly suited to this purpose. Green lucerne may cause game to bloat, although this is the exception rather than the rule, and problems with internal parasites are more commonly encountered in game grazing on cultivated pastures.

Since planted pasture is susceptible to overgrazing by game in the early stages of growth, it may be necessary to allow such grazing to attain a suitable height in fenced off areas of the farm before admitting game into these areas. It may even be advisable to grow this supplementary grazing on a separate part of the farm, and to feed it to the animals in a cut or otherwise processed form.

Controlled rotational grazing, as applied in large game reserves and described above, is of limited value on game farms, particularly smaller ones. The erection of separate camps therefore offers the only viable alternative. Although much can

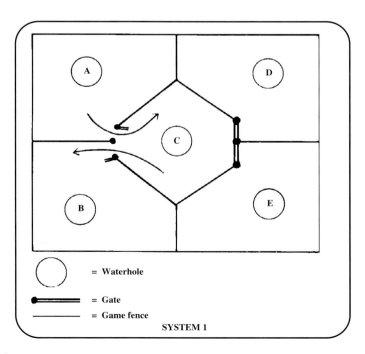

○ = Waterhole

●━━ = Gate

──── = Game fence

SYSTEM 1

be said both for and against one-camp and multi-camp systems, let us for now assume that rotational grazing should be applied.

The Soil Conservation Act of 1969 stipulates that all natural grazing should rest for at least one complete growing season in each four-year cycle. How this legislation affects game farmers, or even stock farmers with free-roaming game on their farms, in terms of practical feasibility is a matter that will have to be taken up with the authorities by the National Game Committee on behalf of the large number of farmers concerned.

In theory, this principle appears to be intrinsically sound, and it may serve as the foundation for applying rotational grazing on game farms — depending, that is, on whether this principle can, in practice, be applied satisfactorily, and on whether the State would be willing, following further representations by game farmers, to allocate the same percentage of aid for the erection of inner fences as is the case in other commercial sectors of the farming industry in South Africa.

The application of rotational grazing systems to game farming has been repeatedly rejected by some experts because it would ostensibly be impossible to move game from one camp to another. Although I concede that it may, in some cases, be difficult or perhaps even impossible to move all the animals from camp to camp, I have mentioned earlier that progress has been made in this area and that further research is receiving attention.

The camp systems shown in the accompanying diagrams should enable a farmer to remove most or all of the game from a specific camp in course of time. According to the first system, the animals are allowed to drink at a central watering point for a certain period of time, so that they become accustomed to the watering point. Salt licks can help to attract game to these watering points. After a while the watering point in Camp A is closed and the animals must go to the central watering point in Camp C to drink. The gate between Camps A and C is shut as soon as a number of animals have entered Camp C, and the gate to Camp B, for example, opened, so that the game can move through to Camp B of their own accord after a day or two, without being disturbed in Camp C. With water already being provided in Camp B, the process is repeated until most or all of the animals have moved out of Camp A. It is important to ensure that Camp C is large enough (approximately 20+ ha) and provides sufficient shelter to prevent the animals from feeling cornered and injuring themselves against the fences in the ensuing panic. The gate to Camp B should also be opened without delay as soon as the gate from Camp A has been shut. If the animals are kept too long in the central camp, they run the risk of being harassed by predators and chased into the fence and caught. This system was employed very successfully by my late father years ago in the Thabazimbi bushveld.

In the second system the animals move from one specific camp to another through V-shaped or other funnels which allow movement in one direction only. Differently shaped funnels can be designed and used for this purpose. It should, however, be noted that, in the Transvaal, for example, funnels may not be used to induce game to enter enclosed camps. Such legislation is intended primarily to prevent farmers from luring neighbours' game onto their farms and appropriating it. Be that as it may, the use of funnels or similar systems to implement rotational grazing on a game farm will probably not be treated as an offence — otherwise I trust that the legislators will make provision for the necessary exceptions.

Game can also be lured or herded from one camp to another in several other ways. I related earlier how lucerne and salt licks were used successfully during a drought to induce almost all the

game to enter a newly erected adjacent camp. Although expensive, a helicopter can also be used to move game along. Farmers should be warned, however, that they risk wasting considerable sums of money if they count on moving game around at will. Although the animals may move voluntarily through game gates and stock fences daily, impala and kudu might, for example, balk when driven along by helicopter. Particularly when certain gates have been shut for a while, the animals often refuse to move through them after too short an interval. It is generally advisable to open gates well in advance, and even to remove fairly large sections of stock or even game fences separating different camps some time before the animals are to be driven through the opening.

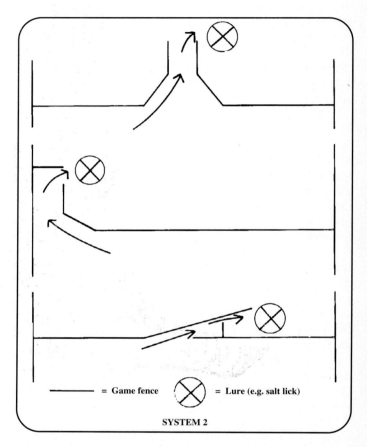

| ——— | = Game fence | ⊗ | = Lure (e.g. salt lick) |

SYSTEM 2

If and when one decides to apply rotational grazing, several other practical aspects have to be considered. It is highly undesirable to attempt to split up game herds during the mating season, and most particularly during the lambing or calving season. Species such as kudu and waterbuck, especially, which conceal their young for a period after birth, should be left alone during the calving and lambing season.

Then, of course, one has to reckon with the species who go through and under fences. It is well nigh impossible to keep warthogs out of a resting camp. Proper maintenance of fences is also essential, as steenbok, duiker and klipspringers regularly find the way to greener pastures. Fortunately these smaller species usually occur in limited numbers and therefore cannot utilise a resting camp excessively.

Finally, it should also be kept in mind that many species do not favour tall grassveld. Sour grassveld, in particular, should therefore not be allowed to grow unchecked during the resting period.

Although in theory it seems a wise policy to allow a period of rest during the growing season every four years, and a standard four-camp system for game may serve as a good starting point for experimental research, many game farms are simply not large enough to justify such a system, and instead the condition of the grazing should determine whether, and, if so, when, a recovery period is needed.

THE ONE-CAMP SYSTEM

Although the principle of rotational grazing is sound both physiologically and ecologically, it is doubtful whether on most game farms more than a one-camp system can be justified for financial and other reasons. In fact, it has already been mentioned that springbok, for example, cause less damage to the grass stratum in given circumstances than sheep, if both species were to be kept permanently in the same camp.

The fact that many of our provincial nature reserves and even some of our national parks are barely larger than most game farms, and after many years are still in an excellent condition despite the relatively large numbers of game they support, without the use of grazing camp systems, surely indicates that an alternative approach is possible.

The number of animals on undivided game farms is, obviously, of the utmost importance, even if the game on a farm cannot be accurately counted. Biomass and carrying capacity figures, energy requirement tables and conversion formulae to determine comparable animal units, etc, may be very interesting, but to my mind find little application in practice unless an eagle eye is continuously kept on the condition of the veld and the animals! It is very much a part of human nature to want to measure and describe everything in terms of figures, and this is no doubt as it should be. However, in nature there are often too many unquantifiable factors which can quickly and funda-

mentally upset the most meticulous calculations.

THE NEW APPROACH

What can and should be measured — and to my mind this is the new approach that ought to be followed by the Department of Agriculture as well as game and even stock farmers — is the condition of the grazing, which is after all the crux of the matter!

Experts on grazing have made considerable advances in recent years in determining quantitatively the plant composition, density and productivity of, in particular, grassveld. Although some techniques, and especially the statistic processing of the data, can be rather complicated, the routine survey techniques are quite straightforward in some cases, and farmers can gather very interesting and useful information with the assistance and guidance of their information officers.

A good example here is the wheel-point survey method proposed by Tidmarsh and Havenga, in terms of which the farmer can determine the increase or decrease in ground cover and in pioneer grasses, which are indicators of an improvement or a deterioration in the condition of the veld. Without discussing this or any other of the many useful survey methods in detail, I appeal strongly to grazing experts employed by the Department of Agriculture to become more actively involved in offering game farmers information and assistance. Their knowledge is of inestimable value and can contribute enormously to quantifying the development or degradation of a farmer's grazing. This can allow the necessary adjustments in terms of game numbers, and can prevent the disastrous collapse of grazing on many farms.

I agree with the view that, ultimately, stock and game farmers

Buffalo grazing in long grassveld areas may open the grassveld to such an extent that it becomes acceptable to other species.

farm with grass and trees, and that both forms of farming depend on the successful management of the vegetation.

Even without the professional services of information officers, most capable farmers are able to notice the signs of veld degradation, even if this has already reached an advanced stage. Bare veld and the absence of foliage within the animals' reach during the growth season usually indicate advanced stages of overutilisation and veld deterioration.

The logical solution is to take off surplus game. Particularly when the animals appeared thin during the preceding winter and the more sensitive species such as kudu were lost, and the summer rains during the following wet season were not satisfactory, sufficient numbers of the surplus game must be taken off at the start of the ensuing game harvesting season in autumn.

In Prof. Tainton's book "Veld and Pasture Management in South Africa", Dr B R Roberts recommends that approximately one third of the stock supported on sweet and mixed veld should be removed fairly quickly when droughts occur. The situation is not so very different for game! A game farmer must keep a constant vigil over the condition of his veld and make the necessary adjustments without delay to prevent his veld and game from perishing during severe droughts.

CONVERSION TABLES: GAME AND LARGE STOCK UNITS

(a) Elephant

Class	Mass (kg)	Estimated number/ Large stock unit
Calf, 5 years	850	0,9
Cow, dry, 15 years	1 850	0,3
Cow, dry, 50 years	3 300	0,3
Cow with calf, 15 years	1 850	0,2
Cow with calf, 50 years	3 300	0,2
Bull, 15 years	2 200	0,3
Bull, 50 years	3 700	0,3

(b) Giraffe

Class	Mass (kg)	Estimated number/ Large stock unit
Calf, 9 months	390	1,3
Cow, dry, 5 years	770	0,7
Cow, dry, 10 years	850	0,8
Cow with calf, 5 years	770	0,6
Cow with calf, 10 years	850	0,6
Bull, 5 years	960	0,6
Bull, 10 years	1 190	0,6

(c) Eland

Class	Mass (kg)	Estimated number/ Large stock unit
Calf, 8 months	200	2,0
Cow, dry, 3 years	460	1,0
Cow, dry, 6 years	500	1,1
Cow with calf, 3 years	460	0,8
Cow with calf, 6 years	500	0,9
Bull, 3 years	760	0,8
Bull, 6 years	815	0,8

(d) Buffalo

Class	Mass (kg)	Estimated number/ Large stock unit
Calf, 8 months	145	2,4
Cow, dry, 4 years	460	1,0
Cow, dry, 10 years	530	1,0
Cow with calf, 4 years	460	0,8
Cow with calf, 10 years	530	0,8
Bull, 4 years	500	0,9
Bull, 10 years	640	0,9

(e) Zebra

Class	Mass (kg)	Estimated number/ Large stock unit
Foal, 5 months	95	3,1
Mare, dry, 4 years	270	1,6
Mare, dry, 7 years	290	1,7
Mare with foal, 4 years	270	1,3
Mare with foal, 7 years	290	1,3
Stallion, 4 years	310	1,4
Stallion, 7 years	335	1,5

(f) Kudu

Class	Mass (kg) Large stock unit	Estimated number/
Calf, 6 months	55	4,8
Cow, dry, 3 years	125	2,7
Cow, dry, 5 years	160	2,5
Cow with calf, 3 years	125	2,2
Cow with calf, 5 years	160	2,0
Bull, 3 years	220	1,8
Bull, 5 years	240	1,9

(g) Waterbuck

Class	Mass (kg)	Estimated number/ Large stock unit
Calf, 5 months	47	5,0
Cow, dry, 3 years	130	2,7
Cow, dry, 5 years	160	2,7
Cow with calf, 3 years	130	2,2
Cow with calf, 5 years	160	2,1
Bull, 3 years	195	2,0
Bull, 5 years	225	2,1

(h) Blue wildebeest

Class	Mass (kg)	Estimated number/ Large stock unit
Calf, 4 months	·51	4,8
Cow, dry, 3 years	145	2,5
Cow, dry, 5 years	160	2,6
Cow with calf, 3 years	145	2,0
Cow with calf, 5 years	160	2,0
Bull, 3 years	195	2,0
Bull, 5 years	215	2,1

(i) Black wildebeest

Class	Mass (kg)	Estimated number/ Large stock unit
Calf, 4 months	40	6,0
Cow, dry, 3 years	105	3,7
Cow, dry, 5 years	115	3,5
Cow with calf, 3 years	105	3,0
Cow with calf, 5 years	115	2,7
Bull, 3 years	125	3,0
Bull, 5 years	135	3,0

(j) Tsessebe

Class	Mass (kg)	Estimated number/ Large stock unit
Calf, 4 months	38	6,2
Cow, dry, 3 years	104	3,9
Cow, dry, 5 years	113	3,6
Cow with calf, 3 years	104	3,1
Cow with calf, 5 years	113	2,8
Bull, 3 years	126	3,1
Bull, 5 years	138	3,1

(k) Blesbok

Class	Mass (kg)	Estimated number/ Large stock unit
Lamb, 4 months	23	9,8
Ewe, dry, 3 years	60	6,1
Ewe, dry, 5 years	67	5,1
Ewe with lamb, 3 years	60	4,9
Ewe with lamb, 5 years	67	4,0
Ram, 3 years	73	5,3
Ram, 5 years	81	5,1

(l) Warthog

Class	Mass (kg)	Estimated number/ Large stock unit
Piglet, 3 months	13	12,0
Sow, dry, 2 years	59	5,0
Sow, dry, 3 years	65	5,4
Sow with piglets, 2 years	59	3,6
Sow with piglets, 3 years	65	3,8
Boar, 2 years	74	4,1
Boar, 3 years	80	4,7

(m) Impala

Class	Mass (kg)	Estimated number/ Large stock unit
Lamb, 4 months	19	12,8
Ewe, dry, 2 years	37	7,0
Ewe, dry, 4 years	45	7,4
Ewe with lamb, 2 years	37	5,4
Ewe with lamb, 4 years	45	5,4
Ram, 2 years	51	6,3
Ram, 4 years	60	6,2

(n) Springbok

Class	Mass (kg)	Estimated number/ Large stock unit
Lamb, 2½ months	12	23,5
Ewe, dry, 18 months	27	12,1
Ewe, dry, 3 years	31	10,5
Ewe with lamb, 18 months	27	9,6
Ewe with lamb, 3 years	31	8,3
Ram, 18 months	30	10,5
Ram, 3 years	36	10,0

(o) Ostrich

Class	Mass (kg)	Estimated number/ Large stock unit
Chick, 3 — 4 months	25	8,5
Bird, 1 year	65	3,9
Bird 3 years	110	2,9
Bird, adult	120	2,7

SUPPLEMENTARY FEEDING IN THE VELD

Supplementary feeding of game in the veld follows the same basic principles as those described in Chapter 12. Mineral licks, feed blocks, feed pellets and concentrated feed mixtures in meal form (see the example on p. 105), which supply additional minerals, energy, nitrogen and other elements, are occasionally used to supplement deficient grazing. In some cases, lucerne and other suitable types of hay should be placed at the animals' disposal during severe droughts and also during the winter months.

17. WATER PROVISION IN GAME RESERVES AND ON GAME FARMS

Game farmers and game rangers have few effective methods at their disposal for controlling the movements of game on a game farm or in a game reserve. Here the availability and efficient utilisation of water is of the utmost importance, since the distribution of watering points has a profound impact on effective veld and pasture management. Poor planning can lead to overgrazing, soil erosion and bush encroachment. In extensive natural areas, the location and spacing of watering points can even contribute to the spread or control of dangerous diseases.

WATER REQUIREMENTS

The water requirements of game vary according to the species and the season. When determining the water consumption of animals, it must be established how much water is consumed at a time by an average sized individual of a particular species. The average interval between drinking times should also be determined and the average daily requirements calculated accordingly.

Research in the Kruger National Park yielded the following results:

EXAMPLES OF THE WATER REQUIREMENTS OF GAME

Species	Consumption (litres)	Average interval between drinking (hours)	Average daily requirement (liters)
Impala	3,92	68,4	1,38
Blue wildebeest	16,29	46,9	8,34
Burchell's zebra	21,11	35,2	14,39
Buffalo	33,75	38,0	21,32
Elephant	160,20	43,4	88,59

These figures give a good indication of the water requirements of the species concerned during winter. Other species of comparable size will require approximately the same amounts of water during winter — an analysis of this information has revealed that the water requirements of the animals correlate well with their mass. Buffalo, blue wildebeest and impala each require approximately 4 kg or 4 litres of water per 100 kg of mass daily. This represents 4 per cent of the animals' mass.

When provision must be made for sufficient water for the game in a given area, a fair indication of the water requirements would be obtained by taking 4 per cent of the total biomass of the animals from the different species in the area. Allowance should be made in these calculations for wastage and evaporation.

As a matter of interest, an average elephant requires as much water in the winter as 4 buffalo or 6 zebra or 11 blue wildebeest or 66 impala of average size.

A large elephant bull can drink up to 315 litres of water at a time, and use another approximately 160 litres for bathing.

In summer game generally consumes much less water. This may be ascribed to various factors, including the high moisture content of green grass and leaves. Impala, for example, can

In the winter, an elephant drinks as much water as four buffalo, six zebra, eleven blue wildebeest or sixty six impala.

survive without any drinking water for a month or more, provided that adequate moisture is ingested through their food.

WATER QUALITY

Water from new boreholes should be analysed chemically to ensure that no toxic or harmful quantities of fluorine and other substances are present which would render it unsuitable for consumption. Effluent from mines and factories can also contain toxic substances, while the run-off from orchards and cultivated lands that have been sprayed with pesticides poses a considerable threat.

Stale drinking water in containers and troughs must regularly be replaced with clean water. These containers should always be cleaned out thoroughly before being replenished.

Water in which snails and disease-causing organisms are present must be treated. Besides occasionally obstructing narrow pipes, snails are often intermediate hosts of bilharzia, which affects both humans and animals, and also cause game and stock to become infested with conical intestinal flukes and liver flukes. Regular cleaning of cement dams and water troughs, together with treatment with copper sulphate, will help to combat this problem.

Contaminated water can also promote the spreading of other contagious diseases such as anthrax and foot-and-mouth disease. In the case of severe outbreaks of anthrax, it has been proved in the Kruger National Park that the disease can be controlled by disinfecting water sources.

DIFFERENT TYPES OF WATERING POINTS FOR GAME

The same types of dams and water troughs as those used on stock farms are suitable for game.

Earth dams and other natural water sources, as well as cement troughs, are all well utilised. Earth dams are generally preferred to cement troughs, and animals who are not used to drinking from the latter usually need time to become accustomed to them while access to other water is still available.

Cement troughs are easy to clean, and the water can be replaced or treated if outbreaks of disease occur. When veld deterioration is observed in an area, it is also a simple matter to drain cement troughs, thus discouraging game from concentrating in that area.

In areas where elephants are likely to damage pump installations, these can be protected by sturdy fences or railings or surrounded by a deep ditch with steep sides.

Water pipes are sometimes damaged by elephants, warthogs and jackals, and plastic pipes, in particular, should be buried sufficiently deep underground to prevent damage. When metal pipes are laid underground, it should be remembered that certain soil types cause the pipes to rust relatively soon. Particularly in the case of major water provision projects, where pipes must be laid across great distances, it is advisable to have the soil analysed and to take preventive steps where possible.

The embankments around earth dams can eventually be broken down if large herds of buffalo cross them regularly. Ripple action on the inside can also considerably shorten the life of an earth embankment. By covering vulnerable areas of the dam wall with concrete or a densely packed layer of stones, one can, however, limit erosion and damage.

Plains-living species such as zebra, wildebeest and impala usually avoid drinking where the vegetation is dense. This is particularly true in areas where predators occur, since they may use the cover of such vegetation to pounce on their prey. For this reason, rivers which flow through unspoilt areas are utilised only where the banks are relatively open. Game populations can be encouraged to spread out more evenly along river courses by clearing more spots along the river, thus making it more accessible to animals which are wary of vegetation.

Kudu, bushbuck, nyala and other secretive species will naturally frequent more densely vegetated river banks and are not influenced to the same extent by the distribution of open spots along river banks.

Large sums of money have been wasted in the past in attempts to sink boreholes in the vicinity of river beds, while copious quantities of water directly beneath the surface of apparently dry river beds were overlooked. Sand pits can be exploited relatively economically, while a bulldozer moving along a dry watercourse can uncover pools by moving aside sand at suitable sites. This is a much cheaper method of making water, and therefore new pastures, available to game.

THE LOCATION AND SPACING OF WATERING POINTS

Excessive concentration of game around a watering point may result in trampling and destruction of the surrounding area. Overgrazing generally leads to soil erosion and bush encroachment.

Watering places for game do not necessarily have to be in the immediate vicinity of a borehole. By means of plastic pipes, water can economically, quickly and efficiently be laid on to various points some distance away from a borehole or concrete dam.

When choosing a suitable site for a watering point, the soil and veld type, as well as the slope of the terrain, should be taken into account. Sites with vulnerable grazing close by, and soil which crumbles easily or forms dust, or which washes away readily, particularly on slopes, should rather be avoided if possible. Watering points also tend to be utilised relatively poorly when placed in tall grassveld and far from the animals' normal pastures. A suitable site for a new watering point should therefore be chosen with care.

Large nature reserves and game reserves: In large areas such

On average, zebra graze some 7,2 kilometres from the nearest water during the winter. For blue wildebeest this figure is 7,36 kilometres, for buffalo 7,84 kilometres, for elephant 5,92 kilometres and for impala only 2,24 kilometres.

as the Kruger National Park, one finds that certain species of game migrate seasonally from one area to another, thus practising a natural form of rotational grazing. In summer, when natural water sources are widespread, the animals can move where they choose, and usually utilise the best grazing available. In winter, however, the animals are generally obliged to graze in the vicinity of permanent water sources such as rivers, where the grazing is not necessarily always optimum. As soon as the rains resume, the herds of game, especially blue wildebeest and zebra, move away to their summer pastures. Rotational grazing and resting are thus effected in the natural way. Large concentrations of worm eggs which accumulated in the manure of game during winter in their winter grazing area usually hatch after the first rains. Since the host species has by then moved to other pastures, millions of parasite larvae die before they are able to infest new hosts, and parasite control is thus also accomplished in a natural way.

When watering points are introduced under the above conditions in the animals' summer grazing areas, game may congregate in this preferred grazing area the whole year round. This can lead to veld deterioration and other problems. Consequently it has already become common practice to encourage game to move out of a particular area by, for instance, shutting off the water supply to water troughs in overgrazed areas.

The spacing of watering points is also of the utmost importance. If the watering points in a large reserve are placed too far apart, strips of grazing between adjacent pastures will not be utilised efficiently, since they are too far from the animals' drinking sites and therefore beyond the animals' normal paths.

Research in the Kruger National Park has revealed that each species usually grazes within a specific radius from a watering point: impala stay within a radius of approximately 2,24 km, elephant within 5,92 km, zebra within 7,20 km, blue wildebeest within 7,36 km and buffalo within 7,84 km. Although the animals may occasionally move further away from the water, the above distances represent the average radius of veld utilisation around a watering point during the winter months. Such information can, theoretically, be used to plan the optimum spacing of watering points.

Placing watering points too close together can also have numerous deleterious consequences. Very little or no reserve grazing is conserved for very dry seasons between the different watering points, since all the grazing is within easy reach of any of the watering points all year round. In these circumstances, more game can be kept in a smaller area because water and feed are utilised to the maximum. In time, however, this may cause game to multiply beyond optimum limits, with the result that, during droughts, game populations may collapse when they exhaust the available grazing and even the water supply. In such circumstances, veld deterioration and the associated ecological disturbances are unavoidable. When watering points are so close together that provision is not made for relatively animal-free zones in between waterholes, contagious diseases such as anthrax and foot-and-mouth disease can also spread rapidly from herd to herd throughout the area. Watering points situated near the borders of neighbouring states where disease may be present can also lead to undesirable contact with infected herds of game from neighbouring regions.

Game farms: The diameter of game farms is often less than twice the grazing radius of impala around a watering point, that is less than 2 x 2,4 = 4,8 km. In the case of most game farms, a single

Although impala are able to survive for long periods without water, they are usually found near water, where they feed on shrubs and other green plant food.

waterhole would therefore be sufficient to place all the grazing on that farm within the reach of impala and most other game.

On game farms, however, there are often other important considerations. Especially with the introduction of new game, it is important to provide water at different spots and especially along boundary fences and in the corners of camps, so that the animals will discover these in good time.

On hunting and safari farms, it is also sometimes desirable to have game gathering at different watering points, where they can easily be observed by visitors. It is not uncommon to have a scenic, natural waterhole close to the camping site, so that visitors may admire the game from the verandah of a restaurant or their bungalows. Alternatively, tree-houses and other hides can be erected near suitable watering points.

Game farms with special and separate capture and holding pens also require special provision for controlled watering points in the different pens. The controlled supply of water to different pens can, to a large extent, allow game to be moved successfully and facilitate rotational grazing.

In exceptional cases, where the convergence of game may demand more drinking space than usual, use can be made of longer or even additional water troughs. Where different species gather at the same water or feed troughs, and some of these species behave aggressively, it is a good policy to provide alternative water and even feed troughs at concentration points.

RESTRICTING PREDATION AND DISTURBANCES AT WATERING POINTS

Particularly in winter, predators such as lion, leopard and caracal use watering points as prime hunting spots. Dense bush, dam walls, rocks and other cover can favour the hunting efforts of predators, to the detriment of the game drinking there. Predation at waterholes can be reduced by removing shrubs and similar cover for a distance of approximately 50 to 100 m from watering points. If alternative watering points are also available in the vicinity, game will also leave a drinking site more readily if they sense danger, and move on to a safer spot.

It has been shown repeatedly that game will avoid watering points on game farms and even in larger nature reserves during the day and instead drink at night if they are disturbed by people during the day. This also applies to farms on which hunting game from hides near waterholes or from vehicles is allowed.

Disturbances in the proximity of waterholes should therefore be kept to the absolute minimum. Hides and other viewing points should be located far enough from the water and adequately concealed, and persons using these shelters should behave quietly and unobtrusively.

Roads and parking areas situated too close to watering points should be rerouted. Road traffic should be planned in such a way that game footpaths leading to and from the water are crossed as little as possible, particularly near waterholes. Wild animals are wary of being cornered between their watering points and potential danger, and consequently it is better that all traffic routes avoid the water by at least a few hundred metres, and that a single road preferably leads from the water to a suitable parking spot nearer to the water.

Although much more remains to be said about the supply of water for game, the above information should suggest that thorough planning must precede any development project in wilderness areas. Just as judicious planning can benefit the veld and the animals in an area, so poor planning or inefficient development can not only drastically damage the environment, but also diminish the recreational value of natural areas quite considerably.

In winter, adult buffalo drink an average of 21,32 litres of water per day, every 38 hours. During summer they often roll in the mud, contributing significantly to the formation of new pans or the enlargement of existing ones.

18. WILDLIFE DISEASE AND ITS CONTROL

Just like domestic stock, game can also be plagued by a wide variety of parasites and germs. In the case of the buffalo, for example, more than forty disease-producing germs and parasites have been described, and twenty in the case of the impala. Despite this, sick animals are normally seldom seen. Preventive measures remain of the greatest importance here. Isolated outbreaks of certain dangerous diseases can decimate the populations of certain species in a country such as South Africa. As in the case of domestic stock, where large losses are normally incurred owing to disease and parasites, sensible management practices and precautions can also contribute to maintaining healthy game breeding stock.

Because game seldom manifest symptoms of disease, and wild animals who are disease-ridden weaken and die quickly, to be rapidly disposed of by predators and scavengers, many farmers hold the mistaken belief that wild animals are not vulnerable to disease to the same extent as livestock.

An analysis of animal losses in a well-known zoo, where daily inspections were carried out by a veterinarian, revealed that 80 per cent of 280 wild animals who died showed no symptoms of disease prior to death. When an animal has contracted some form of disease, the following non-specific symptoms may occasionally be observed in exceptional cases: a staring, open coat, drooping head and ears, unsteady gait, a tendency to lag behind the herd, and to lie down or conceal itself in dense bush or tall grass. Anorexia, emaciation, diarrhoea, dehydration (e.g. sunken eyes), suppurating discharges from the eyes or nose, rapid or laboured breathing, convulsions or paralysis and unconsciousness may also occur.

Without the appropriate experience it is generally extremely difficult to diagnose a specific illness in a a wild animal. This chapter gives examples of some of the most significant and prevalent diseases and parasite afflictions, and the most characteristic symptoms are also briefly described. In view of the more than hundred different types of contagious diseases and parasites threatening South African game and livestock, it should be clearly stated that the following are at best informative examples.

DRASTIC DISEASES

These diseases are generally responsible for large-scale losses, and their onset and progress is rapid. Anthrax and rinderpest are typical of these diseases. Although well-known as livestock diseases, these two afflictions also jeopardise the future survival of game in South Africa! History has shown that isolated outbreaks of either of these diseases can destroy game populations in large areas.

Anthrax: In some major conservation areas such as the Kruger National Park and Etosha, anthrax has repeatedly been responsible for severe losses amongst game in the past. For example, more than a thousand animals have been lost during a single outbreak in a period of four months in the northern parts of the Kruger Park. More than 29 species of wild animals have succumbed to anthrax and nearly all species are potentially susceptible. Certain species do appear to have some resistance, but others, such as the roan antelope and the kudu, are very susceptible to anthrax.

Anthrax is characterised by sudden and large-scale losses.

When dead animals are encountered with blood flowing from the mouth, nose and other body openings, and sometimes even with haemorrhages visible on the skin, the possibility of anthrax should immediately be given serious consideration. The carcasses should be covered or protected with branches to prevent predators and scavengers from reaching them, and the assistance of a state veterinarian or livestock inspector should be summoned without delay to confirm the diagnosis. Anthrax is a notifiable disease and suspected cases must, therefore, be reported by law.

Under no circumstances should a carcass which is suspected of being infected with anthrax be cut open. When the spores are exposed to air, they develop resistance, and may survive in the soil for more than twenty years. Such spores remain infectious, and if the bones of an infected carcass were to end up in a mudhole, for example, it could continue to cause new outbreaks of anthrax for many years. The spores can spread over very great distances in different ways, and theoretically epidemics could occur in any part of the country at any time.

The carcasses of contagious animals should be handled with extreme care, since humans can also be infected, with fatal results. Thick rubber gloves and gumboots, protective overclothing and even masks should be worn to prevent self-contamination.

The flesh of suspected infected carcasses, or of animals who have died in known endemic anthrax areas and where the possibility of anthrax cannot be excluded beyond any doubt, should not under any circumstances be made available for human consumption.

Control measures by the Division of Veterinary Services constantly strive to prevent fresh outbreaks of this disease by periodic immunisation of susceptible livestock. Sufficient quantities of vaccine are made available by the Division of Veterinary Services for the immunisation of domestic livestock in case of an epidemic. Obviously serious consideration should also be given to accummulating sufficient vaccine reserves to ensure the survival of our vulnerable game populations, too.

Although a costly venture, it is possible to immunise game successfully in the field. Such operations have been effectively carried out in the Kruger National Park for years. Vaccine obtained from Onderstepoort is used annually to immunise roan antelope. The same vaccine has also also been used to immunise eland, blue wildebeest, nyala, buffalo, giraffe and other species.

Immunisation techniques and general principles applicable to the control of outbreaks of disease in game are discussed later in this chapter.

Rinderpest: Like a potentially devastating powderkeg with a short fuse, rinderpest continues to smoulder in other parts of Africa, and all possible measures should be taken, also in South Africa, to safeguard game and livestock against this annihilating disease. Millions of head of cattle and innumerable herds of game have already succumbed to rinderpest, and today's patchy distribution of certain game species in Africa can largely be ascribed to earlier outbreaks of this dreaded disease. Even in the Kruger Park, certain species of game such as buffalo were almost annihilated by rinderpest towards the end of the previous century.

Rinderpest is an extremely contagious and deadly disease

afflicting cattle and buffalo, in particular, but also other cloven-hoofed animals. The disease is characterised by inflammation of and lesions on the mouth and digestive tract. Symptoms include lesions in the mouth and throat, as well as fever, discharges from the nose and eyes, the whitening of the eyes and blindness, laboured respiration and severe diarrhoea.

The faeces are generally watery and blood-flecked and have an unusually unpleasant odour. Small amounts of intestinal mucous membrane may be secreted in the faeces. Affected animals rapidly become thin and debilitated.

In the case of some species and in certain individual animals, the symptoms are less obvious, while, by contrast, others may die before the typical clinical signs develop. Although the symptoms can be inconsistent, large-scale losses amongst game and livestock, associated with the above symptoms and particularly with visible lesions of the digestive tract, are most likely ascribable to rinderpest.

When rinderpest last occurred in Southern Africa, the contagion could not be contained. All animals were highly susceptible and most animals which contracted the disease died. When all the livestock and susceptible game had been eradicated from large regions of the country, rinderpest also disappeared — and, together with it, allegedly, the tsetse fly, which until then had still occurred in South Africa and had caused sleeping sickness and nagana in people and livestock in the Transvaal.

In East and West Africa, rinderpest has continued to occur sporadically to this day. It has been claimed that, in extensive areas, these epidemics have been the cause of annual losses of up to 85 per cent of all blue wildebeest calves. The risk always remains that epidemics such as these may once again spread across Africa and, as in the past, wipe out thousands of head of cattle and game.

The South African Division of Veterinary Services has sufficient vaccine and is prepared to protect the country's livestock against a rinderpest epidemic. But what about our game populations? Through co-ordinated action by government departments charged with agriculture and nature conservation, timeous provision should be made to accumulate sufficient vaccine reserves to protect our game populations. In the past it was claimed that, owing to the lack of suitable immunisation techniques, game could not be immunised on a large scale. This is no longer the case. Appropriate research during recent decades has shown that large numbers of game can be immunised within a short space of time. Naturally, proper research is vital to show that available vaccines are efficient and safe for use on all susceptible game species!

EROSION DISEASES

Certain diseases seldom cause dramatic outbreaks of disease. Periodic deaths and production losses due to these contaminations can, however, cause more damage cumulatively in the long term than sporadic outbreaks of the more dramatic diseases. Some of the many examples are briefly described:

Heartwater: Ignorance and, regrettably, the avarice of certain game merchants, have caused the dangers of heartwater to be vastly overplayed. Despite the many stories and allegations in circulation, heartwater has thus far been confirmed as a clinical disease condition only in the eland and the springbok. Certain alien species of game are naturally also susceptible, but most game farmers concern themselves with indigenous species.

Eland possess a remarkable resistance to heartwater and only

succumb to this disease in exceptional cases. Springbok, however, are highly susceptible. When springbok are transported from a heartwater-free zone to one in which heartwater is prevalent, great losses can be anticipated.

Symptoms of heartwater in the species mentioned correspond with those observed in cattle and sheep, and include the following: high fever, rapid respiration and heart rate, hypersensitivity, rapid and erratic blinking of the eyes, prominence of the nictitating membrane, gnashing of the teeth and froth about the mouth and nose. A characteristic feature is the tendency of an affected animal to turn around jerkily with stiff legs, while blinking its eyes constantly. Finally the animal collapses with the head drawn back. Muscular spasms and convulsions are common. The characteristic symptoms described here are not, however, always manifested.

Although it is exceptional, eland may contract heartwater disease. Muscular spasms, jerking of the eyes, foam at the mouth and nose, and other symptoms of this disease in domestic stock, also characterise this disease in eland.

Autopsies reveal accumulation of fluid in the peritoneum and in the chest and abdominal cavities. The lungs contain considerable fluid and froth and the spleen is enlarged. The blood vessels are prominently filled with blood, and haemorrhages in the heart and muscles are common. It is important to note, however, that several other diseases and physiological afflictions produce similar signs during post-mortem examinations. It is therefore imperative to confirm the disease by means of microscopic examination.

Inoculation of springbok with heartwater-contaminated blood has already been carried out successfully. If the animal reacts clinically following artificial contamination or suddenly develops a high fever, it is treated with oxytetracycline (for example Terramycin, Pfizer Labs.) or another suitable preparation to halt the progress of the diseases.

NEW APPROACH

During the last two years, the Veterinary Research Institute at Onderstepoort, has, in collaboration with Geo Schwulst Laboratories, done research to develop and evaluate a new method of vaccination against heartwater.

This method entails the simultaneous infection and treatment of the animal to be vaccinated. Heartwater infected blood is injected intravenously to introduce the organisms that will stimulate immunity. A slow releasing antibiotic (doxycycline) is implanted under the animal's skin, behind the animal's ear, at the same time. As the disease causing organisms multiply in the animal's body, to

Springbok are highly susceptible to heartwater and animals which originate from heartwater-free areas will die almost without exception when they are introduced to areas where heartwater occurs.

develop immunity (and disease), the pill, Doximplant, releases the antibiotic, slowly enough not to kill the heartwater causing organisms before adequate 'immunity' has been developed, and at an adequate concentration to prevent any symptoms.

The advantages of this unique method of vaccination are; less risks of disease and mortality, and less work and trauma to an animal, such as a springbok which otherwise would have had to be caught daily to establish its body temperature.

Existing problems are that, should too high a dose of Doximplant be implanted, the heartwater causing organism could be eliminated before adequate immunity has developed. Alternatively, too low a dose of Doximplant could result in the animal developing heartwater and possibly dying from it. A drawback of the method is that, unless each individual animal is weighed and the Doximplant is administered at the correct dosage level, the exercise may be a total failure.

The dosage rate for Doximplant varies from species to species and all animals have to be weighed in order to calculate the correct dosage rate. Vaccinated/treated animals should be kept under close observation and be observed daily for some time, just in case clinical disease still develops. Vaccinated animals should, however, not be kept in confinement for too long but should preferably be exposed to ticks as soon as possible in order to become infected with natural strains of heartwater in the area, whilst the Doximplant is still affording the animal some protection.

It should also be kept in mind that an animal, vaccinated with a particular strain of heartwater may still acquire the disease if it becomes infected with a different strain of heartwater against which the original 'vaccine strain' may not be effective. Animals removed from heartwater veld for prolonged periods of time may, furthermore, lose their 'immunity' against the disease.

Doximplant, marketed by Rumevite Agricura, was registered for use in sheep and goats under cover of Act no. 36 of 1947. It was recently also registered for use in cattle. Research to evaluate its effectiveness in the vaccination of springbok against heartwater has yielded very positive results but requires follow-up inves-

tigation. Readers must please take note that Doximplant has only been registered for use in domestic animals and should contact Mr. George Schwulst at tel. no. (011) 493 6960 for further information regarding its use in wild animals.

Foot-and-mouth disease: A large-scale outbreak of foot-and-mouth disease can have an extremely detrimental effect on both the game and livestock industries. Although game seldom become seriously ill, and very few animals normally die, foot-and-mouth disease accounts for enormous production losses amongst farm livestock. A severe outbreak of foot-and-mouth disease in South Africa may spread across the borders to other countries in Southern Africa and lead to serious economic difficulties for everyone. Consequently it is in the general interest to do everything possible to prevent the spread of this economically devastating disease. Farmers, game merchants, and other individuals who illegally transport susceptible livestock or game species, or meat and other products from known foot-and-mouth areas to other parts of the country, make themselves guilty of rash obstinacy for which there is absolutely no excuse!

In South Africa, the Division of Veterinary Services has divided the country into different control areas. The Eastern Transvaal bushveld and other potentially dangerous adjacent areas are subject to strict permit control with regard to livestock, game and certain products derived from animals. Antelope and other susceptible game species may, for example, under no circumstances be transported from the Kruger Park and adjacent farms to other parts of the country. Information concerning these control measures, which are constantly being amended in accordance with changing circumstances, are obtainable from the head office of the Division of Veterinary Services in Pretoria, or from your local state veterinarian or livestock inspector.

Foot-and-mouth disease is a highly contagious disease which particularly afflicts cloven-hoofed animals such as cattle, sheep, goats, pigs and game. In the Kruger National Park and adjacent areas, impala are mainly affected, sometimes in epidemic proportions. During several outbreaks in the area over the past 20 years, it was almost exclusively impala and domestic stock that were visibly infected with the disease.

Natural cases of foot-and-mouth disease have, however, already been described in other African game species such as the bushbuck, kudu, eland, grey duiker, waterbuck, reedbuck, sable antelope, roan, gemsbok, tsessebe, red hartebeest, blue wildebeest, grysbok, bush pig, warthog and the buffalo.

In the case of infected buffalo, the lesions are usually relatively unobtrusive, or may even be absent altogether. Like cattle, sheep and goats, the buffalo can also be a carrier of the foot-and-mouth virus without manifesting any symptoms of disease. Therefore, with buffalo as with cattle, sheep and domestic goats, veterinary officials should not lose sight of these potential carrier animals when speculating about the origins of fresh outbreaks and deciding on control measures.

Fortunately it would appear that carrier animals and highly susceptible game or stock are able to cohabit together for long periods without the disease necessarily infecting the susceptible animals clinically. Further research is urgently needed in order to know more of the role of different animal species and environmental factors in transmitting and spreading of foot-and-mouth disease.

Foot-and-mouth disease is characterised in its clinical form by small blisters and/or lesions in the animals' mouths and on their feet, just above or between the hooves. In warthogs, lesions can develop on the knees. Lesions on the nose, teats and other parts

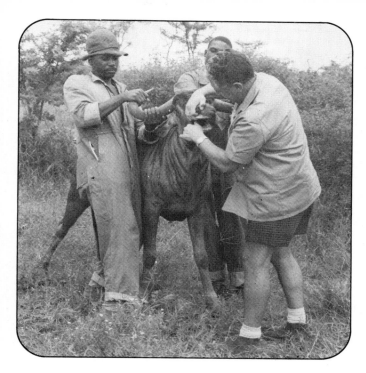
Foot-and-mouth disease inspection under field conditions.

develop on the knees. Lesions on the nose, teats and other parts of the body have also been observed. Since foot-and-mouth disease is known to be one of the most contagious of diseases, these lesions usually occur concurrently in several animals of the same group.

Foot-and-mouth disease has already been artificially induced in elephants. Although the experimental animals responded dramatically, the disease could not be transmitted to other elephants through direct contact. Foot-and-mouth disease does also not occur naturally in African elephants and, in the case of this animal, is largely of academic interest.

In cattle, the lesions can be very pronounced, and it may for instance happen that the entire superficial layer of skin on the tongue is stripped off when the tongue is extended for examination. Lameness, salivation and other signs of disease are usually far more noticeable in stock than in game.

Although in exceptional cases game may react intensely, it is far more likely that a herd of impala, for example, could be infected with foot-and-mouth disease without this being suspected by someone who is not familiar with disease in game.

Foot-and-mouth disease spreads through direct contact between animals. Pastures and watering points can also become infected, however, and thus contribute to the spread of the disease. Fortunately the virus is sensitive to solar radiation, and the contagion cannot survive long in the veld in our South African weather conditions.

Often humans play a very important role in the spread of foot-and-mouth disease. Poachers and other individuals who transport contaminated meat and animal products illegally are only some of the culprits who will never be sufficiently punished for their reprehensible deeds! The clothes and shoes of a person who has handled or slaughtered an infected animal will remain contagious for weeks or even months, and without the necessary disinfection and precautions, foot-and-mouth disease can thus spread over large distances.

At present the shooting of buffalo is allowed in the Transvaal in certain circumstances, without a permit. The purpose of this concession is to prevent the spread of foot-and-mouth disease to livestock. The same legislation, ironically enough, makes no provision for measures to ensure the safe disposal of the carcass. While there is always a slight chance of a live buffalo infecting domestic stock, the shooting of such an animal and the uncontrolled disposal of and handling of contaminated meat and products hold a far greater risk of spreading disease.

More active and directed efforts to make the public aware of the dangers of foot-and-mouth disease, with the emphasis on prevention, would definitely help to contain the spread of this disease.

The control of foot-and-mouth disease remains under the direct supervision of the Division of Veterinary Services of the Department of Agriculture. Since foot-and-mouth disease is notifiable, observance of this regulation is obligatory!

The isolation of contaminated areas, restrictions on the movements of susceptible species and their products, disinfecting of contaminated equipment and the preventive inoculation of stock in adjacent areas all constitute an important part of any control regime.

In contaminated areas, particularly in certain overseas countries and where the outbreaks are of a limited nature, susceptible stock and their carcasses are destroyed. In South Africa, in the case of isolated outbreaks, all susceptible stock in the restricted zone are usually artificially infected with the same type of virus under strictly controlled conditions to avoid prolonging the disease. After a period of quarantine, the control measures are gradually relaxed. In the case of more widespread outbreaks, the susceptible animals in the contaminated and adjacent areas are inoculated.

In the past, all laboratory testing for foot-and-mouth disease had to be done overseas, but South Africa has for some time had its own foot-and-mouth institute. It is hoped that future research will produce accurate information to support more reasonable control measures, which in the past were often based on assumptions rather than factual knowledge, and often imposed unnecessary restrictions on the game industry.

Whereas in the past use had to be made of vaccines which did not always impart the necessary immunity to inoculated stock, locally produced vaccines produced from viruses from dormant contaminations in endemic foot-and-mouth areas in southern Africa should afford local stock populations improved protection.

Through supportive assistance with the testing of buffalo samples, the foot-and-mouth institute can furthermore contribute to the establishment in the country of a number of buffalo herds which can be certified free of foot-and-mouth disease.

Game farmers and game merchants are urgently requested to assist the Division of Veterinary Services wherever possible in the prevention and control of foot-and-mouth disease, not only in the interest of the livestock industry, but also to the benefit of the game industry.

Rabies: Rabies has already been diagnosed in more than 18 different species of wild animal. The widely held conception that, in southern Africa, rabies occurs mainly in jackals, dogs and suricates, and that stock or grazing game are only affected in highly exceptional cases, has in recent years been disproved in an unexpected and baffling manner.

In Namibia, tens of thousands of kudu have in the recent past died of rabies. Eland did not emerge unscathed from the epidemic either. Events such as these show once again that one cannot be dogmatic when, as so often happens, one neglects

Rabies, primarily a disease of dogs, wild carnivores and smaller mammals, caused the death of thousands of kudu in Namibia some years ago. Photo: Transvaal Division of Nature Conservation.

ing up management strategies for nature reserves and game farms.

The degree of indifference to the dangers of disease appear to be directly related to the level of ignorance concerning the subject. The frequently heard excuse that nature should be left undisturbed to run its own course sounds particularly hollow in the mouths of those who do their utmost to increase game production through pasture management, the artificial provision of water, as well as predator control, yet fail to take the necessary precautions against disease and parasites.

Any animal in a known rabies area who manifests behaviour changes, or who shows neurological symptoms such as unusual aggressiveness, convulsions or paralysis, should be regarded with suspicion. Kudu that have been infected with rabies show a heightened urge to mate, and this is suspected to contribute to the spread of the disease.

Wherever large numbers of kudu are lost and the cause of death cannot be positively ascertained, the possibility of rabies should not be excluded. Kudu losses due to a shortage of browse during severe droughts should, however, not give rise to undue panic.

Farmers, game rangers and anyone else living in a known rabies area should ensure that all dogs and cats in the area are immunised regularly and in accordance with veterinary requirements. In my opinion, domestic dogs remain one of the most significant transmitters of rabies. During the eleven years I spent in the Kruger Park, rabid dogs were repeatedly destroyed within a radius of 60 km of the nearest park boundaries. By contrast, research and surveys during the same period failed to reveal a single confirmed case of rabies amongst jackals or other wild animals in this area.

Humans are naturally also susceptible to rabies and the consequences are nearly always fatal. Animals who are suspected of being infected should preferably not be handled, and suspect cases should be reported to the nearest state veterinarian or livestock inspector without delay. Rabies is also a notifiable disease and is therefore controlled by the Division of Veterinary Services.

Tuberculosis: For many years, this well-known disease affecting humans and animals has been dormant in certain kudu populations in the Eastern Cape, in particular. Duiker and a variety of other species are also susceptible to tuberculosis.

In zoos, in particular, tuberculosis can cause serious problems. Otherwise this disease is seldom encountered in wild animals in South Africa.

Suspected cases with enlarged glands and/or pulmonary and other lesions which may indicate the presence of tuberculosis should be examined by a veterinarian. The movement of game and livestock from contaminated areas should only occur with veterinary authorisation and under strict control.

Abscesses and swellings: Abscesses usually develop in body tissue which has been bruised or damaged in some way and infected with pus-forming bacteria. If an abscess occurs in a part of the body where further deterioration may pose an immediate threat to the animal, it is advisable to try to stop the swelling by injecting an antibiotic or sulfonamide. Alternatively it may be wiser to allow the abscess to ripen, after which it should be drained, curetted and disinfected. Follow-up treatment generally entails disinfecting the wound and the administration of antibiotics.

Animals with open, suppurating wounds should not be permitted to roam freely without treatment. Suppurating wounds can infect the environment and may in some cases constitute a threat to other animals. Actinomycosis and Corynebacteriosis are only two examples of specific abscess-producing diseases which can spread from livestock to game.

Actinomycosis, which is also known as lumpy jaw, is characterized by hard, bony swellings under the skin of the lower jaw, or on other bones surrounding the mouth cavity of animals such as cattle, impala and bushbuck. Generally the disease spreads very slowly from one animal to another in a specific camp or environment. In the Kruger Park, for example, an infection present in impala has been localised to a small area between Skukuza and Lower Sabie for many years.

While treatment can be successful, though time-consuming, it may be wiser in the case of the more common species such as impala to destroy infected animals and their carcasses. In any case, even over an extended period, only individual animals are generally affected, and the disease can thus be contained with only minor losses.

In a zoo or in small pens which have floors, these should be thoroughly disinfected. A thick layer of soil over the contaminated earth floors of game pens can also assist in preventing the infection from recurring.

Corynebacteriosis is characterised in sheep, cattle and in domestic goats and antelope by swollen and festering glands. Eventually the infection spreads throughout the body and abscesses are also formed in the lungs, liver and other organs. This type of infection is characterised by yellow-green, slightly granular pus.

When camps or pens which have, for example, been contaminated by sheep suffering from such suppurations are subsequently used for keeping game, the wild animals can develop severe sepsis.

Wild animals, like humans and domestic animals, can also be afflicted with different types of cancer. Swellings on older animals may therefore, in addition to numerous other diseases, animals may therefore, in addition to numerous other diseases, indicate the presence of cancer.

Pneumonia: Wild animals can contract pneumonia even under veld conditions. A survey following severe cold, rain and wind in the Kruger National Park revealed, for example, that most of the impala destroyed during a routine culling operation were suffering from varying degrees of pneumonia. Before being shot, nearly all the animals appeared perfectly healthy. Only in a few cases was the inflammation so severe that the animals concerned were likely to have succumbed from it.

It should be mentioned here that game, particularly impala, nyala, bushbuck and kudu, may die during conditions of extreme cold, even without contracting pneumonia. Losses are especially common during autumn, when late winter rains or early spring rain, aggravated by icy winds, may cause the above-mentioned species to die of exposure. Even buffalo in the Kruger National Park have succumbed under these conditions. In captivity, inadequate nutrition, poor hygiene and cold draughts play a major role in the development of pneumonia. Very old and thin animals are particularly prone to pneumonia, as to most diseases.

Gastro-enteritis and diarrhoea: Worms, coccidiosis, paratyphoid and numerous other factors can cause gastro-enteritis.

Although diarrhoea is seldom observed in animals in the wild, several factors can be responsible for clinical gastro-enteritis in game, for example heavy parasite infestations on cultivated pastures and in small pens, coccidiosis in animals such as blue wildebeest calves or impala, as well as poor hygiene, mouldy hay or too much concentrated feed. Gastro-enteritis is frequently a common and serious condition in hand-reared animals.

In contrast to the treatment of young wild animals (see p. 103), ruminants who have already been weaned or introduced to plant feed, should not be treated orally with antibiotics or sulfonamides. If this is done, these germicides may destroy some of the micro-organisms in the ruminant's stomach which are essential for normal digestion of plant fibre, and this can lead to severe digestive disturbances. It is possible to overcome this problem to some extent by prior dosing with certain chemicals which will assist the germicides in moving directly from the animal's mouth to the abomasum and intestines, bypassing the rumen, omasum and reticulum of the ruminant, where the vital micro-organisms are present.

Recommended alternative treatments are kaolin, tannic acid and, in some cases, calcium hydroxide. Treating animals suffering from diarrhoea is very often problematic. The assistance of a veterinarian should be sought and the cause of the ailment eliminated.

ASYMPTOMATIC INFECTIONS OF GAME WHICH MAY PRODUCE DISEASE IN STOCK

The saying that "game succeeds where livestock succumbs" is particularly apt here.

Opponents of the concept of conservation are quick to point accusing fingers at game farmers and game rangers when livestock perishes in an area where it may well have been ill-advised to attempt to farm with cattle in the first place! It should perhaps be pointed out to such detractors that game possess excellent characteristics which enable them to survive better than livestock in certain areas, without the benefit of the farmer's costly remedies.

It is claimed that, owing to tsetse and nagana infestations, it is impossible or at least very expensive to farm with livestock in more than one third of Africa's potential stock farming regions. Game thrives in these areas!

In the eastern Transvaal, many farmers struggle to farm with cattle against overwhelming natural odds such as foot-and-mouth disease and other difficulties. Yet buffalo, which have an excellent natural immunity to this disease and which can be hunted for between R3 000 and R5 000, as well as daily fees of R500 and more, are remorselessly destroyed at a loss, in futile efforts to rid the Lowveld of foot-and-mouth disease! The question unavoidably arises whether the breeding and utilisation of buffalo would not in certain cases be a far more profitable venture.

The blue wildebeest is immune to bovine malignant catarrh, a disease of cattle, which is transmitted by wildebeest and sheep.

In addition to the above-mentioned diseases, one can also include bovine malignant catarrh, corridor disease and African swine fever in those diseases which normally produce no symptoms or direct harm in their wild hosts, but which can cause devastating losses amongst the more susceptible farm stock species.

Bovine malignant catarrh: At the insistence of cattle farmers in the Transvaal, bovine malignant catarrh has been declared a notifiable disease in South Africa. Control measures instituted in terms of this decision stipulate, amongst others, that wildebeest may no longer be transported freely to farms or areas in which they do not already occur. This stipulation has caused the market value of wildebeest to drop drastically, and farmers were forced, during the punishing drought of 1983, to destroy thousands of wildebeest who had no other refuge. These unfortunate events are especially distressing when one considers that the numbers of blue wildebeest in the Etosha and Kruger National Park had declined by tens of thousands during previous decades owing to anthrax and other causes!

These events were even more deeply to be regretted because wildebeest fulfil an important ecological role on any game farm. Research by Prof. I G Horak of the University of Rhodes has revealed that the development of ticks which occur on blue wildebeest is significantly undermined and that blue wildebeest in fact control tick populations in a natural manner.

for cattle against elephant skin disease was also obtained from the blue wildebeest. The possibility has also not been excluded that horseflies or other insects which parasitise blue wildebeest and subsequently cattle thus immunise the cattle against elephant skin disease in a natural manner.

In contrast to other notifiable diseases, bovine malignant catarrh poses no real threat to the country's economy. In fact, malignant catarrh constitutes one of the least contagious cattle diseases. For example, this disease cannot even be transmitted through contact between individual cattle.

As in the case of blue and black wildebeest, malignant catarrh can be transmitted to cattle via sheep. Up to five or six months after coming into contact with an infected carrier, the animal may only begin to show the first symptoms of malignant catarrh. In countries where blue and black wildebeest do not occur, sheep act as sole carriers of the disease. And yet the restrictions regarding wildebeest have still not been made applicable to sheep as well.

Presently, farmers who wish to introduce wildebeest to their farms or who wish to trade with these animals, have to apply to the Veterinary Head Office in Pretoria for permission. The following requirements have to be met:

* Written permission must be obtained from the immediate neighbours. If they refuse to grant permission, they cannot be forced to do so.
* Approval from the local farmers' association must be obtained. This is also sometimes denied because of the illogical fear that the introduction of wildebeest on a specific farm will introduce the disease to the area, while wildebeest may already occur on nearby properties.
* Approval from the Regional state veterinarian must be obtained.

The application is then sent to the Veterinary Head Office in Pretoria by the regional state vet, after which the property is registered and receives an official number.

Recently, an insurance scheme has been devised by Wildlife Broking Services in conjunction with Dr Hymie Ebedes of the Department of Agriculture. Farmers in an area where there is a known threat of outbreaks may obtain an inexpensive liability insurance policy to indemnify adjoining cattle farmers in the event of an outbreak of confirmed bovine malignant catarrh. Cases must be confirmed microscopically by a veterinarian or pathologist.

Before the devastating drought of a few years ago, some of the largest concentrations of blue wildebeest were to be found in private nature reserves in the eastern Transvaal. In spite of close contact between cattle and the wildebeest, a two-year survey in the area showed not one single confirmed case of bovine malignant catarrh amongst cattle. On several other game farms in the country, wildebeest and cattle have also been kept together for 20 years and more without any stock losses related to malignant catarrh.

All of this does not mean that malignant catarrh may not, after many years, erupt and cause individual farmers to suffer great losses.

Symptoms include the following: Inflammation of the eye and nasal mucosa and excretions from the eye and nose which later become purulent. The cornea of the eyes turn whitish and opaque and blindness can follow. Hard crusts form on the nose, which causes the animal to breathe with difficulty. A raw, bleeding surface is revealed if the scabs are removed. Inflammation in the mouth leads to erosions on the lips, gums, palate and the cavity between the gums and the cheeks. The lymph glands enlarge and glands under the skin become clearly visible. Diarrhoea occasionally occurs. Afflicted animals usually die within one to fourteen days.

In addition to the lesions described above, an autopsy usually reveals haemorrhaging in the mucosa of the stomach and intestines, an enlarged spleen, small white spots in the liver and kidneys, and an abnormal amount of fluid in the cerebral cavity of the skull. Since a small number of other diseases, of which most do not normally occur in South Africa, can cause very similar symptoms and lesions in cattle, it is essential that a clinical diagnosis of malignant catarrh must always be confirmed by laboratory tests.

Although primarily a clinical disease affecting cattle, malignant catarrh has in exceptional circumstances been diagnosed in a kudu, an eland, an African buffalo, a giraffe, hartebeest and a few exotic game species kept in captivity.

Preventive measures should, wherever possible, be directed at avoiding contact between possibly infected wildebeest or sheep and cattle.

It would appear that malignant catarrh is transmitted particularly in circumstances where cattle graze in the same vicinity as wildebeest during the calving time of the latter and for a few months afterwards. In the Serengeti region of Tanzania, the farmers ensure that their cattle do not come into contact with blue wildebeest during this time. However, it would appear that direct contact is not necessary for the disease to be transmitted. Once further research has been done to establish the method(s) of contagion beyond any doubt, more efficient isolation strategies can be worked out.

Onderstepoort's Veterinary Research Institute has a test to determine whether individual wildebeest have malignant catarrh. By making use of this method, the establishment of blue and black wildebeest herds which are free of malignant catarrh could also contribute further to ensure the future of this popular farm game species on farms in the Republic.

Corridor disease: Sudden losses can occur amongst cattle who have grazed on the same contaminated veld as buffalo. All buffalo are not carriers of corridor disease. For example, buffalo from the Addo Elephant National Park are free of the disease. In cattle, corridor disease can be controlled by means of an intensive and strictly monitored dipping programme, since it is transmitted by ticks.

African swine fever: Domestic swine are highly susceptible to this viral disease which is carried in certain regions by warthogs and bushpigs, without, however, the wild pig species being affected by it. African swine fever is a notifiable disease and farmers in swine fever control areas should familiarise themselves with the regulations applicable to their region.

The most significant single control measure is surely a restriction on the transportation of live wild pigs and raw meat and products from endemically infected areas. Guidelines on approved methods for preserving warthog and bushpig trophies for hunters, as well as permits for the transportation of meat and other pork products can be obtained from your local veterinarian and livestock inspector.

PREVENTIVE DISEASE CONTROL MEASURES ON GAME FARMS AND IN GAME RESERVES

Farmers and hunters should be aware of the strict regulations concerning the transport of warthogs, warthog trophies or raw warthog meat.

PREVENTIVE DISEASE CONTROL MEASURES ON GAME FARMS AND IN GAME RESERVES

Since it is much more complicated to control an outbreak of disease in free-roaming game, it is of the utmost importance that every possible precaution must be taken in order to forestall epidemics.

Although circumstances in different nature reserves and on game farms may vary, and the approach to disease prevention will largely be influenced by local conditions, the following principles apply throughout:

Disease occurring in an area: It is particularly important to know which notifiable and dangerous livestock and game diseases usually occur in the area concerned. The local state and private veterinarians and local livestock inspectors are in the best position to supply this information. Local control measures and permit control is also relevant and it is important for all farmers and game rangers to acquaint themselves with the laws and regulations controlling animal diseases and parasitic infestations in their area.

Prevention of contamination from neighbouring areas: Particularly farms and game reserves that border on neighbouring states are exposed to the risks of outbreaks of disease. Our internal control of veterinary diseases and parasites is very efficient, but the same does not necessarily apply to our neighbouring states.

Especially when it is common knowledge that an adjacent neighbouring state suffers regularly from diseases such as foot-and-mouth disease and anthrax, everything possible must be done to restrict direct contact between game and stock on the two sides of the international border.

Naturally in these conditions game-proof fences afford game and livestock the best protection. In some cases an animal-free strip between the contaminated and clean areas is advisable. Where two parallel game fences cannot be afforded or justified, a cattle fence a small distance from and running alongside a game fence may also provide better protection than a single boundary fence. Electrified fences can help to keep animals away from the boundaries. Tall mountains and cliffs, large dams amd lakes and wide and deep rivers which coincide with

boundaries can also sometimes be used beneficially to effect efficient separation.

During active outbreaks of dangerous diseases in adjacent areas, contact between game and livestock herds on either sides of the fence can furthermore be restricted by closing down all the watering points close to the border.

Regular patrols along boundary fences and the periodic dispersal of game from the fences can also help to limit direct contact between infected and susceptible animals. When extremely dangerous diseases such as rinderpest and anthrax occur near a border area, it may even justify the effort and expense of using helicopters to chase game away from the fences.

When an outbreak of disease occurs in a large wilderness area such as the Kruger Park, the spacing and location of game watering plays a very important role in the spread of epidemics (see Chapter 17).

When epidemics of, for example rinderpest or anthrax threaten to annihilate all the game in a specific area, it may however be necessary to intervene very drastically and then to subdivide the whole area, even if only temporarily, into large units by means of game fences. The same control measures for boundaries described above should then be applied to the inner fences to stop the further spread of the epidemic. Regardless of how radical this concept may sound, dire circumstances may arise when such drastic control measures may be the only alternative for ensuring the survival of our larger and more important game areas.

Control over the movement of animals and animal products: In South Africa no wild animal may be transported from one location to another without a veterinary permit. In certain endemic disease areas, raw and unprocessed animal products may also not be transported without a permit. Excuses on the grounds of ignorance concerning local control measures are not accepted in court and fines imposed are generally very high!

These regulations have been instituted in the interest of the stock as well as the game farmer, and should be strictly observed. Once again, it is vital to establish in advance which diseases are relevant in a particular area.

It would be foolhardy in the extreme to risk importing diseases and parasites to a disease-free farm or reserve as a consequence of translocating animals from areas where that risk is present.

When the disease is a notifiable one, quarantining of game or livestock prior to translocation is usually mandatory. Before the animals may be transported, it is necessary to obtain a no-objection permit from the local state veterinarian of the area to which the animals are to be translocated. The no-objection permit is then handed to the state veterinarian of the area from which the animals are to be moved, and he issues a veterinary transportation permit authorising the animals to be transported. Prescriptions regarding quarantine facilities and requirements are described in the transportation permit and must be observed stringently. It may be required that the animals be kept in quarantine for a certain time before despatch, after delivery, or both.

During quarantine the state veterinarian is legally entitled to insist that certain tests be carried out on the animals. For the purposes of foot-and-mouth disease, this may entail collecting throat scrapings and blood samples, and tuberculin skin tests may be carried out on animals from endemic tuberculosis areas.

Immunisation: While it is relatively easy to treat animals in captivity and prior to their release, it is desirable to immunise

The routine immunisation of rare species, in particular, is recommended against diseases such as anthrax, when such animals are to be released in an endemic anthrax area. Mention has already been made of the necessity to inoculate susceptible springbok against heartwater before introducing them into a heartwater-infested area (see p. 143).

Experimental research suggests that outbreaks of certain other livestock diseases may also pose a threat to game. Giraffe and impala have, for example, contracted lumpy-skin disease and buffalo calves have died of blue-tongue, a significant disease in sheep, when the animals were experimentally infected with the virus concerned.

Research on disease in game is still a relatively new field, and much more research is urgently required to determine which livestock diseases are all potentially dangerous to game. All vaccines are not equally effective and safe for use on animals other than those for which they were specifically developed, either. The efficacy and safety of vaccines for use on game will therefore also have to be the subject of further research.

Research over past years has allowed game to be successfully immunised, even under veld conditions. The same method developed more than 20 years ago to immunise lion, leopard, cheetah and other predators in the Pretoria National Zoo against distemper and cat 'flu has since then been adapted very effectively for use in the Kruger National Park to immunise the rare roan against anthrax. In this park, the roan are darted annually from helicopters with darts containing the vaccine.

The basic principles governing the original immunisation darts, are the following: An ordinary game capture dart is used. The barb is removed from the needle, however, so that the dart does not remain in the animal once the vaccine has been injected. The needle opening is relatively large and the volume of vaccine is limited to small volumes (approximately 1 ml), so that the entire contents of the dart can be injected as soon as the animal is hit but before the dart is ejected. By making use of a special high powder charge behind the dart's plunger, the injecting action is accelerated to such an extent that the vaccine is injected within a fraction of a second. Mr Gert van Rooyen of the National Parks Board has developed immunisation darts of a durable type of plastic which are relatively inexpensive and can therefore be discarded in the veld. The contents of the syringe are propelled forward by a compressed spring behind the syringe plunger. As soon as the dart needle hits the animal, a rubber cap fitting tightly over the point of the dart is punctured and the substance is injected into the animal.

A small rubber bulb which fits over the rear end of the needle and which is filled with a brightly coloured fluid, injects the colourant around the wound made by the dart. One can then ascertain that the animal has been successfully immunised.

In Chapter 8, different dart types were illustrated. Mr van Rooyen has also developed a special immunisation rifle with a magazine capable of firing several darts in rapid succession.

Hundreds of wild animals can also be immunised daily by using helicopters to herd them into capture corrals and subsequently vaccinating them in a crush. For this purpose, darts with specially lengthened handles or needles have been designed in order to reach the animals in the crush more easily. Animals that have been immunised in this manner, can simultaneously be colour-marked to avoid being vaccinated accidentally a second time.

Until quite recently, opponents of the conservation concept attempted to dismiss the game farming industry on the grounds that the large-scale immunisation and harvesting of large numbers of wild animals would be an ostensibly impossible task. Undeterred, resolute game farmers, game rangers and even entrepreneurs have worked unceasingly to perfect techniques aimed at overcoming these problems. The possibility of immunisation by means of additions to drinking water and mine-

Diseases such as anthrax and rinderpest, which pose a dire threat to our indigenous game populations, can be contained to a large extent by immunising free ranging wild animals. Helicopters, dart guns and enough darts, as well as sufficient stocks of safe vaccine are required to do this.

aimed at overcoming these problems. The possibility of immunisation by means of additions to drinking water and mineral licks, and by using specially designed immunisation bullets consisting of soluble chemicals, are amongst the proposals put forward. I believe that South Africans will continue to take the lead in the perfection of revolutionary techniques which will benefit not only the game industry, but also the livestock industry across the entire world.

Selective culling: Sickly, deformed and otherwise inferior animals should, as far as possible, be removed from the herd in the interest of the continued survival of healthy breeding stock. In the wild, predators with selective hunting methods take care of this very important selection process. In artificially restricted conditions, where predators are unable to fulfil this role, the farmer or game ranger must eliminate the weaker animals himself.

These genetically weak animals may produce inferior offspring with hereditary deformities. In addition, it is a well-known phenomenon that debilitated and sick animals provide significant reservoirs of internal and external parasites. Such animals are therefore not merely a liability because they are relatively unproductive themselves, but also because they increasingly infest their environment with parasites, which is also to the detriment of the productivity of the rest of the herd. Take the time to examine a thin and sick animal which has been shot, add up the ticks and worms present in the carcass, and multiply these figures with reasonably average egg production rates of the parasite types concerned, which often amounts to thousands or tens of thousands of eggs per female parasite, and then judge for yourself whether it is worth farming with inferior animals!

Diseases and parasites transmitted by humans: All necessary precautions should be taken to ensure that labourers who have to feed and care for animals in captivity are not carriers of tuberculosis or any of the other diseases which may infect the animals. Some years ago, there was even an outbreak of sarcoptic mange amongst a group of sable antelope who had been kept in quarantine and cared for by a labourer who was himself infected with it.

Routine parasite control: Whenever possible, animals should be treated for internal and external parasites before being released in a new environment. Not only does this improve the newly relocated animal's chances of survival, but also prevents undesirable parasites from settling in new areas. The methods and principles of parasite control are discussed in more detail later in this chapter.

Disinfection: Transport trailers, crates, holding pens and camps can be infested with ticks, mange mites and various other disease-producing organisms. When these facilities are subsequently used to transport or hold other animals, the animals can become infected and develop symptoms of disease. It is therefore vital to clean and disinfect all holding facilities regularly.

EMERGENCY ACTION IN CASE OF AN EPIDEMIC

Although epidemic outbreaks of disease are generally controlled by the Division of Veterinary Services of the Department of Agriculture, the farmer and the game ranger, and, in fact, every citizen also has an important contribution to make.

The following steps, arranged in the logical order, serve as general guidelines when large-scale losses are observed amongst game and/or livestock:

Report losses: The local state veterinarian or livestock inspector should be notified of the losses without delay. If neither can be located, the Head Office of the Division of Veterinary Services in Pretoria should be contacted and the necessary information provided.

Correct diagnosis: In the case of certain notifiable diseases, the state veterinary personnel collect the samples themselves. Carcasses of animals who are suspected to have died of diseases such as anthrax and rabies, should be kept in safe isolation until the state veterinarian or livestock inspector arrives. The carcasses should under no circumstances be handled or transported beforehand. In all cases it is necessary for a clinical diagnosis to be confirmed by means of blood smears and laboratory tests.

Immediate organisation of control measures: In the case of notifiable diseases, the Division of Veterinary Services will take responsibility for all control measures. Support personnel can be transferred from other areas, if necessary, depending on the scope and threat posed by an epidemic.

The Veterinary Disease and Parasite Act authorises veterinary personnel to enter private property without permission and to perform certain steps which may be necessary in the execution of their important function. It goes without saying that farmers have a duty to give the necessary assistance to the Division of Veterinary Services when it comes to eradicating dangerous diseases.

Disease survey and isolation of the contaminated area: It is vital to establish as rapidly as possible the extent to which the disease has already spread. On the basis of this information, control boundaries for the region are determined. The movement of susceptible livestock, game and animal products from the contaminated area is strictly controlled. Gate control posts and road blocks are, amongst others used to eliminate loopholes. The control boundaries are patrolled day and night, depending on the circumstances, to prevent contact between animals from the contaminated and adjacent clean areas. As the disease spreads, boundary arrangements are constantly adapted to the changing circumstances.

Disposal of contaminated material: At the discretion of the state veterinarian or his personnel, contaminated carcasses can be incinerated, disinfected or buried, depending on the disease concerned. Vehicles, protective clothing and shoes of personnel, as well as any equipment which may have become contaminated and polluted, must be cleaned and disinfected in accordance with prescriptions before the contaminated area may be left.

The above merely provides a superficial overview of the usual steps taken during the outbreak of a disease. Depending on the specific disease to be contained, the state veterinary personnel may also consider and implement other control measures.

INTERNAL PARASITES

Antelope and other species of farm game, like domestic livestock, are generally infected with a great variety of internal parasites. The most important parts of the body infested by the parasites are:

— tapeworm — seldom significant;
— flukes — seldom significant.

* **other organs** (lungs, liver, etc):
— roundworm — occasionally detrimental to the host and also detracts from the value of the organs for human consumption;
— tapeworm (liver) — detracts from its value for human consumption;
— tapeworm cysts — infest predators;
— flukes — less prevalent than in livestock.

* **the muscles and soft tissue:**
— roundworm — seldom significant;
— tapeworm cysts — economically significant.

Factors which contribute to heavy worm infestations: In their natural environment and on good grazing, game normally shows minimal signs of parasite infestations. Severe and clinically observable infestations can, however, occur, and then in particular in:
— old, sick and debilitated animals
— animals grazing on poor pasture and who are undernourished
— overpopulations of game, especially in restricted areas
— animals which are kept in captivity in unhygienic conditions
— animals which are given supplementary feed on the ground or in feeding troughs which have been polluted with manure.

Manure and manure-soiled pastures and feed are the most important sources of infestation. In the laboratory it is by no means unusual to count 10 000 and even more worm eggs per gram of goat manure.

Symptoms of worm infestations: Antelope with tens of thousands of worms in their intestines may show few, or even no, symptoms of infestation.

All parasites are not equally dangerous to their hosts. Moderate infestations of certain dangerous worms, such as some of the blood-sucking species of hookworm, may be more harmful than severe infestations of other worm species.

Animals who are in a debilitated condition due to malnutrition, disease, pregnancy, nursing young, or other stressing factors, also offer reduced resistance to parasite infestations. Young animals who have recently been weaned are also ideal victims of diseases and parasites.

Under normal circumstances, the symptoms of worm infestations are not only seldom observed, but are also relatively non-specific. The following signs in an animal may, however, be an indication of worm infestations:
— emaciation
— diarrhoea, or even obstipation
— a pot-belly
— a dull, occasionally staring coat
— debilitation, weakness in the hindquarters and a swaying gait.

Most wild animals that die of severe parasite infestations probably show no obvious earlier signs of illness. The growth of young animals who were exposed to heavy infestations for long periods is often affected, and this sometimes prevents such individuals from developing into properly formed, strong and vigorous adults.

Since the genetic composition of individual animals may make certain animals less resistant to disease and parasites, one may find that certain inferior animals are constantly afflicted with problems. Animals who repeatedly or continuously show signs of diseases and parasitism should possibly not be retained as part of the breeding herd, since theoretically they are likely not only to pass on their own inferior traits, but may also cause

infestations in the entire herd. Fortunately natural selection ensures that fewer of these inferior animals occur amongst game than amongst livestock.

Roundworm: As has been indicated, roundworm are surely the most significant group of endoparasites encountered in game. The symptoms described above are mostly associated with severe infestations of roundworm in the digestive tract.

More than 60 different species of worms infest game and livestock in South Africa. A single animal can harbour 60 000 or more worms in its digestive tract. Some parasites infest either game alone or livestock alone. Most worms are harmful to only specific species of game. When a large variety of game or animal species thus occur on the same farm, many of the parasite eggs or larvae are therefore ingested by game or stock in which those parasites are unable to develop any further. In this manner endoparasites are removed from the veld to a certain degree.

Certain types of roundworm are able to infest a wide variety of animal species and can therefore also be transmitted from livestock to game or from game to livestock. The wire-worm or stomach-worm (*Haemonchus contortus*) found in cattle and sheep, for example, is able to infest 19 antelope species as well. Under adverse conditions, severe wire-worm infestations may be responsible for losses amongst eland, blesbok and certain other species of game.

The well-known nodular worm (*Oesophagostomum columbianum*) found in sheep has also been found to infest 14 species of antelope, whereas at least three antelope species are susceptible to one of the most deadly sheep worms, the so-called Sandveld hookworm (*Gaigeria pachyscelis*).

Fortunately game and stock have been living together on the same farms for centuries, and consequently a large degree of symbiosis has developed between parasites and their domesticated and wild hosts.

Liver flukes: Several different types of worms occur mainly in the liver, or pass through the animal's liver as part of their life cycle. The following are examples of parasites which are reasonably obvious and are generally found in the liver. *Monodontella giraffae* in the giraffe and *Grammocephalus clathratus* in the elephant are two types of roundworm which may in exceptional cases cause sufficiently severe liver damage to lead to clinical disease. In both of these hosts, hardening (cirrhosis) of the liver can eventually lead to emaciation and debilitation, and finally death. Even adult elephants may become exceptionally ill. However, young elephants in captivity are generally more noticeably affected.

Cooperioides hepaticae is a thin roundworm which is relatively hard to discern, generally found in the bile ducts of impala. Occasionally mild thickening of the bile ducts, small abscesses, or a purulent fluid in the bile ducts indicate the presence of this parasite. When the liver is dissected and pressed between the fingers, the worms can sometimes be squeezed from the bile ducts. These parasites seldom affect the impala adversely. Infested impala livers may, however, be unsuitable for human consumption for aesthetic reasons.

Stilesia hepatica is a longish tapeworm occurring in the bile ducts of livestock and different species of game. Once again, the adverse effect of this parasite relates more to the decreased value of the slaughtered animal's liver than to significant harm to the live host.

Linguatula serrata is an unusual parasite which spends the adult part of of its life cycle in the noses of carnivores such as dogs and lions. Blue wildebeest and buffalo represent some of the intermediate hosts of this parasite. For example, the livers of approximately 60 to 70 per cent of the blue wildebeest in the Kruger Park are infested with this parasite. Although the longish, soft bodies of the parasites give them the appearance of worms, the "tongue-worm", as this parasite is also known, is more closely related to the scorpion and the tick than to worms.

Echinococcus and other tapeworm cysts occur quite commonly in and on the liver and other organs of livestock and a wide variety of game. These cyst-like growths and attachments on organs represent the immature stages of tapeworm species which occur as adults in dogs or wild predators.

Since parasite infestations on game farms and in nature reserves can be initiated or aggravated when organs infested with these organisms are consumed by dogs or wild predators, parasite-infested organs should preferably be burnt.

Lungworms: The tapeworm cysts are also reasonably often observed in the lungs or attached to the lung surface.

Several of the roundworm species which infest other parts of the body during their adult stages also migrate as immature and microscopically small parasites through the lungs of their hosts. These roundworms, as well as the tapeworm cysts mentioned, are not true "lungworms".

True "lungworms" develop specifically in the lungs of livestock and/or game and can in exceptional cases affect their hosts clinically. Although the worms themselves are sometimes difficult to detect with the naked eye, raised and slightly discoloured swellings on the lung surface, or purulence in the pulmonary tubes, may indicate lungworm infestations.

Impala and other game species infested with lungworm may develop pneumonia. Impala in parts of the eastern Transvaal and Zululand are heavily infested with the lungworm *Pneumostrongylus calcaratus*. As mentioned earlier, these animals showed a very high incidence of acute pneumonia during random culling during severe cold in the Kruger Park. The lesions were particularly concentrated in those parts of the lungs where lungworm lesions were also evident. This research seems to indicate that this parasite may, in unfavourable conditions, contribute to disease and even losses amongst infested impala.

Surveys in the north-western and western Transvaal have shown that the impala in these regions are still relatively free of this parasite. Since severe lungworm infestations can lead to lowered productivity and even to deaths amongst impala, game farmers fear that the unrestricted translocation of impala from lungworm-infested regions to clean parts of the country may pose a threat to clean impala herds.

Tapeworms, measles and other meat parasites: Adult tapeworms are normally seldom encountered amongst farm game species.

"Measles", or rather, the gleaming white tapeworm heads of immature tapeworms in humans or wild predators, which are found in a small bladder of fluid in the muscles, particularly, of their intermediate hosts, may be responsible for considerable economic losses.

Since pork or beef which is infested with measles and is not cooked thoroughly or treated effectively can cause tapeworm infestations in humans, all measle-contaminated meat is usually inspected critically and generally rejected for human consumption. In contrast to beef and pork, venison containing measles poses no threat to humans, since these measles would only develop into adult tapeworms if ingested by a susceptible wild predator species.

Although limited research suggests that the types of tapeworm to which humans are susceptible only exceptionally infest game species such as the eland, it is nevertheless not advisable to use measle-infested venison which has not been properly prepared for human consumption.

Once again, game farmers in the western Transvaal and in other parts of the country where measles do not occur in game are concerned that the large-scale relocation of game from measle-contaminated regions to clean areas may create new infestations. In the Kruger Park and directly adjacent areas, approximately 30 to 80 per cent of the impala, buffalo and blue wildebeest are infested with measles. Although the absence of certain of the larger predators elsewhere in the country limits the natural life-cycles of these parasites, one may expect that some of the smaller species of predator may help to maintain certain of these infestations elsewhere; that is to say, if the parasites were given the opportunity through mass distribution of game from contaminated areas to establish themselves successfully in clean areas.

Buffalo, like cattle, are occasionally infested with a roundworm (*Onchocerca sp.*) which also causes round nodules in the muscles. However, these parasites can be distinguished from measles in that they are not enclosed in water blisters. If a nodule is dissected and the parasite is searched for with a sharp-pointed knife, the very thin and long worm can sometimes be seen with the naked eye. These parasite lumps are especially noticeable under the buffalo's hide, over the breastbone and chest and in the neck muscles. This muscle parasite is relatively insignificant.

As in cattle, filariasis also occurs in buffalo. These parasites cannot be seen with the naked eye. The yellow-greenish discolouration of and even slight haemorrhaging within the subcutaneous tissue of the buffalo may, however, have an adverse effect when the quality of the carcass is evaluated at an abattoir.

Trichinella spiralisis is an extremely dangerous parasite. The small spiral-shaped, curled-up worms can only be seen under a microscope. Trichinosis only occurs in a limited area of the Kruger Park. Since this parasite is transmitted mainly through the eating of raw meat, herbivores such as antelope, like cattle and sheep, are normally not infested with this parasite. The warthog can, however, owing to his scavenging habits, become infested with Trichinella parasites, just like wild predators and rodents. It is therefore advisable to cook warthog venison thoroughly before eating it, particularly in the extreme eastern Transvaal.

Flukes: Bilharzia does not normally cause any serious problems in wild animals. Theoretically, though, numerous species of wild animals are susceptible to infestation by bilharzia parasites (*Schistosoma spp.*). For example, the hippopotamus has its own bilharzia parasite which is not, as far as is known, transmitted to any other mammal.

Conical flukes (*Paramphistomum* and *Cotylophoron spp.*) occur in the rumen and reticulum of livestock and certain species of game, but they are relatively harmless. The smaller, immature parasites in the intestines may, however, cause diarrhoea. Emaciation and progressive weakening can result, and in exceptional cases heavily infested animals may die. It would appear that this parasite can adversely affect the sable antelope, amongst others, when such animals graze in marshy or wetland areas.

amongst others, when such animals graze in marshy or wetland areas.

Liver flukes (*Fasciola spp.*) do not affect game to the same extent as livestock. Game occurring in marshy or wetland areas may, however, become severely infested with liver flukes, which could be fatal in the case of certain animals, such as the eland.

The parasitic flukes described above, each of which consists of different species, are dependent on freshwater snails for the completion of their life-cycles. This is why wet environments promote the infestation of livestock and game with bilharzia, conical flukes and liver flukes.

Bilharzia is, of course, particularly significant to humans. It is therefore apt to warn farmers and game rangers who live in the drier parts of the country that they themselves, as well as the game and stock in their care, may be exposed to the risk of bilharzia infestations even in the absence of pans, wetlands, marshes and earth dams, since the snails which serve as the intermediate hosts for bilharzia parasites can survive even in cement dams and troughs and can thus contaminate the water.

The control of internal parasites: The following general rules apply:

1. Do not import game from areas where parasites and diseases occur which may contaminate your farm or nature reserve and which may later cause disease or losses amongst your game or stock, or other financial losses.
2. As far as possible, treat all purchased animals for parasites before releasing the animals on your farm or in a nature reserve.
3. Avoid cramming too many animals into a small, restricted area and, most particularly, treat all animals regularly for parasites (for example with anthelmintic blocks) when game is kept on cultivated pastures.
4. Control game populations so as not to exceed the limitations imposed by the available grazing and browse in the specific environment.
5. Make provision for adequate supplementary feeding in winter, so that the animals do not grow excessively weak during unusually dry years and thus succumb to parasite infestations.
6. Supplementary feed should be supplied in clean containers, so that the animals are not forced to feed from the ground, where worm-infested feed can lead to severe worm infestations.
7. Feed and water troughs should be sufficiently high above the ground to avoid pollution by excreta, and must be cleaned regularly.
8. Grass hay, teff or straw used in night rooms as bedding should be replaced regularly and the floors kept scrupulously clean and dry.
9. Old, sick, emaciated and debilitated animals are usually a source of parasites and should preferably be removed from the herd.
10. Individual animals suffering from severe parasite infestations should receive the appropriate treatment.
11. Routine deworming of all the game on a game farm is also recommended, to keep parasite numbers down.

Deworming: Anthelmintics can be administered in various ways, but some can only be given orally. If these preparations are tasteless, odourless and particularly safe, they can be given by means of supplementary feed. Otherwise the animals have to be caught and orally dosed.

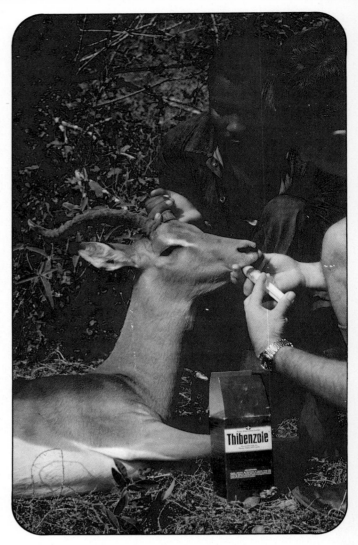

Anthelmintics can be administered to captured game by means of oral dosing, or by intramuscular or subcutaneous injection.

Since oral dosing can lead to choking and even pneumonia, it may be advisable to give broad-spectrum anthelmintic injections instead.

Special anthelmintic blocks or treated concentrated feed or mineral licks, in pellet or powder form, can furthermore be used to administer certain anthelmintics at a low dose over a period of a few days.

Before a preparation has been registered for use specifically on game, the use of such a remedy to treat game can unfortunately not be recommended unconditionally. This applies to all parasiticides, regardless of whether they are for internal or external parasites.

Having said this, it is not inappropriate to mention some of the numerous preparations that have been used successfully to treat wild animals. Until these preparations are registered, they will have to be used at own risk: Thiabendazole (Thibenzole, MSD) is a tasteless and odourless substance for the treatment of roundworms. It can be added to feed mixtures to deworm practically all the South African antelopes, zebra, hippopotamus, rhinoceros and elephant in captivity.

Levamisole hydrochloride (Ripercol-L, Janssen Pharm.) is a particularly useful broad-spectrum remedy for the treatment of roundworms which can be injected intramuscularly. This preparation has already been used very successfully on a wide variety of South African game species and predators. Like *Tetramisole hydrochloride (Tramisol W.M., ICI)*, Ripercol-L is

Free ranging wild animals can be dewormed by including safe and effective anthelmintics in their mineral licks. Rumevite anthelmintic blocks are particularly suitable.

one of the few anthelmintics that effectively eradicate the stubborn liver fluke *Grammocephalus clathratus* in young elephants. Tramisol W.M. has furthermore been used successfully for the treatment of lungworm infestations in bontebok.

Mebendazole (Telmin, Janssen Pharm.) and *dichlorvos (Equigard, Shell)* can be administered in the animals' feed and has been successfully used to deworm various ungulates in the Johannesburg Zoo.

Fenbendazole (Panacur, Hoechst Pharm.) is a relatively safe and very effective remedy for the treatment of roundworms.

Rafoxanide (Ranide, MSD) has been used successfully to treat blesbok for wire-worm by means of oral dosing.

Ivermectin (Ivomec, MSD) has successfully been used on impala. Injected subcutaneously at a dosage level of 200 mg/kg, this preparation is effective against several types of roundworm, as well as certain lice.

Lintex (Bayer) (contains niclosamide) is very effective for the treatment of animals against adult tapeworms. This substance is virtually tasteless and odourless and can be given in the animals' feed or even in the milk of bottle-fed orphans. A wide range of mammals and even birds have been treated successfully with Lintex.

Care should be taken with all the above preparations not to exceed the prescribed doses unnecessarily, as toxic symptoms may develop. This does not mean, however, that certain remedies such as Thibenzole and Lintex do not have reasonably wide safety margins.

Anthelmintic blocks: Rumevite anthelmintic blocks have been used throughout the country for years for the routine deworming of farm game. The active ingredient, fenbendazole (Panacur) is particularly safe for game and effectively eradicates various types of roundworm.

During winter relatively few active worm parasites are found on pastures and the parasites survive chiefly in the digestive systems of game and livestock. The best time to put out anthelmintic blocks is during July.

The following general rules may ensure that game utilise the anthelmintic blocks better and that treatment is therefore more effective:

1. If the animals are not accustomed to mineral licks, first put out coarse salt or salt blocks. (Unfortunately game in certain parts of the country refuse to utilise any form of mineral lick).
2. Thereafter, put out feed blocks (without anthelmintic) at the same spot until the blocks are being well utilised.
3. Now replace these blocks with those containing Panacur.

4. The treated blocks should be available for about 2 to 4 weeks to ensure that most animals do, in fact, ingest sufficient amounts of the preparation.
5. Sufficient anthelmintic blocks should be distributed across the farm so that they are within reach of all the animals. Concentrate particularly on favourite grazing spots and watering points.
6. The blocks can be placed inside metal frames or anchored to the ground by means of metal rods if warthogs or zebra move the blocks around or damage them excessively.

Continuing research in the field of parasite control promises to yield new breakthroughs in the near future.

EXTERNAL PARASITES

Ticks, scabies and mange mites, lice, fleas and various types of flies and their larvae parasitise wild animals. However, external parasites tend to be a far greater problem on domestic stock than on game.

Ticks: With the possible exception of the buffalo, giraffe, eland and, to a lesser degree the waterbuck and the gemsbok, it may appear to the layman that ticks seldom occur on game in any significant numbers.

Dr Ivan Horak , director of the tick research unit at the University of Rhodes, has produced some outstanding research on game parasites. His research will certainly contribute to a more scientific and ecologically sound approach to controlling parasites on game. The contents of this chapter are based largely on his research, and the reader is referred to Dr Horak's publications (see References) for further details.

Dr Horak established that a single buffalo could carry more than 20 000 ticks. Approximately 8 000 ticks were counted on a kudu in the eastern Cape. A single female tick can lay between 2 000 and 20 000 eggs, and this explains why, in certain circumstances, ticks may suddenly assume plague proportions on a game farm. On cattle farms, ticks are able to multiply even faster, since more ticks able to develop to maturity occur on cattle than on any game species.

Factors contributing to severe tick infestations: Natural selection over the ages has ensured the disappearance of the weaker wild animals, amongst which those with a particular susceptibility to infestations by ticks and other parasites. Only the stronger and healthier animals survived to ensure a more robust and viable progeny. This explains to a large degree why wild animals generally have a greater resistance to disease and parasites than domestic stock.

However, various factors may cause weakening of the animals' resistance or exposure to abnormally severe infestation pressure, which may in turn lead to the development of heavy tick infestations. Some of these contributing factors, as well as the phenomenon that tick infestations can be influenced on a particular game farm or in a nature reserve by the species composition, are discussed briefly below:

1. Excessive numbers of game in a specific area promote the degree of infestation by internal and external parasites. Heavy tick infestations can therefore be expected whenever too many animals are kept on poor grazing, in particular.
2. When game is translocated to an unsuitable habitat and the animals do not adapt well to their new environment, they may also succumb to parasite infestations.

It may be necessary to make use of cattle to control tick numbers on farms where eland occur.

3. Parasites may even be introduced via game which is brought in from elsewhere, and thus infest other game already present on the farm or in the nature reserve, to the detriment of these animals.

4. During the breeding season, large numbers of ticks are found on impala rams. Any other circumstances which cause an animal to become emaciated and its resistance to weaken may similarly contribute to heavy parasite infestations.

Certainly one of the most interesting findings arising from Dr Horak's research has been the relative contribution of different game species to existing and new parasite infestations on a game farm or in a nature reserve. Without generalising, or going into detail about the ecological control of tick populations, it is important for the game farmer and game warden to take note of the following facts:

1. Minimal problems with tick infestations will be encountered on game farms on which only the smaller species occur. Small, immature ticks may be found on the small species. Since the larger and mature ticks depend chiefly on cattle and large game species to develop and to complete their life cycles, the absence of these larger hosts will therefore contribute to the less successful multiplication of ticks.

2. When the larger and smaller species are kept together, the ticks multiply faster, and certain species can be particularly adversely affected.

3. The small, immature ticks (some farmers refer to them as "pepper ticks") are particularly active during the autumn, winter and spring. Because they are so small and so hard to see, one could incorrectly conclude that an antelope does not have ticks, while he may in fact be carrying thousands.

4. The large and mature ticks are especially active in summer, and are seen mainly on the larger game species and on livestock.

5. Cattle, eland and buffalo are some of the most important tick reservoirs. Kudu can also carry considerable numbers of ticks. All the ticks on a kudu do not, however, develop to

maturity. For example, some female ticks drop off and die before they can lay eggs. The natural resistance of the kudu to ticks therefore contributes to the fact that tick populations on kudu do not increase as fast as they do on cattle.

6. Eland are particularly suitable hosts for ticks. Not only do they represent an important source of tick infestations, like cattle, but they also suffer from heavy infestations themselves, often dying from the direct or indirect consequences.

7. As has already been mentioned, the blue wildebeest is a remarkable asset on any game farm, in more respects than one. The outstanding resistance of this animal to ticks not only protects it from infestations, but also contributes enormously to eradicating ticks from the environment. As a vacuum cleaner removes dust from a room, so a herd of wildebeest attracts ticks; but, in contrast to suitable hosts such as cattle and the eland, most of the ticks survive on the wildebeest for only a short while, before dropping off and dying before their females can produce eggs.

The game farming industry certainly needs research such as that of Dr Horak in order to implement management practices in a scientific manner.

Tick control: Although tick control is not as important on game as on cattle, the artificial control of tick burdens in a particular area is frequently necessary, especially when losses are suffered. The following are merely intended as hints, and do not represent the final solution to effective control of ticks on game or even stock:

1. Thin, sick or injured and tick-infested animals usually represent a source of tens of thousands of ticks with the potential to infest the veld, and should preferably be removed.

2. Game populations should never be allowed to exceed sensible limits, since this will lead to weaker animals and poorer grazing, which inevitably starts a vicious circle of deterioration unless immediate action is taken.

3. Individual animals that are obviously and chronically infested with unusually high tick burdens may have an inherent and even hereditary susceptibility to ticks and should also not be retained.

4. Taking into account Dr Horak's observations regarding the particular susceptibility of certain game species to tick infestations and the remarkable resistance of others, a game farmer should use his discretion when stocking his farm.

5. Using dipped cattle to clear a farm of ticks is a technique that has been used successfully for years. Cattle are driven into a game camp and thus accumulate ticks on themselves. The cattle are then dipped or sprayed with an acaricide, and driven back into the camp. The process is repeated until the tick burden has been reduced sufficiently. In order for this method of tick control to succeed, it is important to take note of the following facts:

* The blue tick, *Boophilus decoloratus*, is especially prominent from September to November. In order to control this specific tick, it is therefore advisable to drive the cattle into the game pens and dip them during these months.

* However, adults of most other species of ticks are absorbed in greater numbers by cattle during the summer months. Dr Horak therefore recommends that cattle should as a rule be driven into the game camps and dipped in January and February, in order to reduce tick burdens.

* Since cattle of the *Bos taurus* species accumulate more

ticks than those of the *B. indicus* species, the former are more suitable for this purpose. (Cattle which are accustomed to ticks should be used, otherwise the cattle themselves may succumb to diseases transmitted by ticks.)

* The cattle must be dipped every 5 days, or the female ticks may mature and drop off to lay eggs before the dip can kill them.

Although not essential, this cattle-dipping technique is useful when ticks become a problem.

Mange and scabies: Various types of microscopically small mites — organisms related to ticks — can cause dermatitis and hair loss in game and stock. Some of these parasites can affect different animal species, and in exceptional cases even humans, while others occur only on specific animal species.

Scabies or mange has been diagnosed in blue wildebeest, red hartebeest, impala, giraffe, springbok, steenbok, lion, leopard, cheetah and buffalo. Buffalo can be infested by three different parasites, although clinical signs of scabies or mange are seldom observed in this species. Mortalities due to scabies or mange seldom occur, but have been recorded in blue wildebeest, impala, springbok, lion and cheetah. Particularly in the cheetah, the infestation may develop rapidly and prove fatal. Heavily infested sick animals are also easy prey for predators.

Lice and fleas: Bare, almost bald patches along the sides of an animal's neck, particularly in late winter when the animals are

Cattle farmers should make use of dips such as Triatix, which do not pose a threat to oxpeckers, as these birds destroy large numbers of ticks themselves.

thin, can be an indication of a severe lice infestation. This baldness has been observed in kudu, nyala, bushbuck and impala. In contrast with mange lesions, the skin of animals infested with lice shows no noticeable inflammation or thickening, and is not covered in scabs.

Fleas can be a nuisance when predators such as jackals are kept in pens with earth floors. Antelope and other ungulates are generally not significantly plagued by fleas.

Preparations for the treatment of ticks, scabies, mange, lice and fleas: Unless a parasiticide has been registered for use on wild animals, all preparations are used at own risk. With due regard for this reservation, it should nonetheless be mentioned

that *Benzene hexachloride (B.H.C.)* has in the past been used successfully to treat antelope and warthogs.

Similarly, suspensions of the 5 per cent wettable powder of malathion have been used with great success to treat lion, leopard and cheetah for ticks, fleas, and even scabies and mange.

However, a number of cheetah who had been immobilized with phencyclidine hydrochloride (Sernylan, Park-Davis & Co,) developed toxic symptoms when treated with malathion. This is another unfortunate example of the unexpected toxic side-effects that preparations which are safe when used alone can have when used in conjunction with other drugs. It also emphasizes the importance of using registered substances wherever possible, and then only strictly in accordance with the directions.

Over the past few years, Amitras *(Triatix, Coopers)* has been used with increasing success to treat antelope for ticks before transportation or release into new areas. The results thus far indicate that this preparation is remarkably safe for use in antelope. Directions for preparation and use should nevertheless be strictly observed. Triatix possesses numerous properties to recommend it. For example, the animal's entire body need not be treated. If most of the animal's body is sprayed with the dip, ticks on the rest of the animal will also drop off and die. The effect of this preparation also lasts for a few days, which prevents ticks from re-infesting the animal immediately after treatment. This preparation is also not harmful to oxpeckers, who do a great deal to control ticks naturally.

When the animals have been captured and loaded into crates or onto trucks, it is usually quite simple to treat them with a suitable acaricide through slits in the sides or roof of the crate or truck using a suitable spray apparatus. Even if a spray is considered safe, it is still advisable not to contaminate edible plant matter and water.

Tsetse flies: In approximately one third of Africa, the tsetse fly makes cattle farming impossible, or at least non-viable economically.

As was mentioned earlier, the large-scale outbreak of rinderpest in South Africa at the end of the previous century was followed by the disappearance of the tsetse fly in the Transvaal, and, together with this, the two feared diseases nagana and sleeping sickness, which were transmitted by these flies.
However, tsetse flies do still occur in parts of southern Africa, and the South African Division of Veterinary Science is prepared to deal with this problem effectively if it becomes necessary.

Although tsetse flies and nagana pose no direct threat to game, wild animals were killed in very great numbers in an effort to control the tsetse fly. As a fortunate counter-balance, large parts of Africa which have been rendered unfit for cattle farming by the tsetse fly have been preserved for game.

Biting flies: Stable flies *(Stomoxys sp.)* are bloodsucking flies which cause severe irritation in captive wild animals. The ears of wild predators such as lion, leopard and cheetah are bitten until they bleed. In antelope and other ungulates, the flies concentrate on the lower limbs and the animals can often be seen prancing around in an effort to evade these annoying flies.

Numerous other biting flies cause irritation in game and livestock. Some types even transmit contagious diseases.

Larvae of nasal bot flies: The nasal and sinus cavities of blue and black wildebeest, bontebok, blesbok, red hartebeest and tsessebe are often infested with the larvae of *Gedoelstia, Kirkioestrus and Oestrus spp.* Up to 1 200 larvae have been counted around the brain of a single blue wildebeest — and yet wild hosts of these larvae are not necessarily adversely affected by such severe infestations.

In giraffe, springbok and zebra, the larvae of *Rhinoestrus spp.* are able to infest their wild hosts without causing any clinical symptoms.

Bulging eye disease: Cattle and sheep infested with *Gedoelstia* larvae can suffer from a condition known as bulging eye disease. The common name adequately describes the symptoms that can be expected. In exceptional cases, nervous symptoms due to lesions in the central nervous system, as well as heart failure, may occur. Grey rhebok and other antelope species which are not the usual hosts of these larvae may also become blind if infested with these larvae.

Until now, bulging eye disease has been only a minor problem in certain parts of Namibia, where cattle or sheep that were grazed together with infested game became infested themselves and developed the typical symptoms.

When the species mentioned above are relocated from known problem areas to clean areas, it is advisable to treat them for nasal bot larvae before releasing them.

On South Africa's Highveld the flies are particularly active from October to June. In winter few pupae and adult flies are present in the veld, and, almost without exception, the parasites spend the winter as larvae in the nasal and sinus cavities of their wild hosts. On the Highveld and in other temperate regions, where bulging eye disease may occur, it is therefore advisable wherever possible to catch individuals of the wild host species in winter and dose them orally. Blesbok have been treated successfully with rafoxanide (Ranide, MSD) at a dosage level of 7,5 to 15 mg/kg. As mentioned earlier, this treatment is also effective in treating wire-worm infestations in blesbok.

When livestock on a farm contract bulging eye disease, the cattle and sheep should be moved as far as possible away from the infested game herds. Treatment of all the cattle and sheep on the farm with Ranide at approximately three-week intervals should prevent further outbreaks.

Preventive measures should be aimed primarily at separating livestock from infested game herds during those times of the year when the flies are active, and preventing occurrences by the prophylactic treatment of carrier animals.

CONCLUSION

All possible measures should be taken to prevent your animals from contracting diseases and parasites from adjacent contaminated areas, or from game or livestock entering your farm or nature reserve.

If, despite all precautionary measures, a disease does occur in your vicinity, the contents of this chapter will, at most, provide the necessary guidelines for the correct action. Notifiable diseases should immediately be reported to your state veterinarian or livestock inspector, who will initiate the necessary control measures. Other diseases should also be discussed with a veterinarian in order to treat the problem as effectively as possible.

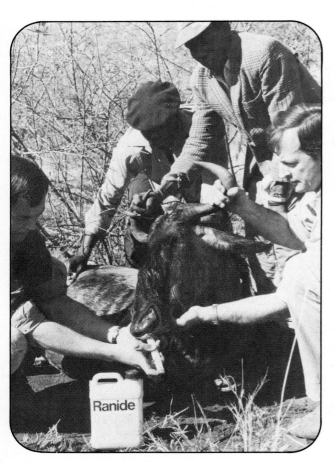

Before game is released into a new area, they should be treated with paraciticides. Here, a blue wildebeest (left) is being treated for nasal bot larvae and worms, while a load of impala (right) are being sprayed with Triatix for external parasites through the roof slats of the transport truck.

19. GAME COUNTS, CROPPING METHODS AND CARCASS DATA

In this chapter, the advantages and disadvantages of the most important game counting and harvesting methods are discussed briefly.

Different methods have been devised for determining game populations on a farm. Most of these are useless and misleading. Some of the most common techniques are discussed below:

GAME COUNTS

A reliable game count is certainly one of the most important requirements for the effective management of any conservation area or game ranch. Yet in spite of this, game counts are frequently conducted without proper understanding of the fundamental problems associated with counts.

An accurate count of animals is extremely difficult to obtain, especially with more cryptic species or in areas with dense vegetation. The emphasis should be on the repeatability of counts which would allow for comparison between different counts and therefore enable population trends of species to be monitored.

Several factors must be considered before a census is made. These include the size of the area, the characteristics of the vegetation and the animal species to be counted. It is important to note that no single method will provide reliable results for all animals in all possible habitat types.

Census methods can be classified into two main groups: ground counts and aerial counts. Several types of ground counts are available and include drive counts, transect counts and road-strip counts.

Road strip counts: This entails counting game from a vehicle during repeated trips along a representative set of roads. The average distance from the road at which animals can be seen, and therefore counted, is calculated and multiplied by the distance travelled, in order to arrive at the area on which the game was seen and counted. If this area is, say, 100 hectares, and 50 impala and 10 kudu were counted, this method would yield a count of 500 impala and 100 kudu on a farm measuring 1 000 hectares (10 x 100 hectares).

Despite the fact that game is not distributed evenly across the veld and that such counts are therefore not representative, and that particularly the more timid species avoid roads and vehicles, and that climatic conditions and numerous other factors render this method inaccurate, it is nevertheless widely used to determine game populations and/or quantify the increase or decrease in game numbers on a farm.

Waterhole counts: This method is time consuming and requires many observers, who man all the waterholes in an area for a continuous period (usually for 24 or 48 hours).

The assumption behind waterhole counts is that each animal will drink water once a day and that all the animals on a farm can therefore be counted if all the watering points are observed on one particular day.

However, facts show that impala, for instance, are able to go without water for a week in winter and even longer than a month in summer. To complicate matters further, during the breeding season impala rams are likely to visit the same watering point several times on the same day in search of female company. In the Kruger Park, impala drink once every approximately 68 hours, blue wildebeest every 47 hours, Burchell's zebra every 35 hours, buffalo every 38 hours and elephant every 43 hours in winter. Numerous factors such as the moisture content of the grazing and browse, the amount of dew on the grazing during the night and early morning hours, and the availability of veld water, cause animals to drink more or less frequently, and waterhole counts will therefore not yield reliable estimates.

Drive counts: Some academics even use game spoor and dungheaps to determine game numbers, which can, of course, be completely deceptive! A more reliable method is to line up sufficient people who are able to identify the different game species, and to move through a game camp approximately 50 m to 100 m apart, with each person counting every animal spotted on either his left or his right, or ahead. A few counters can conceal themselves at look-out points, for example hilltops, near ravines or alongside straight paths or open strips. They can then count the game fleeing before the approaching line, and when all of this data is processed later, a reasonable indication of game populations can at least be obtained. Dense, flat veld and large game farms cannot, however, be covered satisfactorily using this method.

Aerial counts: All of this leaves us with only one alternative, and that is an aerial census! Although expensive, an aerial game census at least every two or three years is usually justified. In my opinion, any large-scale removal of game populations should in any case be preceded by an aerial count, to prevent too much game from being cropped owing to inadequate information. Such counts should be undertaken by an experienced pilot and game counters.

Both helicopters and fixed-wing aircraft are suitable for aerial counts, although fixed-wing aircraft are generally more widely used. Helicopters are particularly useful when the area is relatively small or when dense vegetation or very large herds are present. The helicopter allows enough time to split a large herd into smaller groups and herds can be photographed more easily from a helicopter. However, helicopter counts are expensive and in many instances a fixed-wing aircraft can be used effectively.

Only high wing aircraft should be considered, as a low wing reduces visibility. A six-seater aircraft will allow more observers and should therefore result in more reliable counts. It is important for the aircraft to have slow-flying capabilities as an airspeed of about 160 — 170 km/h is required.

As in the case of ground counts, several variations of aerial counts may be used. Sample or strip counts are used to count animals within strips. The total population is then estimated when the results are extrapolated to the whole area. During a total count an attempt is made to count all the animals and the whole area is therefore systematically covered.

Several important factors must be considered when an aerial count is planned:

✱ A detailed map of the area must be available to ensure accurate navigation and to plot any additional information

* The census must be planned carefully before the first flight. Landmarks may be marked on the maps and the procedure must be discussed in detail with the observers and pilot.

* Some observers should be experienced in census work as certain skills have to be developed. The difficulty of observing and counting with accuracy is often underestimated.

* Safety must always be be a consideration. The pilot must be experienced in low level operations and be able to maintain a constant airspeed at the required height. Particular care must be taken to avoid large birds. Vultures, eagles and other raptors often fly at low levels and do not react to the aircraft's presence until the last moment when their behaviour may be unpredictable.

* Avoid counting when it is more than 40 per cent overcast as low contrast makes it very difficult to observe animals. Counting in strong winds should also be avoided as navigation is more difficult as well as posing a possible hazard.

* Census flights should be restricted to the early morning before animals have moved into the shade and when the air is less turbulent than later in the day. A census session should not exceed 2 — 3 hours as aerial census-taking is tiring and long sessions may result in a poor count.

* The season should also be taken into consideration. The best results are obtained during the winter months when maximum visibility in most vegetation types is possible.

* The parallel flight paths should be narrow enough to allow observers to count all animals. The maximum effective counting distance is considered to be less than 400 m and the best results are normally obtained when the aircraft is flown in an east/west direction.

* Possible restrictions concerning low-flying or general aircraft operations could apply to a particular area. It is advisable to consult the Directorate of Civil Aviation in this regard.

The animals counted during the census may be recorded on a map, thus providing a record of animal distribution and any other important information such as water distribution. Many people prefer to use tape recorders, although this could easily lead to the loss of important information if care is not taken to ensure that equipment operates effectively.

CROPPING METHODS

While meat products remain an important form of game utilization, every effort should be made to improve game culling methods. Regardless of which method is used, the culling of game should always meet the following requirements:

1. The animals should not be chased about and disturbed excessively.
2. Culling on hot days or during hot times of the day should be avoided wherever possible.
3. There is never any excuse for cruelty, and any method used should meet all humanitarian requirements.
4. Where necessary, the method should be sufficiently selective to allow for the removal of only male animals, for instance.
5. Damage to the venison, for example by bullet wounds and injuries, should be kept to a minimum.
6. The carcasses should be bled as soon and as thoroughly as possible.
7. The stomach and intestines should be removed as quickly and as hygienically as possible.
8. Carcasses should be kept cool and protected from flies during handling.
9. The total cost per carcass, in terms of facilities and services, should be kept to a minimum without compromising quality requirements.

Spotlight hunting: Hunting by spotlight at night continues to be popular, for example when culling impala in bushveld regions. While the animals are blinded by a sharp light, it is relatively easy, especially in open veld and with the correct rifle, to shoot only head shots.

Unfortunately, poor marksmen cause too many animals to escape with broken horns and shattered lower jaws, thus doomed to die cruelly from starvation.

The present high cost of fuel renders the spotlight hunting method uneconomical, and in very dense bushveld an improved solution is still being sought. Spotlight hunting is naturally not too successful on moonlit nights, either, and this interrupts the schedule at venison depots.

Smaller hunting camps: The shooting of game on large game farms should preferably be restricted to specific, smaller hunting camps. Mention was made in Chapter 10 of special capture corrals which can be used for capturing farm game. Such enclosures also yield the best results when culling excess game.

The culling process entails the following: Early in the hunting season game is lured into the smaller capture corrals and allowed to grow accustomed to an open hunting vehicle periodically driving past the animals. These enclosures cover approximately 20 hectares and provide sufficient shelter to prevent the animals from feeling trapped and constantly attempting to escape. Adequate grazing is reserved in these camps during the growing season, and a network of roads enables the farmer to reach almost every part of the capture or hunting camp. As soon as the animals have grown accustomed to the camp and the hunting vehicle, a cooling truck is brought in and arrangements finalized for the sale of the carcasses.

With the minimum of disturbance, the hunters eventually drive through the camp and, for example, impala rams are shot from the vehicle one after the other. When an animal goes down, the rest of the herd should be allowed to move away of their own accord, without being startled or chased, before anyone leaves the vehicle to retrieve the carcass. Incredible as it may sound, the animals become increasingly accustomed to the moving vehicle and the reports of the rifles, and they become tamer rather than wilder as a result of the continuous shooting. However, the animals are wilier than we sometimes think, and it has been observed that, when impala rams are being hunted selectively, for example, they begin gradually to avoid the hunting vehicle while the ewes and lambs graze on unperturbed. It is imperative that the people on the vehicle do not talk or make any noise, so that the animals do not begin to associate the moving vehicle and the sound of rifles with the presence of people or the death of their companions.

This method is particularly successful when different hunters conceal themselves near the corners of the camp, or at places where the animals usually seek shelter. To prevent accidents, these hunters shoot only in the opposite direction to that of the hunting camp. In their efforts to escape from the camp, the animals tend to move along the fences, from where they can then be hunted.

The shooting of game in large camps, especially during the day, will excessively bewilder the animals. If there is no other choice and only rams are to be shot, the rams in breeding herds should preferably be left alone. With the necessary knowledge of the behaviour of the different game species, the culling process can be adapted even further to yield the best results. For example, during the breeding season impala rams tend to move up and down along the camp fences during the late afternoons. These are usually bachelor males who can then easily be shot from roads alongside the fences, without unnecessary disturbance to the breeding herds.

Use of a helicopter: The successful use of a helicopter to cull game, particularly springbok and blesbok on the Highveld, is well established. It is not impossible for an experienced pilot and marksman to crop a group of 5 to 6 springbok at a rate of 2 to 4 minutes per animal, including shooting, hooking and delivery to a central point. This is the preferred method used by Kovisco for years, inter alia to hunt a total of approximately 240 000 springbok up to 1983, mostly for export purposes.

Using a helicopter to drive game into capture corrals and shooting the animals there has also been considered, but not yet satisfactorily tested in practice. Although large numbers of game can be shot in this manner at specific points, this method also holds obvious disadvantages. First, the erection and moving of capture corrals is an expensive and time-consuming process. The meat of animals who have been chased for long distances may also not be of a sufficiently high quality. Apart from the

THE BODY AND CARCASS WEIGHTS OF SOUTH AFRICAN GAME SPECIES
(Weights in kilograms as for adult animals)

Species	Body weight	Dressing percentage	Approx. slaughtered carcass weight
ANTELOPE			
Sable antelope	180 - 230	55±	99 - 127
Roan	227 - 272	55±	125 - 150
Gemsbok	180 - 240	55±	99 - 132
Eland	460 - 700	51	235 - 357
Kudu (Greater)	150 - 300	57	86 - 172
Bushbuck	24 - 54	55±	13 - 30
Nyala	55 - 127	55±	30 - 70
Springbok	30 - 48	51 - 58	16 - 26
Impala	39 - 80	58	23 - 46
Klipspringer	9 - 16	55±	5 - 9
Suni	4 - 6	55±	2 - 3
Steenbok	9 - 14	55±	5 - 8
Oribi	10 - 17	55±	6 - 9
Cape grysbok	10	55±	5,5
Sharpe's grysbok	7,5	55±	4,1
Common duiker	15 - 26	55±	8 - 14
Red duiker	11 - 14	55±	6 - 8
Blue duiker	4 - 5	55±	2 - 3
Mountain reedbuck	22 - 38	55±	12 - 21
Reedbuck	40 - 80	55±	22 - 44
Grey rhebok	18 - 25	55±	10 - 14
Tsessebe	120 - 150	55±	66 - 83
Blesbok	60 - 82	53	32 - 44
Bontebok	50 - 64	53	27 - 34
Red hartebeest	105 - 182	55±	58 - 100
Waterbuck	204 - 270	55±	112 - 149
Black wildebeest	90 - 160	55±	50 - 88
Blue wildebeest	180 - 270	58±	104 - 157
OTHER LARGE MAMMALS			
African elephant	up to 6569	55±	up to 3613
Black rhinoceros	up to 1000	55±	up to 550
White rhinoceros	1400 - 2300	55±	770 - 1265
Burchell's zebra	320	55±	176
Cape mountain zebra	204 - 260	55±	112 - 143
African buffalo	up to 800	50	up to 400
Giraffe	703 - 1395	55±	387 - 767
Bushpig	46 - 82	55±	25 - 45
Warthog	44 - 104	55±	24 - 57
Hippopotamus	971 - 1999	55±	534 - 1099

appearance of white spots and haemorrhages in the muscles, such meat also spoils quickly. Bruising can also contribute to further rejections of the meat and carcasses.

CARCASS DATA

As was mentioned earlier, the body mass of the same species sometimes differs from one region to another, and consequently the information supplied in the above table should serve merely as an approximate estimate of expected carcass data.

In the table, the average live masses of different game species have been multiplied by an average carcass yield of 55 per cent, to give an approximation of the expected dressed carcass mass of adult animals of both sexes. In the case of species of which the carcass yields and/or average carcass masses are known, these have been stated accordingly.

A frequent point of discussion is the amount of biltong that the carcass of a particular species will produce. The nutritional value and bacteria numbers found in biltong have also been the subject of interesting news articles and radio programmes.

Biltong contains approximately 3 to 4 times more protein than unprocessed raw meat. Approximately 3,5 kg of raw meat is required to make 1 kg of dried biltong. An impala with a total body mass of 45 kg has a carcass mass of about 26 kg — that is, the mass of the carcass without the head, limbs, skin and viscera. This comprises approximately 6,5 kg (25 per cent) bone and 19,5 kg (75 per cent) deboned meat. Although all the deboned meat is not suitable for biltong, such an impala will yield approximately 5 to 6 kg of biltong. A very large impala ram with a carcass mass of 45 kg will produce approximately 9 to 10 kg of biltong.

It is interesting to note that a large elephant bull will yield approximately 2 500 kg of deboned meat and a large buffalo approximately 140 to 170 kg. In the case of the elephant, only 45 per cent of the deboned meat is suitable for biltong production. The remainder consists of sinewy meat which is more suitable for canning.

Certain random surveys have shown that the biltong bought at certain butcheries contains more than 4 million bacteria per gram of biltong — it is therefore small wonder that the piece of biltong that you had hidden away so carefully disappeared! However, it may be comforting to know that, provided your biltong has not disappeared yet, these bacteria are generally not harmful. If you were to eat venison biltong produced at the Skukuza abbatoir in the Kruger National Park, you would have even less to fear. Here, staff of the National Parks Board and the Division of Veterinary Services have proved that venison can be handled and processed so hygienically that the end product, biltong, contains only a thousandth of the bacteria found in the biltong of the butcheries referred to.

UNIQUE QUALITIES OF VENISON

Research at the Veterinary Research Centre at Skukuza has shown that venison does not spoil easily. Impala carcasses hung in gauze-protected, well ventilated rooms in winter, without refrigeration, showed no signs of decomposition even after a week. Chemical and bacteriological tests carried out after 7 days also revealed no signs of decay. These important observations should be given serious consideration by the appropriate authorities when regulations and prescriptions are laid down regarding deadlines for the freezing or refrigeration of game carcasses. In the Kruger National Park, elephant and buffalo carcasses are often transported as far as 300 km, without refrigeration, and without becoming spoiled.

In addition to the exceptional ability of venison not to spoil, the biochemical composition and remarkable nutritional value of venison make it an excellent health food. The low fat and cholesterol content of venison are two of many properties that recommend it. Further research is needed, however, to determine the comparative nutritional value of the venison obtained from the different species.

Although hunting and farm holidays provides welcome additional income for a game farmer, the success of a game farming enterprise still depends largely on the capture, culling and marketing of surplus animals.

20. TROPHY HUNTING

PREPARATION OF TROPHIES FOR DISPATCH TO THE TAXIDERMIST*

Many an excellent trophy has been ruined because a hunted animal has been wrongly handled or because of the inadequate attention or incorrect treatment given to the animal's skins and horns during or shortly after the hunt.

- The use of good skinning knives by trained skinners should result in a minimum number of accidental cuts.
- Only good quality salt (preferably table salt) in ample quantities should be taken along and used.
- A sufficient number of sacks or cloths in which to transport the treated trophies, should be taken along as well.
- Individual trophies should be easily identifiable by marking them with aluminium or lead tags, preferably attached to the trophies with galvanized wire.

SPECIAL PRECAUTIONS

Particular techniques are described later, but, if you want an undamaged skin make sure that:

- the animal is skinned *as soon as possible* and preferably within an hour or two of being shot;
- if the carcass *has* to be moved before skinning, it is not dragged over stones or sharp objects, and that the skin is not damaged during loading, transport or offloading;
- special care be taken that the skin is not damaged during loading and offloading when the trophy is hauled over the tailgate or over the sharp sides or edges of the carrying vehicle. Lifting the carcass with tarpaulins or hessian and transporting it on these or on a thick layer of soft branches is advisable;
- the carcass is not exposed to the sun or high temperature, because this may enchance `hair slip'. Cover the animal with leafy branches during transport to provide shade, and skin the animal in a cool, shady place;
- the skin of certain species, such as eland, kudu, bushbuck, nyala, impala and gemsbok, which are more prone to damage, be given special attention during handling, transport and storage;
- all fat and pieces of meat be removed from the skin, as these contribute to putrefaction and skin damage. Be particularly sure that the parts below the mane of the zebra and of the ears are thoroughly cleaned of all flesh and fat;
- all dirt and blood be removed and the skin properly washed with clean water;
- the skins be drained of excess liquid by hanging them for a short while in a cool, shady place, before salting.

SALTING

It cannot be overemphasized that only clean, good quality salt, preferably table salt, be used.

- Rub the salt well on to and into all inner parts of the skin, fold the sides of the skin up to the middle and roll it, or simply fold the skin lengthwise to cover the inner, salted surfaces.
- As salt cannot penetrate effectively into the thick hides of elephant, rhino, hippo and other thick-skinned animals, the inner parts of such skins must be shaved more thinly.
- Stretching the skin, hair downwards, over a smooth tree stump or over a piece of wood in the form of a crescent, specially selected for this purpose, aids in the thinning process.
- Salt the thinned parts of the skin as the thinning process progresses.
- Make sure that the skin is carved thin enough for the salt to reach the hair roots so as to prevent decomposition and `hair slip'.
- If it is not possible to thin a skin, make incisions from the inside into the skin, parallel to each other and about 10 millimetres (1/3 inch) apart.
- The depth of these cuts must be about half the skin's thickness to ensure adequate salt penetration.
- When several skins have to be salted simultaneously select a level area (a cement floor in a cool room is preferable) and strew an even layer of salt on the floor, put the first skin, hair down, on the layer of salt, followed by the next skin, hair down, on the layer of salt, followed by the next skin, and keep stacking in this way, making sure that the salt is well worked on to and into the moist inner surface of each skin.
- Store the salted skins for about 24 hours in a cool place before opening them, shaking the loose salt off and hanging the skins in the shade to dry.
- During the hot and humid summer months, and particularly in tropical and subtropical regions, special precautions have to be taken. Try to dry all skins as quickly as possible to avoid fungal discolouration and bacterial putrefaction. Dry the skins during the day only and cover them with plastic or waterproof tarpaulins overnight.
- Never keep or transport a wet skin for any length of time in a plastic bag or a sealed container as this will ruin the trophy.
- Fold the skin, before it is completely dry, into the shape that it will finally be folded for dispatch. With the hairy side now facing upwards, fold the edges inwards to meet in the middle, with the hair facing inwards. Fold it in the required size,

---

* This section is largely based on a hunter's guide (booklet) produced and distributed by Nico van Rooyen Taxidermy, Post Box 217, Rosslyn, 0200.

unfold it again and allow to dry thoroughly in a cool place. Forming the skin folds before the skin is completely dry is important to prevent it from cracking when folding it when it is eventually completely dry.

- Most important — protect the skins, while drying, in a rat-free area and in a place where dogs and hyenas cannot get at them.

SHOULDER MOUNTS

Skin the animal as indicated in the accompanying sketch:

Cut the skin from behind the shoulder, forward along the upper neck to behind the horns (A). Pierce the skin on the back and cut it around the thorax (B). Then cut the skin of both forelegs below the elbow joints in a circular fashion (C).

Exceptions to cut (A):

- If the animal has a mane, cut (A) must be made directly next to and parallel to the mane.

- Rhino, hippo and pigs have cut (A) made *below* the chest and neck, instead of above.

In antelope, cut (A) is split behind the horns and continued in a V-shape to the base of each horn, from where it is continued around each horn (D) to neatly separate skin and horn at the junction.

Now proceed to remove the skin, without leaving much meat, connective tissue or fat on the skin, and without cutting into the skin.

- Start from the shoulder, where (A) and (B) meet, working down towards the lower neck and forelegs.

- Loosen the skin around the forelegs, without cutting into the skin. Cut the limbs at or above (C) and pull them out.

- With the skin detached from the thorax and neck, up to the bases of the ears, cut the ear cartilage off against the skull and leave it attached to the ears.

Now follows the most delicate and difficult part of the skinning process. With the following sketch as a guide, skin the head as follows:

- Expose the inner sides of the eyelids and cut through the mucous membrane where it deflects onto the eyeball (E).
- Gently remove the skin from the skull, from the horn base, downwards.
- When getting nearer the lips, with the skin now turned inside out, cut the lips loose as close to the gums as possible (F).
- With the nose cartilage attached to the skin, and without damaging the nostrils, cut the cartilage loose from the nose bone (G).
- With the scalp removed from the skull, remove all pieces of meat and loose fat from the skin.
- Place the scalp on a clean table for the finer dissection work that follows.
- Split the inner mucous membrane of the lips from the outer skin but do not cut it off or damage it.
- Do not cut too deeply into the lip skins of a carnivore as the root bases of the animal's whiskers may be cut off and result in the hair falling out.
- Remove excess fat, muscle and connective tissue from the lip skins.
- Cuts on the inside of the lip and between the rows of root bases of carnivores' whiskers, not so deep as to penetrate the skin, will aid in salt penetration and better skin preservation
- Next split the nose cartilage along the mid-plane and cut the two halves loose from the skin up to the nostrils.
- Remove excess muscle, connective tissues and fat from the nasal skin and nostrils.

The ears are treated in the following way:

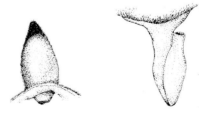

- Cut away all meat and connective tissue between the skin and cartilage, from the base of the ear up to where only the outer skin and cartilage are attached.
- Then separate the skin and cartilage by squeezing your finger, a blunt screwdriver or the handle of a spoon in betweeen, or, by cautious dissection, up to the tip of the ear.

- With the skin and cartilage separated to the tip and to the edges of the ear, push the cartilage, still attached to the skin, inwards to have the ear inside out and ready for washing and salting.
- Remove all blood and dirt by thorough washing, making sure that no blood remains in the hair.
- Drip-dry and salt well (see above). Make sure that all parts, particularly the ears, nose and lips are well salted.

FULL MOUNTS

- Position the animal firmly on its back and make the main incisions straight from the end of the breastbone (all animals, excluding the carnivores) backwards along the lowest part of the abdomen to the tip of the tail (H).
- In carnivores this incision extends from the chin (not cutting through the lower lip) to the tip of the tail.
- Cut along the inner parts of the limbs, from the midline (below) to the elbow and hock-joints, gradually declining to the back surface of the legs and going down in straight lines to the animal's feet. (I), (J).
- In antelope make incision (A/D) as for shoulder mount.
- Remove the skin from the carcass.

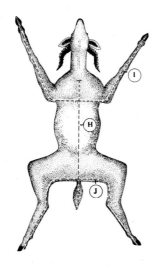

- The limbs must be removed up to the last toe-bone leaving the *empty* hoofs, toes or claws attached to the skin.
- For full mounts of small animals, up to the size of a jackal, it is not necessary to make incisions along the legs. After the longitudinal incision (H) has been made the legs are cut loose from the body and skinned while turned inside out.
- Make sure that the entire skin is preserved, no pieces cut off and thrown away and with all incisions made in such a way that the minimum *scars* will show once the mount has been completed.
- Keep one fore- and one hindleg bone, as well as the pelvis bone. Remove all meat and tendons, and don't boil it, but salt it well.
- Keep, store and pack skin and parts of skeleton separate to avoid oil from the marrow damaging the skin.
- Measurements of different parts of the head, neck, carcass and limbs could be useful and you are recommended to file these with your trophy.

RUG MOUNTS

If you wish to mount a carnivore's skin with the head intact, remove the body skin, as described (see `full mount') and base the skinning of the head on the description for the preparation of a 'shoulder mount' with the following modifications:
- The main incision (A/H), in this instance, must be made from the chin (not cutting through the lower lip) along the lower part of the body to the tip of the tail.
- Clean and detach the skull with the skin.

FEET AS SOUVENIRS

- The feet of zebra, buffalo and of antelope must be cut open at the back, down to the base of the hooves.
- In the case of elephant, rhino and hippo the feet can be cleaned out without cutting down at the back. However, much time can be saved and the job done much easier if the incisions are made.
- Remove *all* bones, including those in the hooves and clean out all the connective tissue and fat.
- Salt, fold and dry in the shade. Do not try to preserve the natural shape of the skin as this will be taken care of by the taxidermist.

STORAGE OF SKINS

- Protect your trophies against dogs, hyenas, rats and skin beetles. Keeping all skins in a lockable, rat- and insect- proof storeroom or storage space is advisable.
- Dried skins should not be allowed to get wet.
- Keep trophies away from fuel containers and do not spill fuel, or other chemicals that can ruin a trophy, over the skins.
- Insecticides, such as 'Karbadust', 'Dazzel' (Agricura) or 'Reskol' or 'Sevkol' (Coopers) can be used to treat dried skins for protection against harmful insects.

TREATMENT OF SKULLS

Most taxidermists require the skull with the lower jaw, while others don't expect clients to provide the jawbones. As a rule the horns should not be cut off, but kept intact on the skull as this will ease the taxidermist's task. The best advice is to consult your taxidermist before setting off on safari, and find out what *he* needs to make a masterpiece of *your* trophy. Handle the skull in the following way:
- Remove the skull from the neck by cutting it loose at the first joint.
- Cut and shave off *all* muscle and connective tissue and remove the lower jaw.
- Remove all brain material through the opening at the base of the skull. This is best done by stirring and scooping with a piece of wire or a special spoon or tool, and by rinsing with water.
- Once properly cleaned, fill the brain cavity, nose and sinus cavities with salt and put the well salted skull away, separately from the skin.
- Please note that boiling is not recommended as it will damage the skull and horns if not done correctly.
- Mark and number tag the skull and other bones and keep good records to avoid confusion.

DISPATCHING IT TO THE TAXIDERMIST OR TANNER

Once the well-treated bones and skins are properly dried, they can be packed for dispatch. If the material orginated from an endemic stock disease area (e.g. foot-and-mouth disease control area) or if the trophies are to be sent to another country, make sure that all veterinary control measures have been complied with. This may entail the treatment of bones and horns with formalin, and of hides and skins with chemicals such as sodium carbonate ('washing soda') and/or sodium fluorosilicate. The local state veterinarian or stock inspector will provide you with the required information. Not complying with veterinary regulations is a serious offence and can lead to a heavy fine and the trophies being confiscated and destroyed.

Here are some general hints regarding packing and dispatch:

● Long horns, particularly of trophies with a wide spread, and which are difficut to fit into a small crate, can be temporarily removed from the skull to facilitate packing and transport.
● Immerse the entire horn in water for one to two days and then pull or 'screw' the horn from the inner bony core.

● The bony core can be sawn off about 30 centimetres (12 inches) from the skull to reduce the parcel size.
● As fresh horns are inclined to shrink, to the extent that it may later not fit over the bony core, it is advisable to push it back over the sawn off core and to let it dry with the core before finally removing it for packing and dispatch.
● Make sure that all marking and numbering tags are properly fixed.
● If skins only are to be dispatched, sew them up tightly in a hessian sack, mark the parcel well and send it off.
● If skulls, horns and bones also have to be sent away, sew up every item separately in hessian, pack these all in straw and dispatch in a sturdy wooden crate.
● If straw is not available, pack the individual items carefully to avoid chafing.
● Make sure that there are no openings in the crate through which horns, bones or small pieces of skin can be lost.
● Take a pride in your work. Don't let a successful safari end in frustration and ill feeling because badly treated, wrongly packed or inadequately addressed parcels have not reached the taxidermist or tanner in the condition that you or your client would have wanted them to.

Photograph: Bennie Lategan

SAFARI CLUB INTERNATIONAL

MEASURING METHODS

The Safari Club system of measurement has been designed as a simple, universal system for scoring all the game trophies of the world. It is easy to use, yet fully reflects the quality of the trophy. It differs from the older systems in that it does not require a sixty day 'drying out' period before a trophy can be measured.

The objective is to establish and preserve a record of outstanding trophies. Obviously, the sooner measurements are taken the more true-to-life and meaningful they will be.

S.C.I. gives credit for all of the horn growth that the animal has produced. Every point is counted and is also measured. There is no penalty for lack of summetry.

The system is a maximum-type system where the intent is to give the trophy the highest possible score. Basal circumferences are usually taken at the hairline — the largest place — rather than at a right angle. Spiral horns are measured around the spiral instead of up the front or side. Buffalo and wildebeest horns are measured around the outer curve instead of by the shorter front curve.

Measurements are recorded in inches. This is the current United States system of measurement and the majority of S.C.I. members and record book buyers are Americans.

Safari Club uses the honour system for accepting entries. No witnesses, affidavits or notarized signatures are required. Unless there is evidence to the contrary, it is assumed that fellow members are honest sportsmen and women who care about the integrity of the Safari Club Record Book and whose entries are truthful.

The following illustrations show the measurements to be taken for the different species

S.C.I. MEASURING METHODS

A. Measure the length of the horns around the spiral, following the top of the spiral ridge from the lowest point in front to the tip, or to a point in line with the tip if the tip is broken or blunted. If the spiral ridge flattens out and disappears, follow the horn surface directly to the tip.
B. Measure the circumference of the horns at the base. Follow the edge of the base as closely as possible, excluding malformations. Keep the tape above any scallops. Form a continuous loop with a tight tape, maintaining the same angle as the edge of the base makes with the axis of the horn. This does not need to be at a right angle to the axis of the horn.
C. Total all scores. Record fractions in 1/8ths.

Spiral horned antelope:
Kudu
Eland
Nyala
Bushbuck
Sitatunga

A. Measure the length of the horns on the front surface from a point in line with the lowest edge of the base to the tip, or to a point in line with the tip if the tip is broken or blunted. Do not push tape into indentations.
B. Measure the circumference of the horns at the base. Follow the edge of the base as closely as possible, excluding malformations. Keep the tape above any scallops. Form a continuous loop with a tight tape, maintaining the same angle as the edge of the base makes with the axis of the horn. This does not need to be at a right angle to the axis of the horn.
C. Total all scores. Record fractions in 1/8ths.

Other Southern African antelope

A. Measure the length of the horns across the forehead with a single measurement. Begin at one horn tip, follow the outside curve of the horn to the lowest part of the horn, incline gradually to the front corner of the boss, bridge the forehead and repeat on the other horn continually, except when bridging the forehead.
B. Measure the circumference of the horns at the largest part of the boss. Form a continuous loop with a tight tape. This does not need to be at a right angle to the axis of the horn.
C. Total all scores. Record fractions in 1/8ths.

Blue wildebeest

A. Measure the length of the horns across the boss crown with a single measurement. Begin at one horn tip, follow the outside curve to the lowest part of the curve, incline gradually to the back curve, which is followed to the crown of the boss. Then bridge the boss gap from crown to crown with a tight tape and repeat on the other horn to its tip.

B. Measure the bosses at the widest part, parallel to the centre line of the boss gap. Begin where the horn meets the skull in front, go over the top of the boss, and end where the horn meets the skull in back. Keep the tape tight, and do not push the tape into depressions. Do not measure the circumference of the boss.

C. Total all scores. Record fractions in 1/8ths.

Black wildebeest

A. Measure the length of the horns across the forehead with a single measurement. Begin at one horn tip, follow the outside curve of the horn to the lowest part of the horn, incline gradually to the front corner of the boss, bridge the forehead, and repeat on the other horn to its tip. Keep the tape in contact with the horn continually, except when bridging the forehead.

B. Measure the bosses at the widest part at a right angle to the long axis of each horn. Begin where the horn meets the skull in front, go over the top of the boss, and end where the horn meets the skull in back. Keep the tape tight, and do not push the tape into depressions. Do not measure the circumference of the boss.

C. Total all scores. Record fractions in 1/8ths.

Buffalo

A. Measure the length of the tusks (hippopotamus and bushpig = lower tusks; warthog = upper tusks) on the outer curve from a point in line with the lowest edge of the base to the tip, or to a point in line with the tip if the tip is broken or broomed.

B. Measure the circumference of the tusks at the largest place at a right angle to the axis of the tusk.

C. Total all scores. Record fractions in 1/8ths.

Hippopotamus
Bushpig
Warthog

A. Measure the length of the horns on the front surface from the lowest point in front to the tip, or to a point in line with the tip if the tip is broken or blunted.

B. Measure the circumference of the horns at the base. Follow the edge of the base as close to the head as possible. This does not need to be at a right angle to the axis of the horn.

C. Total all scores. Record fractions in 1/8ths.

Rhinoceros

A. Weigh each tusk to the nearest ½ pound. Those weights falling halfway or more between ½ pounds will be recorded at the next higher ½ pound. Weights falling less than halfway between ½ pounds revert to the next lower ½ pound.
B. Total all scores.
Note: The length and circumference of the tusks may be given as supplementary data, but will not count in the score.

Elephant

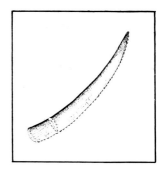

A. Measure the length of the skull in line with the long axis. The lower jaw may be in place, and may include normal teeth.
B. Measure the width of the skull at a right angle to the long axis.
C. Total all scores. Record fractions in $^1/_{16}$ths.
Note: Measurements should be taken with calipers; however, carpenter squares are permitted. Body measurements will not be accepted.
Recording Measurements: All skull measurements are to be recorded in sixteenths of an inch. If a measurement falls halfway or more between sixteenth marks, use the next higher sixteenth. If the measurement is less than halfway between sixteenth marks, revert to the next lower sixteenth.

Carnivores

A. Measure the length of the crocodile across the back from the tip of the nose to the tip of the tail. Follow the centre of the backbone, keeping the tape in contact with the crocodile wherever possible.
B. The total score is the length to the nearest inch.

Crocodile

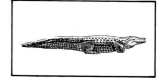

Photograph: Bennie Lategan

THE ROWLAND WARD RECORD SYSTEM

MEASURING METHODS

1. All measurements must be taken with a steel tape or official steel cable approved by Rowland Ward Publications.

2. Field measurements of lengths of crocodiles and of the body size of elephants should be taken at the time and place of the kill and should be attested to by both the professional hunter and the sportsman. For all other measurements a minimum period of 60 days must elapse between the time the trophy is bagged and when the trophy is measured (or weighed), by which time the natural shrinkage of horns and tusks is more or less complete.

3. All measurements of horns must be taken to the nearest $1/8$ inch; if a measurement form for this type trophy is received filled out in sixteenths, the sixteenths will be cut back to the next lower eighth.

   All measurements for skulls will be taken to the nearest $1/16$ inch.

   All measurements for tusk length and body size of elephants will be taken to the nearest $1/4$ inch.

   When measuring in eighths, a measurement falling halfway between eighths, or higher will be recorded at the next higher eighth. Measurements falling less than the halfway mark will be recorded at the lower eighth. Measurements taken in sixteenths or in quarter-inches will be similarly interpolated.

   Weights of elephant tusks will be taken to the nearest pound. For elephant tusks, weights falling at or above the half-pound mark will be recorded at the next higher pound, and weights falling below the half-pound mark will be recorded at the lower pound.

4. Measurements taken in metric will be accepted, and for publication the right is reserved to publish in inches or in centimetres. Any conversion of measurements from centimetres in inches, or vice versa, will be done by the publisher in accordance with a standard conversion table.

5. Many official measurers for the Rowland Ward system are available throughout the world to measure trophies. It is the responsibility of the trophy owner to transport the trophy to the measurer. There is no charge for measuring a trophy and any entry fee charged is a publication charge.

6. A skull which is damaged (by gunshot or blow) will not be accepted for entry unless the skull is measured by an official measurer, and then only when a note is added to the entry form stating that the measurer is satisfied that the damage did not increase any dimension.

7. A horn trophy with a split skull will not be accepted for entry unless the trophy is measured by an official measurer, and then only when a note is added to the entry form stating that the measurer is satisfied that splitting the skull did not increase any dimension.

8. The policy of Rowland Ward is not to assess against a trophy a numerical penalty because of any non-symmetry of the two horns. The basis of this policy is to give credit to the trophy for all horn material grown by the animal, even though it is not distributed symmetrically.

   The inherent hazard in such a policy is that if applied literally and unthinkingly it could result in a freak head becoming number one in the record book in its class. Rowland Ward's policy is that freak heads may be interesting but do not represent excellence in trophy quality.

   In such cases it is the responsibility of the official measurer to record the pertinent data on the entry form and to provide photos illustrating the problem. It is the responsibility of the editor to rule on the acceptance of this trophy, his alternatives being: Rule that the entry is a freak head and reject it as unsuitable for the record book; List the trophy as the new number one head with an explanatory note; List the trophy at the bottom of the list of heads, with an explanatory note.

   In summary, for all abnormal, malformed, appreciably unbalanced or freakish trophies, the official measurer must refer the trophy to the editor for a decision, with appropriate guiding data and photographs.

9. Acceptance by the publisher of an entry form for publication carries no guarantee of an exact date of publication.

10. The *minimum dimensions* listed herein for acceptance of trophies for entry may be modified at any time at the discretion of the publisher.

11. Every trophy entry form must show the exact locality where the trophy was bagged. Local place names are desirable, but are not sufficient. The name of the country must always be given, and the place where the trophy was taken must be tied in with a geographical place name readily identifiable on a standard map of the country concerned. It is sufficient to record simply the location based on the compass quadrant system, viz S.W. Zimbabwe.

12. All entries must be on a standard Rowland Ward entry form, or a reproduction thereof, except field measurements of elephant body size and crocodile lengths, which may be on regular stationery.

13. An official measurer may not score a trophy which he has bagged if it falls within the top ten of that species in the current edition of the record book.

1. Measure the length of the longer horn around the spiral, keeping the tape on top of the spiral ridge, starting at the lowest point in the front of the base and proceeding to the tip. In some cases the spiral ridge may fade out and become indistinct near the tip of the horn. Follow the spiral as long as the spiral form can be distinguished and, when the spiral ridge completely disappears, proceed in a straight line to the horn tip (A-B).
2. Measure the circumference of the base of the longer horn. The measurement must be a true circumference and not elliptical (C).
3. Measure the spread, tip to tip (D-B).
4. Rank on the basis of measurement No. 1 (above).

Spiral horned antelope:
Kudu
Eland
Nyala
Bushbuck
Sitatunga

1. Measure the length of the longer horn on the front surface of the horn from the lowest edge of the base to the tip (A-B).
2. Measure the circumference of the base of the longer horn, at right angles to the axis of the horn. The measurement must be a true circumference and not elliptical (C).
3. Measure the spread, tip to tip (D-B).
4. Rank on the basis of measurement No. 1 (above).

Other Southern African antelope

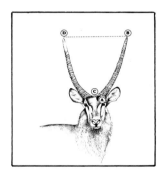

1. Measure greatest width outside at right angles to the axis of the skull and in a straight line (X-Y).
2. Measure greatest width inside at widest point between insides of both horns (S-T).
3. Measure the length of the longer horn on outside curve, starting at the inside corner of the horn boss at narrowest part of horn gap and measuring along the front edge, inclining to the outside surface of the horn and continue to the tip (A-B), see sketch.
4. Measure the spread, tip to tip (C-B)
5. Measure the width of the wider boss at its widest point, taking the measurement parallel to the centre line of the boss gap, beginning where the horn meets the skull in front and going over the top of the boss to end where the horn meets the skull in the back (G-H). See sketch. Keep the tape in contact with the boss.
6. Rank on the basis of measurement No. 1 (above).

Blue wildebeest

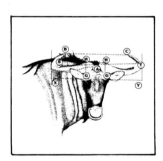

1. Measure the length of the longer horn on outside curve, starting at the front bottom corner of the horn boss and measure along the front edge, inclining to the outside surface of the horn and continue to the tip (A-B). See sketch.
2. Measure the width of the wider boss at its widest point, taking the measurement parallel to the centre line of the boss gap, beginning where the horn meets the skull in front and going over the top of the boss to end where the horn meets the skull in the back (G-H) (see sketch). Keep the tape in contact with the boss.
3. Measure the spread, tip to tip (C-B).
4. Rank on the basis of measurement No. 1 (see above).

Black wildebeest

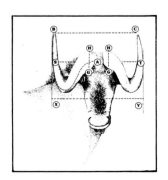

1. Measure greatest width outside at right angles to the axis of the skull and in a straight line (X-Y).
2. Measure greatest width inside at widest point between insides of both horns (S-T).
3. Measure length of longer horn on outside curve, starting at the front bottom corner of the boss and measuring along the front edge, inclining to the outside surface of the horn and continue to the tip (A-B).
4. Measure the spread, tip to tip (D-B).
5. Measure the width of the wider boss at its widest point, beginning where the horn meets the skull in front and going over the top of the boss to end where the horn meets the skull in the back (G-H). The line of measurement is to be parallel to the axis of the skull.
6. Rank on the *sum* of measurement. Nos. 1, 3 and 5.

Buffalo

1. Measure the length on the outer curve of the longest lower tusk, from the lowest edge of the base to the tip.
2. Measure for the longest lower tusk on the outer curve the length of the tusk that protrudes from the gum. This measurement for the record book is taken 60 days or more after the trophy is bagged, at which time the gum line may not be visible, so while this measurement is desired it is not required. This measurement will be acceptable if taken as a field measurement.
3. Rank on the basis of measurement No. 1 (above).

Hippopotamus
Bushpig

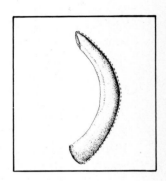

1. Measure the length of the outer curve of the longest upper tusk, from the lowest edge of the base to the tip.
2. Measure for the longest upper tusk on the outer curve the length of the tusk that protrudes from the gum. This measurement for the record book is taken 60 days or more after the trophy is bagged, at which time the gum line may not be visible, so while this measurement is desired it is not required. This measurement will be acceptable if taken as a field measurement.
3. Rank on the basis of measurement No. 1 (above).

Warthog

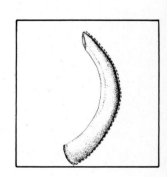

1. Measure the length on the front curve of each horn (A-B).
2. Measure the circumference of the base of each horn (C). Keep as close to the head as possible, which may result in an elliptical measurement.
3. Rank on the basis of the *sum* of the four measurements taken under Nos 1 and 2.

Rhinoceros

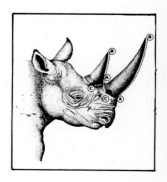

1. Weigh each tusk to the nearest pound. Weights falling at or above the half-pound mark will be recorded at the next higher pound, and weights falling below the half-pound mark will be recorded at the lower pound. Note that the weight of each tusk is to be recorded.
2. Record also the length on outside curve of each tusk and the greatest circumference of each tusk, both measured to the nearest quarter-inch.
3. Rank on the basis of the weight of the heavier tusk.

Elephant (Tusks)

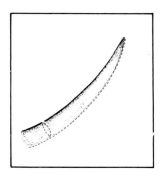

1. Measure the length of the skull in line with the long axis and as shown in the illustration (A-B).
2. Measure the width of the skull over zygomatic arches (Z-Y).
3. Rank on the basis of the *sum* of measurements Nos. 1 and 2 (above).

Carnivores

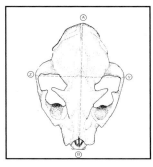

Crocodile

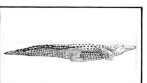

This is a field measurement, taken before skinning, of the total body length including lenth of tail. Pull the nose and tail to get them into a straight line. Then drive in pegs at the end of the nose and tail. Take the measurements between pegs and not by following the line of the body. Measurements should be taken to the nearest quarter inch. This measurement should be taken by the professional hunter, certified by him and by the owner whose trophy has been measured, and the details, giving also date, locality, etc., sent to Rowland Ward Publications. It should be noted that the Publishers will accept measurements of 'full mount' taxidermied specimens using the above system as it has been established that there is very little longitudinal stretching of the skin involved in taxidermied specimens. Lengths of crocodile skins either raw, curred or tanned will not be accepted.

TROPHY HUNTING AND THE LAW

In Southern Africa hunting is regulated by various conservation authorities in the different countries and provinces. The import and export of animal trophies and products are, furthermore, controlled by the respective veterinary authorities. Depending on the presence or absence of foot-and-mouth disease and other important stock diseases, more or less strict veterinary restrictions are applicable. International control to safeguard rare and endangered species may also affect your planning.

CONTROL OF THE TROPHY HUNTING INDUSTRY IN SOUTH AFRICA — A SAFEGUARD FOR OVERSEAS CLIENTS*

In 1981 the four Provincial Nature Conservation Departments (Cape, Natal, Orange Free State and Transvaal) in South Africa introduced legislation to control the hunting, outfitting and professional hunting industries in their provinces.

The object of the legislation was to provide protection for the overseas client by setting a standard of expertise that would be obligatory before a hunting outfitter or professional hunter would be licensed to operate, and to provide for the maintenance of these standards once a licence had been granted.

The standard of expertise of service provided by the hunting outfitter or professional hunter is the same throughout the four Provinces (and in Namibia).

The legal requirements to be met before a hunting outfitter or professional hunter can obtain a licence in South Africa are:

● Candidates must pass two written examinations. The first is to test their general knowledge of game animals, their habits, social behaviour, breeding cycles; the preparation and care of trophies; legal requirements for exporting trophies; trophy

* Contribution by Mr. J.V. Ludbrook, Conservator (Sport Hunting) of the Natal Parks Board, on behalf of the Inter-Provincial Co-ordinating Committee on Professional Hunting for South Africa.

requirements for entering in record books (Safari Club International and Rowland Ward)
- The second written examination requires an intimate knowledge of all the laws pertaining to hunting in each province.

When a candidate has successfully completed the two written examinations he has then to pass a practical test. Provincial nature conservation officers test the candidate in the bush on a variety of aspects, e.g. identification of animal spoor, ability to track, evaluation of horn lengths, skinning, shooting, bush knowledge, first aid, animal behaviour, hunting ability, firearms, preparation and care of trophies.

Having passed the practical examination the 'professional' is then issued a licence to operate, as he has attained the standards set by the nature conservation authorities. A candidate wishing to operate as a hunting outfitter, besides passing these examinations, also must have the facilities he offers to clients inspected. The hunting camp, trophy preparation facilities, vehicles and staff are required to conform to set standards.

Finally, the hunting outfitter has to submit his publicity material to the nature conservation officials before distribution as a check against possibly misleading advertising.

Thereafter, licensing follow-up checks and inspections are carried out by officials on a regular basis.

A further safeguard for the client is the legal requirement that the hunting outfitter enter into a written agreement with the client prior to the hunt covering, among other things, species and sex of game offered and fees charged, fees for services provided, and duration of hunt and daily fees. The enactment of enforcement of legislation on professional hunting has led to a raising of standards in this field. The effect of the legislation has been twofold. It is geared primarily to protect the client from any possible malpractice by the hunting outfitter or professional hunter.

Should a client feel that he has been the subject of unethical practice during a hunt in South Africa, he should contact the nature conservation authorities of the province in which he hunted and request that his complaint be investigated.

THE TRANSPORTATION AND EXPORT OF HUNTING TROPHIES FROM SOUTH AFRICA — VETERINARY CONTROL*

To facilitate the export of hunting trophies obtained in South Africa, prospective hunters should be aware of the fact that it is an internationally accepted procedure that:
- the importing country has the right to determine whether or not it will allow the importation of trophies, and
- if the importation of trophies is allowed, under what conditions it will be allowed, and the certification required.

A prospective hunter should therefore, prior to his departure from his home country, approach the veterinary authorities of his own country and ask for an import permit for the trophies he hopes to obtain. Should the veterinary authorities of the importing country indicate that an import permit is not required in respect of trophies, the hunter should then ask the authorities to give him a note to that effect in writing.

Should veterinary certification in respect of the importation of trophies be required, the hunter should ask the authorities to supply him with these requirements in writing in the form of an import permit.

When the hunter is ready to export his trophies to his home country, he should approach the State Veterinarian of the area where the hunting has taken place and show him the import permit and the veterinary health requirements. If there is compliance with the health requirements, the State Veterinarian will then issue a veterinary health certificate to that effect in respect of the trophies.

If the hunter/exporter is not sure which State Veterinarian to approach, he can contact the Regional Director of Veterinary Services of the region in which the hunting has taken place, who will then inform him of the telephone number/address of the State Veterinarian concerned.

As control measures are subject to change from time to time, depending on the disease situation in any particular region, it is suggested that the Regional Director of Veterinary Services be contacted shortly before hunting arrangements are finalized.

At the time of writing the only movement restrictions on game products in South Africa where those applicable in the foot-and-mouth disease and African swine fever controlled areas. These areas are situated on the northern borders of the country and next to the Kruger National Park. Unfortunately for the game hunter this is the most popular hunting area in the Republic. In the rest of the country game products are allowed to move freely and without a permit.

CONTROL MEASURES

FOOT-AND-MOUTH DISEASE CONTROLLED AREA

The controlled area is shown on the accompanying map.

In this area the control measures are only applicable to the products of cloven-hoofed game and a veterinary movement permit, obtainable from a State Veterinarian, is required for any movement of these products into, out of, or within the controlled area. The permit must accompany every movement and is valid for one movement only.

For control purposes the area is divided into four zones.

The Kruger National Park — an endemic foot-and-mouth disease area. No cloven-hoofed game products are allowed to be moved out of this zone except those which are processed and treated by the Parks Board at their Skukuza abattoir.

The red-line area — a zone of approximately 15 km (10 miles) wide, situated outside and along the Western and Southern borders of the Kruger National Park and the Mozambique border between Komatipoort and the Swaziland border.

Carcasses or meat from any cloven-hoofed animals may not be moved out of this zone. Biltong may be moved to any destination provided it is completely dry and prepared with vinegar.

Skins, hides and trophies of cloven-hoofed animals may be moved to any destination after they have been treated in one of the following ways.
Skins and hides:

---

* Contribution by Dr. G.C. Dent and Dr. J. Krige of the Directorate of Veterinary Services of the Department of Agriculture of South Africa.

Skins and hides:

Treated with salt and 5 per cent washing soda and stored for one month under the supervision of a State Veterinarian;

Immersed and kept in a 1:2 500 sodium silico-fluoride saturated salt solution for 24 to 48 hours (depending on the thickness of the skin), under the supervision of a State Veterinarian;

Salted and dried and stored for a period of three months under the supervision of a State Veterinarian.

Trophies:

Skulls and skeletons — boiled and dried;

Masks — treated as for skins and hides;

Horns — immersed and kept in 5 per cent formalin or 5 per cent washing soda for 24 hours.

The secondary area — a zone of 10 to 20 km (6 to 12 miles) wide, situated to the west of the red-line area. Game products may be moved from this area without any prior treatment provided that in the case of game carcasses they are clean, dressed and without feet, head and entrails.

Remainder of the controlled area — the rest of the controlled area. Game products may be moved freely provided they are accompanied by a veterinary movement permit.

AFRICAN SWINE FEVER CONTROLLED AREA

The controlled area is shown on the accompanying map.

Control measures are applicable to any products of bushpig, warthog and domestic pigs. A veterinary movement permit, as for foot-and-mouth disease, must accompany every movement into, out of, and within the area.

The carcasses and meat of bushpig, warthog and domestic pigs may be moved within the area but may not be taken out of it.

The skins and trophies of these animals can be moved to any destination provided they are treated as follows:

Skins:

All skins must be dipped for at least 60 seconds in a dipping mixture that is known to be effective against the hut tampan, *Ornithodoros moubata,* directly after slaughter. Skins originating from a foot-and-mouth disease controlled area should also be treated as in the paragraph, relating to skins and hides.

Trophies:

Skulls and skeletons — must be treated as indicated above.

Masks — must be treated as indicated in the previous paragraph on skins.

Teeth — must be treated in 5 per cent formalin or 5 per cent washing soda for five minutes.

Veterinary movement permits are obtainable from State Veterinarians or from Regional Directors of the Directorate of Veterinary Services.

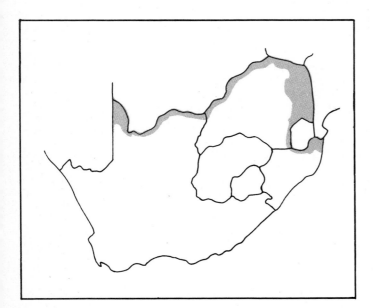

Foot-and-mouth disease controlled area

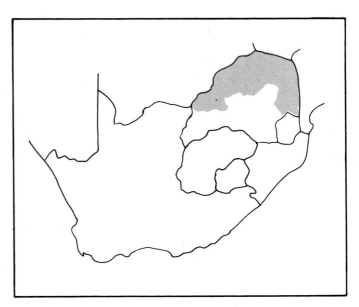

African swine fever controlled area

RIFLE CALIBRES RECOMMENDED FOR HUNTING SOUTHERN AFRICAN GAME SPECIES

It should be noted that the hunting of all the species mentioned is not necessarily recommended but merely that the calibres are recommended (+) or not recommended (—) in relation to the species to be shot.

SPECIES	BODY WEIGHT (KG)	22 Rimfire highspeed	222 Hornet	222 Rem.	223 Rem.	224 Wby. Mag.	22-250 Rem.	220 Swift	243 Win.	240 Wby. Mag.	244 H&H Mag.	250-3000 Sav.	257 Roberts	25-06 Rem.	257 Wby. Mag.	264 Win. Mag.	6,5 X 68 S	270 Win.	270 Wby. Mag.	7 X 57	280 Rem.	284 Win.
Cape fox	2 - 4	–	+	+	+	+	+	+	+	+	+	+	+	+	+	+	+	+	+	+	+	+
Bat-eared fox	3 - 5	–	+	+	+	+	+	+	+	+	+	+	+	+	+	+	+	+	+	+	+	+
Blue duiker	4 - 5	–	+	+	+	+	+	+	+	+	+	+	+	+	+	+	+	+	+	+	+	+
Suni	4 - 6	–	+	+	+	+	+	+	+	+	+	+	+	+	+	+	+	+	+	+	+	+
Sharpe's grysbok	6 - 9	–	+	+	+	+	+	+	+	+	+	+	+	+	+	+	+	+	+	+	+	+
Aardwolf	8 - 10	–	+	+	+	+	+	+	+	+	+	+	+	+	+	+	+	+	+	+	+	+
Black-backed jackal	5 - 10	–	+	+	+	+	+	+	+	+	+	+	+	+	+	+	+	+	+	+	+	+
Side-striped jackal	7 - 12	–	+	+	+	+	+	+	+	+	+	+	+	+	+	+	+	+	+	+	+	+
African civet	9 - 13	–	+	+	+	+	+	+	+	+	+	+	+	+	+	+	+	+	+	+	+	+
Serval	8 - 14	–	+	+	+	+	+	+	+	+	+	+	+	+	+	+	+	+	+	+	+	+
Caracal	8 - 20	–	+	+	+	+	+	+	+	+	+	+	+	+	+	+	+	+	+	+	+	+
Cape grysbok	9 - 11	–	+	+	+	+	+	+	+	+	+	+	+	+	+	+	+	+	+	+	+	+
Steenbok	9 - 14	–	+	+	+	+	+	+	+	+	+	+	+	+	+	+	+	+	+	+	+	+
Red duiker	11 - 14	–	+	+	+	+	+	+	+	+	+	+	+	+	+	+	+	+	+	+	+	+
Klipspringer	9 - 16	–	+	+	+	+	+	+	+	+	+	+	+	+	+	+	+	+	+	+	+	+
Oribi	10 - 17	–	+	+	+	+	+	+	+	+	+	+	+	+	+	+	+	+	+	+	+	+
Common duiker	15 - 26	–	+	+	+	+	+	+	+	+	+	+	+	+	+	+	+	+	+	+	+	+
Grey rhebok	18 - 25	–	–	+	+	+	+	+	+	+	+	+	+	+	+	+	+	+	+	+	+	+
Wild dog	26 - 28	–	–	+	+	+	+	+	+	+	+	+	+	+	+	+	+	+	+	+	+	+
Mountain reedbuck	22 - 38	–	–	+	+	+	+	+	+	+	+	+	+	+	+	+	+	+	+	+	+	+
Chacma baboon	14 - 44	–	–	+	+	+	+	+	+	+	+	+	+	+	+	+	+	+	+	+	+	+
Springbok	30 - 48	–	–	+	+	+	+	+	+	+	+	+	+	+	+	+	+	+	+	+	+	+
Bushbuck	24 - 54	–	–	+	+	+	+	+	+	+	+	+	+	+	+	+	+	+	+	+	+	+
Brown hyena	42 - 47	–	–	–	+	+	+	+	+	+	+	+	+	+	+	+	+	+	+	+	+	+
Cheetah	36 - 60	–	–	–	–	+	+	+	+	+	+	+	+	+	+	+	+	+	+	+	+	+
Leopard	30 - 71	–	–	–	–	+	+	+	+	+	+	+	+	+	+	+	–	+	+	+	+	+
Antbear	42 - 65	–	+	+	+	+	+	+	+	+	+	+	+	+	+	+	+	+	+	+	+	+
Impala	39 - 80	–	–	–	–	+	+	+	+	+	+	+	+	+	+	+	+	+	+	+	+	+
Reedbuck	40 - 80	–	–	–	+	+	+	+	+	+	+	+	+	+	+	+	+	+	+	+	+	+
Spotted hyena	49 - 80	–	–	–	–	+	+	+	+	+	+	+	+	+	+	+	+	+	+	+	+	+
Bontebok	50 - 64	–	–	–	–	–	–	–	+	+	+	+	+	+	+	+	+	+	+	+	+	+
Blesbok	60 - 82	–	–	–	–	–	–	–	+	+	+	+	+	+	+	+	+	+	+	+	+	+
Bushpig	46 - 82	–	–	–	–	–	–	–	–	+	+	+	+	+	+	+	+	+	+	+	+	+
Warthog	44 - 104	–	–	–	–	–	–	–	+	+	+	+	+	+	+	+	+	+	+	+	+	+
Nyala	55 - 127	–	–	–	–	–	–	–	–	–	–	–	–	–	–	+	+	+	+	+	+	+
Black wildebeest	90 - 160	–	–	–	–	–	–	–	–	–	–	–	–	–	–	–	–	+	+	+	+	+
Tsessebe	120 - 150	–	–	–	–	–	–	–	–	–	–	–	–	–	–	–	–	+	+	+	+	+
Red hartebeest	105 - 182	–	–	–	–	–	–	–	–	–	–	–	–	–	–	–	–	+	+	+	+	+
Sable antelope	180 - 230	–	–	–	–	–	–	–	–	–	–	–	–	–	–	–	–	–	–	+	+	+
Lion	up to 238	–	–	–	–	–	–	–	–	–	–	–	–	–	–	–	–	–	–	–	–	–
Gemsbok	180 - 240	–	–	–	–	–	–	–	–	–	–	–	–	–	–	–	–	–	–	+	+	+
Blue wildebeest	180 - 270	–	–	–	–	–	–	–	–	–	–	–	–	–	–	–	–	–	–	+	+	+
Cape mountain zebra	204 - 260	–	–	–	–	–	–	–	–	–	–	–	–	–	–	–	–	–	–	+	+	+
Waterbuck	204 - 270	–	–	–	–	–	–	–	–	–	–	–	–	–	–	–	–	–	–	+	+	+
Kudu (Greater)	150 - 300	–	–	–	–	–	–	–	–	–	–	–	–	–	–	–	–	–	–	+	+	+
Roan	227 - 272	–	–	–	–	–	–	–	–	–	–	–	–	–	–	–	–	–	–	+	+	+
Burchell's zebra	270 - 430	–	–	–	–	–	–	–	–	–	–	–	–	–	–	–	–	–	–	+	+	+
Nile crocodile	up to 700+	–	–	–	–	–	–	–	–	–	–	–	–	–	–	–	–	–	–	+	+	+
Cape buffalo	up to 800	–	–	–	–	–	–	–	–	–	–	–	–	–	–	–	–	–	–	–	–	–
Eland	460 - 910	–	–	–	–	–	–	–	–	–	–	–	–	–	–	–	–	–	–	–	–	–
Black rhino	up to 1 000	–	–	–	–	–	–	–	–	–	–	–	–	–	–	–	–	–	–	–	–	–
Giraffe	703 - 1 395	–	–	–	–	–	–	–	–	–	–	–	–	–	–	–	–	–	–	–	–	–
Hippopotamus	971 - 1 999	–	–	–	–	–	–	–	–	–	–	–	–	–	–	–	–	–	–	–	–	–
White rhino	1 400 - 2 300	–	–	–	–	–	–	–	–	–	–	–	–	–	–	–	–	–	–	–	–	–
African elephant	up to 6 569	–	–	–	–	–	–	–	–	–	–	–	–	–	–	–	–	–	–	–	–	–

7 X 64	7 mm Rem. Mag	7 mm Wby. Mag.	300 Savage	308 Win.	30-06 Springfield	300 H & H	308 Norma Mag.	300 Win. Mag.	300 Wby. Mag.	303 British	8 X 57	8 mm — 06	8 X 60 S	8 X 68 S	8 mm Rem. Mag.	338 Win. Mag.	340 Wby. Mag.	9,3 X 62	9,3 X 64	358 Norma Mag.	375 H & H Mag.	378 Wby. Mag.	404 Jeffery	458 Win. Mag.	460 Wby. Mag.	500 Jeffery	505 Gibbs	77 Nitro Exp.	600 Nitro Exp.
+	+	+	+	+	+	+	+	+	+	+	+	+	+	+	+	+	+	+	+	+	+	+	+	+	+	+	+	+	+
+	+	+	+	+	+	+	+	+	+	+	+	+	+	+	+	+	+	+	+	+	+	+	+	+	+	+	+	+	+
+	+	+	+	+	+	+	+	+	+	+	+	+	+	+	+	+	+	+	+	+	+	+	+	+	+	+	+	+	+
+	+	+	+	+	+	+	+	+	+	+	+	+	+	+	+	+	+	+	+	+	+	+	+	+	+	+	+	+	+
+	+	+	+	+	+	+	+	+	+	+	+	+	+	+	+	+	+	+	+	+	+	+	+	+	+	+	+	+	+
+	+	+	+	+	+	+	+	+	+	+	+	+	+	+	+	+	+	+	+	+	+	+	+	+	+	+	+	+	+
+	+	+	+	+	+	+	+	+	+	+	+	+	+	+	+	+	+	+	+	+	+	+	+	+	+	+	+	+	+
+	+	+	+	+	+	+	+	+	+	+	+	+	+	+	+	+	+	+	+	+	+	+	+	+	+	+	+	+	+
+	+	+	+	+	+	+	+	+	+	+	+	+	+	+	+	+	+	+	+	+	+	+	+	+	+	+	+	+	+
+	+	+	+	+	+	+	+	+	+	+	+	+	+	+	+	+	+	+	+	+	+	+	+	+	+	+	+	+	+
+	+	+	+	+	+	+	+	+	+	+	+	+	+	+	+	+	+	+	+	+	+	+	+	+	+	+	+	+	+
+	+	+	+	+	+	+	+	+	+	+	+	+	+	+	+	+	+	+	+	+	+	+	+	+	+	+	+	+	+
+	+	+	+	+	+	+	+	+	+	+	+	+	+	+	+	+	+	+	+	+	+	+	+	+	+	+	+	+	+
+	+	+	+	+	+	+	+	+	+	+	+	+	+	+	+	+	+	+	+	+	+	+	+	+	+	+	+	+	+
+	+	+	+	+	+	+	+	+	+	+	+	+	+	+	+	+	+	+	+	+	+	+	+	+	+	+	+	+	+
+	+	+	+	+	+	+	+	+	+	+	+	+	+	+	+	+	+	+	+	+	+	+	+	+	+	+	+	+	+
+	+	+	+	+	+	+	+	+	+	+	+	+	+	+	+	+	+	+	+	+	+	+	+	+	+	+	+	+	+
+	+	+	+	+	+	+	+	+	+	+	+	+	+	+	+	+	+	+	+	+	+	+	+	+	+	+	+	+	+
+	+	+	+	+	+	+	+	+	+	+	+	+	+	+	+	+	+	+	+	+	+	+	+	+	+	+	+	+	+
+	+	+	+	+	+	+	+	+	+	+	+	+	+	+	+	+	+	+	+	+	+	+	+	+	+	+	+	+	+
+	+	+	+	+	+	+	+	+	+	+	+	+	+	+	+	+	+	+	+	+	+	+	+	+	+	+	+	+	+
+	+	+	+	+	+	+	+	+	+	+	+	+	+	+	+	+	+	+	+	+	+	+	+	+	+	+	+	+	+
+	+	+	+	+	+	+	+	+	+	+	+	+	+	+	+	+	+	+	+	+	+	+	+	+	+	+	+	+	+
+	+	+	+	+	+	+	+	+	+	+	+	+	+	+	+	+	+	+	+	+	+	+	+	+	+	+	+	+	+
+	+	+	+	+	+	+	+	+	+	+	+	+	+	+	+	+	+	+	+	+	+	+	+	+	+	+	+	+	+
+	+	+	+	+	+	+	+	+	+	+	+	+	+	+	+	+	+	+	+	+	+	+	+	+	+	+	+	+	+
+	+	+	+	+	+	+	+	+	+	+	+	+	+	+	+	+	+	+	+	+	+	+	+	+	+	+	+	+	+
+	+	+	+	+	+	+	+	+	+	+	+	+	+	+	+	+	+	+	+	+	+	+	+	+	+	+	+	+	+
+	+	+	+	+	+	+	+	+	+	+	+	+	+	+	+	+	+	+	+	+	+	+	+	+	+	+	+	+	+
+	+	+	+	+	+	+	+	+	+	+	+	+	+	+	+	+	+	+	+	+	+	+	+	+	+	+	+	+	+
+	+	+	+	+	+	+	+	+	+	+	+	+	+	+	+	+	+	+	+	+	+	+	+	+	+	+	+	+	+
+	+	+	+	+	+	+	+	+	+	+	+	+	+	+	+	+	+	+	+	+	+	+	+	+	+	+	+	+	+
+	+	+	+	+	+	+	+	+	+	+	+	+	+	+	+	+	+	+	+	+	+	+	+	+	+	+	+	+	+
+	+	+	+	+	+	+	+	+	+	+	+	+	+	+	+	+	+	+	+	+	+	+	+	+	+	+	+	+	+
+	+	+	+	+	+	+	+	+	+	+	+	+	+	+	+	+	+	+	+	+	+	+	+	+	+	+	+	+	+
+	+	+	+	+	+	+	+	+	+	+	+	+	+	+	+	+	+	+	+	+	+	+	+	+	+	+	+	+	+
+	+	+	+	+	+	+	+	+	+	+	+	+	+	+	+	+	+	+	+	+	+	+	+	+	+	+	+	+	+
+	+	+	+	+	+	+	+	+	+	+	+	+	+	+	+	+	+	+	+	+	+	+	+	+	+	+	+	+	+
+	+	+	+	+	+	+	+	+	+	+	+	+	+	+	+	+	+	+	+	+	+	+	+	+	+	+	+	+	+
−	−	−	−	−	−	−	−	−	−	−	−	−	−	−	−	−	−	+	+	+	+	+	+	+	+	+	+	+	+
+	+	+	+	+	+	+	+	+	+	+	+	+	+	+	+	+	+	+	+	+	+	+	+	+	+	+	+	+	+
+	+	+	+	+	+	+	+	+	+	+	+	+	+	+	+	+	+	+	+	+	+	+	+	+	+	+	+	+	+
+	+	+	+	+	+	+	+	+	+	+	+	+	+	+	+	+	+	+	+	+	+	+	+	+	+	+	+	+	+
+	+	+	+	+	+	+	+	+	+	+	+	+	+	+	+	+	+	+	+	+	+	+	+	+	+	+	+	+	+
+	+	+	+	+	+	+	+	+	+	+	+	+	+	+	+	+	+	+	+	+	+	+	+	+	+	+	+	+	+
+	+	+	+	+	+	+	+	+	+	+	+	+	+	+	+	+	+	+	+	+	+	+	+	+	+	+	+	+	+
+	+	+	+	+	+	+	+	+	+	+	+	+	+	+	+	+	+	+	+	+	+	+	+	+	+	+	+	+	+
+	+	+	+	+	+	+	+	+	+	+	+	+	+	+	+	+	+	+	+	+	+	+	+	+	+	+	+	+	+
−	−	−	−	−	−	−	−	−	−	−	−	−	−	−	−	+	+	+	+	+	+	+	+	+	+	+	+	+	+
+	+	+	+	+	+	+	+	+	+	+	+	+	+	+	+	+	+	+	+	+	+	+	+	+	+	+	+	+	+
−	−	−	−	−	−	−	−	−	−	−	−	−	−	−	−	−	−	−	−	+	+	+	+	+	+	+	+	+	+
−	−	−	−	−	−	−	−	−	−	−	−	−	−	−	−	+	+	+	+	+	+	+	+	+	+	+	+	+	+
−	−	−	−	−	−	−	−	−	−	−	−	−	−	−	−	−	−	−	−	+	+	+	+	+	+	+	+	+	+
−	−	−	−	−	−	−	−	−	−	−	−	−	−	−	−	−	−	−	−	+	+	+	+	+	+	+	+	+	+
−	−	−	−	−	−	−	−	−	−	−	−	−	−	−	−	−	−	−	−	−	+	+	+	+	+	+	+	+	+

21. HORN SHAPE AND SPOOR

THE HORN SHAPE OF ADULT ANTELOPE
(Symbols: H = Females with horns; — = Females usually without horns)

SABLE (H) ROAN (H) GEMSBOK (H) NYALA (—)

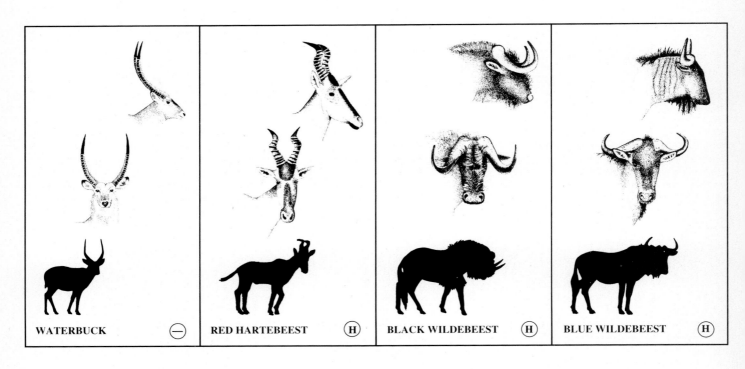

WATERBUCK (—) RED HARTEBEEST (H) BLACK WILDEBEEST (H) BLUE WILDEBEEST (H)

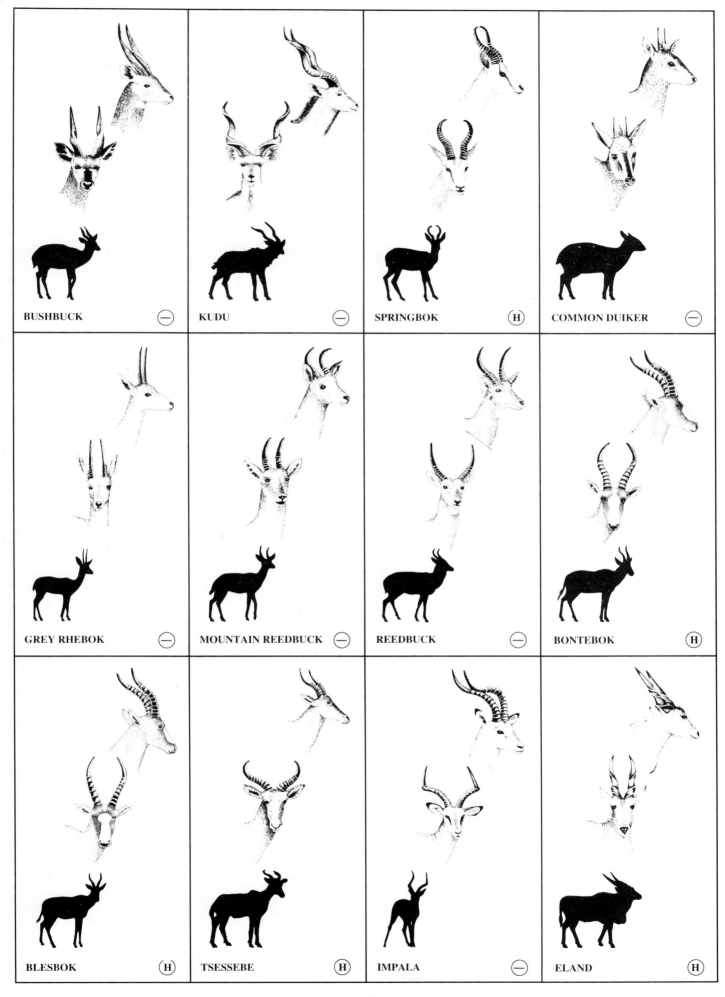

BUSHBUCK ⊖

KUDU ⊖

SPRINGBOK Ⓗ

COMMON DUIKER ⊖

GREY RHEBOK ⊖

MOUNTAIN REEDBUCK ⊖

REEDBUCK ⊖

BONTEBOK Ⓗ

BLESBOK Ⓗ

TSESSEBE Ⓗ

IMPALA ⊖

ELAND Ⓗ

KNOW THEM FROM THEIR SPOOR

The more commonly encountered wild animal species dealt with in this book, can easily be identified by bundu experts from their characteristic spoor. Without seeing the animals themselves, a fair knowledge of animal spoor will enable the explorer to obtain first-hand information on the species occurring in a particular area.

To the experienced bush dweller, it is easy to distinguish between the spoor of animals closely resembling those of other species. However, to put this knowledge into words or even attempt to produce characteristic sketches of spoor, revealing all the variable features to be found in nature, can never be a good substitute for practical experience.

The spoor of the fore and hindfeet of the same animal are usually different as can be the spoor of different individuals of the same species.

Taking into consideration the shortcomings of a schematic representation of animal spoor, the keen student should, nevertheless, with the assistance of the sketches provided here, find it relatively easy to learn to identify the animals from the spoor they leave behind.

To facilitate differentiation, a somewhat arbitrary subdivision of spoor is followed, i.e. dividing the spoor according to structure and actual size.

Animals with hard hooves are divided into two groups — those with cloven hooves (e.g. all the antelope, the giraffe, buffalo and wild pigs), and those with horse-like (cup-shaped) spoor, such as the two zebra species.

The cloven-hoofed species are subdivided, according to the approximate length of the front spoor of adult animals. In this

way, spoor very similar in shape may be differentiated by their size. As the smaller spoor of young animals may confuse the inexperienced, the largest spoor of a group of animals should always be selected and measured. Bear in mind that in nature everything is relative, and even the measurements given here are but rough indications of spoor size.

Also remember that the shape and size of spoor can be affected considerably by the terrain. Spoor in sand or mud can, for instance, be larger than on hard ground.

The elephant, two rhino species and the hippopotamus (the 'big four') have soft undersides to their feet and the shape of their spoor differs markedly from those of the hoofed animals and of other smaller soft-soled species.

From the front to the back, the spoor of a large 'desert elephant' can measure up to about 800 mm. The length of the spoor (front foot) of a white rhino can be about 280 mm and that of the black rhino and of the hippopotamus about 250 mm.

The spoor of the smaller soft-soled species are, at times, very difficult to differentiate. Among the larger carnivores quite marked differences in the structure of their spoor occur. If in doubt, look for the shape and alignment of the individual pads. Also remember that the front spoor of the brown hyena is considerably larger than the hind spoor, frequently misleading the uninformed, who might believe that two different animals had walked in the same tracks.

Consult other reference books on animal spoor and trail signs. If still in doubt ask the local residents, especially the older people, to help you to clarify the mystery about that unidentifiable wild beast which shares their domain.

HARD-HOOFED ANIMALS

CLOVEN-HOOFED

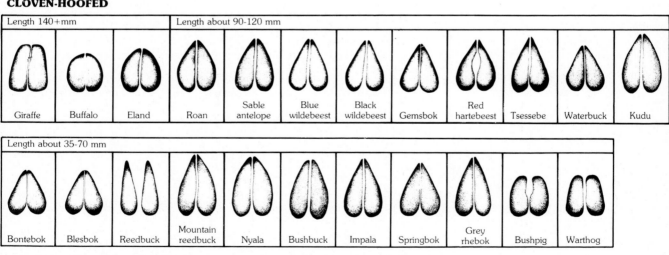

Length 140+mm	Length about 90-120 mm										
Giraffe	Buffalo	Eland	Roan	Sable antelope	Blue wildebeest	Black wildebeest	Gemsbok	Red hartebeest	Tsessebe	Waterbuck	Kudu

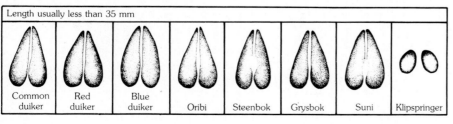

Length about 35-70 mm										
Bontebok	Blesbok	Reedbuck	Mountain reedbuck	Nyala	Bushbuck	Impala	Springbok	Grey rhebok	Bushpig	Warthog

Length usually less than 35 mm

Common duiker	Red duiker	Blue duiker	Oribi	Steenbok	Grysbok	Suni	Klipspringer

ODD-TOED

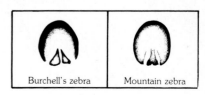

Burchell's zebra	Mountain zebra

180

SOFTER-SOLED ANIMALS

THE 'BIG FOUR'

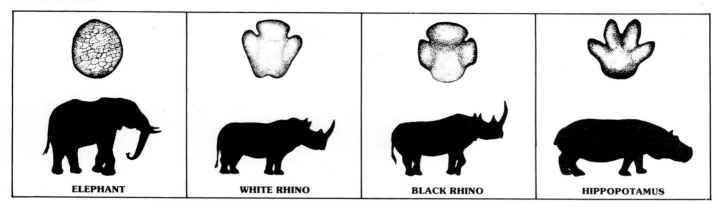

| ELEPHANT | WHITE RHINO | BLACK RHINO | HIPPOPOTAMUS |

CARNIVORES

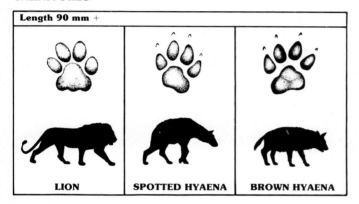

Length 90 mm +

| LION | SPOTTED HYAENA | BROWN HYAENA |

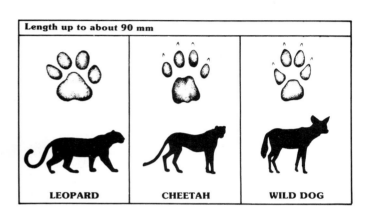

Length up to about 90 mm

| LEOPARD | CHEETAH | WILD DOG |

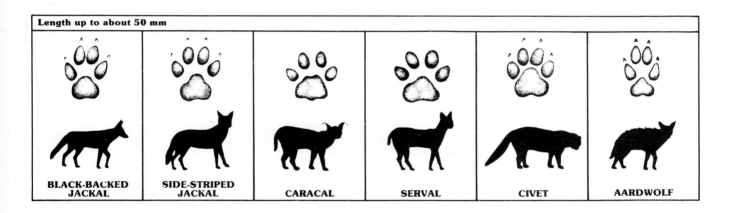

Length up to about 50 mm

| BLACK-BACKED JACKAL | SIDE-STRIPED JACKAL | CARACAL | SERVAL | CIVET | AARDWOLF |

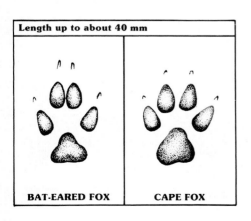

Length up to about 40 mm

| BAT-EARED FOX | CAPE FOX |

CHACMA BABOON

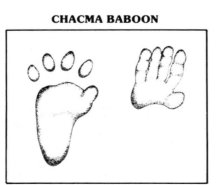

ANTBEAR

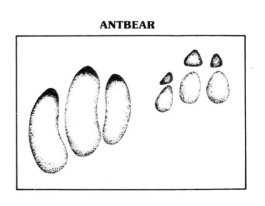

CHEMICAL NAMES / ACTIVE INGREDIENTS: BRAND NAMES AND THE MANUFACTURERS OF SOME OF THE MOST IMPORTANT DRUGS WHICH ARE MENTIONED IN THE TEXT

Chemical name/ Active ingredient	Brand name	Manufacturer/ Distributor
Acepromazine maleate	Acetylpromazine	Boots Pure Drug Co.
Amitras	Triatrix	Coopers
Azaperone	Stresnil	Janssen Pharm.
Chlordiazepoxide	Librium	Roche
Chlorpromazine hydrochloride	Largactil	Maybaker
Diazepam	Tranimal	Roche
Dichlorvos	Equiguard	Shell Chemical Co.
Diprenorphine hydrochloride	Revivon M5050	Reckittt & Sons
Doxapram hydrochloride	Dopram	A.H. Robins & Co.
Fentanyl	Fentanyl	Janssen Pharm.
Glucuronic acid	Guronsan	Chugai Pharm. Co.
Haloperidol	Serenace	G.D. Searle & Co.
Heptaminol	Cortensor	Wander Ltd.
Hydrocortisone	Efcortelan	Glaxo Labs.
Ivermectin	Ivomec	MSD
Ketamine hydrochloride	Ketalar	Park-Davis & Co.
Levamisole hydrochloride	Ripercol-L	Janssen Pharm.
Mebendazole	Telmin	Janssen Pharm.
Methylphenidate hydrochloride	Ritalin	Ciba
Methyridine	Promintic	Imperial Chemical Industries
Nalorphine hydrobromide	Lethidrone	Burroughs Wellcome & Co.
Naloxone hydrochloride	Narcan	Endo Labs.
Niclosamide	Lintex	Bayer
Nikethamide	Coramine	Ciba
Nor-oripavine hydrochloride or cyprenorphine hydrochloride	Cyprenorphine M285	Reckitt & Sons
Oripavine hydrochloride or etorphine hydrochloride	Etorphine M99	Reckitt & Sons
Oxytetracycline hydrochloride	Terramycin	Pfizer Labs.
Phenbendazole	Panacur	Hoechst Pharm.
Phencyclidine hydrochloride	Sernyl/Sernylan	Park-Davis & Co.
Phthyalsulphathiazole	Thalazole	Maybaker
Promethazine hydrochloride	Phenergan	Maybaker
Propionylpromazine hydro-chloride	Combelen	Bayer
Rafoxanide	Ranide	MSD
Succinylcholine chloride	Scoline	Glaxo-Allenburys
Tetramisole hydrochloride	Tramisol W.M.	Imperial Chemical Industries
Thiabendazole	Thibenzole	Merck, Sharp & Dohm
Xylazine hydrochloride	Rompun	Bayer

182

AFRIKAANS AND TECHNICAL NAMES OF GAME SPECIES DISCUSSED IN THE TEXT

English	Afrikaans	Technical name
Impala	Rooibok	Aepyceros melampus
Springbok	Springbok	Antidorcas marsupialis
Blesbok	Blesbok	Damaliscus dorcas phillipsi
Bontebok	Bontebok	Damaliscus dorcas dorcas
Tsessebe	Basterhartbees	Damaliscus lunatus
Red hartebeest	Rooihartbees	Alcelaphus buselaphus
Eland	Eland	Taurotragus oryx
Gemsbok	Gemsbok	Oryx gazella
Kudu	Koedoe	Tragelaphus strepsiceros
Bushbuck	Bosbok	Tragelaphus scriptus
Nyala	Njala	Tragelaphus angasi
Waterbuck	Waterbok	Kobus ellipsiprymnus
Reedbuck	Rietbok	Redunca arundinum
Mountain reedbuck	Rooiribbok	Redunca fulvorufula
Grey rhebok	Vaal ribbok	Pelea capreolus
Blue wildebeest	Blouwildebees	Connochaetes taurinus
Black wildebeest	Swartwildebees	Connochaetes gnou
Sable	Swartwitpens	Hippotragus niger
Roan	Bastergemsbok	Hippotragus equinus
Blue antelope	Bloubok	Hippotragus leucophaeus
Steenbok	Steenbok	Raphicerus campestris
Sharpe's grysbok	Tropiese (Sharpe se) grysbok	Raphicerus sharpei
Grysbok	Kaapse Grysbok	Raphicerus melanotis
Oribi	Oorbietjie	Ourebia ourebi
Suni	Soenie	Neotragus moschatus
Klipspringer	Klipspringer	Oreotragus oreotragus
Common duiker	Gewone duiker	Sylvicapra grimmia
Red duiker	Rooiduiker	Cephalophus natalensis
Blue duiker	Blouduiker	Cephalophus monticola
Elephant	Olifant	Loxodonta africana
Square-lipped (white) rhinoceros	Witrenoster	Ceratotherium simum
Hook-lipped (black) rhinoceros	Swartrenoster	Diceros bicornis
Hippopotamus	Seekoei	Hippopotamus amphibius
Buffalo	Buffel	Syncerus caffer
Giraffe	Kameelperd	Giraffa camelopardalis
Burchell's zebra	Bontsebra	Equus burchelli
Cape mountain zebra	Kaapse bergsebra	Equus zebra
Quagga	Kwagga	Equus quagga
Warthog	Vlakvark	Phacochoerus aethiopicus
Bushpig	Bosvark	Potamochoerus porcus

LENGTH

1 kilometre	=	0,6 miles
	=	1 000 metres
1 metre	=	1 000 millimetres
	=	100 centimetres
	=	3 feet 3 inches
	=	1,1 yards
1 mile	=	1,6 kilometres
	=	1 760 yards
1 yard	=	0,9 metres
	=	3 feet
1 foot	=	30 centimetres
	=	12 inches
1 inch	=	2,5 centimetres
	=	25 millimetres
1 millimetre	=	1 000 microns (micrometre)

MASS

1 metric ton	=	1 000 kilograms
	=	2 200 pounds
1 kilogram	=	1 000 grams
	=	2,2 pounds
1 pound	=	0,45 kilograms
	=	454 grams
	=	16 ounces
	=	3 teacups ±
1 teacup	=	5 ounces ±
1 ounce	=	30 grams ±
	=	2 tablespoons ±
	=	4 dessertspoons ±
	=	8 teaspoons ±
1 teaspoon	=	4 grams ±
1 gram	=	1 000 milligrams
	=	15 grains
1 grain	=	65 milligrams

SURFACE AREA

1 square kilometre	=	1,0 mil. sq. metres
	=	100 hectares
	=	0,4 sq. miles
1 square mile	=	3,1 mil. sq. yards
	=	310 morgen
	=	2,6 kilometres
1 hectare	=	10 000 sq. metres
	=	2,5 acres
	=	1,2 morgen
1 morgen	=	10 000 sq. yards
	=	2,1 acres
	=	0,85 hectares
1 acre	=	0,4 hectares
	=	0,5 morgen
1 sq. metre	=	1,2 sq. yards
1 sq. yard	=	0,8 sq. metres
	=	9 sq. feet
1 sq. foot	=	144 sq. inch
	=	929 sq. centimetre

VOLUME

1 cubic metre	=	1 000 litres
1 litre	=	1 000 millilitres
	=	35,2 fluid ounces ±
	=	5 full glasses ±
	=	1,8 pints
1 gallon	=	4,5 litres
	=	8 pints
1 pint	=	0,57 litres
	=	568 millilitres
	=	3 - 4 teacups ±
	=	20 fluid ounces ±
1 fluid ounce	=	28,4 millilitres
	=	2 tablespoons ±
	=	4 dessertspoons ±
	=	8 teaspoons ±
1 teaspoon	=	4 millilitres ±
1 millilitre	=	15 drops ±
1 medicine measure	=	5 millilitres

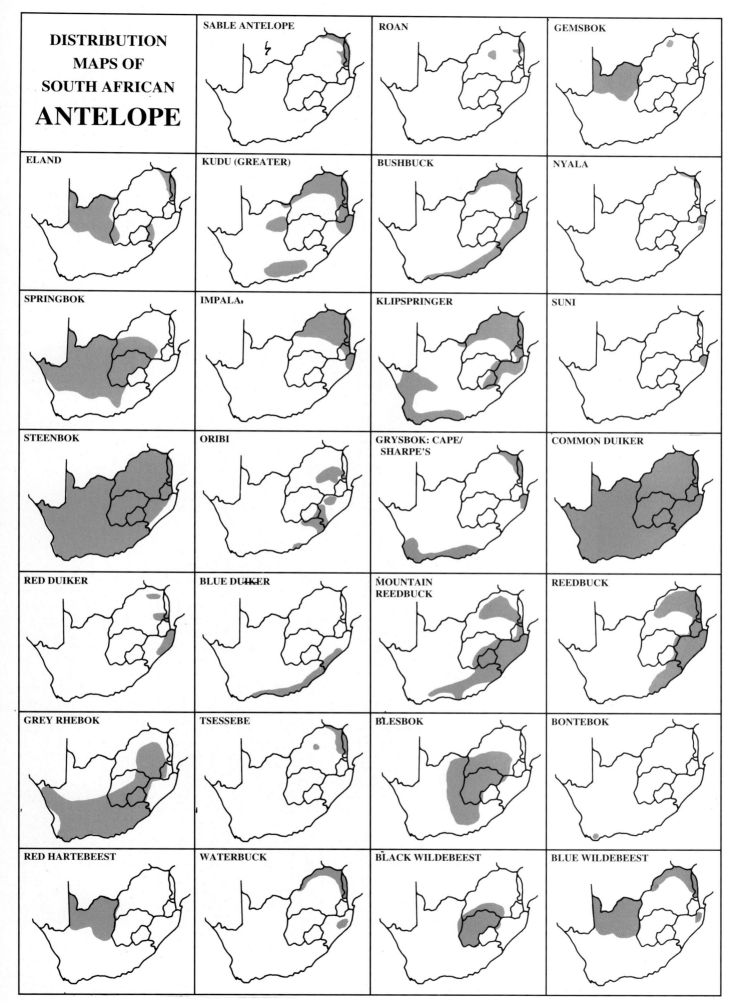

DISTRIBUTION
MAPS OF
SOUTH AFRICAN
ANTELOPE

SABLE ANTELOPE

ROAN

GEMSBOK

ELAND

KUDU (GREATER)

BUSHBUCK

NYALA

SPRINGBOK

IMPALA

KLIPSPRINGER

SUNI

STEENBOK

ORIBI

GRYSBOK: CAPE/ SHARPE'S

COMMON DUIKER

RED DUIKER

BLUE DUIKER

MOUNTAIN REEDBUCK

REEDBUCK

GREY RHEBOK

TSESSEBE

BLESBOK

BONTEBOK

RED HARTEBEEST

WATERBUCK

BLACK WILDEBEEST

BLUE WILDEBEEST

ACKNOWLEDGEMENTS

Sincere appreciation is expressed to the following people (in alphabetical order) for their help in supplying or checking information and/or facilitating the printing of the book:

Mr Pikkie Baard, Dr George Barkhuizen, Dr Pierre Bester, Prof Koos Bothma, Dr Bourquin, Miss Marie Breitenbach, Miss Fifi Bierman, Mr Schalk Burger, Dr Chris Coetzee, Dr Lynn Colly, Mr Gary Davies, Mr Francois de Klerk, Dr Valerius de Vos, Mr Flip du Plooy, Dr Hymie Ebedes, Dr Anthony Ferrar, Mr Willie Gertenbach, Mr Koos Giliomee, Dr Dudley Gradwell, Mr Johan Haasbroek, Mr Louis Heysteck, Dr Ian Hofmeyr, Mr Fred Hoppert, Prof Iavn Horak, Mr Eric Horvitch and staff, Dr Brian Huntley, Prof Andre Immelman, Mr Stoffel Jacobsz, Mr Jorrie Jordaan, Dr Salomon Joubert, Mr Johan Kloppers, Mr Bennie Lategan, Mr Johan Lensing, Dr Hans Meissner, Dr Piet Mulder, Dr Johan Neethling, Mrs M Orton, Dr Howard Pettifer, Dr u de V Pienaar, Dr Pat Pullinger, Mr Dirk Reselman, Mr Alec Rough, Mr Kobus Roux, Mr Willie Roux, Prof John Skinner, Dr Dalibor Slavik, Mrs Sharon Slavik, Dr Butch Smuts, Dr Gordon Strick, Dr Blackie Swart, Mr K van Deventer, Mr Gert van Rooyen, Mr Nico van Rooyen, Mr Vicky van Schalkwyk, Dr Piet van Wyk, Dr Petri Viljoen, Mrs Ruth Viljoen, Mr Boompie Viljoen, Dr John Vincent, Mr Piet Vorster, Miss Denise Woods and Mr Sagie Young.

I would like to make special mention of three people, whose help and encouragement were indispensable: Mrs Sharon Slavik, for her excellent translation, enthusiastic help and constant encouragement, without which this book would not have been completed. Thank you Shanny! Dr Dalibor Slavik, for his support and the sacrifices he so willingly made while Sharon was working on the book — many thanks Dalibor. And last, but certainly not least, Dr Hymie Ebedes, who made me realise that I could finish this task for Eddie and told me to get on with it! Thanks Hym.

Special thanks to the friendly and efficient staff at Promedia Printers for their excellent service.

LITERATUURLYS

Ables E D and Ables J 1969. Field immobilization of free-ranging impala in Northern Kenya. *E Afr Wildl J* 7, 61-66.

Abrams J T 1968. In: Crawford M A 1968. *Comparative nutrition of wild animals.* London, Academic Press.

Adelaar T F 1965. Die invloed van brakwater op vee. In: G J Stander (Red). 1965 *Water.* Pretoria, SA Akad vir Wet en Kuns (Afd Chemie).

Adolph E F 1933. The metabolism and distribution of water in body and tissues. *Physiol Rev* 13, 336.

Adolph E F 1947. Tolerances to heat and dehydration in several species of mammals. *Amer J Physiol* 151, 564.

Allden W G 1962. Rate of herbage intake and grazing time in relation to herbage availability. *Aust Soc Anim Prod* 4, 163-166.

Allee W C, Emerson A E, Park O, Park T and Schmidt K P 1950. *Principles of animal ecology.* Philadelphia, Saunders, 2nd ed. 837 pp.

Allen G M 1939. A check list of African mammals. *Bull Mus comp Zool Harv* 83, 763.

Altman P L and Dittmer D S 1966. *Environmental Biology.* Bethesda, Maryland, Fed of Am Societies for Experimental Biology.

Anderson C F 1961. Anaesthetizing deer by arrow. *J Wildl Mgmt* 25(2), 202-203.

Anderson G D and Talbot L M 1965. Soil factors affecting the distribution of the grassland types and their utilization by wild animals on the Serengeti Plains, Tanganyika. *J Ecol* 53, 1.

Anderson J L 1965. Annual change in testis and kidney fat weight of impala (*Aepyceros m melampus* Lichtenstein). *Lammergeyer* 3(2), 56-59.

Anderson J L 1972. Seasonal changes in the social organization and distribution of the impala in Hluhluwe Game Reserve, Zululand. *J Sth Afr Wildl Mgmt Ass* 2(2), 16-20.

Anderson J L 1972. The impala rut. *Afr Wild Life* 27(2), 79-82.

Anderson W A D 1966. *Pathology,* 5th ed, Saint Louis, C V Mosby Co.

Andrewartha H G and Birch L C 1954. *The distribution and abundance of animals.* University of Chicago Press, Chicago.

Anon 1961. A table of paralytic drugs used to restrain animals at the Bloemfontein zoo, South Africa. *Int Zoo Yb* 3, 121.

Anon 1963. Toxic substances present in plants and their effect of grazing animals. *Biochem J* 88, 55.

Ansell W F H 1959. Further data on Northern Rhodesian ungulates. *Mammalia,* Paris 23, 332-349.

Ansell W F H 1960. The breeding of some larger mammals in Northern Rhodesia. *Proc Zool Soc London* 134, 251-274.

Ansell W F H 1960. *Mammals of Northern Rhodesia.* Lusaka, Government Printer. 155 pp.

Ansell W F H 1960. Mammals of Northern Rhodesia. *Puku* 1.

Ansell W F H 1960. Contributions to the mammalogy of Northern Rhodesia. *Occ Pap nat Mus S Rhod* 24B, 351-398.

Antonius O 1937. On the geographical distribution in former times and today, of the recent Equidae. *Proc zool Soc Lond B* 107, 557-564.

Antonius O 1951. Die Tigerpferde: die zebras. *Monogr Wildsäugetiere (Berl)* 11, 1-148.

Armstrong G G 1965. *An examination of the cementum of the teeth of bovidae with special reference to its use in age determination.* MSc Thesis, University of Alberta.

Asdell S A 1946. *Patterns of mammalian reproduction.* Ithaca, NY Comstock Publishing Co, Inc; London, Constable & Co Ltd 437 pp.

Asibey E O A 1974. Wildlife as a source of protein in Africa south of the Sahara. *Biological Conservation* 6(1), 32.

Astley-Maberley C T 1959. *The game animals of southern Africa.* Cape Town, Nelson.

Astley-Maberly C T 1959. *Animals of South Africa.* Timmins, Cape Town.

Azavedo J C S and Agnew A D Q 1968. Rift Valley impala food preferences. *E Afr Wildl J* 6, 145-146.

Babault G 1949. Notes éthologiques sur quelques mammifères africains. *Mammalia* 13, 57-68.

Baker J R 1937. Light and breeding season. *Nature* (Lond) 139, 414.

Baker M K and Boomker J 1973. Helminths from the mountain reedbuck *Redunca fulvorufula* (Afzelius, 1815). *Onderstepoort J vet Res* 40(2), 69-70.

Balch C C, Balch D A, Johnson V W and Turner J 1953. Factors affecting utilization of food by dairy cows. 1. The effect of limited water intake on the digestibility and rate of passage of hay. *Br J Nutr* 7, 212.

Bandy P J, Cowan IMcT and Wood A J 1956. A method for the assessment of the nutritional status of wild ungulates. *Can J Zool* 34, 48-52.

Bang F B 1969. Variation in disease susceptibility. In: Sladen B K and Bang F B (Ed) 1969. *Biology of populations.* New York, American Elsevier Publishing Co, Inc.

Bang F B 1969. The evolution of disease. In: Sladen B K and Bang F B (Ed) 1969. *Biology of populations.* New York, American Elsevier Publishing Co, Inc.

Barker M K and Keep M E 1970. Checklist of ticks found on the larger game animals in the Natal game reserves. *Lammergeyer* 12, 41-47.

Barnard P J 1961. The phenomenon of game migration in the Kalahari-Gemsbok National Park with a discussion of various marking methods to facilitate a study of the routes followed. *Koedoe* No 4, 178-194.

Barnard P J and Van der Walt K 1961. Translocation of the bontebok, *Damaliscus pygargus* from Bredasdorp to Swellendam. *Koedoe* 4, 105-109.

Basch W S B 1964. Gestation period of impala. *Afr Wild Life* 18(2), 162.

Basson P A, McCully R M, Kruger S P, Van Niekerk J W, Young E and De Vos V 1970. Parasitic and other diseases of the African buffalo in the Kruger National Park. *Onderstepoort J vet Res* 37, 11.

Basson P A, McCully R M, De Vos V, Young E and Kruger S P 1971. Some parasitic and other natural diseases of the African elephant in the Kruger National Park. *Onderstepoort J vet Res* 38, 239-254.

Basson P A, McCully R M, Kruger S P, Van Niekerk J W, Young E, De Vos V, Keep M E and Ebedes H 1971. Disease conditions of game in South Africa: Recent miscellaneous findings. *Veterinary Medical Review* 2/3, 313-340.

Basson P A, McCully R M, Kruger S P, Van Niekerk J W, Young E, De Vos V, Keep M E and Ebedes H 1971. Krankheiten beim Südafrichanischen wild neuere untersuchungen. *Veterinär-Medizinische Nachrichten* 2/3, 305-332.

Bateman J A 1971. *Animal traps and trapping.* David and Charles, Newton Abbot. 286 pp.

Beaton W G (Ed) 1963. Symposium on wildlife in East Africa, its economic development and the veterinary implications. *Bull epiz Dis Afr* 11, 139-176.

Beland O P 1952. How long do they live? *Nat Hist (NY)* 61, 131-134, 141-142.

Benedict F G 1936. *Physiology of the Elephant.* Carnegie Inst Wash Publ 474, 302 pp.

Benson C W 1963. The problem of the cropping of lechwe on the Kafue Flats, Northern Rhodesia. *Publ IUCN, NS,* No 1, 88-89.

Bentley K W, Boura A L A, Fitzgerald A E, Hardy D G, Mccoubrey A, Aikman M L and Lister R E 1965. Compounds possessing morphine-antagonizing or powerful analgesic properties. *Nature* 206, 102-103.

Berry M P S 1975. Game ranching in Natal. *J Sth Afr Wildl Mgmt Ass* 5(1), 33-37.

Biance W, Findlay J D and McLean J A 1965. Responses of steers to water restriction. *Res Vet Sci* 6, 38.

Bigalke R C 1958. On the present status of ungulate mammals in South West Africa. *Mammalia* 22, 478-497.

Bigalke R C and Neitz W O 1954. Indigenous ungulates as a possible source of new domesticated animals. *J S Afr vet med Ass* 25(4), 45-54.

Bigalke R C and Bateman J A 1962. On the status and distribution of ungulate mammals in the Cape Province, South Africa. *Ann Cape prov Mus* 2, 85-109.

Bigalke R C, Liversidge R and Schijf J 1975. *Springbokbestuur.* Noord-Kaaplandse Tak van die Natuurlewevereniging van Suidelike Afrika, Kimberley.

Bissonnette T H 1935. Modification of mammalian sexual cycles. IV. Delay of oestrus and induction of anoestrus in female ferrets by reduction of intensity and duration of daily light periods in the normal oestrous season. *J exp Biol* 12, 315-320.

Biswell H H 1963. Research in wildlife fire ecology in California. *Proc Second Tall Timbers Fire Ecol Conf Tallahassee Fla,* 63-97.

Blaine G 1922. Notes on the zebras and some antelopes of Angola. *Proc zool Soc Lond* 1922, 317-339.

Blaine G 1934. Hartmann's zebra. *J Soc Pres Fauna Emp, NS* 22, 15-17.

Blancou L 1951. La protection de la faune sauvage en Afrique Èquatoriale Française. *Mammalia* 15, 157-169.

Blancou L 1952. Some mammals of French Equatorial Africa. *Afr wild Life* 6, 210-211.

Blancou L 1954. Buffles d'Afrique. *Zooleo, NS* 27, 425-434.

Blancou L 1963. A propos de la distribution de la girafe en Afrique. *Mammalia* 27, 311-312.

Bland S J 1888. Cited by Scott P P 1968. In: Crawford M A 1968. *Comparative nutrition of wild animals.* London, Academic Press.

Blane G F and Dobbs H E 1967. Distribution of tritium-labelled etorphine (M99) and dihydromorphine in pregnant rats at term. *Br J Pharmac Chemother* 30, 166-172.

Blane G F, Boura A L A, Fitzgerald A E and Lister R E 1967. Actions of etorphine hydrochloride (M99), a potent morphine-like agent. *Br J Pharmac Chemother* 3(1), 11.

Blaxter K L and Mitchell H H 1948. The factorization of the protein requirements of ruminants of the protein values of feeds, with particular reference to the significance of the metabolic fecal nitrogen. *J Anim Sci* 7, 351-372.

Bligh J and Harthoorn A M 1965. Continuous radio-telemetric records of the deep body temperature of some unrestrained African mammals under near-natural conditions. *J Physiol* 176, 145.

Blood D C and Henderson J A 1960. *Veterinary Medicine.* London, Baillière, Tindall and Cox.

Blower J H 1959. Topi. *Uganda Wildl Sport* 1, 16-23.

Blower J H 1961. The impala. *Wildl & Sport* 2(4), 26-27.

Blower J H 1961. Wildlife of Uganda. 1. The roan antelope. *Uganda Wildl Sport* 2, 11-13.

Blower J J and Brooks A C 1961. Development and utilization of wildlife resources in Uganda. *IUCN Publ New Series* 1.

Blower J H and Brooks A C 1963. Development and utilisation of wildlife resources in Uganda. *Publ IUCN, NS* 1, 96-101.

Bodenheimer F S 1938. *Problems of animal ecology.* London, Oxford University Press. 179 pp.

Bodenheimer F S 1954. Problems of physiology and ecology of desert animals. In: J L Cloudsley-Thompson (Ed). 1954. *Biology of Deserts.* Proceedings of a symposium on the biology of hot and cold deserts organized by the Institute of Biology, London.

Bolwig N 1958. Aspects of animal ecology in the Kalahari. *Koedoe* 1, 115-135.

Bolwig N 1959. Further observations on the physiological and behavioural characteristics of small animals in the southern Kalahari. *Koedoe* 2, 70-76.

Bonsma F N 1951. Livestock production. In: Welsch A (Ed) 1951. *Africa south of the Sahara.* London, Oxford University Press.

Bonsma J 1976. Bosveldbome en weistreke. Pretoria, J L van Schaik Bpk.

Boomker J, Horak I G and Alves R 1979. Cooperia connochaeti sp Nov (Nematoda, Trichostrongylidae) from the blue wildebeest, *Connochaetes taurinus* (Burchell, 1823). *Onderstepoort J vet Res* 46, 83-86.

Bourlière F 1955. *Mammals of the world: their life and habits.* New York, Knopf.; London, George G Harrap Co Ltd. 223 pp.

Bourlière F 1955. *The natural history of mammals.* London, George G Garrap & Co Ltd. 363 pp.

Bourlière F 1961. Le sex-ratio de la girafe. *Mammalia* 25, 467-471.

Bourlière F 1963. The wild ungulates of Africa: ecological characteristics and economic implications. *Publ IUCN NS* No 1, 102-105.

Bourlière F 1963. Specific feeding habits of African carnivores. *Afr Wild Life* 17, 21-27.

Bourlière F 1963. Conservation and management of game stock. In: UNESCO, 1963. *A review of the natural resources of the African Continent,* pp 395-401.

Bourquin O 1973. Utilisation and aspects of management of the Willem Pretorius Game Reserve. *J Sth Afr Wildl Mgmt Ass* 3(2), 65-73.

Bourquin O, Vincent J and Hitchins P M 1971. The vertebrates of the Hluhluwe Game Reserve-Corridor (State Land) — Umfolozi Game Reserve Complex. *Lammergeyer* 14, 5-58.

Boyazoglu P A, Barret E L, Young E and Ebedes H 1971. Liver mineral analyses as indicator of nutritional adequacy. 2nd World Congress on Animal Feeding, 23-28 October 1972, Madrid, Spain.

Bramley P S and Neaves W B 1972. The relationship between social status and reproductive activity in male impala *Aepyceros melampus. J Reprod Fert* 31, 77-81.

Brand D J 1963. Records of mammals bred in the National Zoological Gardens of South Africa during the periods 1908-1960. *Proc Zool Soc Lond* 140(4), 617-659.

Brocklehurst H C 1931. *Game animals of the Sudan, and their habits and distribution.* London, Gurney & Jackson. 170 pp.

Brody S 1945. *Bioenergetics and Growth.* New York, 1023 pp.

Brook A H and Short B F 1960. Regulation of body temperature of sheep in a hot environment. *Austr J agric Res* 11, 402.

Brooks A C 1961. *A study of the Thomson's gazelle (Gazella thomsonii Gunther) in Tanganyika.* London, HMSO. 147 pp.

Brooks A C and Buss I O 1962. Past and present status of the elephant in Uganda. *J Wildl Mgmt* 26, 38-50.

Brooks A C and Buss I O 1962. Trends in tusk size of the Uganda elephant. *Mammalia* 26, 10-34.

Brown C E 1936. Rearing wild animals in captivity, and gestation periods. *J Mammal* 17, 10-13.

Brown L H 1963. Wild animals, agriculture and animal industry. *Publ IUCN NS* No 1, 109-112.

Brundrett J M and Elvie Turner Jr 1961. Surgical procedures used on wild animals in captivity. *Int Zoo Yb* 3, 111.

Bruner D and Gillespie J 1966. *Hagan's infectious diseases of domestic animals.* Itaca, Cornell Univ Press.

Bryden H A 1889. *Kloof and Karoo.* London, Longmans, Green & Co. 435 pp.

Bryden H A 1897. *Nature and sport in South Africa.* London, Chapman & Hall. 314 pp.

Bryden H A (Ed) 1899. *Great and small game of Africa.* London, Rowland Ward. 612 pp.

Bryden H A 1900. *Animals of Africa.* London, Sands. 240 pp.

Bryden H A 1936. *Wild life in South Africa.* London, George G Harrap & Co Ltd. 283 pp.

Buckley T E 1876. On the past and present geographical distribution of the large mammals of South Africa. *Proc zool Soc Lond* 1876, 277-293.

Buechner H K 1958. Elephant census, II. *Uganda Wildl Sport* 1(4), 17-25.

Buechner H K 1961. Territorial behaviour in Uganda kob. *Science* 133, 698-699.

Buechner H K, Buss I O, Longhurst W M and Brooks A C 1963. Numbers and migration of elephants in Murchison Falls National Park, *Uganda. J Wildl Mgmt* 27, 36-53.

Buechner H K, Harthoorn A M and Lock J A 1960. Immobilizing Uganda kob with succinyl choline chloride. *Can J Comp Med* 24(11), 317-324.

Buechner H K, Harthoorn A M and Lock J A 1960. Recent advances in field immobilization of large mammals with drugs. *Trans N Amer Wildl Conf* 25, 415-422.

Buechner H K, Harthoorn A M and Lock J A 1960. Control of African wild animals. *Nature (Lond)* 185, 47-48.

Buechner H K, Harthoorn A M and Lock J A 1960. The immobilization of African animals in the field, with special reference to their transfer to other areas. *Proc Zool Soc Lond* 135(2), 261-264.

Bullock W R 1962. The weight of the African Elephant. *Proc zool Soc Lond* 138, 133-135.

Burgess H J L 1961. A note on the possible use of wild game as a source of food. Uganda Game Department Ms, 11 pp.

Buss I O 1959. Wildlife research in Murchison Falls National Park and vicinity, Uganda. *Fulbright Progr Rep* No 2.

Buss I O 1959. Elephant census, III. *Uganda Wildl Sport* 1(5), 25-32.

Buss I O 1961. Some observations on food habits and behaviour of the African elephant. *J Wildl Mgmt* 25, 131-148.

Buss I O and Brooks A C 1963. Observations on number, mortality and reproduction of elephants in Uganda. *Publ IUCN NS* 1, 117-122.

Buss I O, Rasmussen L E and Smuts G L 1976. The role of stress and individual recognition in the function of the African elephant's temporal gland. *Mammalia* 40(3), 437-451.

Butynski T M and Von Richter W 1975. Wildlife management in Botswana. *Wildl Soc Bulletin* 3(1), 19-24.

Buxton P A 1955. *Animal life in deserts.* London, Edward Arnold, Ltd.

Cabrera A 1936. Subspecies and individual variation in the Burchell zebras. *J Mammal* 17, 89-112.

Cabrera A and Ruxton A E 1926. On mammals from Luluabourg, Southern Congo. *Ann Mag nat Hist,* Ser 9, 17, 591-602.

Cabrera V M 1965. Tooth trimming in two vicious lions. *Int Zoo Yb* 5, 192-193.

Cameron C M, Tustin R C and Meeser M J N 1963. *Salmonella typhimurium* infection in blue wildebeest calves. *Jl S Afr vet med Ass* 34, 53-55.

Cansdale G S 1946. *Animals of West Africa.* London, Longmans, Green & Co. 144 pp.

Carmichael J 1938. Rinderpest in African game. *J Comp Path Therap* 51, 264.

Carmichael I H, Patterson L, Dräger N and Breton D A 1977. Studies on reproduction in the African buffalo *(Syncerus caffer)* in Botswana. *S Afr J Wildl Res* 7(2), 45-52.

Carpenter K P 1968. In: Graham-Jones O (Ed) 1968. *Some diseases of animals communicable to man in Britain.* Proceeding of a symposium, London 1966. Oxford, Pergamon Press.

Carpenter L H and Williams G L 1972. A literature review of the role of mineral fertilizers in big game range improvement. Special Report No 28, Colorado Division of Game, Fish and Parks, 25 pp.

Carrington R 1958, *Elephants*. London, Chatto & Windus. 272 pp.

Carter N 1961. Progress in drugging technique. *Wild Life* 2(4), 9.

Cater J C 1954. The Nyika plateau, Nyasaland. *Oryx* 2, 298-302.

CCTA/CSA 1959. The eland as a domestic animal. *Science-Afrique,* 17, 7-8.

Chalmers G 1963, Breeding data: Steinbok *(Raphicerus campestris* Thunberg). *E Afr Wildl J* 1, 121-122.

Chapman A, 1921. *Savage Sudan — its wild tribes, big game and bird life.* London, Curney & Jackson, 452 pp.

Chew R M 1961. Water metabolism of desert inhabiting vertebrates. *Biol Rev* 36, 1-31.

Chew R M 1965. Water metabolism of mammals. In: V W Mayer and R G van Gelder (Eds). 1965. *Physiological Mammalogy,* Academic Press, New York and London, Vol. 2.

Child G 1964. Growth and ageing criteria of impala, *Aepyceros melampus.* Occasional Papers of the National Museums of Southern Rhodesia No 27B, 28 May 1964, 128-135.

Child G 1970. Wildlife utilization and management in Botswana. *Biological Conservation* 3(1), 18-22.

Child G 1970. Game ranching. *Proc S Afr Soc Anim Prod* 9, 47-51.

Child G and Fothergill R 1962. *Techniques used to rescue black rhinoceros* (Diceros bicornis) *on Lake Kariba, Southern Rhodesia.* Kariba Studies, Manchester University Press, pp 37-41.

Child G and Savory C R 1964. The distribution of large mammal species in Southern Rhodesia. *Arnoldia Rhod* 1(14), 1-15.

Child G F T 1964. Growth and ageing criteria of impala *Aepyceros melampus. Occ Pap Nat Mus S Rhod* 4(27b), 128-135.

Child G F T 1968. *Behaviour of large mammals during the formation of Lake Kariba.* Kariba Studies. Trustees of the National Museums of Rhodesia, Salisbury, Rhodesia.

Child G F T 1968. An ecological survey of northeastern Botswana. A report to the Government of Botswana. *UN Development Programme, FAO, No TA 2563, Rome.*

Child G F T 1969. The incidence of abnormal tooth formulae in two impala populations. *Mammalia* 33, 541-543.

Christian J J 1963. Endocrine adaptive mechanisms and the physiologic regulation of population growth. In: Mayer W V and van Gelder R G (Ed) 1963, *Physiological mammalogy, Vol 1, Mammalian populations.* New York and London, Academic Press.

Christy C 1929. The African buffaloes. *Proc zool Soc Lond* 1929, 445-462.

Cillie B 1987. *Soogdiere van Suider-Afrika.* 182.pp

Clarenburg A 1964. Salmonellosis. In: Van der Hoeden J (Ed) 1964. *Zoonoses.* Amsterdam, London and New York, Elsevier Publishing Co.

Clark R and Quin J I 1949. Studies on the water requirements of farm animals in South Africa. 1. The effect of intermittent watering on merino sheep. *Onderstepoort J Vet Sci* 22, 335.

Clarke J R 1953. The hippopotamus in Gambia, West Africa. *J Mammal* 34, 299-315.

Clement A J 1965. Who'll exploit the eland? *Farmer's Weekly,* March 3, 59-61.

Cloudsley-thompson J L 1961. *Rhythmic activity in animal physiology and behavior.* New York, Academic Press.

Cloudsley-Thompson J L 1965. *Animal conflict and adaptation.* London, G T Foulis and Co Ltd.

Cloudsley-Thompson J L and Chadwick M J 1964. *Life in deserts.* Philadelphia, Dufour Edition.

Codd L E W 1951. *Bome en struike van die Nasionale Krugerwildtuin.* Pretoria, Die Staatsdrukker.

Coetzee C J 1982. Snotsiekte by beeste. *Vleisbeeste* E 11.

Collier F 1940. Field notes on Nigerian mammals. *Niger Fld* 9, 10-16.

Colman E A 1953. *Vegetation and watershed management.* Ronald Press Co NY, 412 pp.

Condy J B 1963. Internal parasitism of animals in Wankie National Park. *S Afr J Sci* 59, 415.

Condy J B 1964. The capture of black rhinoceros *(Diceros bicornis)* and buffalo *(Syncerus caffer)* on Lake Kariba. *Rhodesian J Agric Res* 2(1), 31-34.

Condy J B 1972. Observations on levels of internal parasites in free living Rhodesian wild life. I Kudu *(Tragelaphus strepsiceros)* (Pallas, 1766). *Zoologica Africana* 7(2), 413-418.

Condy J B and Vickers D B 1972. Brucellosis in Rhodesian wildlife. *Jl S Afr vet med Ass* 43, 175.

Cook C W, Stoddard L A and Harris L E 1954. The nutritive value of winter range plants. *Utah Ag Exp Sta Bull* 372.

Cook C W, Stoddard L A and Harris L E 1956. Comparative nutritive value and palatability of some introduced and native forage plants for spring and summer grazing. *Utah Ag Exp Sta Bull,* 385.

Cook C W, Taylor K and Harris L E 1962. The effect of range condition and intensity of grazing upon daily intake and nutritive value of the diet of desert ranges. *J Range Mgmt* 15, 1-6.

Cotton C B 1933. The giant eland *(Taurotragus derbianus). Proc zool Soc Lond* 1933, 1037-1038.

Crake T 1980. Game farming is taking off. *Farmer's Weekly,* June 25, 59-61.

Crampton E W and Lloyd L E 1959. *Fundamentals of nutrition.* W H Freeman Co, San Francisco, Calif, 494 pp.

Crandall L S 1964. *The management of wild mammals in captivity.* Chicago, University of Chicago Press.

Crawford M A (Ed) 1968. *Comparative nutrition of wild animals.* London and New York, Academic Press.

Crockford J A, Hayes F A, Jenkins J H and Feurt S D 1957. Field application of nicotine salicylate for capturing deer. *Trans N Am Wildl Conf* 22, 579-583.

Crockford J A, Hayes F A, Jenkins J H and Feurt S D 1957. Nicotine salicylate for capturing deer. *J Wildl Mgmt* 21(2), 213-220.

Crockford J A, Hayes F A, Jenkins J H and Feurt S D 1958. An automatic projectile type syringe. *Veterinary Medicine* 53, 115-119.

Croft P G 1959. Use of suxamethonium for restraint. *Vet Rec* 71, 354-355.

Cronwright-Schreiner S C 1925. *The migratory springbucks of South Africa.* London; T Fisher Unwin. 140 pp.

Curry-Lindahl K 1956. Ecological studies on mammals, birds, reptiles and amphibians in Eastern Belgian Congo, I. *Ann Mus roy Congo belge, Sci zool* 42, 79 pp.

Daniel Marie and Ling C M 1972. The effect of an etorphine/acepromazine mixture on the heart rate and blood pressure of the horse. *Vet Rec* 90(12), 336-339.

Darling F F 1958. Conservation and the ungulates. *Mammalia* 22, 317-322.

Darling F F 1960. Wildlife husbandry in Africa. *Sci Amer* 203, 123-128.

Darling F F 1960. *Wild life in an African territory.* London, Oxford University Press. 160 pp.

Darling F F 1960. An ecological reconnaissance of the Mara plains in Kenya Colony. *Wildl Monogr* No 5. 41 pp.

Darling F F 1961. African wild life as a protein resource. *Span (Lond)* 4, 100-103.

Dasmann R F 1959. *Environment Conservation.* John Wiley & Sons Inc NY, 307 pp.

Dasmann R F 1962. Game ranching in African land-use planning. *Bull epiz Dis Afr* 10, 13-17.

Dasmann R F 1963. Game ranching in African land-use planning. *Publ IUCN, NS,* No 1, 133-136.

Dasmann R F and Mossman A S 1960. The economic value of Rhodesian game. *Rhod Fmr* 30, 17-20.

Dasmann R F and Mossman A S 1961. Commercial use of game animals on a Rhodesian ranch. *Wild Life* 3(3), 7.

Dasmann R F and Mossman A S 1962. Reproduction in some ungulates in Southern Rhodesia. *J Mammal* 43(4), 533-537.

Dasmann R F and Mossman A S 1962. Population studies of impala in Southern Rhodesia. *J Mammal* 43(3), 375-395.

Dasmann R F and Mossman A S 1962. Road strip counts for estimating numbers of African ungulates. *J Wildl Mgmt* 26, 101-104.

Dasmann R F and Mossman A S 1962. Abundance and population structure of wild ungulates in some areas of Southern Rhodesia. *J Wildl Mgmt* 26(3), 262-268.

David J H M 1969. The ecology and behaviour of the bontebok, *D d dorcas,* cited by Lynch C S 1974. Memoir 8 of the National Museum, Bloemfontein.

Davidson F T 1934. Elephants, lions and airplanes. Collecting and studying wild life in Kenya Colony and Tanganyika with the aid of man-made wings. *Nat Hist (NY),* 34, 105-116.

David R 1966. R05-2807/B10 (Vallium) as a tranquilizer in zoo animals. *Int Zoo Yb 6,* 270-273.

Davis D E 1960. Estimating the numbers of game populations. Sect 5 in: Mosby H S (Ed) 1960. *Manual of game investigational techniques.* Washington, D C, Wild Life Society. 27 pp.

Davis J W and Anderson R C (Ed) 1971. *Parasitic diseases of wild animals.* Ames, Iowa, The Iowa State University Press.

Davis J W, Karstad L H and Trainer D O (Ed) 1970. *Infectious diseases of wild animals.* Ames, Iowa, The Iowa State University Press; London, Tindall and Cassell, Ltd.

Denney R N 1969. Black rhinoceros immobilization utilising a new tranquillizing agent. *E Afr Wild J* 7, 159-165.

Deshler W 1963. Cattle in Africa: distribution, types and problems. *Geogr Rev* 53, 52-58.

De Vos V 1978. Immobilisation of free-ranging wild animals using a new drug. *The Veterinary Record* 103, 64-68.

De Vos V 1978. A new potent analgesic for chemical immobilization of gemsbok, *Oryx gazella gazella*. *Koedoe* 21, 173-180.

De Vos V and Lambrechts M C 1971. Emerging aspects of wildlife diseases in Southern Africa. Proc SARCCUS symposium on nature conservation as a form of land use. Gorongosa National Park, Mocambique, 13-17 Sept 1971, p 97.

De Vos V and Van Niekerk C A W J 1969. Brucellosis in the Kruger National Park. *Jl S Afr vet med Ass* 40, 331.

Dixon J E W 1964. Preliminary notes on the mammal fauna of the Mkuzi Game Reserve. *Lammergeyer* 3(1), 40-58.

Dixon J E W 1966. Notes on the mammals of Ndumu Game Reserve. *Lammergeyer* 6, 24-40.

Dixon J E W 1968. Notes on horned female impala. *Lammergeyer* 8, 4-6.

Dixon J E W 1968. Prey of large raptors. *Ostrich* 39, 203-204.

Domino E F 1964. Neurobiology of phencyclidine (Sernyl) — a drug with an unusual spectrum of pharmacological activity. *Int Rev Neurobiol* 6, 303.

Dorst J (Ed) 1958. Investigation upon the present status of ungulates in Africa South of the Sahara. *Mammalia* 22, 357-503.

Dougall H W 1963. On the chemical composition of elephants faeces. *E Afr Wildl J* 1, 123.

Dougall H W, Drysdale V M and Glover P E 1964. The chemical composition of Kenya browse and pasture herbage. *E Afr Wildl J* 2, 86-121.

Dowling D F 1955. The hair follicle and apocrine gland populations of zebu (*Bos indicus* L) and shorthorn (*B taurus* L) cattle skin. *Aust J agric Res* 6, 645.

Dozsa I 1962. Durch Chlorpromazin potentierte Narkose bei Felidae. *Nord Vet Med* 14 (Suppl 1), 107-111.

Dräger N 1975. A severe outbreak of interdigital necrobacillosis in gemsbok (*Oryx gazella*) in the northern Kalahari (Botswana). *Trop Anim Hlth Prod* 7, 200.

Dräger N and Mehlitz D 1978. Investigations on the prevalence of trypanosome carriers and the antibody response in wildlife in northern Botswana. *Tropenmed Parasit* 29, 223-233.

Dräger N and Paine G D 1980. Demodicosis in African buffalo *Syncerus caffer caffer* in Botswana. *Journal of Wildlife Diseases* 16(4), 521-524.

Dräger N, Paterson L and Breton D 1976. Immobilization of African buffaloes (*Syncerus caffer caffer*) in large numbers for veterinary research. *E Afr Wildl J* 14, 113-120.

Du Plessis S S 1968. *Ecology of blesbok (Damaliscus dorcas phillipsi) on the Van Riebeeck nature Reserve, Pretoria, with special reference to productivity*. DSc (Wildlife Management) Thesis, University of Pretoria.

Du Toit P J 1947. Game in relation to animal diseases. *Jl S Afr vet med Ass* 18, 59.

Dyson R F 1965. Experience with succinylcholine chloride in zoo animals. *Int Zoo Yb* 5, 205-206.

Ebedes H 1962. Practical experience in the use of the cap-chur gun. *Jl S Afr vet med Ass* 33, 87.

Ebedes H 1966. Notes on the immobilization and biology of zebra (*Equus burchelli antiquorum*) in the Etosha Game Park, South West Africa. *Jl S Afr vet med Ass* 37(3), 299-303.

Ebedes H 1969. Notes on the immobilization of gemsbok in South West Africa using etorphine hydrochloride (M99). *Madoqua* 1, 35-45.

Ebedes H 1971. The capture of plains zebra *Equus burchelli antiquorum*, H Smith 1841, with M-99 (Reckitt) and tranquillizers in the Etosha National Park. *Madoqua* 1(3), 67-76.

Ebedes H 1972. The nomadic plains zebra (*E b antiquorum*, H Smith 1841) of the Etosha Salina. Cited by Smuts G L 1972. MSc Thesis, University of Pretoria.

Ebedes H 1975. The immobilisation of adult male and female elephant *Loxodonta africana*, Blumenbach with etorphine and observations on the action of diprenorphine. *Madoqua* 9(2), 19-24.

Ebedes H 1975. The capture and translocation of gemsbok *Oryx gazella gazella* in the Namib Desert with the aid of fentanyl, etorphine and tranquillizers. *Jl S Afr vet med Ass* 46(4), 359-362.

Ebedes H 1976. Anthrax epizoötics in Etosha National Park. *Madoqua* 10(2), 99-118.

Ebedes H and Burroughs R E J 1992. The use of Tranquillizers in wildlife. 31 — 37. *Bulletin no 423*.

Ebedes H, Leibnitz E and Joubert J 1977. The immobilisation of wildebeest *Connochaetes taurinus* with etorphine and the use of diprenorphine as an etorphine antagonist. *Madoqua* 10(1), 71-73.

Eggers G W N 1965. The immediate postanaesthetic period. *Curr Res Anesth* 44, 226-235.

Elder D F 1956. Watering patterns of some desert game animals. *J Wildl Mgmt* 20, 368-378.

Ellerman J R, Morrison-Scott T C S and Hayman R W 1953. *Southern African mammals, 1758 to 1951, a reclassification*. London, British Museum (Natural History). 363 pp.

Eloff F C 1959. Observations on the migration and habits of the antelopes of the kalahari Gemsbok Park — Pts I and II. *Koedoe* 2, 1-29, 30-51.

Eloff F C 1961. Observations on the migration and habits of the antelopes of the Kalahari-Gemsbok Park — Pt III. *Koedoe* 4, 18-30.

Eloff F C 1962. Observations on the migration and habits of the antelopes of the Kalahari-Gemsbok Park — Pt IV, *Koedoe* 5, 128-136.

Elton C S and Miller R S 1954. The ecological survey of animal communities with a practical system of classifying habitats by structural characters. *J Ecol* 42, 460-496.

Eriksen E 1963. Om Cap-chur instrumentariet. *Medlemsbl danske Dyrlaegeforen* 3, 53-72.

Erasmus T 1967. *Water metabolism studies with ruminants*. Submitted to the Faculty of Agriculture, University of Pretoria, in partial fulfilment of the requirements for the degree of DSc (Agric).

Eriksen E 1970. Einfangen von Hirschwild durch immobilisierungen mit neuroleptika. *Nord Vet Med* 22, 385-400.

Estes R D 1966. Behaviour and life history of the wildebeest (*Connochaetes taurinus* Burchell). *Nature* 212(5066), 999-1000.

Fairall N 1968. The reproductive seasons of some mammals in the Kruger National Park. *Zool Afr* 3(2), 189-210.

Fairall N 1969. The use of the lens technique in deriving the age structure and life table of an impala (*Aepyceros melampus*) population. *Koedoe* 12, 90-96.

Fairall N 1969. Prental development of the impala. *Koedoe* 12, 97-103.

Fairall N 1970. Research on the reproduction of wild ungulates. *Proc S Afr Soc Anim Prod* 9, 57-61.

Fann W E 1966. Use of methylphenidate to counteract acute dystonic effects of phenothiazines. *Am J Psychiat* 122(11), 1293.

F A O 1963. Wild life management and economic development: possibilities and limitations. *Publ IUCN, NS No* 1, 152-157.

Fatti L P, Smuts G L Starfield A M and Spurdle A A 1980. Age determination in African elephants. *J Mamm* 61, 547-551.

Feely J M 1965. A game-cropping scheme in the Luangwa Valley. *Zoologica Africana* 1(1), 227-230.

Ferrar A A 1973. Wildlife utilization in Rhodesia. Part 1. A planning schedule for wildlife utilization on a Rhodesian cattle ranch. *Rhodesian Science News* 7(1).

Ferrar A A 1973. Wildlife utilization in Rhodesia. Part 2. Some economic and ecological attributes of Rhodesia's large mammals. *Rhodesian Science News* 7(1).

Field C R 1974. Scientific utilization of wildlife for meat in East Africa: A Review. *J Sth Afr Wildl Mgmt Ass* 4(3), 177-183.

Field C R and Blankenship L H 1973. On making the game pay. *Africana* 5(4), 22.

Fiennes R 1966. Feeding animals in captivity. *Int Zoo Yb* 6, 58-67.

Fiennes R 1968. Potentially dangerous pets. *New Scientist* 37, 10.

Fitzsimmons F W 1920. *The natural history of South Africa*. London; Longmans, Green & Co. 4 vols.

Fitzsimons V 1955. An effective baboon trap. *Fauna and Flora* 6, 79-84.

Flower S S 1931. Contributions to our knowledge of the duration of life in vertebrate animals. V. Mammals. *Proc zool Soc Lond* 1931, 145-234.

Flower S S 1932. Notes on the recent mammals of Egypt with a list of the species recorded from that Kingdom. *Proc zool Soc Lond* 1932, 369-450.

Forbes R M and Garrigus W P 1948. Application of lignin ratio technique to the determination of the nutrient intake of grazing animals. *J Anim Sci* 7, 373-382.

Foster J C and Kearney D 1967. Nairobi National Park census, 1966. *E Afr Wildl J* 5, 112-120.

Fox M W 1971. Psychopathology in man and lower animals. *J Amer Vet med Ass* 159, 66.

Frade F 1933. Éléphants d'Angola. *Bull Soc portug Sci nat* 11, 319-333.

Frade F 1933. Éléphants du Mozambique. *Bull Soc portug Sci nat II*, 307-318.

Frankel S H 1963. Some economic aspects of the conservation and development of wild life resources in modern African states. *Publ IUCN, NS No* 1, 166-169.

Fraser A 1968. *Reproductive behaviour in ungulates*. London, Academic Press.

Fraser A D 1958. On the present status of ungulates in Southern Rhodesia. *Mammalia* 22, 469-475.

Fraser Darling F 1961. African wildlife as a protein resource. *Span* 4(3), 100-103.

French M H 1956. The effect of infrequent water intake on the consumption and digestibility of hay by Zebu cattle. *Emp J Exp Ag* 24, 128.

Fuhrman F A 1963. Environmental physiology and psychology in arid conditions. Cited by: Grosskopf J F W et al 1969. Jl S Afr vet med Ass 40, 51.

Gaerdes J H 1965. The impala in South West Africa. Afr Wild Life 19(2), 109-113, 145.

Gammon D M 1962. Veld fire control. Rhodesia Ag J 59, 177-191.

Gandal C P 1966. White muscle disease in a breeding herd of nyala antelope (Tragelaphus angasi) at New York Zoo. Int Zoo Yb 6, 277-278.

Ganong W F 1969. Review of medical physiology, 4th ed, Los Altos, Large Medical Publications, pp 509-511.

Gardocki J F, Yelnosky J, Kuehn W F and Gunster J C 1964. A study of the interaction of nalorphine with fentanyl and innovan. Toxicol Exptl Pharmacol 6, 593-601.

Gaukler A and Kraus M 1970. Zur immobilisation von wildwiederkäuern mit Xylazin (Bay Va 1470). Der Zoologische Garten 38, 37-46.

Gertenbach W P D and Potgieter A L F 1979. Veldbrandnavorsing in die struikmopanieveld van die Nasionale Krugerwildtuin. Koedoe 22, 1-28.

Ghobrial L I and Cloudsley-Thompson J L 1966. Effect of deprivation of water on the dorcas gazelle. Nature Lond. 212, 306.

Gillet H 1966. The scimitar oryx and the addax in the Tchad Republic. (Part 1.) Afr Wild Life 20, 103.

Glass B P 1965. The mammals of Eastern Ethiopia. Zool Afr 1(1), 177-179.

Glover J 1963. The elephant problem at Tsavo. E Afr Wildl J 1, 30-39.

Golley F B and Buechner H K 1968. A practical guide to the study of the productivity of large herbivores. Oxford, Blackwell Scientific Publications.

Government of Nyasaland (Malawi) 1963. Note on the problems surrounding the implementation of a wild life utilization policy in a densely populated country. Publ IUCN, NS, No 1, 250-252.

Graaff A 1960. Handling and storage of animal foods in zoos. Int Zoo Yb 2, 102-104.

Grafton R N 1963. Age determination methods for the impala antelope in Transvaal, South Africa. MA Thesis, University of Missouri.

Graham-Jones O 1964. Restraint and anaesthesia of some captive wild animals. Vet Rec 76(44), 1216-1248.

Graupner E D and Graupner O F 1971. Predator-prey interrelationships in a natural big game population. Final report, Nature Conservation Division, Transvaal Provincial Administration, 36 pp.

Greenwald L I 1967. Water economy of the desert dwelling springbok (Antidorcas marsupialis). Submitted in partial fulfilment of the requirements for the degree of master of Science in Zoology in the graduate School of Syracuse University, USA.

Grimwood I R 1963. The fauna and flora of East Africa. In Conservation of nature and natural resources in modern African states. IUCN Publ New Series 1, 179-188.

Grimwood I R, Benson C W and Ansell W F N 1958. The present day status of ungulates in Northern Rhodesia. Mammalia 22, 451-467.

Grosskopf J P W 1958. Hartwater-immunisasie van elande, Taurotragus oryx. Jl S Afr vet med Ass 29, 329.

Grosskopf J F W, Fairall N and Visser D 1969. The influence of various tranquillizing agents on the body temperature of sheep at high and low ambient temperatures. Jl S Afr vet med Ass 40, 51-56.

Grosskopf J F W and Smuts G L 1975. Serum gonadotrophin activity of pregnant zebra and horse mares. Jl S Afr vet Ass 46(4), 367-368.

Grzimek M and Grzimek B 1960. A study of the game of the Serengeti Plains. Z Säugetierk 25, 1-61.

Grzimek M and Grzimek B 1960. Serengeti shall not die. Collins, St James Place, London.

Guilbride P D L, Coyle T J, Mcanulty E G, Barber L and Lomax G D 1962. Some pathogenic agents found in hippopotamus in Uganda. J Comp Path Therap 72, 137.

Guilbride P D L, Rollinson D H L and Mcanulty E G 1963. Tuberculosis in free living (Cape) buffalo (Syncerus caffer Sparrman). J Comp path Therap 73, 337.

Haagner A 1920. South African mammals. London, Witherby. 248 pp.

Hafez E S E, Badreldin A L and Shafei M M 1955. Skin structure of Egyptian buffaloes and cattle with particular reference to sweat glands. J agri Sci 46, 19.

Hall L W 1964. Anaesthetic accidents and emergencies. Vet Rec 76(26), 713.

Hall T C, Taft E B, Baker W A and Aub J C 1953. A preliminary report on the use of Flaxedil to produce paralysis in the white-tailed deer. J Wildl Mgmt 17(4), 516-520.

Hall-Martin A J 1973. A note on the seasonal utilization of different vegetation types by giraffe. S Afr J of Sci 70, 122-123.

Hall-Martin A J 1974. Food selection by Transvaal lowveld giraffe as determined by analysis of stomach contents. J Sth Afr Wildl Mgmt Ass 4(3), 191-202.

Hall-Martin A J 1977. Giraffe weight estimation using dissected leg weight and body measurements. J Wildl Mgmt 41(4), 740-745.

Hall-Martin A J and Skinner J D 1978. Observations on puberty and pregnancy in female giraffe (Giraffa camelopardalis). S Afr J Wildl Res 8, 91-94.

Hall-Martin A J, Skinner J D and Smith A 1977. Observations on lactation and milk composition of the giraffe Giraffa camelopardalis. S Afr J Wildl Res 7(2), 67-71.

Hall-Martin A J, Von la Chevallerie M and Skinner J D 1977. Carcass composition of the giraffe Giraffa camelopardalis giraffa. S Afr J Anim Sci 7, 55-64.

Halloran A F and Deming O V 1958. Water development for desert bighorn sheep. J Wildl Mgmt 22, 1.

Haltenorth T and Trense W 1956. Big game of the world and its trophies. Bonn, Bayerischer Landwirtschaftsverlag. 436 pp.

Hamilton C L and Jepson H G 1940. Stockwater developments: wells, springs and ponds. Farmers Bull 1859, US Dept of Ag.

Hammond J 1941. Fertility in mammals and birds. Biol Rev 16, 165-190.

Hanks J 1967. Crossbow darting. Animals — The international wildlife magazine, No 248.

Hanks J 1967. The use of the new "hypodart" for animal immobilization. Puku 5, 228-231.

Hanks J 1967. The use of M99 for the immobilization of the Defassa waterbuck. East Afr Wildl J 5, 96-105.

Hanks J and Dowsett R J 1969. The use of etorphine (M99) for the immobilization and translocation of the puku. The Puku 5, 123-130.

Hanson W R 1963. Calculation of productivity, survival and abundance of selected vertebrates from sex and age ratios. Wild Life Monogr No 9. 60 pp.

Harper F 1945. Extinct and vanishing mammals of the old world. Spec Publ Amer Comm int Wild Life Prot No 12, 850.

Harrison H 1936. The Shinyanga game experiment: a few of the early observations. J Anim Ecol 5, 271-293. 70(46), 939-940.

Harthoorn A M 1962. Capture of white (square-lipped) rhinoceros, Ceratotherium simum simum (Burchell), with the use of the drug immobilization technique. Can J Comp Med 26(9), 203-208.

Harthoorn A M 1963. The use of translocation as a means of preserving wild animals and an integral factor in the solution to certain problems of national parks and nature reserves. Publ IUCN, NS, No 1, 198-202.

Harthoorn A M 1963. The value of neuroleptic narcosis in restraint, compared with that of anaesthesia, sedation or paralysis. Proc Symp Afr Mammals Zool Soc S Afr, Cape Town.

Harthoorn A M 1965. Application of pharmacological and physiological principles in restraint of wild animals. Wildlife Monographs 14, 78 pp.

Harthoorn A M 1967. Comparative pharmacological reactions of certain wild and domestic mammals to thebaine derivatives in the M-series of compounds. Fed Proc 26(4), 1251-1261.

Harthoorn A M 1970. The flying syringe. London, Geoffrey Bles.

Harthoorn A M 1976. Chemical capture of animals. Cox and Wyman, London.

Harthoorn A M and Bligh J 1965. New potent morphine analogues for the restraint of large hoofed animals. Res Vet Sci 6, 290-299.

Harthoorn A M and Bligh J 1965. The use of a new oripavine derivative with potent morphine like activity for the restraint of hoofed animals. Res Vet Sci 6(3), 290-299.

Harthoorn A M and Lock J A 1960. A note on the prophylactic vaccination of wild animals. Brit Vet J 116, 252.

Harthoorn A M, Lock J A and MacKeand J 1960. Translocation of wild animals as a means of game control. Nature (Lond) 187-518.

Harthoorn A M and Player I C 1964. The narcosis of the white rhinoceros. A series of eighteen case histories. Proc Fifth Intern Symp Dis Zool Anim (1963). Tyd Diergen 89, 225-229.

Harthoorn A M, Van der Walt K and Young E 1973. Possible therapy for capture myopathy in captured wild animals. Nature 247(5442), 577.

Harthoorn A M and Young E 1974. A relationship between acid-base balance and capture myopathy in zebra (Equus burchelli) and an apparent therapy. Vet Record 95, 337-342.

Harthoorn A M, Young E and York W 1974. Blood enzyme levels as indications of capture stress in zebra, Equus burchelli. Proc Cong Amer Ass Zoo Vets, Atlanta.

Hawthorne V M 1971. Coyote movements in Sagehen Creek Basin, northeastern California. *Calif Fish and Game* 57(3), 154-161.

Hayman R W 1951. Notes on some Angolan mammals. *Publ Cult Comp Diament Angola,* No 11, 31-36.

Hayman R W 1955. Mammals of Sierra Leone. *Zoo Life* 1955, 2-6.

Hayne D 1949. An examination of the strip census method for estimating animal populations. *J Wildl Mgmt* 13, 145-157.

Hazzard L K 1958. *A review of literature on big game census methods.* Colorado Game and Fish Dept, pp 1-75.

Heady H F 1960. *Range management in East Africa.* Nairobi, Government Printer. 125 pp.

Heape W and Marshall F H A 1931. *Emigration, migration and nomadism.* London, W. Heffer and Sons Ltd.

Hecker J F, Budtz-Olsen O E and Ostwald M 1964. The rumen as a water store in sheep. *Aust J agric Res* 15, 961.

Hedger R S 1972. Foot-and-mouth disease and the African buffalo (*Syncerus caffer*). *J Comp Path* 82, 19.

Hedger R S, Condy J B and Falconer J 1969. The isolation of FMDV from African buffalo (*Syncerus caffer*). *Vet Rec* 84, 516.

Hegner R 1938. *Big fleas have little fleas, or who's who among the protozoa.* Baltimore, Williams and Wilkins Co.

Henning M W 1956. *Animal diseases in South Africa,* 3rd ed. South Africa, Central News Agency.

Heuschele W P 1960. Immobilization of captive wild animals with succinylcholine chloride using the projectile type syringe. *Int Zoo Yb* 2, 308-309.

Heuschele W P 1961. Chlordiazepoxide for calming zoo animals. *J Amer vet med Ass* 139(9), 996-998.

Heuschele W P 1961. Chlordiazepoxide for calming zoo animals. *Int Zoo Yb* 3, 116-119.

Howell P G, Young E and Hedger R S 1973. Foot-and-mouth disease in the African elephant. *Onderstepoort J vet Res* 40(2), 41-52.

Hill J E and Carter T D 1941. The mammals of Angola, Africa. *Bull Amer Mus nat Hist* 78, 1-212.

Hime T M and Jones D M 1970. The use of xylazine in captive wild animals. *Verhandlungsbericht des XII Int Symp über die Erkrankungen der Zootiere, Budapest,* 1970, pp 143-146.

Hirst S M 1966. Immobilization of the Transvaal giraffe (*Giraffa camelopardalis*) using an oripavine derivative. *Jl S Afr vet med Ass* 37(1), 85-89.

Hirst S M 1969. Predation as a regulating factor of wild ungulate populations in a Transvaal lowveld nature reserve. *Zoologica Africana* 4(2), 199-230.

Hirst S M 1969. Road strip census techniques for wild ungulates in African woodland. *J Wildl Mgmt* 33(1), 40-48.

Hirst S M, Kettlitz W K and Visagie G P 1963. The use of Ro 5-2807 (Roche) as a tranquillizer in wild ungulates. *Zool Afr* 1(1), 231-238.

Hitchins P M 1966. Body weights and dressed carcass yields of impala and wildebeest in Hluhluwe Game Reserve. *Lammergeyer* 6, 20-23.

Hitchins P and Vincent J 1972. Observations on range extension and dispersal of impala (*Aepyceros melampus* Lichtenstein) in Zululand. *J Sth Afr Wildl Mgmt Ass* 2(1), 3-8.

Hofmeyr C F B 1956. Two hundred and eighty four autopsies at the National Zoological Gardens, Pretoria. *Jl S Afr vet med Ass* 27, 263.

Hofmeyr J M and de Bruine J R 1973. The problems associated with the capture, translocation and keeping of wild ungulates in South West Africa. *The Lammergeyer* 18, 21-29.

Hofmeyr J M 1974. Developments in the capture and airlift of roan antelope *Hippotragus equinus equinus* under narcosis to the Etosha National Park. *Modoqua* 1(8), 37-48.

Hofmeyr J M, Ebedes H, Fryer R E M and De Bruine J R 1975. The capture and translocation of the black rhinoceros *Diceros bicornis* Linn in South West Africa. *Madoqua* 9(2), 35-44.

Hofmeyr J M and Lenssen J 1975. The capture and care of eland *Taurotragus oryx oryx* (Pallas) using the boma method. *Madoqua* 9(2), 25-33.

Hofmeyr J M, Luchtenstein H G and Mostert P K N 1977. Capture, handling and transport of springbok and the application of haloperidol as a long acting neuroleptic. *Madoqua* 10(2), 123-130.

Horak I G 1978. Parasites of domestic and wild animals in South Africa. X. Helminths in impala. *Onderstepoort J vet Res* 45, 221-228.

Horak I G 1979. Parasites of domestic and wild animals in South Africa. XII. Artificial transmission of nematodes from blesbok and impala to sheep, goats and cattle. *Onderstepoort J vet Res* 46, 27-30.

Horak I G 1980. The control of parasites in antelope in small game reserves. *Jl S Afr vet med Ass* 51(1), 17-19.

Horak I G 1981. The seasonal incidence of the major nematode genera recovered from sheep, cattle, impala and blesbok in the Transvaal. *Jl S Afr vet med Ass* 52(3), 213-223.

Horak I G 1981. Host specificity and the distribution of the helminth parasites of sheep, cattle, impala and blesbok according to climate. *Jl S Afr vet med Ass* 52(3), 201-206.

Horak I G 1982. Parasites of domestic and wild animals in South Africa. XV. The seasonal prevalence of ectoparasites on impala and cattle in the Northern Transvaal. *Onderstepoort Journal of Veterinary Research* 49(2), 85-94.

Horak I G 1983. The internal and external parasites of kudu. *Pelea* 2, 22-26.

Horak I G, Biggs H C, Hanssen T S and Hanssen R E 1983. The prevalence of helminth and arthropod parasites of warthog, *Phacochoerus aethiopicus*, in South West Africa/Namibia. *Onderstepoort J vet Res* 50, 145-148.

Horak I G, Boomker J and De Vos V 1980. A description of the immature stages of *Kirkioestrus minutus* (Rodhain and Bequaert, 1915). (Diptera: Oestridae), and the life cycle and seasonal prevalence of this fly in blue wildebeest. *Onderstepoort J vet Res* 47, 23-30.

Horak I G, Boomker J, Kingsley S A and De Vos V 1983. The efficacy of ivermectin against helminth and arthropod parasites of impala. *Jl S Afr vet med Ass* 54(4), 251-253.

Horak I G and Butt M J 1977. Parasites of domestic and wild animals in South Africa. III. *Oestrus* spp and *Gedoelstia hässleri* in the blesbok. *Onderstepoort J Vet Res* 44(2), 113-118.

Horak I G, De Vos V and Brown M R 1983. Parasites of domestic and wild animals in South Africa. XVI. Helminth and arthropod parasites of blue and black wildebeest (*Connochaetes taurinus* and *Connochaetes gnou*). *Onderstepoort J vet Res* 50, 1-13.

Horak I G, Potgieter F T, Walker J B, De Vos V and Boomker J 1983. The ixodid tick burdens of various large ruminant species in South African nature reserves. *Onderstepoort J vet Res* 50, 221-228.

Hornocker M G 1970. An analysis of mountain lion predation upon mule deer and elk in the Idaho Primitive Area. *Wildl Monogr* 21, 13.

Houpt T R 1959. Utilization of blood urea in ruminants. *Am J Physiol* 197, 115-120.

Howard D A 1964. The copper content of the liver of some game animals in Kenya. *E Afr Wildl J* 2, 47-50.

Howell P G and Young E 1970. Experimental foot-and-mouth disease in the African elephant. *Jl S Afr vet med Ass* 42, 94.

Hubbard W D 1926. Notes on the antelopes and zebra of Northern Rhodesia and Portuguese East Africa. *J Mammal* 7, 184-193.

Hubbard W D 1929. Further notes on the mammals of Northern Rhodesia and Portuguese East Africa. *J Mammal* 10, 294-297.

Huntley B J 1972. A note on food preferences of a steenbok. *J Sth Afr Wildl Agmt Ass* 2(1), 24-26.

Huntley B J 1973. Ageing criteria for tsessebe (*Damaliscus l. lunatus*). *J Sth Afr Wildl Mgmt Ass* 3(1), 24-26.

Huxley J 1961. *The conservation of wild life and natural habitats in Central and East Africa.* Paris, UNESCO; New York, Columbia University Press. 133 pp.

I B A H 1962. The geographical distribution of the warthog and domestic pigs in Africa. *Bull epiz Dis Afr* 10, 91-94.

Imes G D and Smuts G L 1975. Gross and microscopic observations of ovarian abnormalities from five Burchell's zebra, *Equus burchelli antiquorum*, Smith 1841. *Onderstepoort J vet Res* 42(4), 109-116.

Immink R J 1970. From crossbow to crossbow. *Custos* 1(3), 23.

Ingles J M 1965. Weight and shoulder height of impala. *Puku* 3, 75-86.

Ingoldby C M 1929. On the mammals of the Gold Coast. *Ann Mag nat Hist,* 10th Ser 3, 511-529.

Innes J R M and Saunders L Z 1962. *Comparative neuropathology,* 1st ed, New York and London, Academic Press.

Innis A C 1958. The behaviour of the giraffe, *Giraffa camelopardalis*, in the eastern Transvaal. *Proc zool Soc Lond* 131, 245-278.

International Zoo Yearbook 1960. Doses and effects of succinylcholine chloride delivered with projectile syringe to immobilize several species of wild animals at the San Diego Zoo. *Int Zoo Yb* 2, 319-321.

Irby L R 1973. A preliminary report on the mountain reedbuck (*Redunca fulvorufula*) in the Loskop Dam Nature Reserve. *J Sth Afr Wildl Mgmt Ass* 3(2), 53-58.

Irby L R 1975. Meat production potential of mountain reedbuck. *S Afr J of Animal Science* 5, 67-76.

Kare M R 1955. Water, electrolytes and acid-base balance. In: Dukes H (Ed) 1955. *The physiology of domestic animals*. New York. Comstock Publishing Associates.

Kayanja F I B 1969. The ovary of the impala, *Aepyceros melampus* Lichtenstein 1812. *J Reprod Fert Suppl* 6, 311-317.

Kanyanja F I B 1969. The ovary of the impala (*Aepyceros melampus* Lichtenstein, 1812). *J Reprod Fert Suppl* 6, 311-317.

Kay R N B 1968. Water metabolism. In: Golley F B and Buechner H K (Ed) 1968. *A practical guide to the study of the productivity of large herbivores*. Oxford, Blackwell Scientific Publications.

Kayll A J 1974. Use of fire in land management. In: Kozlowski T T and Ahlgren C E (Eds) 1974. *Fire and Ecosystems*, Academic Press Inc, NY, 483-511.

Keep M E 1973. Factors contributing to a population crash of nyala in Ndumu Game Reserve. *The Lammergeyer* 19, 16-23.

Keep M E and Keep P J 1967. Immobilization of waterbuck. *Vet Rec* November 18th, 1967, p 552.

Keep M E and Keep P J 1968. The immobilization of eland using new drug combinations. *The Lammergeyer* 9, 18-23.

Keith M E and Stoltz L P 1971. *Baboon capture using cages*. Pretoria, Wallachs Printing Co, pp 1-10.

Kellas L M 1954. Observations on the reproductive activity and growth rate of the dik dik (*Rhynchotragus kirkii* Neumann). *Proc zool Soc Lond* 124, 751-784.

Kennan T C D 1961. Veld management in the farming areas of S. Rhodesia with special reference to veld-burning. Paper read at the Wildlife Conference Course, University College of Rhodesia and Nyasaland, 19-26, May, 1961.

Kenneth J H 1943. *Gestation periods: A table and bibliography*. Edinburgh: Imperial Bureau Animal Breeding and Genetics. 23 pp.

Kerr M A 1965. The age at sexual maturity in male impala. *Arnoldia Rhod* 1(24), 1-6.

Kettlitz W K 1954. 'n Voorlopige verslag van die verspreiding van sekere wildsoorte in Transvaal. *Fauna and Flora* 124-134.

Kettlitz W K 1955. A preliminary report on the distribution of certain species of game in the Transvaal. *Fauna & Flora* 6, 125-134.

Kettlitz W K 1962. The capture of giraffe without immobilization. *Fauna and Flora* 13, 24-27.

Kettlitz W K 1962. The distribution of some of the larger game mammals in the Transvaal (excluding the Kruger National Park). *Ann Cape Prov Mus II*, 118-137.

Kettlitz W K 1967. The blesbok (*Damaliscus dorcas phillipsi*) with special reference to the herd in the P F N R. *Fauna and Flora* 18, 36-46.

Khamis M Y and Saleh M S 1970. Beitrag zur Anwendung des Präparates Bay Va 1470 (Rompun) beim Büffel. *Vet med Nachr* 4, 274-284.

King J M 1969. The capture and translocation of the black rhinoceros. *E Afr Wildl J* 7, 115-130.

King J M and Carter B H 1965. The use of the oripavine derivative M-99 for the immobilization of the black rhinoceros (*Diceros bicornis*) and its antagonism with the related compound M-285. *E Afr Wildl J* 3, 19-27.

Kling J M and Klingel H 1965. The use of the oripavine derivative M99 for the restraint of equine animals and its antagonism with the related compound M285. *Res Vet Sci* 6, 335-447.

Kleiber M 1965. Metabolic body size. In: K L Baxter (Ed) 1965. Section 7 of *Energy Metabolism*, Publ No 11, European Assoc Anim Prod, Academic Press, New York.

Kleyhans C J and Van Hoven W 1976. Rumen protozoa of the giraffe with a description of two new species. *E Afr Wildl J* 14, 203-214.

Klingel H and Klingel Y 1966. Tooth development and age determination in the plains zebra (*Equus quagga boehmi* Matschie). *Der Zool Garten (NF)* 33, 34-54.

Knowles F A 1911. The distribution of game in Uganda *J E Afr Nat Hist Soc* 2, 18-22.

Knowles J E 1959. Notes on the distribution of game in Northern Rhodesia, 1904-1913. *N Rhod J* 4, 139-146.

Komarek R 1963. Fire and the changing of wild-life habitat. *Proc Second Tall Timbers Fire Ecol Conf Tallahassee, Fla*, 35-43.

Kok O B 1973. Etorphine (M-99) immobilisation and associated behaviour of the red hartebeest (*Alcelaphus buselpahus caama*). *J Sth Afr Wildl Mgmt Ass* 3(1), 9-15.

Korein J, Codden D R and Mowrey F H 1959. The clinical syndrome of paroxysmal paralytic myoglobinuria. Report of 2 cases and an analytical review of the literature. *Neurol* 9, 767.

Kritzinger L 1990. Heartwater disease — A new solution to an old problem? *Natura* 20, 37.

Kroll W R 1962. Experience with Sernylan in zoo animals. *Int zoo Yb* 4, 131-141.

Kruger J C, Skinner J D and Robinson T J 1979. On the taxonomic status of the black and white springbok, *Antidorcas marsupialis*. *SA Journal of Science* 75, 411-412.

Kruger National Park 1960. Annual Report of Biologist 1958/1959. *Koedoe* 3, 1-205.

Krumbiegel I 1939. Die Giraffe. *Monogr Wildsäugetiere* 8. 98 pp.

Küpper W, Dräger N, Mehlitz D and Zillmann U 1981. On the immobilization of hartebeest and kob in upper Volta. *Tropenmed Parasit* 32, 58-60.

Labuschagne R J 1968. *Die Krugerwildtuin en ander Nasionale Parke*. Johannesburg, Da Gama-uitgewers (Edms) Bpk.

Lambrechts A V W 1974. Beraamde digthede en biomassas van sekere wildsoorte in 'n oos-Transvaalse laeveldgebied. Tweede Verslag, Transvaalse Afdeling Natuurbewaring, 16 pp.

Lambrechts M C, Buhr W H and Van der Merwe J P 1956. Observations on the transmission of foot-and-mouth disease to game and controlled transmission from game to cattle and vice versa by means of contact. *Jl S Afr vet med Ass* 27, 133.

Lamprey H F 1963. Ecological separation of the large mammal species in the Tarangire Game Reserve, Tanganyika. *E Afr Wildl J* 1, 63-92.

Lamprey H F 1963. The survey and assessment of wild animals and their habitat in Tanganyika. *Publ IUCN NS No 1*, 219-222.

Lamprey H F 1964. Estimation of the large mammal densities, biomass and energy exchange in the Tarangire Game Reserve, and the Masai Steppe in Tanganyika. *E Afr Wildl J* 2, 1-46.

Lancaster D G 1953. *A checklist of the mammals of Northern Rhodesia*. Lusaka, Government Printer, 56 pp.

Lang H 1923. Recent and historical notes on the square-lipped rhinoceros (*Ceratotherium simum*). *J Mammal* 4, 155-163.

Lang H 1924. Threatened extinction of the white rhinoceros (*Ceratothermium simum*). *J Mammal* 5, 173-180.

Langman V A 1973. The immobilization and capture of giraffe. *S Afr J of Sci* 69, 200-203.

Langman V A 1973. Radio-tracking giraffe for ecological studies. *J Sth Afr Wildl Mgmt Ass* 3(2), 75-78.

Larsen L H 1963. Restraint and anaesthesia of wild animals in captivity. *Australian Journal* 39, 73-80.

Lawrence B and Loveridge A 1953. Mammals from Nyasaland and Tete. *Bull Mus comp Zool Harv* 110, 1-80.

Laws R M 1966. Age criteria for the African elephant *Loxodonta africana*. *E Afr Wildl J* 4, 1-37.

Lawton R F 1963. Palaecological and ecological studies in the northern province of Northern Rhodesia. *Kirkia* 3, 46-77.

Laycock G 1969. Moving day for sea otters. *Audubon* 71(1), 58-78.

Ledger H P 1963. A note on the relative body composition of wild and domesticated ruminants. *Bull epiz Dis Afr* 11, 163-165.

Ledger H P 1963. The importance of stock selection for increasing the productivity of semi-arid areas. *Publ IUCN NS No 1*, 223-231.

Ledger H P 1963. Weights of some East African mammals. *E Afr Wildl J* 1, 123-124.

Ledger H P 1963. Animal husbandry research and wildlife in East Africa. *E Afr Wildl J* 1, 18-29.

Ledger H P 1964. The role of wildlife in African agriculture. Working Paper, No 41. First FAO African Regional Meeting on Animal Production and Health, Addis Ababa. (Rome): FAO. 8pp. Also in *E Afr agric For J* 30, 137-141.

Ledger H P, Payne W J A and Talbot L M 1961. A preliminary investigation of the relationship between body composition and productive efficiency of meat producing animals in the dry tropics. *VIIIth int Congr Anim Prod (Hamburg, 1961)*. 5 pp (Mimeograph).

Ledger H P, Payne W J A, Talbot L M and Zaphiro D R P 1961. The use of carcass analysis techniques for investigating the meat production potential of game and domesticated animals in semi-arid areas. In: Conf on land management problems in areas containing game, Lake Manyara, Tanganyika. 10 pp. (Mimeograph).

Leistner O A 1959. Notes on the vegetation of the Kalahari-Gemsbok National Park with special reference to its influence on the distribution of antelopes. *Koedoe* 2, 128-151.

Leopold A 1933. *Game management*. New York and London, Charles Scribner's Sons. 481 pp.

Leuthold W 1970. Observations on the social organization of impala. *Z Tierpsychol* 27, 693-721.

Lewis H E and Masterson S P 1957. The food value of blitong (S A dried meat). *Brit J Nutr* 11, 5-12.

Liversidge R 1980. Why game farming? *Farmer's Weekly*, May 28, 18-19.

Livingston H G, Payne W J A and Friend M T 1962. Urea excretion in ruminants. *Nature (Lond)* 194, 1057-1058.

Lister R E 1964. Structure activity requirements in some novel thebaine-derived analgesics. *J Pharm Pharmacol* 16, 364-366.

Lister R E 1966. The toxicity of some of the newer narcotic analgesics. *J Pharm Pharmacol* 18, 364-382.

Lombard J 1966. Game Ranching? *Meat Industry,* January — March 1966, 21-27.

Longhurst W 1957. Elephant census *Uganda Wildl Sport,* 1.

Longhurst W 1958. Wildlife research in Uganda. *Fulbright Program Progr Rep No* 3, 42 pp.

Louw P A 1964. Bodemkundige aspekte van die Kalahari-Gemsbokpark. *Koedoe* 7, 156-172.

Lovell R 1955. Intestinal diseases of young calves with special reference to infection with *Bacterium coli. Vet Rev Annot* 1, 1.

Lovemore D F 1963. The effects of anti-tsetse shooting operations on the game populations as observed in the Sebungwe District, Southern Rhodesia. *Publ IUCN NS* No 1, 232-234.

Lydekker R 1908. *The game animals of Africa.* London, Rowland Ward. 484 pp.

Lydekker R 1926. *The game animals of Africa.* London, Rowland Ward.

Lyell D D 1913. *Wild life in Central Africa.* London. 284 pp.

Lynch C D 1974. A behavioural study of blesbok, *Damaliscus dorcas phillipsi,* with special reference to territoriality. Memoir 8 of the National Museum, Bloemfontein.

MacFarlane W V 1964. Terrestrial animals in dry heat: Ungulates. *Handbook of Physiology* Sec 4, Dill DB Am Physiol Soc, Wash.

Maloiy G M O 1973. Water metabolism of East African ruminants in arid and semi-arid regions. *Züchtgsbiol* 90, 219-228.

Mann I 1963. Vitamin content and amino-acid composition of some African game animals. Kabete, Kenya: Department of Veterinary Services. 6 pp.

Manville R H 1949. Techniques for capture and marking of mammals. *J Mammal* 30(1), 27-33.

Marsboom R, Mortelmans J, Vercruysse J and Thienpont D 1962. Effective sedation and anaesthesia in gorillas and chimpanzees. *Nordisk Vet Med* 14(1), 95-101.

Marsboom R and Mortelmans J 1964. Small animal anaesthesia (Proc London 1963). Cited by: Grosskopf J F W *et al* 1969. Jl S Afr vet med Ass 40, 51.

Marsboom R and Symoens J 1968. Azaperone (R1929) as a sedative for pigs. *Tijdschr Diergeneesk* 93(1), 3-15.

Marsh R E and Clark W R 1968. An effective weasel trap. *J Mamm* 49(1), 157.

Marshall F H A and Bowden F P 1936. The further effects of irradiation on the oestrous cycle of the ferret. *J exp Biol* 13, 383-386.

Martini G A and Siegert R (Ed) 1931. *Marburg virus disease.* Berlin, Springer.

Martinaglia G 1937. Some considerations regarding the health of wild animals in captivity. *S Afr J Sc* 33, 833.

Mason D R 1977. Notes on social, ecological and population characteristics of mountain reedbuck in the Jack Scott Reserve. *S Afr J Wildl Res* 7(1), 31-35.

Massopust L C, Wolin L R and Albin M S 1972. Electrophysiological and behavioural responses to ketamine hydrochloride in the rhesus monkey. *Anesth Analg Curr Res* 51, 329

Matschie P 1898. Die geographische verbreitung der tigerpferde und das zebra des Kaokofeldes in Deutsch-Südwest-Afrika. *S B Ges naturf Fr Berl* 1898, 169-181.

Maydon H C (Ed) 1932. *Big game shooting in Africa.* Lonsdale Library Vol. 14. London, Seeley. 445 pp.

McCain R 1939. The development and use of game drives for determining whitetail deer populations on Allegheny National Forest. *Trans N Amer Wildl Conf* 4, 221-230.

McCane R A and Young W F 1944. The secretion of urine during dehydration and rehydration. *J Physiol* 102, 415.

McCaughey C A 1961. Diseases of elephants. *Ceylon Vet J* 9, 94.

McClintic D and Henkes R 1980. probing animal behaviour. *The Furrow* 85(4), 3-4.

McDiarmid A 1962. *Diseases of free-living wild animals.* FAO Agricultural Studies No 57, Rome, Food and Agricultural Organization of the United Nations.

McDiarmid A (Ed.) 1969. Diseases in free-living wild animals. *Proc Symp Zool Soc Lond,* No 24, London, Academic Press.

McDiarmid A 1972. The role of the veterinary profession in wildlife research and management. *Br vet J* 128, 277.

McCulloch B and Achard P L 1965. Mortality in the capture of game animals. *Oryx* 8, 131.

McCully R M, Basson P A, Pienaar J S, Erasmus B, Young E and Pieterse L M 1969. Herpes Lesions in elephants. *Jl S Afr vet med Ass* 40, 422.

McCully R M, Basson P A, Pienaar J S, Frasmus B J and Young E 1971. Herpes nodules in the lung of the African elephant, *Loxodonta africana. Onderstepoort J vet res* 38, 225-236.

Meeser M J N 1962. Foot-and-mouth disease in game with special reference to the impala *(Aepyceros melampus). Jl S Afr vet med Ass* 33, 351.

Meeser M J N 1963. The role of the veterinarian in wildlife conservation and preservation. *Jl S Afr vet med Ass* 34, 255.

Meester J 1965. The origins of the southern African mammal fauna. *Zool Afr* 1(1), 87-93.

Meinertzhagen R 1938. Some weights and measurements of large mammals. *Proc zool Soc Lond* A 108, 433-439.

Meinertzhagen R 1957. *Kenya Diary, 1902-1906.* Edinburgh and London, Oliver & Boyd. 347 pp.

Meissner H H 1982. Klassifikasie van plaasdiere en wild om weidingskapasiteit te beraam. *Boerdery in Suid-Afrika.* 4 pp.

Melland F 1938. *Elephants in Africa.* London, Country Life Ltd. 186 pp.

Mentis M T 1970. Estimates of natural biomasses of large herbivores in the Umfolozi Game Reserve area. *Mammalia* 34, 363-393.

Mentis M T 1972. A review of some life history features of the large herbivores of Africa. *Lammergeyer* 16, 1-89.

Mentis M T 1977. Stocking rates and carrying capacities for ungulates on African rangelands. *S Afr J Wildl Res* 7(2), 89-98.

Mentis M 1978. Economically optimal species — mixes and stocking rates for ungulates in South Africa. *Proceedings of the First International Rangeland Congress,* 146-149.

Mentis M T 1981. In: Tainton N M (Ed.) 1981. *Veld and pasture management in South Africa.* Shuter and Shooter, Pietermaritzburg.

Mentis M T and Duke R R 1974. Stocking rates of game on private land in Natal. *Natal Parks Board Research Communication* No 17; 8 pp.

Mentis M T and Duke R R 1976. Carrying capacities of natural veld in Natal for large wild herbivores. *S Afr J Wildl Res* 6(2), 65-74.

Merck G 1961. A look at wildlife in Sudan. *Anim Kingd* 64, 82-88.

Mettam R W M 1923. Snotsiekte in cattle. *9th and 10th Rep Dir Vet Educ Res, U of S Africa,* p 393.

Mettam R W M and Carmichael J 1933. Microbacillosis in a recently captive antelope in Uganda. *J Comp path Therap* 46, 16.

Miller H A 1963. Use of fire in wildlife management. *Proc Second Tall Timbers Fire Ecol Conf Tallahassee, Fla,* 19-30.

Miller W L and Robertson E D S 1959. *Practical animal husbandry,* London, Oliver and Boyd.

Mitchell B L 1953. Game preservation in Nyasaland. *Oryx* 2(2), 98-110.

Mohan R N and Gotts M G 1970. Diseases and parasites of the African buffalo *(Syncerus caffer). Vet Bull* 40, 157.

Mönnig H O 1934. *Veterinary Helminthology and Entomology.* London, Baillière, Tindall and Cox.

Monro R H and Skinner J D 1979. A note on condition indices for adult male impala *Aepyceros melampus. S Afr J Anim Sci* 9, 47-51.

Montgomery G G 1961. A modification of the nicotine dart capture method. *J Wildl Mgmt* 25(1), 101-102.

Mosby H S (Ed.) 1960. *Manual of game investigational techniques.* Washington, D C, Wildlife Society.

Mossman A S 1961. Wildlife ranching in Southern Rhodesia. *IUCN Publ New Series* I.

Mossman A S 1963. Wildlife ranching in Southern Rhodesia. *Publ IUCN, NS,* 1, 247-249.

Mossman A S and Dasmann R F 1962. *Game ranching handbook for Southern Rhodesia.* National Museum of Southern Rhodesia. 15 pp.

Mossmann A S and Mossmann H W 1962. Ovulation, implantation and fetal sex ratio for impala. *Science* 137, 869.

Murray A 1866. *The geographical distribution of mammals.* London, Day & Son. 420 pp.

Napier Bax P and Sheldrick D L W 1963. Some preliminary observations on the food of elephant in the Tsavo Royal National Park (East) of Kenya. *E Afr Wildl J* 1, 40-53.

Neitz W O 1935. The blesbuck *(Damaliscus albifrons)* and black wildebeest *(Connochaetes gnou)* as carriers of heartwater. *Onderstepoort J Sci Anim Ind* 5, 35.

Neitz W O 1936. Anthrax: Death in blesbok following the use of goat anthrax vaccine. *Jl S Afr vet med Ass* 7, 119.

Neitz W O 1944. The susceptibility of the springbok to heartwater. *Onderstepoort J vet Sci Anim Ind* 20, 25.

Neitz W O 1944. The susceptibility of the springbok *(Antidorcas marsupialis)* to heartwater. *Onderstepoort J vet Sci Anim Ind* 20, 25.

Neitz W O 1963. African swine fever. In: *Emerging diseases of animals.* Rome, FAO Agricultural Studies No 61, p 3.

Neitz W O 1965. A check-list and host-list of the zoonoses occurring in mammals and birds in South and South West Africa. *Onderstepoort J vet res 32*, 189.

Newton R F 1958. Elephant census. *Uganda Wildl Sport* 1, 28-30.

Nicholson B D 1955. The African elephant (*Loxodonta africana*). *Afr Wild Life* 9, 31-40.

Noe F E, Borillo N and Greifenstein F E 1965. Use of a new analeptic, doxapram hydrochloride, during general anaesthesia and recovery. *Curr Res Anesth* 44, 206-213.

Oates L G 1972. Food preferences of giraffe in Transvaal Lowveld mopane woodland. *J Sth Afr Wildl Mgmt Ass* 2(2), 21-23.

Odum E P 1959. *Fundamentals of ecology*. Philadelphia and London, W B Saunders Co.

Oelofse J 1969. Het vangen van wilde dieren met behulp van blauw plastisch materiaal. Tijdschrift *"Zoo"* van de Kon. Mij voor Dierkunde van Antwerpen 35(1) 6 pp.

Offermann P P M 1953. The elephant in the Belgian Congo. In: *The elephant in East Central Africa*, London, Rowland Ward, pp 114-125.

Osterhoff D R and Young E 1966. Blood groups in African buffalo *Syncerus caffer*. *Polymorphismes bio-chimiques des animaux, XC Congres Européen sur les groupes sanguins et le polymorphisme biochimique des animaux. Paris, 5-8 July, 133-135.*

Osterhoff D R, Young E and Ward-Cox I S 1970. A study of genetical blood variants in African buffalo. *Jl S Afr vet med Ass* 41, 33.

Osterhoff D R, Petrie I A and Young E 1972. Haemoglobins in wild animals. *Jl S Afr vet med Ass* 43(4), 361-362.

Osterhoff D R, Ward-Cox I S and Young E 1972. Bio-chemical polymorphism in the South African impala (*Aepyceros melampus*). *Koedoe* 15, 55-59.

Osterhoff D R, Young E and Ward-Cox I S 1972. Transferrin and haemoglobin types in the African elephant (*Loxodonta africana*). *Koedoe* 15, 61-65.

Osterhoff D R, Schoeman S, Op't Hof J and Young E 1974. Genetic differentiation of the African elephant in the Kruger National Park. *South African Journal of Science* 70(8), 245-247.

Osterhoff D R, Schoeman S, Op't Hof J and Young E 1974. Genetic markers as tools in wildlife population studies. *1st World Congress on Genetics applied to Livestock Production, Madrid, Spain, 7-11 September 1974.*

Owen M and Owen D 1980. The fences of death. *Afr Wild Life* 34(6), 25-27.

Paine R and Martinaglia G 1928. Tuberculosis in wild buck living under natural conditions. *Jl S Afr vet med Ass* 1, 87.

Payne W J A 1964. The origin of domestic cattle in Africa. *Emp J exp Agric* 32, 97-113.

Payne W J A 1964. Specific problems of semi-arid environments. *Proc 6th int Congr Nutr (Edinb)* 1963, 213-226.

Pearson R M and Smith J A B 1943. The utilization of urea in the bovine rumen. 2. The conversion of urea to ammonia. *Biochem J* 37, 148-153.

Pearsall W H 1954. Biology and land-use in East Africa. *New Biol* 17, 9.

Pearsall W H 1957. *Report on an ecological survey of the Serengeti National Park, Tanganyika.* London, Fauna Preservation Society. 64 pp.

Percival A B 1924. *A game rangers note book.* London. Nisbet and Co Ltd.

Pereira H C 1961. Conference on land management problems in areas containing game: Lake Manyra, Tanganyika. Pt II, Sect V. The disease problems of wild animals in relation to domestic stock. (Summ.) *E Afr agric For J* 27, 100-102.

Perry J S 1952. The growth and reproduction of elephants in Uganda. *Uganda J* 16, 51-66.

Perry J S 1953. The reproduction of the African elephant, *Loxodonta africana*. *Phil Trans B* 237, 93-149.

Perry J S 1954. Some observations on growth and tusk weight in male and female African elephants. *Proc zool Soc Lond* 124, 97-104.

Petrides G A 1955. *Report on Kenya's wildlife resource and the National Parks.* Royal National parks of Kenya. 31 pp.

Petrides G A 1956. Big game densities and range carrying capacity in East Africa. *Trans N Amer Wildl Conf* 21, 525-537.

Petrides G A 1958. Uganda's priceless heritage. *Uganda Wildl Sport* 1. 4 pp.

Petrides G A 1960. The management of wild hoofed animals in the United States in relation to land use. In: *Ecology and management of wild grazing animals in temperate zones*, 8th Techn meet, IUCN, Warsaw, 181-202.

Petrides G A 1963. Ecological research as a basis for wildlife management in Africa. *Publ IUCN, NS*, No 1, 284-293.

Petrides G A and Swank W G 1958. management of the big game resource in Uganda, East Africa. *Trans N Amer Wildl Conf* 23, 461-477.

Petrides G A and Swank W G 1965. Population densities and the range-carrying capacity for large mammals in Queen Elizabeth National Park, Uganda. *Zoologica Africana* 1(1), 209-225.

Petrides G A and Swank W G 1966. Estimating the productivity and energy relations of an African elephant population. *Proc Ninth International Grassland Contress, Sao Paulo, Brazil, January 1965, 831-482.*

Pettifer H L and Stumpf R H 1981. An approach to the calculation of habitat preference data: Impala on Loskop Dam Nature Reserve. *S Afr J Wildl Res* 11, 5-13

Phillips J 1959. *Agriculture and ecology in Africa.* London, Faber & Faber, 424 pp.

Phillips J F V 1925. The Knysna elephants, a brief note on their history and habits. *S Afr J Sci* 22, 287-293.

Phillips J F V 1930. Fire: its influence on biotic communities and physical factors in South and East Africa. *S Afr J Sci* 27, 352-367.

Philippson P 1934. Domesticating the African elephant. Experiments in the Belgian Congo. *Field* 163, 1527.

Pienaar J G, Bigalke R D, Tustin R C and Naude T W 1964. The occurrence of coccidiosis in impala, *Aepyceros melampus* (Lichtentein, 1912). *Jl S Afr vet med Ass* 35, 333.

Pienaar U de V 1961. A second outbreak of anthrax amongst game animals in the Kruger National Park. *Koedoe* 4, 4.

Pienaar U de V 1963. The large mammals of the Kruger National Park — their distribution and present day status. *Koedoe* 6, 1-37.

Pienaar U de V 1967. Epidemiology of anthrax in wild animals and the control of anthrax epizootics in the Kruger National Park, South Africa. *Federation Proceedings* 26, 1496-1502.

Pienaar U de V 1967. The field-immobilization and capture of hippopotami in their aquatic element. *Koedoe* 10, 149-157.

Pienaar U de V 1967. Operation "Khomandlopfu". *Koedoe* 10, 158-164.

Pienaar U de V 1968. The use of immobilizing drugs in conservation procedures for roan antelope. *Acta Zool et Path Antv* 46, 39-51.

Pienaar U de V 1968. Recent advances in the field immobilization and restraint of wild ungulates in South African National Parks. *Antwerp Zoo J* 46, 17-38.

Pienaar U de V 1969. In: Golley F B and Buechner H K (Ed) 1969. *A practical guide to the study of the productivity of large herbivores.* Oxford and Edinburgh, Blackwell Scientific Publications, pp 132-144.

Pienaar U de V 1969. The use of drugs in the field immobilization and restraint of large wild animals in South African National Parks. *Acta Zool et Path Antv* 48, 163-177.

Pienaar U de V 1969. Predator-prey relationships among the larger mammals of the Kruger National Park. *Koedoe* 12, 108-176.

Pienaar U de V 1969. Observations on developmental biology, growth and some aspects of the population ecology of African buffalo in the Kruger National Park. *Koedoe* 12, 29.

Pienaar U de V 1970. The drug-immobilizing technique on the game farm or ranch. Game owners Ass of SA and SWA information sheet No 1, 9 pp.

Pienaar U de V and Van Niekerk J W 1963. The capture and translocation of three species of wild ungulates in the E. Transvaal with special reference to Ro 5-2807/B-SF (Roche) as a tranquillizer in game animals. *Koedoe* 6, 83-91.

Pienaar U de V, Van Niekerk J W, Young E, Van Wyk P and Fairall N 1966. Neuroleptic narcosis of large wild herbivores in South African National Parks with the new potent morphine derivatives, M99 and M183. *Jl S Afr vet med Ass* 37, 277-291.

Pienaar U de V, Van Niekerk J W, Young E, Van Wyk P and Fairall N 1966. The use of oripavine hydrochloride (M-99) in the drug immobilization and marking of wild African elephant in the Kruger National Park. *Koedoe* 9, 108-124.

Pienaar U de V, Van Wyk P and Fairall N 1966. An aerial census of elephant and buffalo in the Kruger National Park and the implications thereof on intended management schemes. *Koedoe* 9, 40.

Pitchford R J, Visser P S, Du Toit J F, Pienaar U de V and Young E 1973. Observations on *Schistosoma mattheei* in portion of the Kruger National Park and surrounding area using a new quantitive technique. *Jl S Afr vet med Ass* 44(4), 405-420.

Pitchford R J, Visser P S, Pienaar U de V and Young E 1974. Further observations on *Schistosoma mattheei*, Veglia and le Roux, 1929, in the Kruger National Park. *Jl S Afr vet med Ass* 45(3), 211-218.

Pitman C R S 1934. *A report on a faunal survey of Northern Rhodesia.* Livingstone, Government Printer. 500 pp.

Player I C 1967. The translocation of the white rhinoceros: a success in wildlife conservation in South Africa. *Oryx* 9(2), 137-150.

Plowright W 1963. The role of game animals in the epizootiology of rinderpest and malignant catarrhal fever in East Africa. *Bull epizoot dis Afr* 11, 149.

Plowright W, Ferris R D and Scott G R 1960. Blue wildebeest and the aetiological agent of bovine malignant catarrhal fever. *Nature* 188, 1167.

Plowright W, Parker J and Pierce M A 1969. The epizootiology of African swine fever. *Vet Rec* 85, 668.

Posselt J 1963. The domestication of the eland. *Rhod J agric Res* 1, 81-87.

Potgieter L 1984. Slaankrag van gewilde geweerkalibers. *Natura* 2, 15.

Pritchard G I, Folkins L P and Pigden W J 1963. The in vitro digestibility of whole grasses and their parts at progressive stages of maturity. *Can J Plant Sci* 43, 79-87.

Protasenja T P 1956. New method of study of digestion of carbohydrates, proteins and fats in animals with fistulae. *Fiziol Z SSR Secenova* 42, 420-433.

Pugh D M 1964. Acepromazine in veterinary use. *Vet Rec* 76(16), 439-442.

Quin J I, Oyaert W and Clark R 1951. The effect of fasting on the activity of the ruminal flora of sheep and cattle. *Onderstepoort J vet Res* 25, 51.

Rabb G G 1958. Some longevity records of captive mammals. *Journal of Mammalogy* 41, 1.

Rabb G B 1960. Longevity records for mammals at the Chicago Zoological Park. *J Mammal* 41, 114.

Rankin J D and McDiarmid A 1968. Mycobacterial infections in free-living wild animals. *Symp zool Soc Lond* 24, 119.

Ratcliff H L 1956. Cited by Scott P P 1968. In: Crawford M A 1968. *Comparative nutrition of wild animals*. London, Academic Press.

Rautenbach I L 1978. Ecological distribution of the mammals of the Transvaal (Vertebrata: mammalia). *Annals of the Transvaal Museum No 10, Vol 31, 30 November, 1978.* pp 131-156.

Reid J T and Kennedy W K 1956. Measurement of forage intake by grazing animals. *Int Grassland Congr Proc* 7, 3-8.

Riney T 1961. Utilization of wildlife in the Transvaal. *IUCN Publ New Series* 1.

Riney T 1963. Utilization of wildlife in the Transvaal. *Publ IUCN, NS, No 1, 303-305.*

Riney T 1963. The impact of introductions of large herbivores on the tropical environment. *Proc 9th tech Meet, IUCN*, Nairobi, 1963.

Riney T 1964. The economic use of wildlife in terms of its productivity and its development as an agricultural activity. *Working paper, No 49. First FAO African Regional meeting on Animal Production and Health, Addis Ababa. (Rome), FAO.* 8 pp.

Riney T and Child G 1960. Breeding season and the ageing criteria for the common duiker (*Sylvicapra grimmia*). *Proc 1st Fed Sci Congr (Salisbury S Rhod)*: 291-299.

Riney T and Kettlitz W L 1964. Management of large mammals in the Transvaal. *Mammalia* 28(2), 189-248.

Riney T and Smithers R 1960. Wildlife and human values in Southern Rhodesia. *Proc 1st Fed Sci Congr (Salisbury S Rhod)*, 307-317.

Roberts A 1937. The old surviving types of mammals found in the Union. *S Afr J Sci* 34, 73-78.

Roberts A 1937. The South African antelopes. *S Afr J Sci* 33, 771-787.

Roberts A 1951. *The mammals of South Africa.* Trustees of "The mammals of South Africa". 700 pp.

Robertshaw D and Taylor C R 1969. A comparison of sweat gland activity in eight species of East African bovids. *J Physiol* 203, 135.

Robertson-Bullock W 1962. The weight of the African elephant *Loxodonta africana*. *Proc Zoological Soc London* 138(1), 133-135.

Robinette W L 1963. Weights of some of the larger mammals of Northern Rhodesia. *Puku* 1, 207-215.

Robinette W L, Gashwiler J S, Louw J B and Jones D A 1957. Differential mortality by sex and age among mule deer. *J Wildl Mgmt* 21, 1-16.

Robinson T J 1979. Influence of a natritional parameter on the size differences of the three springbok subspecies. *S Afr J Zool* 14, 13-15.

Robinson T J and Skinner J D 1976. A karyological survey of springbok subspecies. *S Afr J of Sci* 72, 147-148.

Roetcher D and Hofmann R R 1970. The ageing of impala from a population in the Kenya Rift Valley. *E Afr Wildl J* 8, 37-42.

Roetcher v D, Hofmann R R and Kanyanja F I B 1970. Ergebnisse der prae — und postnatalen Altersbestimmung beim ostafrikanischen Impala *Aepyceros melampus* Lichtenstein, 1812. *Z Säuertierk* 35, 289-305.

Rogerson A 1968. Energy utilization by the eland and wildebeest. *Symp zool Soc Lond* 21, 153-161.

Rollinson D H L 1962. Brucella agglutinins in East African game animals *Vet Rec* 74, 904.

Roosevelt T and Heller E 1914. *Life histories of African game animals*. New York, Charles Scribner's Sons. (2 vols.) 798 pp.

Rosevear D R 1938. The antelopes of Nigeria. *Niger Fld* 7, 16-17.

Rosevear D R 1939. The hoofed mammals of Nigeria. *Niger Fld* 8, 104-107.

Roth H H 1966. Game utilization in Rhodesia in 1964. *Extrait de Mammalia Tome* 30(3), September 1966.

Roth H H 1970. Studies on the agricultural utilization of semi-domesticated eland (*Taurotragus oryx*) in Rhodesia. *Rhod J agric Res* 8, 67-70.

Round M C 1968. *Check-list of the helminth parasites of African mammals*. Technical communication No 38 of the Commonwealth Bureau of Helminthology St Albans. Farnham Royal, Bucks, England, Commonwealth Agricultural Bureau.

Rowe-Rowe C T 1973. Social behaviour in a small blesbok population. *J Sth Afr Wildl Mgmt Ass* 3(2), 49-52.

Russell E W (Ed) 1962. *The natural resources of East Africa*. D A Hawkins Ltd, in association with East African literature bureau, Nairobi, 144 pp.

Rzasnicki A 1951. Zebra and quaggas. *Ann Mus zool Polon* 14, 203-251.

Sachs R 1967. Live weights and body measurements of Serengeti game animals. *E Afr Wildl J* 5, 24-36.

Sachs R and Sachs C 1968. A survey of parasitic infestations of wild herbivores in the Serengeti regions in Northern Tanzania and the Lake Rukwa region in Southern Tanzania. *Bull epizoot dis Afr* 16, 455.

Sachs R, Staak C and Groocock C M 1968. Serological investigation of brucellosis in game animals in Tanzania. *Bull epizoot dis Afr* 16, 93.

Safar P (Ed) 1965. *Respiratory therapy*, 2nd printing (1966), Philadelphia, F A Davis Company, pp 30-31.

Sagner G and Haas G 1969. Ein neues Mittel zur Anästhesie und Immobilisation von Haus und Wildtieren. Verhandlungsbericht des XI *Int Symp über die Erkrankungen der Zootiere, Zagreb*, 1969, pp 131-133.

Sauer J J C, Theron G K and Skinner J D 1977. Food preferences of giraffe *Giraffa camelopardalis* in the arid bushveld of the western Transvaal. *S Afr J Wildl Res* 7(2), 53-59.

Saugstad S 1942. Aerial census of big game in North Dakota. *Trans N Am Wild Conf* 7, 343-356.

Savory C R 1965. Game utilisation in Rhodesia. *Zoological Africana* 1(1), 321-337.

Schenkel R 1966. On sociology and behaviour in impala (*Aepyceros melampus*, Lichtenstein). *E Afr Wildl J* 4, 99.

Schmidt-Nielsen K 1964. *Desert Aninmals*. Oxford, Clarendon Press.

Schmidt-Nielsen K 1959. The physiology of the camel. *Sci Amer* 201(6), 140-151.

Schmidt-Nielsen K 1964. *Desert Animals. Physiological problems of heat and water*. Clarendon Press, Oxford.

Schmidt-Nielsen K and Schmidt-Nielson B 1952. Water metabolism of desert mammals. *Physiol Rev* 32, 135.

Schwabe C W 1969. *Veterinary medicine and human health*. London, Baillière, Tindall and Cassel.

Scialdo R C, Reinecke R K and De Vos V 1982. Seasonal incidence of helminths in the Burchell's zebra. *Onderstepoort Journal of Veterinary Research* 49(2), 127-130.

Scott P P 1968. In: Crawford M A 1968. *Comparative nutrition of wild animals*. London, Academic Press.

Scott G R 1970. Rinderpest In: Davies J W, Karstad L H and Trainer D O (Ed) 1970. *Infectious diseases of wild animals*. Ames, Iowa, USA, The Iowa State Univ Press.

Sclater W L 1900-1901. *The mammals of South Africa*. London, R N Porter, (2V.)

Sclater P L and Thomas O 1900. *The book of antelopes*, Vol I. London, R H Porter. 220 pp.

Selye H 1950. *Stress*, 1st ed, Montreal, Acta Inc Medical Publishers, pp 82-99.

Setzer H W 1956. Mammals of the Anglo-Egyptian Sudan. *Proc U S nat Mus* 106, 447-585.

Shah K V 1969. Vertebrate populations as reservoirs of disease. In: Sladen B K and Bang F B (Ed) 1969. *Biology of populations*. New York, American Elsevier Publishing Co, Inc.

Shantz H L and Marbut C F 1923. The vegetation and soils of Africa. *Res Ser Amer geogr Soc* No 13. 263 pp.

Shaul D M B 1963. The composition of the milk of wild animals. *Int Zoo Yb* 4, 333-342.

Short D J 1968. In: Crawford M A 1968. *Comparative nutrition of wild animals*. London, Academic Press.

Short R V 1963. A syringe projectile for use with a bow and arrow. *Vet Rec* 75(35), 883-885.

Short R V and King J M 1964. The design of a crossbow and dart for the immobilization of wild animals. *Vet Rec* 76(23), 628-630.

Short R V and Spinage C A 1967. Drug immobilization of the Defassa waterbuck. *Vet Rec* 81, 336-340.

Shortridge G C 1934. The mammals of South West Africa. London, Heinemann. (2 vols.) 779 pp.

Shortridge G C 1934. Hartmann's mountain zebra. *J Soc Pres Fauna Emp*, Pt 22, 13-15.

Siegmund O H (Ed) 1961. *The Merck Veterinary Manual*. New Jersey, Merck and Co, Inc.

Simon N M 1962. *Between the sunlight and the thunder; the wild life of Kenya*. London, Collins. 384 pp.

Simon N M 1963. The Galana river game management scheme. *Publ IUCN NS* No 1, 325-328.

Simpson C D 1968. Reproduction and population structure in greater kudu in Rhodesia. *J of Wildl Mgmt* 32(1), 149-161.

Simpson C D 1972. An evaluation of seasonal movement in greater kudu populations — *Tragelaphus strepsiceros* Pallas — in three localities in southern Africa. *Zoologica Africana* 7(1), 197-205.

Simpson C D 1972. Some characteristics of Tragelaphine horn growth and their relationship to age in greater kudu and bushbuck. *J Sth Afr Wildl Mgmt Ass* 2(2), 1-8.

Simpson C D and Cowie D 1967. The seasonal distribution of kudu — *Tragelaphus strepsiceros* pallas — on a southern lowveld game ranch in Rhodesia. *Arnoldia* 18(3) 1-12.

Simpson V R and Dräger N 1979. African swine fever antibody detection in warthogs. *The Veterinary Record* 105, 61.

Simpson C D and Elder W H 1968. Lens weights related to estimated age in greater kudu. *J of Wildl Mgmt*, 32(4), 764-768.

Simpson C D and Elder W H 1969. Tooth cementum as an index of age in greater kudu (*Tragelaphus strepsiceros*). *Arnoldia* 20(4), 1-10.

Skinner J D 1967. An appraisal of the eland as a farm animal in Africa. *Animal Breeding Abstracts* 35(2), 177-186.

Skinner J D 1970. Game ranching in Africa as a source of meat for local consumption and export. *Trop Anim Hlth Prod* 2, 151-157.

Skinner J D 1971. Productivity of the eland: an appraisal of the last five years' research. *Suid-Afrikaanse Tydskrif vir Wetenskap*, December 1971.

Skinner J D 1971. The sexual cycle of the impala ram *Aecyperos melampus* Lichenstein. *Zoo. Afr* 6(1), 75-84.

Skinner J D 1971. Lifetime production of an impala. *Afr Wild Life* 23, 78-79.

Skinner J D 1971. The effect of season on spermatogenesis in some ungulates. *J Reprod Fert, Suppl* 13, 29-37.

Skinner J D 1973. An appraisal of the status of certain antelope for game farming in South Africa. *Zeitschrift für Tiersüchtung und Züchtungsbiologie* 90(3), 263-277.

Skinner J D 1978. Breeding cycles in three species of African ungulates. In: Assenmacher I, and Farner D S (Eds) 1978. *Environmental Endocrinology*, Springer-Verlag, Berlin, pp 64-72.

Skinner J D 1980. Productivity of mountain reedbuck *Redunca fulvorufula* (Afzelius 1815) at the Mountain Zebra National Park. *Koedoe* 23, 123-130.

Skinner J D and Huntley B J 1971. The sexual cycle in the blesbok ram *Damaliscus dorcas phillipsi*. *Agroanimalia* 3, 23-26.

Skinner J D and Huntley B J 1971. A report on the sexual cycle in the kudu bull *Tragelaphus strepsiceros* Pallas and a description of an intersex, *Zoologica Africa* 6(2), 293-299.

Skinner J D, Scorer J A and Millar R P 1975. Observations on the reproductive physiological status of mature herd bulls, bachelor bulls, and young bulls in the Hippopotamus *Hippopotamus amphibius amphibius* Linnaeus, *General and Comparative Endocrinology* 26, 92-95.

Skinner J D and Van Zyl J H M 1970. The sexual cycle of the springbok ram (*Antidorcas marsupialis*, Zimmerman). *Proc S Afr Soc Anim Prod* 9, 197-202.

Skinner J D, Von le Chevallerie M and Van Zyl J H M 1971. An appraisal of the springbok for diversifying animal production in Africa. *Animal Breeding Abstracts*, 39(2), 215-224.

Sladen B K and Bang F B (Ed) 1969. *Biology of populations, Section IV: Disease in populations*. New York, American Elsevier Publishing Co., Inc.

Sloan J E N 1965. Helminths in ungulates. *Int Zoo Yb* 5, 24-28.

Smit F 1890. The histology of the skin of the elephant. *J Anat Lond* 24, 493.

Smit P J 1964. Die geohidrologie van die Nasionale Kalahari Gemsbokpark. *Koedoe* 7, 153.

Smithers R H N 1971. *The mammals of Botswana*. DSc Thesis, University of Pretoria.

Smithers R H N 1985. *The Mammals of the Southern African Subregion*. 736 pp.

Smuts G L 1972. *Seasonal movements, migration and age determination of Burchell's zebra (Equus burchelli antiquorum, H smith, 1841) in the Kruger National Park*. MSc Thesis, University of Pretoria.

Smuts G L 1973. Xyazine hydrocholride (rompun) and the new retractable-barbed dart ("drop-out" dart) for the capture of some nervous and aggressive antelope species. *Koedoe* 16, 159-173.

Smuts G L 1974. Age determination in burchell's zebra (*Equus burchelli antiquorum*) from the Kruger National Park. *J Sth Afr Wildl Mgmt Ass* 4(2), 103-115.

Smuts G L 1974. Game movements in the Kruger National Park and their relationship to the segregation of sub-populations and the allocation of culling compartments. *J Sth Afri Wildl Mgmt Ass* 4(1), 51-58.

Smuts G L 1974. *Growth, reproduction and population characteristics of Burchell's zebra (Equus burchelli antiquorum, H Smith 1841) in the Kruger National Park*. DSc dissertation, University of Pretoria. 268 pp.

Smuts G L 1975. Home range sizes for Burchell's zebra from the Kruger National Park. *Koedoe* 18, 139-146.

Smuts G L 1975. Pre- and postnatal growth phenomena of Burchell's zebra (*Equus burchelli antiquorum*) from the Kruger National Park. Koedoe 18, 69-102.

Smuts G L 1975. An appraisal of naloxone hydrochloride as a narcotic antagonist in the capture and release of wild herbivores. *J A V M A* 167(7), 559-561.

Smuts G L 1975. Reproduction and population characteristics of elephants (*Loxodonta africana*) in the Kruger National Park. *J Sth Afr Wildl Mgmt Ass* 5(1), 1-10.

Smuts G L 1976. Population characteristics of Burchell's zebra (*Equus burchelli antiquorum*, 1841) in the Kruger National Park. *S Afr J Wildl Res* 6(2), 99-112.

Smuts G L 1976. Reproduction in the zebra mare (*Equus burchelli antiquorum*) from the Kruger National Park. *Koedoe*. 19, 89-132.

Smuts G L 1976. Some reproductive abnormalities of the zebra stallion (*Equus burchelli antiquorum*). *Zoologica Africana* II(I), 221-225.

Smuts G L 1976. Reproduction in the zebra stallion (*Equus burchelli antiquorum*) from the Kruger National Park. *Zoologica Africana* II(I), 207-120.

Smuts G L 1978. Interrelations between predators, prey and their environment. *BioScience* 28, 316-320.

Smuts G L 1979. The diet of lions and spotted hyaenas assessed from stomach contents. *S Afr J Wildl Res* 9, 19-25.

Smuts G L, Bryden B R, De Vos V and Young E 1973. Some practical advantages of CI-581 (Ketamine) for the field immobilisation of larger wild felines, with comparative notes on baboons and impala. *The Lammergeyer* 18, 1-14.

Snijders A J and Horak I G 1972. Trials with Rafoxanide. 4. Efficacy against the larvae of the oestrid fly *Gedoelstia hässleri* in the blesbuck (*Damaliscus dorcas phillipsi* Harper, 1939). *Jl S Afr Vet Med Ass* 43(3), 295-297.

Soma L R and Shields D R 1964. Neuroleptanalgesia produced by fentanyl and droperidol. *J Amer Vet Med Assoc* 145, 897-902.

Sommer F 1953. *Man and beast in Africa*. London, Herbert Jenkins. 206 pp.

Southwick C H 1969. Fluctuations of vertebrate populations. In: Sladen B K and Bang F B (Ed.) 1969. *Biology of populations*. New York, American Elsevier Publishing Co. Inc.

Spinage C A 1962. *Animals of East Africa*. London, Collins.

Spinage C A 1971. Geratodontology and horn growth of the impala (*Aepyceros melampus*). *J Zool Lond* 164, 269-270.

Spinage C A 1972. Age estimation of zebra. *E Afr Wild J* 10, 273-277.

Spinage C A 1973. The role of photoperiodism in the seasonal breeding of tropical African ungulates. *Mammal Review* 3(3), 71-84.

Spinage C A 1974. Territoriality and population regulation in the Uganda defassa waterbuck. In: The behaviour of ungulates and its relation to management. *IUCN Publications New Series* 24, 635-643.

Spinage V A 1962. Rinderpest and faunal distribution patterns. *African Wild Life* 16,55.

Stander G J (Red). 1965. *Water*. Pretoria, S A Akad vir Wet en Kuns (Afd Chemie).

Starfield A M, Smuts G L and Shiell J D 1976. A simple wildebeest population model and its application. *S Afr J Wildl Res* 6(2), 95-98.

Stephansson V 1949. Economic utilization of wildlife through partial or complete domestication. *Trans 14th N Am Wildlife Conf*, 31.

Stevenson-Hamilton J 1912. *Animal life in Africa*. London, William Heinemann.

Stevenson-Hamilton J 1929. *The Low veld: its wild life and its people.* London, Cassel and Company Ltd.

Stevenson-Hamilton J 1947. *Wild Life in South Africa.* London, Cassel and Co Ltd.

Steyn D G 1949. *Vergiftiging van mens en dier met gifplante, voedsel en drinkwater.* Pretoria, J L van Schaik Bpk.

Steyn D G 1965. Skeikundige en toksikologiese aspekte van drinkwater vir mens en dier. In: Stander G J (Red.) 1965. *Water.* Pretoria, S A Akad vir Wet en Kuns (Afd Chemie).

Stewart D R M 1963, Wildlife census — Lake Rudolf. *E Afr Wildl J* 1, 121.

Stewart D R M 1963. The Arabian oryx (*Oryx leucoryx* Pallas). *E Afr Wildl J* 1, 103.

Stewart D R M 1963. Development of wildlife as an economic asset. *Bull epiz Dis Afr* 11, 167-171.

Stewart D R M 1964. Rinderpest among wild animals in Kenya, 1960-2. *Bull epizoot dis Afr* 12, 39.

Stewart D R M 1971. Food preferences of an impala herd. *J Wildl Mgmt* 35, 86-93.

Stewart D R M and Stewart J 1963. The distribution of some large mammals in Kenya. *J E Afr Nat Hist Soc* 24, 1-52.

Stewart D R M and Stewart J 1966. The use of sex and age ratios in estimating abundance and productivity of impala *Lammergeyer* 6, 9-19.

Stewart D R M and Stewart J 1970. Food preference data by faecal analysis for African plains ungulates. *Zool Afr* 5, 115-129.

Stewart D R M and Talbot L M 1962. Census of wildlife on the Serengeti, Mara and Loita Plains. *E Afr Agric For J* 28, 58-60.

Stewart D R M and Zaphiro D R P 1963. Biomass and density of wild herbivores in different East African habitats. *Mammalia* 27, 483-496.

Stigand C H 1909. *The game of British East Africa.* London, Horace Cox, 310 pp.

Stigand C H and Lyell D D 1909. *Central African game and its spoor.* London, Horace Cox. 315 pp.

Stoddart L A and Smith A D 1955. *Range management.* McGraw-Hill Book Company Inc, NY, 433 pp.

Stolk A 1963. Ovulation, implantation and foetal sex ratio in the Uganda kob. *Nature (Lond)* 198, 606.

Storm G L 1965. Movements and activities of foxes as detemined by radio-tracking. *J Wildl Mgmt* 29(1), 1-13.

Sullivan E G 1956. Gray fox reproduction, denning, range, and weights in Alabama. *J Mamm* 37(3), 346-351.

Swank G W and Petrides G A 1957. Hippopo-determine the effects of vegetation and other factors of game populations in Queen Elizabeth Park, Uganda. Fulbright program. Entebbe, Uganda Game and Fisheries. 3 pp. (Mimeograph).

Swank G W and Petrides G A 1957. Hippopotamus population densities in Queen Elizabeth National Park and the effect of a local reduction in their numbers. Fulbright program. Entebbe, Uganda Game and Fisheries. 4 pp. (Mimeograph).

Sweatman G K 1971. Mites and pentastomes. In: Davis J W and Anderson R C (Ed.) 1971. *Parasitic diseases of wild animals.* Ames, Iowa, The Iowa State University Press.

Swynnerton C F M 1936. The tsetse flies of East Africa. *Trans R Ent Soc Lond* 84, 1-579.

Swynnerton G H 1958. Fauna of the Serengeti National Park. *Mammalia* 22, 435-450.

Swynnerton G H and Hayman R W 1950. A checklist of the land mammals of the Tanganyika Territory and Zanzibar Protectorate. *J E Afr Nat Hist Soc* 20, 1-392.

Szappanyos M, Gemperle M and Isard A 1970. Utilization of ketamine (Ketalar) as an anaesthetic in veterinary surgery. *Bull Soc Sc Vet et de Med Comparèe,* Lyon, 72, 149-164.

Taber R D and Cowan I Mc T 1966. In: Giles R H (Ed.) 1969. *Wildlife Management Techniques,* Washington, D C, The Wildlife Society.

Taber R D and Cowan I McT 1971. In: Giles R H (Ed.) 1971. *Wildlife management Techniques* 3rd ed, Washington, D C. The Wildlife Society.

Taber R D and Dasmann R F 1958. The black-tailed deer of the chaparral. *Game Bull Calif Dep Fish and Game* No 8. 163 pp.

Tainton N M 1981. *Veld and pasture management in South Africa.* Shuter and Shooter, Pietermaritzburg.

Talbot L M 1956. Report on the Serengeti National Park, Tanganyika. Brussels, International Union for Protection of Nature, Washington DC, National Parks Association. 9 pp. (Mimeograph).

Talbot L M 1960. Report on field experiments with Palmer Cap-Chur equipment and drugs carried out with and by Mr Palmer in the Narok district and Ngong National Reserve of Kenya. Nairobi, Royal National Parks of Kenya. 7 pp. (Mimeograph).

Talbot L M 1960. Field immobilization of some East African wild animals and cattle. *E Afr Agric For J* 26, 92-102.

Talbot L M 1960. *A look at threatened species.* Fauna Preservation Society (London) for the International Union for Conservation, Morges, Switzerland. 137 pp.

Talbot L M 1961. Preliminary observations on the population dynamics of the wildebeest in Narok District, Kenya. *E Afr Agric For J* 27, 108-116.

Talbot L M 1962. Food preferences of some East African wild ungulates. *E Afr Agric For J* 27, 131-138.

Talbot L M 1963. Comparison of the efficiency of wild animal and domestic livestock in the utilization of East African rangelands. *IUCN New Series* No 1, 229-335.

Talbot L M 1964. Wild animals as sources of food. *Proc 6th int Congr Nutr (Edinb),* 1963, 243-251.

Talbot L M et al 1965. The meat production potential of wild animals in Africa. *Technical Communication No 16, Commonwealth Agricultural Bureaux.*

Talbot L M and Lamprey H 1961. Immobilization of free-ranging East African ungulates with succinylcholine chloride. *J Wild Mgmt* 25, 303-310.

Talbot L M, Ledger H P and Payne W J A 1962. The possibility of using wild animals for animal production in the semi-arid tropics of East Africa. VIIIth Int Congr Anim Prod (Hamburg 1961), III(Final Rep.), 205-210.

Talbot L M and McCulloch J S G 1961. A method for determining body weight of wild animals from external body measurements. In: Conf on land management problems in areas containing game: Lake Manyara, Tanganyika. 8 pp. (Mimeograph).

Talbot L M and McCulloch J S G 1965. Weight estimations for East African wild animals from body measurements. *J Wildl Mgmt* 29, 84-89.

Talbot L M and Stewart D R M 1964. First wildlife census of the entire Serengeti-Mara Region, East Africa. *J Wildl Mgmt* 28, 815-827.

Talbot L M and Talbot M H 1961. A review of the current position of field immobilization in East Africa. In: Conf on land management problems in areas containing game: Lake Manyara, Tanganyika. 8 pp. (Mimeograph).

Talbot L M and Talbot M H 1961. How much does it weigh? *Wild Life, Nairobi* 3(1), 47-48.

Talbot L M and Talbot M H 1962. Food preferences of some East African wild ungulates. *E Afr Agric J* 27(3), 131-137.

Talbot L M and Talbot M H 1962. A hoisting apparatus for weighing and loading large animals in the field. *J Wildl Mgmt* 26, 217-218.

Talbot L M and Talbot M H 1962. Flaxedil and other drugs in field immobilization and translocation of large mammals in East Africa. *J Mammal* 43, 76-88.

Talbot L M and Talbot M H 1963. The high biomass of wild ungulates on East African savanna. *Trans N Amer Wildl Conf* 28, 465-476.

Talbot L M and Talbot M H 1963. The wildebeest in Western Masailand, East Africa. *Wildl Monogr* No 12. 88 pp.

Talbot L M and Zaphiro D R P 1961. Aerial analysis of wildlife population structures. In: Conf on land management problems in areas containing game: Lake Manyara, Tanganyika. 4 pp. (Mimeograph).

Tarshis I B and Penner L R 1960. Treatment of ectoparasites in captive wild animals *Int Zoo YB* 2, 107-109.

Taylor C R 1968. The minimum water requirements of some East African bovids. *Symp zool Soc Lond* 21, 195.

Taylor C R 1968. Hygroscopic food: a source of water for desert antelopes? *Nature, Lond* 219, 181.

Taylor C R 1969. The eland and the oryx. *Scientific American* 220, 89.

Taylor P, Hopkins L, Young M and McFayden I R 1972. Ketamine anaesthesia in the pregnant sheep. *Vet Rec* 90(2), 35-36.

Taylor C R and Lyman C P 1967. A comparative study on the environmental physiology of an East African antelope the eland, and the Hereford steer. *Physiol Zool.* 40, 280.

Teer, J G, Thomas J W and Walker E A 1965. Ecology and management of white-tailed deer in the Llano Basin of Texas. *Wildl Monogr* 15, 62 pp.

Theiler G 1962. The Ixodoidea parasites of vertebrates in Africa south of the Sahara. (Ethiopian Region). Projects S 9958. Report to the Director of Veterinary Services, Onderstepoort, S Afr.

Thomas O 1894. On the mammals of Nyasaland, third contribution. *Proc Zool Soc Lond* 1894, 136-146.

Thomas A D and Reid N R 1944. Rinderpest in game. A description of an outbreak and an attempt at limiting its spread by means of a bush fence. *Onderstepoort J Vet Sci Anim Ind* 20, 7.

Thorburn J A and Thomas A D 1940. Tuberculosis in the Cape kudu. *Jl S Afr Vet Med Ass* 11, 3.

Thurlbeck W M, Butas C A Mankiewicz E M and Laws R :A 1965. Chronic pulmonary disease in the wild buffalo (Syncerus caffer) in Uganda. Am Rev Resp Dis 92, 801.

Tidmarsh C E M and Havenga C M 1955. The wheel-point method of survey and measurement of semi-open grasslands and karoo vegetation in South Africa. Bot Surv of S A Memoir 29, 49 pp.

Tierkel E S 1964. Rabies. In: Van der Hoeden J (Ed). 1964. Zoonoses. Amsterdam, London and New York, Elsevier Publishing Co.

Treichel G 1959. Africa and our wildlife heritage. Anim Kingd 62, 23-28.

Treus V and Kravchenko D 1968. Methods of rearing and economic utilization of eland in the Askaniya-Nova Zoological Park. Symp Zool Soc London 21, 395-411.

Trouessart E L 1904. Catalogues Mammalium. Berlin, Friedlander & Son, 1929 pp.

UNESCO 1963. A review of the natural resources of the African continent. Natural Resources Research Publ No 1. Paris, UNESCO 437 pp.

Uspenskii G A and Saglanskii A D 1952. Domestication of the eland in the USSR. Precis of translation, included as Editor's Note. Rhod J Agric Res 1, 87.

Van Aarde R J 1976. A note on the birth of a giraffe. S Afr J of Sci 72, 307.

Van der Hoeden J 1964. Brucellosis. In: Van der Hoeden J (Ed.) 1964. Zoonoses. Amsterdam, London and New York, Elsevier Publishing Co.

Van der Hoeden J (Ed.) 1964. Zoonoses. Amsterdam, London and New York, Elsevier Publishing Co.

Van der Schyff H P 1957. Ekologiese studie van die flora van die Nasionale Krugerwildtuin. Deel 1. Proefskrif ingehandig ter gedeeltelike voldoening van die vereistes vir die graad Doctor Scientiae in die Fakulteit van Natuurwetenskappe van die Potchefstroomse Universiteit vir Christelike Hoër Onderwys.

Van der Schyff H P 1959. Weidingsmoontlikhede en weidingsprobleme in die Nasionale Krugerwildtuin. Koedoe 2, 96.

Van der Walt K and Ortlepp R J 1960. Moving the bontebok from Bredasdorp to Swellendam. Jl S Afr Vet Med Ass 31, 456-463.

Van Gelder R G 1977. An eland X kudu hybrid, and the content of the genus Tragelaphus. The Lammergeyer 23, 1-5.

Van Hoven W 1974. Ciliate protozoa and aspects of the nutrition of the Hippopotamus in the Kruger National Park. S Afr J of Sci 70, 107-109.

Van Hoven W 1975. Rumen ciliates of the tsessebe (Damaliscus lunatus lunatus) in south Africa. J Protozool 22(4), 457-462.

Van Niekerk J W 1963. Immobilizing drugs used in the capture of wild animals in the Kruger National Park. Jl S Afr Vet Med Ass 34, 568.

Van Niekerk J W and Pienaar U de V 1962. Adaptations of the immobilizing technique in the capture, marking and translocation of game animals in the Kruger National Park. Koedoe 5, 137-142.

Van Niekerk J W and Pienaar U de V 1963. A report on some immobilizing drugs used in the capture of wild animals in the Kruger National Park. Koedoe 6, 126-133.

Van Niekerk J W, Pienaar U de V and Fairall N 1963. A report on some immobilizing drugs used in the capture of wild animals in the Kruger National Park. Koedoe 6, 126-134.

Van Niekerk J W, Pienaar U de V and Fairall N 1963. Enkele gedagtes oor die versorging en verpleging van wilde diere tydens die vang-, vervoer en vrylatingsproses. Jl S Afr Vet Med Ass 34(3), 413-416.

Van Niekerk J W, Pienaar U de V and Fairall N 1963. A preliminary note on the use of Quiloflex (benzodioxane hydrochloride) in the immobilization of game. Koedoe 6, 109-114.

Van Niekerk J W, Pienaar U de V and Fairall N 1963. Immobilizing drugs used in the capture of wild animals in the Kruger National Park. Jl S Afr Vet Met Ass 34(3), 403-411.

Van Rooyen J 1957. Eland and buffaloes to be bred to cattle Entebbe: Uganda Game and Fisheries Dep. 4 pp. (Mimeograph).

Van Rooyen N 1984. Trofee-rekords van SA wildsoorte. Natura 3, 16.

Van Zyl J H M 1962. The meat production of South African game animals. 1. The eland. Fauna & Flora 13, 35-40.

Van Zyl J H M 1963. A preliminary report on the physical characteristics of the springbok (Antidorcas marsupialis Zimmerman) on the S A Lombard Nature Reserve, Bloemhof District, Transvaal, with special reference to the rate of growth in captivity. Proc Symp Afr Mammals. Zoological Society of Southern Africa.

Van Zyl J H M Von la Chevallerie M and Skinner J D 1969. A note on the dressing percentage in the springbok and impala. Proc S Afr Soc Anim Prod (1969), 199-200.

Vesey-Fitzgerald D F 1954. Wildlife in Tanganyika. Oryx 2, 357-365.

Vesey-Fitzgerald D F 1955. The topi herd. Oryx 3, 4-8.

Vesey-Fitzgerald D F 1960. Grazing succession among East African game animals, J Mammal 41, 161.

Vesey-Fitzgerald D F 1961. Drought — How do wild animals survive. Wild Life 2, 36.

Vesey-Fitzgerald D F 1965. The utilization of natural pastures by wild animals in the Rukwa Valley, Tanganyika. W Afr Wildl J 3, 38-48.

Vidler B O, Harthoorn A M, Brocklesby D W and Robertshaw D 1963. The gestation and parturition of the African buffalo (Syncerus caffer caffer Sparrman). E Afr Wildl J 1, 122-123.

Viljoen P C 1981. Fentanyl citrate for the field immobilization of oribi. S Afr J Wildl Res 11(2) 56-58.

Viljoen P and Joubert S 1988. Game counting — advice to game farmers. Natura 15, 8, 45.

Vincent J 1979. The population dynamics of impala, Aepyceros melampus (Lichtenstein) in Mkuzi Game Reserve. PhD Thesis, University of Natal.

Visagie G P 1968. The transportation of live blesbok (Damaliscus dorcas phillipsi). Fauna and Flora 19, 58-60.

Vogt C and Specht F 1896. The natural history of animals Mammalia Vol 1 & 2. London, Blackie & Sons.

Von la Chevallerie M 1970. Meat production from wild ungulates. Proc S Afr Soc Anim Prod 9, 73-87.

Von la Chevallerie M, Erasmus J M Skinner J D and Van Zyl J H M 1971. A note on the carcass composition of the common eland (Taurotragus oryx). S Afr J Anim Sci 1, 129-131.

Von la Chevallerie M and Van Zyl J H M 1971. Some effects of shooting on losses of meat and meat quality in springbok and impala. S Afr J Anim Sci 1, 113-116.

Von la Chevallerie M and Van Zyl J H M 1971. Growth and carcass development of the springbok. Agroanimalia 3, 115-124.

Von Richter W 1979. Wildlife utilization and management as a form of land use in Botswana. Aplied Sciences and Development, 13, 145-157.

Von Richter W and Butynski T M 1974. Wildlife utilization in Botswana: A review and evaluation of hunter returns as a source of administrative and biological data. J Sth Afr Wildl Mgmt Ass 4(3), 167-176.

Von Richter W, Dräger N, Patterson L and Sommerlatte M 1978. Observations on the immobilization and marking of African elephant (Loxodonda Africana) in Botswana. Proceedings of the XX Internationalen Symposium über die Erkrankungen der Zootiere, Dvure Kralové, Akademie Verlag, Berlin, 185-191.

Wackernagel H 1960. Complete nutrition of zoo animals Int Zoo Yb 2, 95-102.

Wackernagel H 1964. Die Basler Grant-Zebragruppe. Bulletin des Zoologischen Gartens, Basel 12, 13.

Wackernagel H 1968. In: Crawford M A 1968. Comparative nutrition of wild animals. London, Academic Press.

Walker B H 1976. An assessment of the ecological basis of game ranching in southern African savannas. Proc Grassld Soc Sth Afr 11, 125-130.

Wallach J D, Frueh R and Lentz M 1967. The use of M-99 as an immobilizing and analgesic agent in captive wild animals. J A V M A 151(7), 870-876.

Walters C J and Bandy P J 1972. Periodic harvest as a method of increasing big game yields. J of Wildl Mgmt 36(1), 128-134.

Ward R 1962. Records of big game. London, Rowland Ward Ltd (11th ed.) 373 pp.

Watson R M 1979. Reproduction of wildebeest (Connochaetes taurinus albojubatus Thomas) in the Serengeti region, and its significance to conservation. J Reprod Fert Suppl 6, 287-310.

Weiner J S 1954. Human adaptibility to hot conditions of deserts. In: Cloudsley-Thompson J L (Ed.) 1954. Biology of deserts. Proceedings of a symposium on the biology of hot and cold deserts organized by the Institute of Biology, London.

Weir J and Davison E 1965. Daily occurrence of African game animals at water holes during dry weather. Zool Afr 1, 353.

Whalley R C R 1932. Southern Sudan game and its habitat. Sudan Notes Rec 15, 261-267.

Whyte I J 1973. Shingwidzi, the orphaned baby elephant. Custos 1(9), 42-45.

Wilkinson R C and Van Hoven W 1976. Geographical distribution and population structure of springbok Antidorcas marsupialis rumen protozoa in southern Africa. Koedoe 19, 17-26.

Wilkinson R C and Van Hoven W 1976. Rumen ciliate fauna of the springbok (Antidorcas marsupialis) in southern Africa. Zoologica Africana 11(1), 1-22.

Williamson G and Payne W J A 1959. An introduction to animal husbandry in the tropics. London, Longmans, Green & Co Ltd. 435 pp.

Willoughby J C 1889. *East Africa and its big game*. London, Longmans, Green & Co. 312 pp.

Wilson D E and Hirst S M 1977. Ecology and factors limiting roan and sable antelope populations in South Africa. *Wildlife Monographs* 54, 1-111.

Wilson V J 1967. The use of oripavine hydrochloride (M99) in the drug immobilization of grey duiker. *Arnoldia* 3(20), 1-6.

Wilson V J 1970. Data from the culling of kudu, *Tragelaphus strepsiceros* pallas in the Kyle Natinal Park, Rhodesia. *Arnoldia* 36(4), 1-26.

Wilson V J and Clarke J E 1962. Observations on the common duiker (*Sylvicapra grimmia*) based on material collected from a tsetse control game elimination scheme. *Proc Zool Soc Lond* 138, 487-497.

Winkler W G and Gale N B 1970. Tuberculosis. In: Davis J W, Karstad l H and Trainer D O 1970. *Infectious diseases of wild mammals*. Ames, Iowa, USA, The Iowa State Univ Press.

Worthington E B 1961. *The wild resources of East and Central Africa. Colonial No 352*. London, H M S O. 26 pp.

Wright B S 1960. Predation on big game in East Africa. *J Wildl Mgmt* 24, 1 - 15.

Wright J G and Hall L W 1961. *Veterinary anaesthesia and analgesia*. London, Baillière, Tindall and Cox.

Wright S 1950. Genetic structure of populations. *Nature* 166, 247-249.

Wylie W D and Churchill-Davidson H C 1960. *A practice of anaesthesia*, London, LLoyd-Lute (Medical Books) Ltd.

Wynne-Jones A 1980. *Hunting on Safari in East and Southern Africa*. 194 pp

Young E 1964. Echinococcosis in man and beast. *Zoön* 3, 12.

Young E 1965. Lesions in the vicinity of the eye of the white rhinoceros, *Diceros simus. Int Zoo Yb* 5, 194-195.

Young E 1965. A suspected case of tetanus in a waterbuck (*Kobus ellipsiprymnus*). *Jl S Afr Vet Med Ass* 36(4), 580.

Young E 1965. 'n Verslag oor die versameling van saad van 'n swart renosterbul, *Diceros bicornis. Jl S Afr Vet Med Ass* 36, 385-386.

Young E 1966. The use of anaesthetics in the transport of animals. *Int Zoo Yb* 6, 273.

Young E 1966. Muscle necrosis in captive red hartebeest, *Alcelaphus buselaphus. Jl S Afr Vet Med Ass* 37, 101-103.

Young E 1966. A preliminary report on blood findings in twenty species of wild mammals. *Jl S Afr Vet Med Ass* 37, 95-98.

Young E 1966. Notes on the blood composition of the red hartebeest, *Alcelaphus buselaphus. Int Zoo Yb* 6, 291-292.

Young E 1966. Treatment of cutaneous granulomata in the black rhinoceros. *Int Zoo Yb* 6, 276.

Young E 1966. Nutrition of the hippopotamus. *Afr Wild Life* 20, 165-167.

Young E 1967. Semen extraction by manipulative technique in black rhinoceros, *Diceros bicornis. Int Zoo Yb* 7, 166-167.

Young E 1967. *Trichinella spiralis* (Owen, 1835) Railiet, 1895 infestation of wild carnivores and rodents in South Africa. *Jl S Afr Vet Med Ass* 38, 441-443.

Young E 1968. Management of adult wild African ungulates. *Afr Wild Life* 22, 217-230.

Young E 1968. Care of young wild ungulates. *Afr Wild Life* 22, 126-140.

Young E 1969. The significance of infectious disease in African game populations. Zool Afr 4, 275-281.

Young E 1970. The diagnosis and control of game diseases. *Zool Afr* 5, 16.

Young E 1970. *Water as faktor in die ekologie van wild in die Nasionale Krugerwildtuin.* DSc (Wildlife Management) Thesis, University of Pretoria, 192 pp.

Young E 1970. Water in game management. Proceedings of the National Water Convention: Water for the future. University of Pretoria, November 1970.

Young E 1971. The elephants of the Eastern Cape. *Custos* 1(1), 15-23.

Young E 1971. Management of animal populations which move across international boundaries. Published proceedings: SARCCUS. Gorongosa National Park, Mocambique, 13-17 September 1971, 91-96.

Young E 1972. A useful marking method for free living mammals. *Koedoe* 14, 131-136.

Young E 1972. Buffaloes — Their role in forming natural watering places. *Custos* 1(2), 14-16.

Young E 1972. The elephant's temperature control mechanisms. *Custos* 1(5), 32-37.

Young E 1972. The water requirements of wild animals in the Kruger National Park. *Custos* 1(6), 31-35.

Young E 1972. The value of waterhole counts in estimating wild animal populations. *Jl S Afr Wildl Mgmt Ass* 2(1), 22-23.

Young E 1972. Observations on the movement patterns and daily home range size of impala, *Aepyceros melampus* (Lichtenstein) in the Kruger National Park. *Zool Afr* 7(1), 187-195.

Young E 1972. Considerations on large scale vaccination of free living game. *Jl S Afr Vet Med Ass* 43(2), 189-191.

Young E 1972. Overstraining disease (capture myopathy) in the tsessebe *Damaliscus lunatus* and oribi *Ourebia ourebi. Koedoe* 15, 143-144.

Young E 1972. Notes on the chemical immobilization and restraint of the Addo elephant (*Loxodonta Africana*). *Koedoe* 15, 97-99.

Young E (Ed.) 1973. *The capture and care of wild animals.* Human and Rousseau, Cape Town, 224 pp.

Young E 1973. Technological aspects of game management and utilization in Africa. *Proc IIIrd World Conf on Animal Production 2, l(c) 30, Melbourne, Australia, August 1973.*

Young E 1975. Echinococcosis (hydatidosis) in wild animals of the Kruger National Park. *Jl S Afr Vet Med Ass* 46(3), 285-286.

Young E 1982. Moderne wildboerdery. Artikelreeks: *Landbouweekblad,* 5 Maart tot 10 September 1982.

Young E 1984. Water vir wild. *Natura* 2, 36.

Young E 1984. Droogtehulp vir wildboere. *Natura* 1, 19.

Young E 1984. Wildvoeding. *Natura* 3, 10.

Young E 1984. Before buying your own dart gun. *Natura* 1, 5.

Young E 1984. The buffalo. *Natura* 3, 38.

Young E 1984. Spesifikasies vir wildheinings. *Natura* 1, 2.

Young E 1984. Bastergemsbok. *Natura* 1, 22.

Young E 1984. Rooibok. *Natura* 3, 6.

Young E 1984. Standaardheinings vir plaaswild. *Natura* 3, 23.

Young E 1984. Blouwildebees. *Natura* 2, 6.

Young E 1984. How to use your dart gun. *Natura* 2, 9.

Young E 1984. Bosluisbeheer by wild. *Natura* 2, 26.

Young E 1984. Springbok. *Natura* 4, 6 — 8.

Young E 1985. Koedoe. *Natura* 5, 8 — 9.

Young E 1985. Eland. *Natura* 6, 8 — 9.

Young E 1985. Sebras. *Natura* 7, 24 — 25, 30.

Young E 1986. Die Kameelperd. *Natura* 11, 6, 34.

Young E 1986. Die Njala. *Natura* 10, 13, 22 — 23.

Young E 1987. The Waterbuck. *Natura* 13, 16 — 17, 46.

Young E 1987. The African buffalo. *Natura* 14, 7, 17, 28.

Young E 1988. The Gemsbok. *Natura* 16, 9, 30 — 31.

Young E 1988. The Blue Duiker. *Natura* 15, 4, 30, 43.

Young E 1989. White rhino. *Natura* 19, 14, 16, 44 — 45

Young E 1989. The Sable Antelope. *Natura* 18, 7, 12, 32.

Young E 1990. The Blesbok and Bontebok. *Natura* 20, 7, 28.

Young E and Basson P A 1973. Heartwater in the eland. *JL S Afr Vet Med Ass* 44(2), 185-186.

Young E, Basson P A and Weiss K E 1970. Experimental infection of game animals with lumpy skin disease virus (Prototype Strain Neethling). *Onderstepoort J Vet Res* 37, 79-88.

Young E and Bronkhorst P J L 1971. Overstraining disease in game. *Afr Wild Life* 25, 51-52.

Young E, Burger P J and Whyte I J 1972. The use of Dopram-V (doxapram hydrochloride), a potent analeptic, on newly captured wild animals. *Veterinary Clinician* 11, 11-13.

Young E and Groenewald A A v J 1972. Abnormal colouration in wild animals. *Custos* 1(11), 33-38.

Young E, Hedger R S and Howell P G 1972. Clinical foot-and-mouth disease in the African buffalo (*Syncerus caffer*). *Onderstepoort J Vet Res* 39(3), 181-183.

Young E and Lombard C J 1967. Physiological values of the African elephant. *The Veterinarian* 4, 169-172.

Young E and N 1987. *African Wildlife and Safari Guide.* 160 pp.

Young E and Oelofse J 1969. Management and nutrition of twenty newly captured young African elephants in the Kruger National Park. *Int Zoo Yb* 9, 179-184.

Young E and Penzhorn B L 1972. The reaction of the Cape Mountain zebra (*Equus zebra zebra*) to certain chemical immobilization drugs. *Koedoe* 15, 95-96.

Young E and Van den Heever L W 1969. The African buffalo as a source of food and by-products: Production potential, parasites and pathology. *JL S Afr Vet Med Ass* 40, 83-88.

Young E and Wagener L J J 1968. The impala as a source of food and byproducts: Data on production potential, parasites and pathology of free-living impala of the Kruger National Park. *JL S Afr Vet Med Ass* 39, 81-86.

Young E, Wagener L J J and Bronkhorst P J L 1969. The blue wildebeest as a source of food and byproducts. The production potential, parasites and pathology of free living wildebeest in the Kruger National Park. *JL S Afr Vet Med Ass* 40, 315-318.

Young E and Whyte I J 1973. The use of xylazine hydrochloride (Rompun, Bayer) in the capture, management and treatment of some African wildlife species. *JL S Afr Vet Med Ass* 44(2), 177-184.

Young E and Whyte I J 1975. Trichinosis (*Trichinella spiralis* infestation) in wild animals of the Kruger National Park. *JL S Afr Vet Med Ass* 46(3), 233-234.

Young E, Zumpt F, Basson P A, Boyazoglu P A, Erasmus B and Boomker J 1973. Notes on the parasitology, pathology and biophysiology of springbuck in the Mountain Zebra National Park. *Koedoe* 16, 195-198.

Young E, Zumpt F, Boomker J, Penzhorn B L and Erasmus B 1973. Parasites and diseases of Cape mountain zebra, black wildebeest, mountain reedbuck and blesbuck in the Mountain Zebra National Park. *Koedoe* 16, 77-81.

Zaloumis E A and Cross R 1974. *Antelope of Southern Africa*. Wildlife Society Publication.

Zaphiro D R P 1959. The use of a light aircraft to count game. *Wild Life (Nairobi)* 1, 31-36.

Zaphiro D R P and Talbot L M 1961. The use of light aircraft in East African wildlife research and game management. *Oryx* 6, 190-199.

Zeuner F E 1963. *A history of domesticated animals*. London, Hutchinson & Co (Publishers) Ltd. 560 pp.

Zimmermann I 1979. The efficiency of Africander steers (*Bos indicus*) on a mixed tree savanna. *Jl S Afr biol Sco* 20, 66-78.

Zimmermann I 1980. Factors influencing the feed intake and live-weight change of beef cattle on a mixed tree savanna in the Transvaal. *J of Range Mgmt* 33(2), 132-136.

Zoological Society of Southern Africa 1962. Proc Symposium on causes and problems of animal distribution. *Ann Cape prov Mus* 2, 1-317.

Zumpt F (Ed.) 1961. *The arthropod parasites of vertebrates in Africa south of the Sahara (Ethiopian Region)*. Vol. 1-3, Johannesburg, South African Institute for Medical Research.

Foto: Transvaalse Afdeling Natuurbewaring.